Architects of the Resurrection

MANCHESTER
1824

Manchester University Press

Gearóid Ó Cuinneagáin speaking at the General Post Office, Dublin, 1942. *Source*: Gearóid Ó Cuinneagáin papers, Department of Defence Military Archives.

Architects of the Resurrection

Ailtirí na hAiséirghe and the fascist 'new order' in Ireland

R. M. DOUGLAS

Manchester University Press

Manchester and New York

distributed exclusively in the USA by Palgrave Macmillan

Published by Manchester University Press
Oxford Road, Manchester M13 9NR, UK
and Room 400, 175 Fifth Avenue, New York, NY 10010, USA
www.manchesteruniversitypress.co.uk

Distributed exclusively in the USA by
Palgrave Macmillan, 175 Fifth Avenue, New York,
NY 10010, USA

Distributed exclusively in Canada by
UBC Press, University of British Columbia, 2029 West Mall,
Vancouver, BC, Canada V6T 1Z2

British Library Cataloguing-in-Publication Data
A catalogue record for this book is available from the British Library

Library of Congress Cataloging-in-Publication Data applied for

ISBN 978 0 7190 7973 3 *hardback*
ISBN 978 0 7190 7998 6 *paperback*

First published 2009

18 17 16 15 14 13 12 11 10 09   10 9 8 7 6 5 4 3 2 1

The publisher has no responsibility for the persistence or accuracy of URLs for external or any third-party internet websites referred to in this book, and does not guarantee that any content on such websites is, or will remain, accurate or appropriate.

Typeset in Palatino
by Koinonia, Manchester
Printed in Great Britain
by the MPG Books Group

I gcuimhne m'athair
Seoirse Ó Dúbhghlas, 1924–2002
Iriseoir

One must remember that in Ireland the time lag which appears in architecture appears equally in everything else, and when Fascism and Nazism have ceased to exist in Europe they will probably be just starting in Ireland, which will be a little museum piece for the rest of the world.

John Betjeman, July 1943

Contents

List of figures   *page* vii
Map: location of Aiséirghe branches, 1945   viii
Acknowledgements   ix

Introduction   1

1 Anti-democratic influences in Ireland, 1919–39   5

2 'New' and 'newer' orders   43

3 The ideology of Aiséirghe   92

4 The green totalitarian band   147

5 Democratic deficit   184

6 Autumn of discontent   220

7 The 'Cunningham circus'   247

   Conclusion   287

   Select bibliography   297
   Index   313

List of figures

1 Gearóid Ó Cuinneagáin (left) and Proinsias Mac an Bheatha
(second from right) lead a Craobh na hAiséirghe parade. *page* 143

2 Craobh na hAiséirghe publicity poster. 143

3 Ailtirí na hAiséirghe meeting in Dublin, 1943. 144

4 The Aiséirghe cartoonist Seán Ó Riain comments on Irish
democracy's achievements. 144

5 Aiséirghe youth on the march. 145

6 Aiséirghe's approach to the partition problem. 145

7 Tomás Ó Dochartaigh (left) and Gearóid Ó Broin (right). 146

8 The Jewish menace: a constant theme in Aiséirghe propaganda. 146

Source: Gearóid Ó Cuinneagáin papers, Department of Defence
Military Archives.

Acknowledgements

Most of the credit for the existence of this book belongs to Fionán and Anne Ó Cuinneagáin. When I contacted them in 1998 to ask whether any of Gearóid Ó Cuinneagáin's papers had survived, neither they nor I knew that a full-length book project would be the result. From the first cursory examination of those papers, however, it became clear that a detailed history of Ailtirí na hAiséirghe would be valuable not only in itself, but to a still greater degree as a lens through which the society and culture from which it emerged could be examined. The extraordinary generosity with which the Ó Cuinneagáin family during the following nine years greeted my quest for information about their late father and his associates; their help in arranging meetings and contacts with former Aiséirghe members; and – as the process of research was overtaken by a cataloguing enterprise that proved almost as time-consuming as writing the book itself – the patience with which they tolerated the creeping invasion successively of their garden shed, their garage and finally their house of an ever-growing mass of papers behind which an increasingly distracted historian could occasionally be observed, is beyond all praise. Their friendship has been the most pleasant and unexpected outcome of a research effort that has proven longer and more complex than any of us ever imagined.

I wish particularly to thank the former officers and members of Ailtirí na hAiséirghe whom I interviewed during the course of research, especially Deasún Breathnach ['Rex Mac Gall'], Liam Ó Cochláin, Síle Bean Uí Chuinneagáin [Síle Ní Chochláin], Caoimhín de Eiteagáin, Tom Mageean, Dónall Ó Maolalaí, Nora Bean Uí Mhaolalaí [Nora Ní Chochláin], Risteárd de Róiste, and Aindrias Ó Scolaidhe. Prionsías Ó Conluain, Risteád Ó Glaisne, Hugo Hamilton, Derry Kelleher, Attracta Maher [née Brennan-Whitmore], Terry Spillane and Pádraig Ó hUiginn also gave generously of their time and insight.

I should like to pay special tribute to Aislinn Ní Chuinneagáin, whose first tentative idea for a short student film on Gearóid Ó Cuinneagáin would ultimately bear fruit in the acclaimed 2004 documentary *Mo Sheanathair, an Führer Gaelach?* [*My Grandfather, the Gaelic Führer?*]. The result bore eloquent tribute to her remarkable and precocious talents as a film-maker. Bernardine Nic Giolla Phádraig and the rest of the staff at Kairos Communications also earned my gratitude for their good-natured tolerance as I worked my way through the catalogue of neophyte blunders in front of their cameras.

Any comprehensive list of the archivists and librarians who helped me would be formidably if not impossibly long; my appreciation of them is on no less substantial a scale. It would, however, be especially remiss of me not to mention the immense kindness and efficiency with which I was assisted by the late and much-missed Commandant Peter Young of the Department of Defence Military Archive, as well as by his successor, Commandant Victor Laing, and their staffs. John E. Taylor of the National Archives and Records Administration at College Park, MD, whose knowledge of the wartime American intelligence documents is greater than that of any other living human, was also indefatigable in his pursuit of OSS materials relating to this topic.

My thinking about Aiséirghe was sharpened and refined by discussions with many scholars in the field. I learned a great deal from presenting portions of this work before the Irish Cultural Association of Rhode Island; the American Conference for Irish Studies; the Conference on Women, Gender and the Extreme Right in Europe at Cardiff University; the Conference on Women in Irish Culture and History at University College, Dublin; and the Centre for Contemporary Irish History at Trinity College, Dublin. I am especially indebted to Professors L. P. Curtis Jr of Brown University, Martin Durham of the University of Wolverhampton, and Bruce Nelson of Dartmouth College, who read the manuscript in whole or part and offered invaluable advice. My colleagues in the History Department at Colgate University, as always, created by their example a supportive and inspiring environment in which to think and write. The completion of this project was also materially assisted by a Harvey Picker Research Grant from the Colgate University Research Council.

The greater part of the manuscript was written in the congenial surroundings of Valeria Sassanelli's house in Via David Silvagni above Trastevere; her hospitality and that of her family will not soon be forgotten. Completion of the remainder would not have been possible without the matchless support and enthusiasm of my wife Elizabeth, who cheerfully assumed the entire burden of domestic responsibilities while the remainder was composed in the monastic seclusion of one or another of Columbus, Ohio's many economically-priced chain motels. Our baby daughter Aoife, who arrived during the closing stages of this project, provided both much-needed diversion and additional incentive to finish it.

A section of Chapter 2 was previously published in the December 2006 issue of *Historical Journal*; I am grateful to the Syndics of the Cambridge University Press for permission to reproduce it here. Crown copyright material in the Public Record Office, Kew, is reproduced by permission of Her Majesty's Stationery Office.

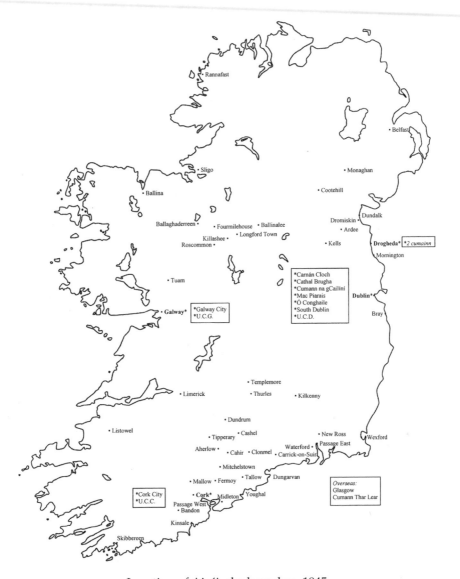

Location of Aiséirghe branches, 1945

The following place names and labels appear on the map:

- Rannafast
- Belfast
- Sligo
- Monaghan
- Cootehill
- Ballina
- Dundalk
- Ballaghaderreen
- Dromiskin
- Fourmilehouse
- Ballinalee
- Ardee
- Longford Town
- Killashee
- Kells
- Drogheda* *2 cumainn
- Roscommon
- Mornington
- *Carnán Cloch
- *Cathal Brugha
- *Cumann na gCailíní
- *Mac Piarais
- *Ó Conghaile
- *South Dublin
- *U.C.D.
- Dublin*
- Tuam
- *Galway City
- *U.C.G.
- Galway*
- Bray
- Templemore
- Limerick
- Thurles
- Kilkenny
- Dundrum
- Listowel
- Cashel
- Tipperary
- New Ross
- Wexford
- Aherlow
- Cahir
- Clonmel
- Waterford
- Passage East
- Carrick-on-Suir
- Mitchelstown
- Mallow
- Fermoy
- Tallow
- Dungarvan
- *Cork City
- *U.C.C.
- Cork*
- Midleton
- Youghal
- Passage West
- Bandon
- Kinsale
- Skibbereen
- Overseas: Glasgow Cumann Thar Lear

Introduction

One of the more anomalous aspects of modern Irish history is the supposed non-emergence of any significant fascist or extreme-right movement during the twentieth century. This is all the more curious in light of the fact that independent Ireland before the Second World War, with its underperforming peasant economy, its sizeable Northern irredenta and its variety of political and paramilitary groups contesting the legitimacy of the state, conformed more closely in many respects to the profile of the authoritarian states of Eastern Europe than to the liberal-democratic systems of the West. A growing scholarly consensus nevertheless maintains that no significant Irish counterpart of the ultra-rightist Continental movements of the interwar period ever arose, and that the most likely candidates for consideration under this heading – members of General Eoin O'Duffy's Blueshirt organisation of the early 1930s – were not in fact fascists, appearances to the contrary. Although O'Duffy's movement continues in some quarters to be taken for an extreme-right body on the Continental model,[1] most scholars, following the groundbreaking work of Maurice Manning (whose conclusions have recently been reinforced by Mike Cronin) accept that those who have sought to find in the Blueshirts an Irish manifestation of fascism have been looking in the wrong place.[2] As J. J. Lee has remarked, perhaps with more epigrammatic felicity than strict accuracy, 'Fascism was far too intellectually demanding for the bulk of the Blueshirts'.[3]

To date, however, no historian has looked beyond O'Duffy and his retinue for other possible varieties of ultra-right extremism in Ireland,

1 See, e.g., R. Griffin, ed., *Fascism* (Oxford: Oxford University Press, 1995).
2 M. A. Manning, *The Blueshirts*, 3rd edn (Dublin: Gill & Macmillan, 2006); M. Cronin, *The Blueshirts and Irish Politics* (Dublin: Four Courts Press, 1997). Tom Garvin, however, goes some distance in the direction of the other extreme by describing the Blueshirts as 'in large part ... [a] free speech movement'. T. Garvin, *1922: The Birth of Irish Democracy* (Dublin: Gill & Macmillan, 1996), p. 22.
3 J. J. Lee, *Ireland 1912–1985: Politics and Society* (Cambridge: Cambridge University Press, 1989), p. 181.

nor beyond the 1930s as the decade during which such a threat was likely to arise. In part this is a consequence of the well-marked tendency to treat Irish history as proceeding along a distinct and separate course from that followed by the rest of the European continent. Thus what appears normal in a European context is perceived as anomalous in an Irish one, and vice versa. Robert Stradling has noted wryly in this connection, 'The popular imagination is not capable of sustaining the shock which juxtaposing the adjectives "Irish" and "fascist" administers'.[4] Furthermore, Anglophone historians have consistently de-emphasised, or more often entirely ignored, those political organisations that conducted their business in the Irish language, concentrating instead on more accessible movements like the Blueshirts that used English as their lingua franca. This omission is no doubt explained by the fact that, for entirely understandable reasons, few scholars in the field of European fascist studies have found it necessary to acquire a reading knowledge of Irish. In light of the strong correlation of cultural and political nationalism, however, the consequence has been that the milieu out of which an authentically Irish fascism was always most likely to arise has been precisely the one that has received the least attention.

The political movement at the centre of this study, Ailtirí na hAiséirghe ['Architects of the Resurrection'], has as a result been virtually overlooked in English-language studies of Irish political history. Although several modern works refer to its sudden rise and success in the 1945 local government elections, none has offered any explanation for, or analysis of, its popular appeal. The most detailed account of the movement to appear thus far is Aoife Ní Lochlainn's MA thesis, a version of which was published as part of an essay collection edited by Dermot Keogh and Mervyn O'Driscoll.[5] The party has also recently been mentioned in Clair Wills' stimulating cultural history of wartime Ireland, although this account is factually inaccurate at several points.[6] Otherwise, Aiséirghe is discussed in print only in various autobiographies and memoirs, principally by former members or others associated with the organisation.

Until recently, a comprehensive study of this movement would not have been possible, inasmuch as all of its records were presumed to have been lost or destroyed. Fortunately, the discovery of a very

---

4 R. A. Stradling, *The Irish and the Spanish Civil War 1936–1939: Crusades in Conflict* (Manchester: Manchester University Press, 1999), p. 1.

5 A. Ní Lochlainn, 'Ailtirí na hAiséirghe: A Movement of Its Time?', in D. Keogh and M. O'Driscoll, eds, *Ireland in World War Two: Diplomacy and Survival* (Cork: Mercier, 2004).

6 C. Wills, *That Neutral Island: A Cultural History of Ireland Duing the Second World War* (London: Faber & Faber, 2007), pp. 364–8.

extensive collection of Aiséirghe documents – including member-ship rolls, account-books, executive committee minutes, records of subsidiary bodies, drafts of published and unpublished party propa-ganda, copies of incoming and outgoing correspondence, and a large quantity of miscellaneous political ephemera and photographs – now makes it possible for a long-overdue history of the Aiséirghe phenom-enon finally to be written. In electoral terms, Ailtirí na hAiséirghe was one of the more successful fascist parties to appear in a Western democratic country; the reasons for its rise, at a time when fascism was being comprehensively discredited elsewhere, provide an explanation for the hitherto-unappreciated prevalence of right-wing extremism, xenophobia and anti-Semitism in mid-twentieth-century Ireland.

Notwithstanding its ultimate – though, as I aim to show, far from inevitable – passing from the political scene, Aiséirghe's history challenges a number of prevalent assumptions about Irish politics and society in the middle of the twentieth century. The first of these is the belief that independent Ireland was virtually predestined to become, and to remain, a member of the family of Western liberal-democratic states. Aiséirghe's rise – and, no less importantly, the cultural envir-noment in which it emerged – indicates that Ireland's supposed immunity from political extremism directed not merely against the legitimacy of the regime but the ideology upon which the state itself was constructed, is due for re-evaluation. The appearance of Aiséirghe and other pro-Axis and anti-democratic movements in the early 1940s shows that discontent with the system of parliamentary democracy itself, as distinct from the performance of individual governments, ran much deeper in Irish life than has ever been recognised, and that explanations of the regime's survival in the turbulent mid-century years must take into consideration the incompetence of its enemies as well as the sagacity of its defenders.

A study of Aiséirghe also sheds considerable light on what has for long been the most under-researched and poorly understood period in modern Irish history: the so-called 'Emergency' and its immediate aftermath. Even today, many historians continue to accept F. S. L. Lyons' evocative but misleading description of the Second World War era as a period during which 'an entire people [were] condemned to live in Plato's cave, backs to the fire of life and deriving their only knowledge of what went on outside from the flickering shadows thrown on the wall before their eyes by the men and women who passed to and fro behind them'. It is further taken for granted that Irish sympathies, to the extent that they were engaged with either of the combatants, lay overwhelmingly with the Allied cause. These assessments, however, are based largely upon the policies adopted by the de Valera government, rather than any systematic study of Irish public opinion. Few attempts have thus far been made to gauge the extent of popular pro-Axis sentiment – nor how the wholly reasonable expectation during the first half of the war of a German victory impacted Irish domestic politics. Aiséirghe's emergence and growth during this period indicates that a far-from-insignificant element within Irish society, far from being indifferent to the outcome of the conflict, was anxious to bring Ireland into conformity with the requirements of what it considered to be an emerging post-democratic world order.

The Aiséirghe phenomenon also represents a contradiction of the familiar stereotype of Ireland during the 1940s as a country suffering from political sclerosis, notable only for its conservatism, unimaginativeness and ideological stasis. Although the history of generational conflict in modern Ireland is a topic that deserves its own separate study, the rise of Aiséirghe – a movement whose members were almost entirely in their 'teens and early twenties, openly contemptuous of their elders' failings, and resentful of the attention accorded to the revolutionary struggle of 1916–21 in which they had been too young to participate – can be seen as one of the first manifestations of 'youth rebellion' in independent Ireland, taking the form of a rejection of the ideological, rather than behavioural, mores of mainstream society and the cultivation of an explicitly political counterculture.

Lastly, and perhaps most importantly, a study of Aiséirghe sheds valuable new light on the rise of fascism as a global phenomenon. To date, historical and theoretical approaches to fascism have focused overwhelmingly on its manifestations in the principal European countries, and its development in response to the combined traumas of the Great War, the Bolshevik Revolution, and the worldwide economic crisis of the 1920s and 1930s. Only very recently have scholars become aware of the commonalities, no less than the many significant particularites and permutations, to be found among fascist movements outside Continental Europe that did not take either the German or Italian variants as their ideological and methodological lodestone. Like some of these, Aiséirghe belongs to a discrete category of fascism that saw its historical mission as the bridging of the ideological gap between Christian social teaching and the concept of the totalitarian state. In what follows, I seek to contribute to the work of historians and political scientists who are charting the spread of fascism beyond its traditional Continental European hinterland, and beginning to recognise it as a doctrine that was capable of flourishing in political cultures whose polarities did not lie along the familiar axis of 'right' and 'left'.

1

Anti-democratic influences in Ireland, 1919–39

On the afternoon of 21 January 1919, the newly elected Members of Parliament from Ireland's republican party, Sinn Féin, assembled at the Mansion House in Dublin. In accordance with their election pledges and long-standing party policy, the successful candidates repudiated their seats in the British House of Commons at Westminster and instead formally constituted themselves as 'Dáil Éireann', or the 'Assembly of Ireland'. The Dáil read aloud a Declaration of Independence in Irish, English and French, asserting that as the national parliament it alone had authority to legislate for the Irish people. It adopted a provisional constitution of the Irish Republic – fewer than four hundred words in length – and issued a manifesto calling upon the nations of the world to support Ireland's right to representation at the Paris Peace Conference, which had commenced its deliberations three days previously. After electing a President of the Republic and a five-member Executive, the Dáil adjourned. 'Everything', as the correspondent of the London *Times* acknowledged, 'was done decently and in order – indeed, the circumstances of the opening of the Irish Parliament were entirely prosaic'.[1]

At the end of the Great War, similar scenes were being played out across the European continent. Less than a week after the Armistice, a self-styled Czechoslovak National Assembly had chosen a government, president and constitution. Hungary, Latvia and the 'Kingdom of Serbs, Croats and Slovenes' (the future Yugoslavia) were soon to follow suit. In at least one significant respect, however, the circumstances in which Ireland's first democratically elected constituent assembly had come into being were less mundane than the *Times* report indicated. Of the seventy-three Sinn Féin parliamentarians elected to the Dáil, only twenty-seven were present at its inauguration to answer their names.

---

1 *The Times*, 22 January 22 1921. For a detailed analysis of the actions of the first Dáil, see B. Farrell, ed., *The Creation of the Dáil* (Dublin: Blackwater, 1994).

The remainder were in British prisons, or on the run.[2] Most had no specific charge preferred against them, but were, in the comprehensive formula of the relevant emergency legislation, 'suspected of acting, having acted or being about to act in a manner prejudicial to the public safety and the defence of the realm'. Before the end of the year, as a guerrilla War of Independence raged throughout Ireland, Dáil Éireann would be declared an illegal organisation and its members made liable to summary arrest and imprisonment.

From its earliest days, therefore, a question mark hung over the Irish democratic experiment. Future events would do little to dispel it. During the two-year-long War of Independence, the Dáil was able to convene on only twelve occasions, which for reasons of security were normally not publicised.[3] At the conclusion of the guerrilla campaign in December 1921, negotiations with the British yielded not the thirty-two-county Irish Republic to which members of the Dáil had pledged their allegiance, but an Anglo-Irish Treaty providing for a partitioned Irish Free State whose titular sovereign remained the British King. In 1922 a bitter year-long Civil War erupted between those prepared to accept the Treaty as the best deal available and the substantial minority of republicans who rejected it as a betrayal of the Irish Republic proclaimed in 1916 by the martyred leaders of the Easter Rising. The Sinn Féin party split, with pro-Treatyites establishing a new political vehicle, Cumann na nGaedheal ['Society of the Gaels'] and setting up a provisional government in Dublin under Michael Collins and Arthur Griffith. Though neither man was to live to see the end of the Civil War, by 1923 the Cumann na nGaedheal administration had succeeded in putting down armed republicanism and asserting its control over the twenty-six counties. The price of victory, though, was great. Around 1,200 Irishmen and women had been killed, many of them in brutal circumstances. More than 10,000 were detained in prisons and internment camps. Five years of war, revolutionary and civil, had devastated the economy and the infrastructure on which it depended. Roads, bridges and railways were destroyed; all the principal cities and many large towns featured sizeable burned-out areas; factories and creameries across the country had been razed to the ground. The long-standing structural problems making for Irish poverty were still in place, with a heavy overdependence on agriculture, a sector that employed no fewer

---

2 Twenty-six Ulster Unionist MPs had also been elected in 1918; understandably, none accepted the Dáil's invitation to participate in its proceedings.
3 P. Mair, 'The Break-up of the United Kingdom: The Irish Experience of Regime Change, 1918–1949', *Journal of Commonwealth and Comparative Politics* 16:3 (November 1978): 290.

than one in two members of the workforce. The Free State was further burdened by the erection of the border with Northern Ireland, which was even more illogical economically than it was politically and which cut across natural lines of distribution and exchange. The industrial northeast, experiencing severe economic problems of its own, was now isolated from its hinterland and long-established domestic markets. Lastly, the death during the Civil War of Collins and Griffith on the pro-Treaty side, and the internment of such figures as Éamon de Valera and Seán Lemass from among the republicans, depleted the available pool of Irish political talent at a critical moment in the nation's history. Although the twenty-six counties now enjoyed a peace of exhaustion, at least a third of the population remained disaffected to some extent from the institutions of the state. Because there never had been a negotiated settlement to the Civil War, a real possibility remained that hostilities would be renewed at some future stage.

Like the 'Succession States' of central and southeastern Europe that came into existence at approximately the same time, therefore, independent Ireland faced immense political, social and economic challenges. It is to the credit of the Cumann na nGaedheal government, headed by William T. Cosgrave, that some of the most pressing of these were met. Institutions of state – many of them facsimiles of their British predecessors – were established. An impartial and, according to its bureaucratic lights, efficient civil service was created. The new unarmed police force, the Garda Síochána, gained broad public acceptance. In other respects, though, the performance of Cosgrave's government offered few grounds for satisfaction. Little effort was made to heal the festering wounds of the Civil War, or to seek even the smallest measure of common ground with the defeated republican element; rather, in governmental circles a tone of triumphalism tinged with paranoia prevailed. Fiscal orthodoxy of the most rigid and unimaginative kind frustrated any attempt to address the structural deficiencies of the Irish economy.[4] The result was to deprive those at the bottom of the social ladder not merely of the means of subsistence, but of any real hope for the future. Patrick McGilligan, Minister of Industry and Commerce, encapsulated Cumann na nGaedheal's take-no-prisoners approach to economic policy when he declared in 1924 before the Dáil that rather than face the prospect of an unbalanced budget, '[p]eople may have to die in this country and may

---

4 Mary Daly points out, however, that Irish political and social institutions were so weak in the 1920s that an aggressive growth-oriented policy might have had a serious, and perhaps dangerous, destabilising impact. See M. E. Daly, *Industrial Development and Irish National Identity, 1922–1939* (Syracuse, NY: Syracuse University Press, 1992).

have to die through starvation' – perhaps the most comprehensively asinine statement ever made by an Irish public representative.[5] The innovations introduced by the Sinn Féin shadow government during the War of Independence, including land redistribution, were rolled back to such an extent that John Regan has characterised the period 1921–36 as an 'Irish Counter-Revolution'.[6]

That Cumann na nGaedheal survived in office can be attributed to the inadequacy of its opposition rather than the popularity of its policies. As Diarmuid Ferriter points out, 'At no election did C[umann na] nG[aedheal] secure even two fifths of valid first-preference votes'.[7] Its continuation in power was the consequence of the anti-Treaty wing of Sinn Féin's decision not to assume its seats in the Dáil, which would have required republican *Teachtaí Dála* [Dáil Deputies, or TDs] to take the Oath of Allegiance pledging fidelity to the British monarch. Until 1926, parliamentary opposition to Cumann na nGaedheal had been provided by the politically active but numerically small Irish Labour Party. In that year, however, Éamon de Valera, recognising the futility of abstentionism, broke with his colleagues in Sinn Féin and founded Fianna Fáil ['Warriors of Fál'[8]] as a republican party committed to the completion of the independence struggle by political means. Brushing aside their signature of the Oath of Allegiance as an 'empty political formula', de Valera and his followers took up their seats in the Oireachtas [parliament] after the 1927 general election. Fianna Fáil's combination of republican aspirations and redistributionist social policies quickly gained a broad appeal, and the party took office as a minority administration in March 1932.

This first alternation of government has correctly been seen as a turning-point in the history of Irish democracy. Despite exhortations from some of their wilder supporters to call out the army rather than turn power over to Fianna Fáil, Cosgrave and his ministers retired peacefully to the opposition benches. It is true that they did so in the firm conviction that Fianna Fáil's policies were unworkable and its tenure in consequence would be short. Nevertheless, their decision to place the country's fate, and their own, in the hands of men they had recently imprisoned, whose comrades they had shot and who in turn had been responsible for the deaths of some of their own friends and

---

5 9 *Díospóireachtaí Páirliminte–Dáil Éireann* (hereafter *DP–Dáil*), c. 562 (30 October 1924).
6 J. M. Regan, *The Irish Counter-Revolution: Treatyite Politics and Settlement in Independent Ireland, 1921–1936* (Dublin: Gill & Macmillan, 1999).
7 D. Ferriter, *The Transformation of Ireland 1900–2000* (London: Profile, 2004), pp. 302–3.
8 'Fál' is one of the fourteen mythological names of Ireland recorded in Geoffrey Keating's *Foras Feasa ar Éirinn* (c. 1640). The name 'Fianna Fáil' is often (mis)translated as 'Soldiers of Destiny'.

colleagues demonstrated both integrity and courage. In the event, their trust was not misplaced. The incoming government resisted pressure from some of its own grass roots for a policy of *revanche*. Despite winning absolute majorities in the 1933 and 1938 general elections, de Valera's administration engaged in no purges of the public service and maintained the rule of law.

Indeed, during the mid-1930s the most visible threat to Irish democracy seemed to emanate from the professed parliamentarians of Cumann na nGaedheal rather than the 'Red Republicans' of Fianna Fáil. Frustrated by their political reverses, Cosgrave and his associates increasingly turned for support to a recently-formed ex-servicemen's organisation, the Army Comrades' Association or 'Blueshirts', headed by General Eoin O'Duffy. During the Cumann na nGaedheal era, O'Duffy had served as Commissioner of the Garda Síochána, a position from which he was removed by the incoming Fianna Fáil administration. No public explanation was offered by the new government, but the fact that O'Duffy's had been one of the leading voices urging Cosgrave in 1932 to organise a *coup d'état* no doubt figured in de Valera's calculations.[9] Before long, the Blueshirts had acquired a nationwide membership whose numbers have been variously estimated between 30,000 and 60,000. Despite its fascist trappings – a paramilitary structure, a coloured-shirt uniform, and above all the straight-arm salute – its growth owed more to economic discontent than Mussolinian or Hitlerite enthusiasm. Three months after Fianna Fáil's accession to power a dispute between the Irish and British governments over the payment of land annuities escalated into an exchange of punitive tariffs upon each other's exports – the 'Economic War'. The brunt of the sanctions, which the British government imposed in part in the hope of bringing down de Valera and securing the return of the presumably more tractable Cosgrave, fell disproportionately on the rural graziers from whom Cumann na nGaedheal derived a vital element of its support. Already deeply fearful that de Valera's rise to power would be the precursor to the widespread victimisation of pro-Treatyites, a Communist revolution, a resumption of the Civil War or some combination of these, Cumann na nGaedheal supporters flocked into the Blueshirts and embarked on a campaign to withhold payment of rates, or taxes on real property, until the Economic War

---

9 The Cumann na nGaedheal government had also resolved to fire the increasingly insubordinate O'Duffy if it regained office. De Valera offered the outgoing Commissioner a number of alternative government appointments equivalent in rank and pay, but he chose to retire from the public service on a generous state pension. See F. McGarry, *Eoin O'Duffy: A Self-Made Hero* (Oxford: Oxford University Press, 2005), pp. 189–90, 197–9.

was terminated. Anxious not to be left on the sidelines by a mass popular movement drawn from their own followers, Cosgrave and his colleagues agreed to the merging of Cumann na nGaedheal with the Blueshirts and the creation of a new party, Fine Gael ['Tribe of the Gaels'] under O'Duffy's leadership.

It soon became apparent that they had made an immense blunder in doing so. Though several careful studies have established that few individual Blueshirts were drawn to the organisation because of fascist sympathies, the same was not at all true of its leader. The increasingly erratic O'Duffy had already begun his drift toward the far right of politics, as evidenced by a number of intemperate public speeches and the extremist rhetoric of his published writings. Of greater concern to the moderates of Fine Gael was his apparent readiness to contemplate a showdown between the Blueshirts and the government and the growing affinity of O'Duffy's rural supporters for violence, some of it directed against the party's own leaders.[10] In September 1934 Fine Gael frontbench efforts to rein in O'Duffy had the desired effect of provoking him to resign. Cosgrave resumed the leadership of a discredited and demoralised party, which would not return to office for another fourteen years. The entire episode had been a boon to Fianna Fáil, and in more than party-political terms alone. Declaring the Blueshirts a threat to democracy and the rule of law, de Valera persuaded the Oireachtas to suppress them. But in the process, he also took the opportunity to crack down on extra-parliamentary and paramilitary movements of all kinds, including the still-illegal Irish Republican Army. Though he had placed himself beyond the republican pale by entering the Dáil, de Valera was expected by many Sinn Féin supporters to resume the task of destroying the Treaty by all possible means, including physical force. When he showed no sign of doing so, IRA activists had become steadily more assertive and menacing, as their frequent street clashes with Blueshirt bands demonstrated. Banning political paramilitarism of whatever stripe, ostensibly as part of an anti-Blueshirt crackdown, enabled the Fianna Fáil government simultaneously to deal with the irreconcilables in its own camp. Paradoxically, no greater service to the cause of democracy was rendered by the Blueshirts than enabling de Valera to depict himself as its impartial defender.

The eclipse of Blueshirtism marked the last moment when the infant Irish democracy might have been overthrown from within. However remote the likelihood of O'Duffy leading an insurrection in 1933–34, or of the majority of Fine Gael supporters backing him had he sought to do so, his was the last extra-parliamentary organisation

10 *Ibid.*, pp. 258–62.

with a realistic prospect of toppling the elected government of the day. The almost certain outcome of any such attempt would have been a renewal of the Civil War, a vista that even de Valera's most extreme antagonists were unwilling to contemplate. Numerous commentators, for that reason, have seen the mid-1930s as the moment when Irish democracy was placed on a firm foundation and 'regime stabilisation' finally achieved. From this point, Irish political history is perceived as diverging decisively from that of the Succession States, and as conforming to the 'Anglo-Saxon' model of limited parliamentary government maintained by popular consensus.

This conclusion, however, takes for granted what requires to be proven. The absence of powerful anti-democratic movements is treated as evidence of a positive endorsement by the Irish people of constitutional party-political governance. Leaving aside the methodologically dubious nature of arguments from the negative, such an approach causes us to ignore or dismiss as marginal those voices that in the 1930s and even the 1940s remained unconvinced of either the merits or the sustainability of popular sovereignty. These were far more numerous – and far closer to the political mainstream – than is conventionally supposed. As the history of the Third Republic in France reminds us, a system of government may function adequately over a period of decades or even generations, attracting high levels of participation in the political process, without ever being regarded as wholly legitimate. The comparison is not an inapposite one, given the hostility and contempt in which the Third Republic was held in Ireland and the enthusiasm generated by its Vichyite successor. Likewise in Ireland, acquiescence in 'the form of government that divided Irishmen the least' did not signify that the constitutional future of the country had been definitively resolved. Nor was there any reason to suppose that it should have done, inasmuch as the historical forces tending to undermine and discredit liberal democracy were at least as strong in newly independent Ireland as those tending to support it.

The strange death of liberal Ireland?

A considerable amount of scholarly attention has been devoted in recent years to the paradox of Irish democracy in the twentieth century. Basil Chubb, Brian Farrell, Tom Garvin, Jeffrey Prager and Bill Kissane are among the most prominent representatives of a school of political scientists and historians that has attempted to explain how a Western liberal-democratic system emerged in a country in which, at the close of the revolutionary era, so many correlates of authoritarianism appeared to exist.[11] It is no reflection upon the valuable work done by these scholars to observe that structural factors have featured much more prominently in their analyses than cultural ones; or that with the single exception of the Blueshirt phenomenon, little attention has been devoted to the extent to which anti-democratic attitudes continued to flourish in the aftermath of, and notwithstanding, the achievement of regime stabilisation.

A strong argument can nonetheless be made that even the structure of Irish politics in the nineteenth century was far from conducive to the establishment of constitutionalism. Notwithstanding Basil Chubb's assertion that the era of British rule under the Union served to inculcate the Irish people with democratic habits and practices, and Brian Farrell's related argument that the constitutional nationalist struggle was a school of democracy that left a lasting impression even on the republican militants who founded the first Dáil in 1919, other scholars have called into question the degree to which a meaningful conceptual distinction can be considered to exist between proponents of 'moral' and 'physical' force in the nineteenth century.[12] One may further legitimately inquire as to the precise nature of the 'lessons' imparted by political activism in Ireland under the Union. In the mid-nineteenth century, as Jonathan Sperber reminds us, Ireland represented the closest approximation in all of Europe to a 'police state', with fourteen times as many armed policemen per capita as in 'absolutist' Prussia.[13]

The fact that independent Ireland did ultimately succeed in establishing a stable democratic regime on the Westminster model has led to a degree of Whiggism, if not outright self-congratulation, on the part of some commentators. Such a teleological perspective causes us to lose sight not only of the improbability of that outcome, but of the degree to which Ireland's peculiar constitutional trajectory differed from that of the larger polity within which it was formerly subsumed. While it is not my purpose here to posit the existence of an Irish *sonderweg* predis-

11 B. Chubb, *The Government and Politics of Ireland*, 2nd edn (Palo Alto, CA: Stanford University Press, 1982); B. Farrell, 'The First Dáil and After', in B. Farrell, ed., *The Irish Parliamentary Tradition* (Dublin: Gill & Macmillan, 1973); T. Girvin, *1922: The Birth of Irish Democracy* (Dublin: Gill & Macmillan, 1996); J. Prager, *Building Democracy in Ireland: Political Order and Cultural Integration in a Newly Independent Nation* (Cambridge: Cambridge University Press, 1986); B. Kissane, *Explaining Irish Democracy* (Dublin: University College Dublin Press, 2002). See also J. G. A. Pocock, 'The Union in British History', *Transactions of the Royal Historical Society*, vol. 10 (6th series) (Cambridge: Cambridge University Press, 2000).
12 See especially L. P. Curtis Jr, 'Moral and Physical Force: The Language of Violence in Irish Nationalism', *Journal of British Studies* 27:2 (April 1988): 150–89.
13 J. Sperber, *The European Revolutions, 1848–1851* (Cambridge: Cambridge University Press, 1984), p. 242.

posing the population to anti-democratic attitudes, it is nonetheless important to bear in mind how very frequently in modern Irish history the evolution of democratic processes was retarded, frustrated or undermined by state policy.[14] The disenfranchisement of the 'forty-shilling freeholders' in 1829, seemingly as a collective punishment for their having voted in excessive numbers in support of Daniel O'Connell's Catholic Association, represented merely the most glaring example of a tendency throughout the nineteenth century to countenance the operation of democratic principles only to the extent that it did not conflict with executive authority.[15] In the same category can be included the vetoing of the expressed will of the Irish majority on the Home Rule question, first by the House of Commons in 1886 and then by the unelected House of Lords in 1893; the denial to Ireland of a system of local government until 1898; and the passage of more than 100 so-called 'coercion acts' granting emergency powers to the executive between 1800 and 1921. During these years, the suspension of civil liberties and of the subject's right to protection from the exercise of arbitrary state power became almost a permanent feature of British administration, to a degree that excited comment from even so inveterate a Hibernophobe as Benjamin Disraeli.[16] The most frequently targeted rights affected by these statutes included trial by jury, protection against self-incrimination, *habeas corpus* (powers enabling the government to imprison citizens without charge or trial were sanctioned some nineteen times during the first four decades

14 As Tom Garvin observes, 'the fact that pre-independence Ireland had no democratic politics has become occluded … The experience of living under such a regime distorted Irish political culture and twisted the way many Irish people thought about politics'. T. Garvin, 'The Rising and Irish Democracy', in M. Ní Dhonnchadha & T. Dorgan, eds, *Revising the Rising* (Derry: Field Day, 1991), p. 22.

15 As a result of this measure, six-sevenths of the Irish electorate were stripped of the parliamentary vote. See M. Goldring, *Tu ne voteras point: l'exclusion du suffrage universel dans l'Irlande du XIXe siècle* (Biarritz: Atlantica, 2005), p. 68.

16 Speaking at Newport Pagnell in 1874, Disraeli observed that the law then prevailing 'permitted the police to enter without notice into private homes and examine writings in order to see whether they could fix the authorship of anonymous letters upon individuals … strangers sojourning in a district may be arrested by a constable … and unless their answers are satisfactory, or they can produce persons to find security for their good behaviour, they may be sent to gaol … newspapers may be warned, and afterwards become forfeited … Ireland at this moment … is governed by laws of coercion and stringent severity that do not exist in any other quarter of the globe'. *The Times*, 5 February 1874.
    As Marie-Louise Legg notes, in the period 1887–89 alone, ten successful prosecutions were brought against newspaper proprietors under the Criminal Law and Procedure Act for publishing accounts of the meetings of Parnell's organisation, the Irish National League. The usual sentence was 'three months imprisonment, with or without hard labour'. M.-L. Legg, *Newspapers and Nationalism: The Irish Provincial Press 1850–1892* (Dublin: Four Courts Press, 1999), pp. 168–9.

of the Union), freedom of the press, and freedom of movement and association. While the proliferation of emergency legislation under the Union has been the subject of several important historical studies,[17] no scholar to date has systematically examined the impact of these laws in eroding public confidence in the impartiality of the state and the responsiveness of nominally democratic systems to popular concerns.

Similarly, the immensely turbulent decade 1913–23 which witnessed the eventual rupture of the Union can have done little to reinforce the confidence of Irish citizens in the efficacy or sanctity of parliamentary procedures. As David Fitzpatrick observes of the immediate pre-Great War period, a 'private army ruled in Ulster with the acquiescence of the state'.[18] Of this organisation, the Ulster Volunteer Force, one Protestant Ulsterman in three was a member; across the entire island the comparable figure among Catholics for its nationalist counterpart, the Irish National Volunteers, was one in eight.[19] The UVF's attempt, with the connivance and, in some cases, the active assistance, of leading figures in British military and political circles to overturn a parliamentary majority in favour of Home Rule for Ireland by the threat of force has been described as constituting perhaps 'the most devastating blow struck against constitutional democracy in modern Ireland or Britain, the most notorious case of running off the pitch with the ball when losing in the game'.[20] Whether or not this is so, the ease with which democratic procedures could be defeated by armed minorities was carefully noted by members of both communities.

The norms of majority rule and the rule of law suffered further erosion during the three bitter armed conflicts in which Ireland was involved in rapid succession: the Great War, the War of Independence and the Civil War. In August 1914, the Imperial Parliament at Westminster passed without debate a Defence of the Realm Act (DORA) that conferred upon so-called Competent Military Authorities of field rank the power to make regulations having the force of law. Extending over the United Kingdom as a whole, DORA bore especially heavily upon

17 See especially C. Campbell, *Emergency Law in Ireland, 1918–1925* (Oxford: Clarendon Press, 1994); S. H. Palmer, *Police and Protest in England and Ireland 1750–1850* (Cambridge: Cambridge University Press, 1988).
18 D. Fitzpatrick, 'Militarism in Ireland', in T. Bartlett & K. Jeffery, eds, *A Military History of Ireland* (Cambridge: Cambridge University Press, 1996), p. 384.
19 *Ibid.*, p. 383.
20 R. V. Comerford, 'Republicans and Democracy in Modern Irish Politics', in F. McGarry, ed., *Republicanism in Modern Ireland* (Dublin: University College Dublin Press, 2003), p. 18. Comerford observes that ,'As against this, it might be argued that the proposal for Home Rule failed to meet one of the other rules of the democratic game, namely that provision should be made for minorities'.

Ireland after the Easter Rising of 1916. As well as providing the legal basis for the execution of the Rising's leaders by Sir John Maxwell, the Competent Military Authority for Ireland, DORA made possible the introduction by 1918 of internment without trial, the prohibition of meetings or assemblies other than those expressly authorised by the executive, and the trial of civilians by courts-martial. The still more draconian Restoration of Order in Ireland Act, adopted at the height of the War of Independence in August 1920, empowered the state to suppress the operation of local government in Irish towns and counties by confiscating the tax revenues payable to local author-ites; to replace coroners' courts with military tribunals; and to impose internal economic blockades by means of restrictions on the passage of persons or goods.[21] Many of these powers were retained, in substance if not in the letter, by the provisional government of the Irish Free State during and after the Civil War, especially under a series of Public Safety Acts adopted between 1923 and 1931.[22] North of the Border, as Colm Campbell points out, most of the emergency provisions of DORA and the Restoration of Order in Ireland Act became part of the domestic legislation of the new Stormont administration under the Civil Authorities (Special Powers) Act, 1922, with the Minister for Home Affairs in Belfast exercising the functions previously discharged by the Competent Military Authority.

Such a legacy could not fail to leave its mark upon the two Irish polities created in the early 1920s. Numerous commentators have noted the high degree of administrative centralisation and executive control that characterised both the Dublin- and Belfast-based jurisdictions. In Northern Ireland, this was accentuated by the abolition of propor-tional representation, the dissolution of local authorities that persisted in returning nationalist majorities, and the unabashed exercise of the gerrymander. The Irish Free State, for its part, similarly eviscerated local government; ended the directly elected judiciary and the institution of the popular initiative;[23] made extensive use of its Special Infantry Corps to suppress peaceful labour disputes; and acquiesced in the Garda Special Branch's subjection of political opponents to persistent and

---

21 Campbell, *Emergency Law in Ireland*, pp. 9–30.
22 The most sweeping of these emergency laws, the Public Safety Act of October 1931, 'suspended habeas corpus, introduced internment without trial, trial by military tribunal, death sentences for the possession of firearms, and reprisal executions'. Kissane, *Explaining Irish Democracy*, p. 207.
23 Under Article 48 of the Free State constitution, any proposition supported by 50,000 signatories was entitled to be placed before the electorate in a popular referendum. When the opposition Fianna Fáil party attempted in 1927 to invoke this provision to force a referendum on the Oath of Allegiance, it was deleted from the constitution by an Act of the Oireachtas.

illegal harassment, detention and assault. The Cumann na nGaedheal government, as John Regan observes, 'remained dependent on a system of law implemented through emergency powers and military courts which made a nonsense of the constitution'.[24] That constitution had itself been amended by act of parliament no fewer than twenty-seven times in fifteen years, lending an unhealthy relativism to the political system. When its de Valera-drafted successor was presented to the electorate in 1937, it was adopted by the affirmative votes of a mere 50.9% of those casting ballots. At the time there seemed little reason to believe that the new constitutional dispensation would prove any more durable than its predecessor had done.

Internal opposition

After the conclusion of the Civil War, the principal danger to the survival of the new Irish regime was thought to derive from the IRA and other republican organisations. But despite isolated and largely unco-ordinated attacks, such as those against Garda barracks in Munster in November 1926 and the assassination of the Cumann na nGaedheal Minister for Home Affairs, Kevin O'Higgins, the following July, the threat to the security of the state from this quarter had largely been contained by the mid-1920s, although its nuisance value thereafter remained high.[25]

The official army, on the other hand, could not fully be relied upon. Too much has been made of the so-called 'army mutiny' of 1924 which, despite its melodramatic name, constituted more a display of insubordination – albeit of a very serious nature – on the part of certain mid-ranking officers aggrieved at the government's post-Civil War demobilisation scheme and its failure to pursue an aggressive republican policy than an attempt to overthrow the institutions of state.[26] The suppression of the 'mutiny' did not, however, curb the proclivity of military leaders from time to time to engage in activities that were definitely inimical to the welfare of Ireland's infant democracy. A case in point, as noted above, was the abortive effort made by Eoin O'Duffy, Garda Commissioner and former army commander-in-chief, to orchestrate a *coup* rather than turn over power to the incoming Fianna Fáil administration in 1932. As Eunan O'Halpin observes, 'at least for the state's first twenty years, no government could be absolutely certain of

24 Regan, *The Irish Counter-Revolution*, p. 303.
25 R. English, *Armed Struggle: The History of the IRA* (New York: Oxford University Press, 2003), ch. 2.
26 M. G. Valiulis, *Almost a Rebellion: The Irish Army Mutiny of 1924* (Cork: Tower, 1985); Regan, *The Irish Counter-Revolution*, pp. 163–97.

the complete loyalty of the defence forces'.[27] This incertitude accounts in large measure for the practice of Cumann na nGaedheal and Fianna Fáil ministries alike of running down the armed forces to the lowest possible level consistent with the maintenance of internal security.[28] In light of the unhappy record of military intervention in the political life of most other European countries established in the aftermath of the Great War, it is hard to condemn them for doing so. Armed services, however, stand as the ultimate guarantor of the state's existence. That the Irish army could not be trusted for this purpose demonstrated the continuing fragility of the political structure.

Civil War tensions, exacerbated by the manifest failure of the new Irish state adequately to address, far less to resolve, the country's chronic under-performance across the gamut of social and economic measures, contributed powerfully to the sense of instability that pervaded the Irish political scene. As a result, criticism and outright condemnation of parliamentary democracy as a system of government became an increasingly common feature of public discourse in the post-independence years. C. S. 'Todd' Andrews noted that there had always been an element of republicanism holding that 'the people had no right to do wrong', a conviction that had been reinforced between the wars by the abject failure of republican political movements other than Fianna Fáil. Its quarrel, though, was less with the principle of democratic decision-making than its outcome in one specific instance, and there is little to suggest that it would have occurred even to the most extreme republicans to repudiate the concept of majority rule had the vote on the Treaty in 1922 gone the other way. The description by Brian Girvin of the republican element during the Treaty controversy as 'anti-democratic forces' is thus at best misleading, inasmuch as the question at issue between the two sides was as much about the legitimacy of the process by which the vote on the Treaty had been conducted as about the acceptability or otherwise of the Treaty itself.[29] As John Regan notes: 'The assumption that democracy is synonymous with majoritarianism was and remains suspect. The Irish electorate

---

27 E. O'Halpin, 'Army, Politics and Society in Independent Ireland, 1923–1945', in T. G. Fraser & K. Jeffrey, eds, *Men, Women and War: Papers Read Before the XXth Irish Conference of Historians, Read at Magee College, University of Ulster, 6–8 June, 1991* (Dublin: Lilliput, 1993), p. 159.

28 Article 8 of the Anglo-Irish Treaty imposed limits on the size of the armed forces that the Irish Free State was permitted to maintain. Except during the Civil War years 1922–23, however, these were never approached in practice.

29 B. Girvin, *From Union to Union: Nationalism, Democracy and Religion in Ireland – Act of Union to EU* (Dublin: Gill & Macmillan, 2002), p. 63. For a contrary view, see P. Hart, 'Parliamentary Politics and the Irish Revolution', in F. McGarry, ed., *Republicanism in Modern Ireland* (Dublin: University College Dublin Press, 2003), pp. 29–30.

explicitly in 1922, and implicitly thereafter, remained under the threat of British violence should it decide to express its aspiration to national self-determination in a manner contrary to British interests'.[30]

If the losing side in the Civil War cannot be categorised as 'anti-democrats' by definition, the 'democratic' credentials of the winners must also be considered from a more nuanced perspective. Luke Gibbons has noted that 'the Arthur Griffith who shouted down Synge's *Playboy* in 1907, and who stated that no excuse is "needed for an Irish nationalist declining to hold the negro his peer" is also the Arthur Griffith who pushed through the Treaty in 1922'.[31] As Tom Garvin points out, moreover, 'The attitude towards the Irish people as being essentially unworthy of their heroic leaders, which so permeated the anti-Treaty side, existed in a rather different form on the pro-Treaty side as well'.[32] Eoin O'Duffy, in commencing a second career in the 1930s as leader of the Blueshirts, was by no means the only prominent Treatyite who looked to extremist movements overseas as role-models for the independent Irish state. In 1922 and 1923, the government's chief law adviser, Hugh Kennedy, and his deputy, Kevin O'Shiel, individually drew ministers' attention to the effectiveness of the *Freikorps* in eradicating left-wing rebellion in Weimar Germany.[33] One of those ministers, James Joseph (J. J.) Walsh, called at a Cumann na nGaedheal parliamentary party meeting for the creation of an Irish version of the *Fasci di combattimento*.[34] As Eunan O'Halpin concludes of Cumann na nGaedheal's tenure in office: 'Making hostages of condemned men, tolerating murder by state forces, shooting unconvicted republican leaders, using civil war legislation and the army to quell social and industrial unrest – all this set a grim precedent which some future government confronted with disorder might follow'.[35] Having been turned out of office in 1932, Cumann na nGaedheal's attachment to itself of a private paramilitary force and its installation of the leader of that force, the eccentric and autocratic O'Duffy, as head of the party betrayed, to say the least, a highly equivocal attitude to the electorate it claimed to serve. So too did the secret meetings of Cumann na nGaedheal representatives with British officials for the purpose of

30 Regan, *The Irish Counter-Revolution*, p. 69.
31 L. Gibbons, 'Labour and Local History: The Case of Jim Gralton, 1886–1945', in *Transformations in Irish Culture* (South Bend, IN: University of Notre Dame Press, 1996), p. 105.
32 Girvin, *From Union to Union*, p. 60.
33 P. Murray, *Oracles of God: The Roman Catholic Church and Irish Politics 1922–37* (Dublin: University College Dublin Press, 2000), p. 88; Regan, *The Irish Counter-Revolution*, p. 121.
34 Regan, *The Irish Counter-Revolution*, p. 122.
35 E. O'Halpin, *Defending Ireland: The Irish State and Its Enemies Since 1922* (Oxford: Oxford University Press, 1999), p. 38.

proferring advice as to how the de Valera government might best be brought down.[36] Seán Lemass' notorious description of Fianna Fáil as 'a slightly constitutional party' might with some justice be applied to Cumann na nGaedheal in those years also.

Among ordinary citizens, too, a profoundly cynical attitude to the political system often prevailed. Even before the War of Independence, Todd Andrews noted the widespread perception in advanced nationalist circles that 'all politicians were ... low, dirty and treacherous. This was the attitude of the Volunteers as well as of the members of the Sinn Féin clubs'. As for the democratic process, 'The only democracy we knew of was British democracy and that had less than nothing to commend itself to me'.[37] His stance, while especially characteristic of post-Civil War republicans, came to be shared by many on the right in the 1930s as they realised that the electoral success of Fianna Fáil was not a passing phase. Whether its adherents shared the *weltanschauungen* of 'shirted' movements in Italy and Germany – the available evidence, as we have seen, suggests that most did not – the rise of the Blueshirt movement represented at least in part a vote of no confidence in the conventional political process. Though the Blueshirts chose not to press their differences with the government to the point of outright insurrection, the number prepared to acknowledge the *de jure* legitimacy of the de Valera administration remained small even after the latter's sweeping victory in the 1933 general election. Comparatively few were as outspoken as O'Duffy's successor to the Blueshirt leadership, Ned Cronin, who proclaimed the following year that 'if a dictatorship is necessary for the Irish people we are going to have one. It will be better than the so-called democratic Government we have, run by foreigners and Jews'.[38] Nonetheless, assertions that the government of the day – as the supposed instrument of the IRA, of crypto-Communists or of de Valera's own 'dictatorial' ambitions – had no rightful claim to the allegiance of the Irish people were so commonplace in the mid-1930s as not to invite attention. Many of these expressions of defiance were the direct counterpart of republicans' rejection of the Free State, and should not in themselves be taken as evidence of a right-wing reaction in favour of totalitarianism. But even at the level of rhetoric, reflexive dismissals of the electorate's verdict could not but erode confidence in the validity of parliamentary politics. The result

36 See D. McMahon, *Republicans and Imperialists: Anglo-Irish Relations in the 1930s* (New Haven, CT: Yale University Press, 1984), pp. 80–1.
37 C. S. Andrews, *Autobiography*, vol. 1, *Dublin Made Me* (Dublin: Mercier, 1979), pp. 101, 116.
38 Garda Síochána report of a speech by Cronin at Arbour Hill, 16 July 1934, quoted by Éamon de Valera. 55 *DP–Dáil*, c. 664 (7 March 1935).

was an increased willingness by mid-decade, among the intelligentsia and 'respectable' political opinion no less than those on the paramilitary extremes, to entertain the possibility that independent Ireland had embarked upon the wrong constitutional path. The proposition that democratic systems were fatally flawed, either as a result of their internal contradictions or their propensity to open the door to a debased ultra-modern cosmopolitanism, became the basis in turn for a more fundamental critique of the Irish constitutional experiment.

On the right wing of Irish politics, anti-democratic and anti-parliamentary sentiment has traditionally been associated almost exclusively with Blueshirtism. Certainly it would be a mistake to understate the seriousness of the Blueshirt challenge to the regime. 'There should be no doubt', John Newsinger contends, 'that if the Blueshirts had been successful, Irish parliamentary democracy would have been replaced by some kind of authoritarian government reflecting the balance of forces between the conservatives and fascists in the movement'.[39] While fascist ideas were undoubtedly represented within Blueshirt ranks, especially among its intellectual element, Maurice Manning and Mike Cronin have convincingly demonstrated that the movement represented to a far greater extent a continuation of the Civil War – or even the Land War of 1879–81 – by less violent means than an Irish manifestation of ultra-rightist activism.[40] By mid-decade the remnant of Blueshirtism, represented by its political wing the National Corporate Party, had indeed become a vehicle for the promotion of totalitarian doctrines,[41] while O'Duffy's increasingly extreme activities and associations were going far to belie Manning's recent contention that there was 'nothing sinister' about his political makeup.[42] However, the most outspoken attacks upon parliamentarianism in the 1930s were as likely to come from personages who were entirely unassociated with Blueshirtism – although, paradoxically, hostility to the democratic system was capable of uniting those who differed on every other significant issue in national politics. Joseph Hanly, a former inspector of schools, anticipated the most radical wing of Blueshirtism with his

39 J. Newsinger, 'Blackshirts, Blueshirts, and the Spanish Civil War', *Historical Journal* 44:3 (September 2001): 838–9.
40 M. A. Manning, *The Blueshirts*, 3rd edn (Dublin: Gill & Macmillan, 2006); M. Cronin, *The Blueshirts and Irish Politics* (Dublin: Four Courts Press, 1997).
41 Typical of which was an editorial in the party organ asserting that 'Fascism stands for justice between individuals as well as classes'. *Blueshirt* 1:17 [N.S.] (26 January 1935). For an analysis of the NCP, see M. White, 'The Greenshirts: Fascism in the Irish Free State 1935–1945', PhD diss., University of London, 2004.
42 M. A. Manning, *James Dillon: A Biography* (Dublin: Wolfhound, 1999), p. 85. In fairness, it should be noted that much information has come to light about O'Duffy's anti-democratic activities since the publication of Manning's book.

call, in a widely read polemic of 1931, for 'more and still more compulsion in the proper direction of national forces … In our circumstances, vigorous, varied, and unequivocal national compulsion is not only desirable, but is urgently required'.[43] From the opposite end of the political spectrum, the republican Francis Stuart, who would spend the Second World War in Berlin broadcasting Nazi propaganda to Ireland, observed contemptuously: 'Democracy is the ideal of those whose lives as individuals are failures and who, feeling their own futility, take refuge in the mass and become arrogant in the herd'.[44] James Hogan, one of the Blueshirts' would-be ideologues, similarly condemned liberal parliamentary systems in 1935 for the moral vacuum at their core resulting from their refusal to acknowledge and uphold transcendent or absolute truths. Democracy, he observed, was 'not for all societies and all times'.[45]

> The malady which is now on the point of destroying civilization in any sense in which that word is worth using, has definitely commenced to attack us, as is evident from the cinema infested condition of our cities, the increasing vulgarisation of outlook even in the countryside, and the assimilation on all hands of a cosmopolitanism that must in the end poison our national existence at its source.[46]

Critics of the democratic system saw at least some hope for the future, believing that a properly led and disciplined Ireland might not merely stand aside from, but even ultimately be the instrument of reversal of, the advance of twentieth-century materialism and decadence. Notwithstanding his own denatured Hibernian variant of 'cultural despair',[47] Francis Stuart in a futuristic 1932 novel set in an Ireland at war with an unnamed Continental combination placed a soliloquy against the horrors of decadent, value-free modernity in the mouth of one of his female protagonists: 'We're not just fighting an army on the Continent; we're fighting a civilisation that has been refined to rottenness. It's swamping the world like a second flood. It's only Ireland that's withstanding it'.[48] Others expressed the hope that Ireland and other peripheral societies, as in the 'Dark Ages', could once again become 'reservoirs of hope for civilisation' in Europe and the world.

43 J. Hanly, *The National Ideal: A Practical Exposition of True Nationality Appertaining to Ireland* (Dublin: Dollard, 1931), pp. 70–1.
44 F. Stuart, *Things to Live For: Notes for an Autobiography* (London: Jonathan Cape, 1934), p. 254.
45 J. Hogan, *Modern Democracy* (Cork: Cork University Press, 1938), p. 60.
46 *Ibid.*, p. 84.
47 See F. Stern, *The Politics of Cultural Despair: A Study in the Rise of the Germanic Ideology* (Berkeley, CA: University of California Press, 1961).
48 F. Stuart, *Pigeon Irish* (New York: Macmillan, 1932).

Fr Patrick O'Leary, writing in the *Catholic Mind* in 1932, drew upon 'ancient prophecies' to predict that 'under the guidance of Heaven we are going to rebuild Jerusalem in Erin'. Ireland's divinely ordained mission as an independent state, he asserted, was to exemplify the compatibility of Catholic ideals and material prosperity.[49] As Aodh de Blacam, literary editor of the *Irish Press*, asserted in 1935,

> We see the European urban civilisation going down to-day in corruption of body and mind, in merciless warfare, and in unbelief … Only 'green' Europe, the peasant lands behind the big cities, promises to live on after the ruin … The ideal natural life of Homer, in Ireland revivified by the natural Faith – may not this be the model and hope of the world of the future?[50]

But such a national revival, in the view of many observers, could hardly take place so long as the nation was divided against itself by a party-political system whose organising principle was the setting of Irishmen and women at each other's throats. Nor could its economic counterpart, liberal capitalism, address the challenges presented by the Great Depression and the Economic War. In both spheres the country's difficulties were traceable to its having entered the twentieth century with an ideological apparatus more appropriate to the nineteenth. Democracy, the journalist J. M. O'Sullivan lamented, was 'dying in Ireland', yet 'we'll have none of autocratic Continental methods, no matter how much ultimately to the advantage of the country'.[51] As events were to show, however, many Irish citizens were more than willing in the 1930s to adopt 'autocratic Continental methods' on their own initiative, should the government prove reluctant to do so.

The 'Rosary Riots'

The potential in Ireland for right-wing extremism, even in the absence of a significant challenge to the established order from the political left, was thrown into sharp relief by the Dublin anti-Communist riots of March 1933, which featured the most serious disturbances to take place in the capital since the Civil War. Among the principal causes of these clashes were the increasingly close links, fostered by organisers from the Communist Party of Great Britain, between the IRA and the nascent Irish Communist movement; the aftershocks of the bitter general election campaign in February, which had featured a considerable

---

49　Fr. P. O'Leary, 'Destiny of the Irish Nation', *Catholic Mind* 3:4 (April 1932): 87.
50　A. de Blacam, *Gentle Ireland: An Account of a Christian Culture in History and Modern Life* (Milwaukee, WI: Bruce, 1935), pp. 21–2.
51　*Kerryman*, 4 February 1939. The author is not to be confused with his namesake Professor J. M. O'Sullivan, Minister of Education in the Cumann na nGaedheal administration.

amount of public disorder between Blueshirts and republicans and much 'Reds under the bed' electoral propaganda[52] from Cumann na nGaedheal; and, above all, the encouragement given to a 'Red scare' by leading Catholic clergymen, who feared that class politics, exacerbated by the unemployment crisis, were for the first time beginning to gain a degree of popular appeal. Disquieted by the emergence of anti-clerical governments in such traditional bulwarks of Catholicism as Mexico and Spain, Irish bishops and priests feared that unless constant vigilance were exercised, the extreme left might succeed in establishing a foothold even in Ireland. A number of ominous straws in the wind, from the hierarchy's perspective, included the appearance of Saor Éire ['Free Ireland'], a political body composed of Marxist republicans; the formation of an Irish Unemployed Workers' Movement, a counterpart to the similarly named British organisation headed by the Communist Wal Hannington; a series of controversial public interventions by the Irish Friends of the Soviet Union, headed by Dónal O'Reilly, a 1916 veteran and Communist activist, and the English ex-suffragette, Charlotte Despard,[53] seeking to depict the USSR in a positive light as a country supportive of religious freedom;[54] and the activities of James Gralton, a Leitrim-born IRA member who had emigrated to the United States before the Great War. A convert to Communism, Gralton returned to Ireland in 1932 and assumed a prominent role in extreme-left and anti-clerical agitation. Taking advantage of his earlier renunciation of Irish nationality, the government promptly served a deportation order upon him. On 5 March 1933, a meeting at Gralton's birthplace in Drumsna, convened to protest against his removal from the country, ended in chaos when the speaker, Peadar O'Donnell of Saor Éire, was showered with stones and clods of earth and was rescued from a worse fate only through the intervention of the Gardaí; according to O'Donnell, the local parish priest, Fr Cosgrove, had led the assault on him. A second meeting, scheduled to be held at the nearby village of Gowel on the same day, 'had to be abandoned owing to the hostile attitude of the people'.[55]

52 The use of this term is not meant to imply that its authors were unpersuaded by their own rhetoric. In a March 1933 letter to Jacques Maritain, the erstwhile Minister for Defence Desmond Fitzgerald confided his 'fear that the country may go Bolshevist'. Quoted in Regan, *The Irish Counter-Revolution*, p. 280.

53 For particulars of Despard's eventful career, see A. Linklater, *An Unhusbanded Life: Charlotte Despard: Suffragette, Socialist, and Sinn Féiner* (London: Hutchinson, 1980).

54 Absurdly, O'Reilly and Despard contended that 'Nobody in Russia has suffered because of their religion; no priest has suffered because he was a priest'. *Irish Independent*, 3 March 1933.

55 *Irish Press*, 6 and 13 March 1933. For a discussion of the implications of the Gralton affair, see Gibbons, 'Labour and Local History'.

It was not surprising, therefore, that the Lenten pastorals issued by the Catholic hierarchy at the beginning of March should have adverted to the menace of Communism, and the necessity for all to be on their guard against subversive elements financed from abroad that, by the use of seductive phrases like 'land', 'bread' or 'the Republic', might seek to draw the Irish people away from their historic allegiance to faith and fatherland. More unusual was the extremism of language of many of these clerical denunciations, some of which, as the historian of Irish Communism Mike Milotte has observed, 'might, at another time and in another place, have occasioned numerous prosecutions for incitement to violence'.[56] Matthew Cullen, Archbishop of Kildare and Leighlin, declared in his pastoral: 'There is no reason why anyone who undertakes to propagate Communism should be allowed to do so with impunity'.[57] In his St Patrick's Day address, the Primate of All Ireland, Joseph Cardinal MacRory, expressed himself almost as immoderately when he warned Communist agitators that 'there is no room for them or their blasphemies among the children of St. Patrick'.[58] Clergymen of lesser prominence, for their part, often translated these episcopal anathemas into even more provocative terms for the benefit of their own flocks, as in the case of Archdeacon P. Donohoe, speaking at Carrick-on-Shannon on 6 March, who promised his listeners that the 'children of martyred forefathers would give short shrift to the allies of Satan'.[59]

The growing intensity of anti-Communist feeling was also expressed in Irish responses to political developments overseas. Commenting on Adolf Hitler's campaign of repression in Germany after the burning of the Reichstag, the *Irish Times*, while deploring his anti-Semitic excesses, declared in an editorial that, 'In reasoned warfare against the Communists Herr Hitler will have the support of all civilised nations. At the moment he is Europe's standard-bearer against Muscovite terrorism, and, although some of his methods certainly are open to question, nobody doubts his entire sincerity'.[60] Seeking elsewhere for an anti-Marxist role model – and no doubt with one eye to the fortunes of its Italian-inspired Blueshirt allies – the *Irish Independent* suggested that Mussolini's fascist regime provided an example of the diversion of socialist impulses into constructive channels from which Irish advocates of a new political order might profitably learn: 'this Italian

56 M. Milotte, *Communism in Modern Ireland: The Pursuit of the Workers' Republic Since 1916*
     (Dublin: Gill & Macmillan, 1984), p. 118.
57 *Irish Times*, 6 March 1933.
58 *Irish Press*, 18 March 1933.
59 *Irish Independent*, 6 March 1933.
60 *Irish Times*, 6 March 1933.

achievement, which provides all the advantages of real democratic control, with stable government and disciplined national life, divorced from any danger of subversive disorder, seems to be more worthy of attention and study by would-be political guides for this Catholic country than does the godless venture of Moscow in materialistic Statecraft'.[61]

It was not long before these appeals to anti-Communist action, given practical direction by Bishop Matthew Collier of Kilkenny's exhortation to form anti-Bolshevik 'Vigilance Committees in every parish', were answered. On 4 March, the newly founded Irish Unity Association (IUA), a Blueshirt splinter, issued a public appeal to the leaders and members of all parties, creeds and organisations to organise a national convention 'to consider and discuss Constitutional ways and means of safeguarding Christianity in Ireland from the menace of Communism'.[62] Twelve days later, a public meeting was held at 41 Parnell Street in Dublin to establish a second body, with similar objectives, named St Patrick's Anti-Communist League (SPACL). This latter society was formed on the initiative of an octogenarian ex-butler from the Catholic University School, Patrick Glennon, who since his retirement had occupied himself with distributing anti-socialist tracts and pamphlets around Dublin and who now assumed the presidency of the movement. Although like the IUA the League was nominally non-sectarian, claiming to represent 'Christians of all Creeds', its denominational character was made clear by the adoption of a rule requiring members to wear a badge or emblem 'with the device of the Sacred Heart thereon'.[63] Adherents were also enjoined to pray daily for the defeat of the Communist menace, and to do everything in their power to ensure the achievement of the League's objectives.

Within weeks of the foundation of the IUA and St Patrick's Anti-Communist League, socialist and Communist premises in Dublin became targets of a series of increasingly serious attacks by riotous mobs singing hymns and chanting papal slogans as an accompaniment to their assaults. On 24 March, a meeting in the city centre addressed by James Larkin Jr was violently broken up by the crowd, a section of which sang 'Faith of Our Fathers'; the Gardaí escorted the speakers away for their own protection, pursued by an angry mob.

61 *Irish Independent*, 25 March 1933.
62 Headed by Con Brosnan, the IUA called for a reconciliation between the two factions in the Civil War. Its aims were stated to be 'to promote national unity, to conduct a vigorous campaign against Communism, and to support Irish-made goods and encourage new industries'. *Irish Press*, 20 February 1933; *Irish Independent*, 4 March 1933.
63 Memorandum by Chief Supt. T. Clarke, 8 April 1933, JUS 8/711, National Archives of Ireland, Dublin (hereafter NAI).

Two days later, a Communist speaker outside the General Post Office was howled down by spectators who forced the abandonment of the meeting.[64] On the 27th, police were called to a disorderly assembly of between 300 and 400 people who were trying to break down the door of Connolly House in Great Strand Street, the national headquarters of the Communist Revolutionary Workers' Groups (RWG).[65] The crowd fled upon the arrival of the Gardaí, but not before they had shattered most of the panes of glass in the front of the building with bricks and burnt in the street literature removed from the ground-floor window display.[66] The following evening, a hymn-singing party gathered to throw stones at Mrs Despard's Irish Workers' College in Eccles Street, but were persuaded to depart 'in military formation' by a priest from the adjacent nursing home. The disappointed stone-throwers thereupon joined forces with a 400-strong mob which earlier in the evening had renewed the attack on Connolly House, and on this occasion, with the assistance of the Eccles Street rioters, succeeded in penetrating the police cordon around the premises. The occupants of the building aggravated the situation by hurling back at the crowd some of the projectiles thrown at them, and it was only with difficulty and the arrival of Garda reinforcements that order was finally restored. At least two people were injured in the mêlée, which the *Irish Workers' Voice*, the journal of the RWG, alleged to have been 'directed by A.C.A. men'.[67] Later that night, bands of young men roamed the streets of the city centre looking for Communists to attack; chancing across what it took to be two left-wingers on Aston Quay, one such vigilante group was poised to hurl them into the River Liffey when Gardaí came to their rescue.[68]

By 29 March it had become clear to the authorities that 'the movement against Communism is gaining strength and Police precautions will be necessary to prevent clashes between rival parties and to prevent damage to property'.[69] In anticipation of further disturbances,

64 *Irish Press*, 25 and 27 March 1933.
65 The Revolutionary Workers' Groups, founded in November 1930, represented an unsuccessful attempt by the Irish Communist movement to boost membership by adopting a decentralised structure and giving greater autonomy to local organisations. They were dissolved upon the relaunch of the Communist Party of Ireland in June 1933. For a detailed discussion, see E. O'Connor, *Reds and the Green: Ireland, Russia and the Communist Internationals 1919–43* (Dublin: University College Dublin Press, 2004).
66 *Irish Press*, 28 March 1933. The official police report stated that all thirty-one panes of glass facing the street had been broken by the crowd, but press photographs show that some windows survived this initial assault.
67 i.e. Army Comrades' Association. *Irish Workers' Voice*, 1 April 1933.
68 Memoranda by Sergeant T. Finlay, 28 March 1933; Inspector P. Heffernan, 29 March; Station Sergeant T. Fitzgerald, 29 March, JUS 8/711, NAI; *Irish Independent*, 29 March.
69 Unsigned Garda memorandum, 29 March 1933, JUS 8/711, NAI.

a mobile squad of two inspectors, five sergeants and sixty officers was assembled that evening at the Store Street Garda station. Around seven o'clock, a serious fire broke out at a furniture warehouse on the corner of Bachelor's Walk and North Lotts, at which so large a crowd gathered to spectate that the fire brigade was obliged to turn its hoses upon them to keep them at a safe distance.[70] As the fire was slowly brought under control, members of the crowd began to filter down to Connolly Hall, only a few hundred yards away, where they launched the third, and by far the most violent, onslaught upon the building in as many days. The riot once again commenced with an exchange of missiles between the crowd and the defenders of the hall, followed by an attempt to rush the Garda cordon. Although the mobile unit at Store Street was quickly deployed the situation deteriorated rapidly. When the newly-appointed head of the Dublin police force, Chief Superintendent Clarke, arrived to survey the scene an hour later, he found such serious disorders in progress that he ordered 'all available police on and off duty … to be sent to Great Strand Street immediately'. This was, however, only the overture to what was to develop into a four-hour-long pitched battle between a crowd estimated at between five and six thousand, and an increasingly beleaguered cordon of police officers. After the initial unsuccessful onslaught upon the hall, the occupants, who had barricaded themselves inside the building since the previous day and had taken the precaution of arming themselves with a large supply of 'bricks, stones and slabs of mortar', poured down a continuous rain of projectiles upon the crowd in the street below. The rioters hurled these missiles back and 'roared encouragement' to the young men who were attempting to overwhelm the police cordon from both ends of the street. Despite energetic resistance, the Garda contingent was unable to prevent members of the mob from climbing to the roof of the hall, gaining access to the interior through the skylight, and setting the building on fire using cans of petrol. Although the Dublin Fire Brigade arrived quickly from the scene of the warehouse fire and extinguished the blaze, the Gardaí had by now become virtually 'besieged', and were frantically attempting to beat off their assailants, some thirty of whom were removed to Jervis Street hospital with head injuries.[71] About eleven o'clock, as the battle between protesters and police reached its zenith, a defender inside

70 *Irish Press*, 30 March 1933.
71 The evacuation of the wounded by members of the St John Ambulance Brigade was resisted by the crowd, who believed that 'the removal of men on the stretchers was a ruse to evacuate Communists from the besieged area'. An ambulance thought to be carrying a Communist was also attacked and damaged. *Irish Times*, 31 March 1933.

the hall opened fire on the rioters with a gun, hitting one in the leg, while another part of the crowd made 'desperate efforts…to reach the hall from the Capel St. and Swift Row ends of G[rea]t Strand Street'. A large number of raiders were able to gain access to the building and proceeded to set it alight for a second time, although once again the fire brigade managed to bring the conflagration under control. At that point, the Gardaí decided in the interests of preventing potential loss of life to evacuate the occupants of the hall for their own safety to the Bridewell, taking with them a number of rioters who had been placed under arrest. This tactical withdrawal was accomplished only with great difficulty, the crowds continuing to attack the police as they withdrew with their prisoners. At last, around midnight, the mob began to disperse, and the Gardaí were able to regain control of the area. In the subsequent search of the hall, revolvers, ammunition and a number of discharged shell-casings were recovered.[72]

The scale and severity of the disturbances raised suspicions – shared by some recent historians – that they had been orchestrated in advance, although in his report on the Connolly House siege Chief Superintendent Clarke noted that the crowd had been made up of 'persons of different walks of life in the City, including a very large percentage of respectably dressed young women'.[73] A fortnight before the beginning of the riots, J. E. O'Brien, secretary of the Management Committee at Connolly House, stated publicly that he had learned that 'an attempt is to be made to wreck our premises', and warned that any attack would meet with resistance.[74] Certainly the attitude taken by the leadership of St Patrick's Anti-Communist League in the aftermath of the disturbances was highly equivocal: whereas in a letter to the press Glennon denied that members of his organisation had been involved, two days later he declared that 'while he would not condone violence the people should not tolerate Communist speakers or others who blasphemed'.[75] Other eyewitnesses at the scene, however, considered that the violence, though fierce, had been spontaneous. Hanna Sheehy Skeffington, who had arrived just as the rioting was beginning and had been attacked and slightly injured by two working-class women

72 Mike Milotte incorrectly states that 'Throughout the attack [on Connolly Hall] the police had watched from a distance, making only one arrest … Only when the crowds moved to O'Connell Street and started looting shops did the Gardaí intervene to halt them'. Milotte, *Communism in Modern Ireland*, p. 119.

73 Dónal Ó Drisceoil is among those who consider that the Rosary Riots were 'co-ordinated' by St Patrick's Anti-Communist League. No evidence, however, is cited in support of this assertion. See D. Ó Drisceoil, *Peadar O'Donnell* (Cork: Cork University Press, 2001), pp. 80–1.

74 *Irish Independent*, 11 March 1933.

75 *Irish Press*, 1 and 3 April 1933.

at the scene, testified that the 'active mobbers were drunken women and young street "toughs" of both sexes'. Passers-by had been called upon to give a demonstration of Catholic allegiance, and set upon if they refused: 'If one was not prepared to intone a hymn one was marked out for violence'. The crowd, she concluded, had acted in a 'mad frenzy ... recalling the "separation allowance" gangs of Easter Week'.[76]

Despite the extent of injury to persons and property, a distinctly unapologetic note was struck by individuals who in other circumstances were swift to condemn any breach of law and order. In a letter criticising the *Irish Press* for its editorial condemnation of the riots, one correspondent maintained that the disturbances 'were not to be taken as an indication of a law-breaking propensity on the part of the individuals concerned, but rather as an inclination of the general will regarding the prevention of the spread of Communism'. Another held the government responsible for compelling the citizenry to seize the initiative, warning ominously that free speech was not an end in itself but merely a means to an end, 'the happiness of the people ... It is the duty of the Government to put down agitation subversive of public morality and loyalty. Why does it not?'[77] Nor were such responses merely the product of the heat of the moment. More than two years afterwards, Professor James Hogan of University College Cork continued to defend the rioters as 'Catholic citizens who took the law into their own hands in default of Government action'.[78]

Anti-Red herrings

Although St Patrick's Anti-Communist League continued its activities, in the spring of 1934 issuing another statement disclaiming responsibility for a series of attacks on Communist Party of Ireland meetings in Dublin, the movement declined as its leadership passed from the decrepit Glennon to his still less capable lieutenant, Patrick McCormack.[79] Mass assaults on premises associated with pro-Communist bodies or against those who were believed to be aiding and abetting Bolshevism by printing far-left literature nonetheless continued to be a feature of Irish political life throughout the 1930s. In April 1936, for example, a Communist Party of Ireland contingent attaching

76 *Ibid.*, 31 March 1933.
77 *Ibid.*, 1 April, 31 March 1933.
78 J. Hogan, *Could Ireland Become Communist? The Facts of the Case* (Dublin: Cahill, n.d. [1935]), p. 64.
79 Memorandum by Station Sergeant D. E. McCarthy, 29 April 1934, JUS 8/342, NAI.

itself to the rear of the annual Easter Rising commemorative parade to Glasnevin cemetery in Dublin came under sustained attack by the crowds en route. Despite the efforts of the Gardaí to protect the demonstrators by encircling them completely as they marched, the cordon was repeatedly breached and 'many of the combatants were to be seen bleeding freely from the face'.[80] Shortly afterward, a Dublin meeting to have been addressed by Peadar O'Donnell and the British Communist MP Willie Gallacher was assailed by a crowd of approximately '2,000 young men and women … shrieking wildly'. Most of the intended platform speakers were injured in the mêlée that followed; Gallacher was able to save himself only by taking advantage of the fact that his features were unknown to the people of Dublin and fleeing through the crowd. Later the same day, separate mobs, each several hundred strong, smashed the windows of the Middle Abbey Street headquarters of the Republican Congress, a movement established to bridge the gap between Marxism and IRA paramilitarism, and of the Freemasons' Hall in Molesworth Street.[81] More than four months later, a standing Garda presence outside the Republican Congress premises was still required to protect it from renewed public onslaughts.[82]

The Irish people's propensity to pursue anti-Red herrings was sustained by apocalyptic predictions in the mid-1930s of the inevitability of attempts at a Communist *coup*. The essayist T. M. Donovan was one of many conservative commentators to warn that 'there is nothing more certain than that a communist revolution [in Ireland] will take place within a decade, and sooner if England is involved in a war'.[83] Though a considerable proportion of these jeremiads represented the continuation of Cumann na nGaedheal politics by other means – and tended to be discounted by Fianna Fáil partisans as a result – forewarnings of an imminent Communist onslaught were also widely employed to reinforce the argument in favour of more rapid social and economic change. Unless the inequities upon which left-wing extremism fed were urgently addressed, it was contended, a violent upheaval was certain to occur. However well-intended they may have been, assertions of this kind did little to foster confidence in the political system. On the contrary, pronouncements of the bankruptcy of 'liberal' forms of government and their impotence in the face of the challenge of the Great Depression conceded much of the case for radical alternatives.

80 *Irish Independent*, 13 April 1936.
81 *Ibid.*, 16 April 1936.
82 *Irish Press*, 22 August 1936.
83 T. M. Donovan, *Revolution: Christian or Communist?*, n.d. [c. 1937], p. 39.

An example of how deep-seated was the anxiety of Irish elites over the threat of left-wing upheaval was provided by the formation of the League of Christian Social Justice in January 1936. Its leaders and supporters included Dr Frank O'Reilly, Executive Secretary of the Catholic Truth Society; Professor Alfred O'Rahilly of University College, Cork; Liam de Róiste, one of Cumann na nGaedheal's founder-members and an ex-TD; and Frank Duff of the Legion of Mary. The League contended that the only way to prevent Bolshevist revolution in Ireland was the organisation by the state of a pre-emptive 'people's revolution' to secure the right of every man 'to marry, and ... to provide for his wife and children'.[84] Through a Fabian process of permeation of the existing parties, the movement aspired to transcend the bitter divisions of Irish politics. It had made little progress, though, before the outbreak of the Spanish Civil War in July relegated virtually all domestic issues to the background.

The conflict in Spain rekindled anti-Communist sentiment in Ireland almost to the levels that it had reached in 1933. Shocked equally by the unprecedented scale of the wave of republican violence against Spanish priests and religious in the summer of 1936 and by the cynicism with which left-leaning commentators like George Orwell justified such atrocities,[85] the majority of Irish citizens regarded the war as a clear-cut struggle between civilisation and Communist-inspired barbarism. Once again the Irish clergy worked assiduously to fan the flames of public passion, albeit with significantly more justification than had been the case on the previous occasion. Dr Edward Mulhern, Bishop of Dromore, was typical of his episcopal colleagues in characterising the contest, in a pastoral letter of 20 September 1936, not as 'a struggle between political parties as to which shall rule, but between God and His enemies'.[86] The Dean of Cork, Monsignor Sexton, spoke for many clerical colleagues in detecting the Hidden Hand at work on the Iberian peninsula: 'Through well-paid agents in Spain, this gang of renegade

84 Minutes of the founding meeting of the League of Christian Social Justice, 24 January 1936; 'Specimen Address to the Public', n.d. [c. April 1936]; LCSJ circular letter, 24 July 1936, Liam de Róiste papers U/271/N/6/19, Cork Archive Institute.
85 A total of 6,832 bishops, priests, monks and nuns are recorded as having been killed by republican forces and irregular militias during the war, in what Stanley Payne has called 'the most extensive and violent persecution of Catholicism in Western history'. Displaying one of the ideological blind spots that he properly condemned in others, Orwell brushed aside the massacres on the ground that 'the Spanish Church was part of the capitalist racket'. H. Thomas, *The Spanish Civil War* (Harmondsworth, Middlesex: Penguin, 1979), p. 270; S. G. Payne, *Franco and Hitler: Spain, Germany, and World War II* (New Haven, CT: Yale University Press, 2008), p. 13; G. Orwell, *Homage to Catalonia* (Harmondsworth, Middlesex: Penguin, 1989), p. 194.
86 *Irish Christian Front*, 24 October 1936.

Jews in Moscow is striving to rob the Spanish people of their Faith, to make them atheists'.[87]

With the active encouragement of the hierarchy, especially in Munster, and in response to an appeal by Frank Geary, editor of the *Irish Independent* daily newspaper, a nationwide organisation was launched in August 1936 to mobilise Irish support for the Nationalist cause. The Irish Christian Front (ICF) underwent a meteoric rise in its first months of existence. Promoted vigorously by the *Independent*, which functioned as the house organ of the ICF,[88] the organisation held a series of massive public meetings across the country in the autumn of 1936. The claimed attendances of 15,000 at its rally in Dublin on 30 August; 40,000 at the Grand Parade, Cork, on 20 September; and 15,000 in Waterford and 10,000 in Longford on 11 October may well have represented the truth.[89] At these assemblies, participants demonstrated their devotion to Christian ideals in public life by crossing their wrists above their heads,[90] and listened to speeches of an anti-Communist, anti-Semitic and occasionally pro-fascist character. Rhetorical violence was sometimes supplemented by its physical counterpart, with hecklers and dissentients being hunted through the streets by would-be ICF lynch mobs.[91] The movement, however, failed to sustain its initial momentum. The prominence within the leadership of former Blueshirts like Patrick Belton and Alec McCabe raised suspicions that the ICF was intended as an anti-Fianna Fáil front organisation. The Catholic bishops likewise feared, with much justification, that Belton aimed at converting the ICF into a political vehicle for his own brand of populist anti-Semitism.[92] Episcopal support was quietly withdrawn and from the spring of 1937 the ICF began a rapid and ultimately terminal decline.

The ICF's failure owed more to the shortcomings of its self-promoting president, Belton, than to any diminution in popular support for Franco. Some 7,000 Irishmen volunteered their services for an Irish

87 *Irish Independent*, 21 September 1936.
88 The ICF did launch its own eponymous journal, but only a single issue seems ever to have appeared.
89 *Irish Christian Front*, 24 October 1936.
90 No doubt coincidentally, the same salute (to Big Brother during the Two Minutes' Hate) was used in the Michael Radford-directed film version of *Nineteen Eighty-Four* starring John Hurt and Richard Burton.
91 F. McGarry, *Irish Politics and the Spanish Civil War* (Cork: Cork University Press, 1999), pp. 118–19.
92 Belton's address at the founding meeting of the ICF branch in Finglas, Co. Dublin, was a typical expression of his political preoccupations: 'We know the *Protocols* [*of the Elders of Zion*] and we know what they mean ... We know their [Jews'] methods and means of digging in. It is our duty to see that they get no farther, and perhaps the day is not too far distant when we will dig them out'. *Irish Independent*, 10 October 1936.

Brigade headed by Eoin O'Duffy, although only a tenth of that number actually reached Spain.[93] Throughout Catholic Ireland, the Generalissimo's image was displayed and the success of his armies petitioned in prayer. But Franco was only one of a number of authoritarian Catholic (or supposedly Catholic) leaders whose regimes were held up as examples in the 1930s. Benito Mussolini in Italy, Engelbert Dollfuss in Austria and, above all, António de Oliveira Salazar in Portugal featured in innumerable journalistic, political and clerical treatments as models for an independent Ireland to emulate. All had come to head countries in the throes of economic and political crisis; all professed respect for the Catholic Church; and all had dealt robustly, and when necessary extrajudicially, with socialism, liberalism and parliamentarianism. The relevance to Ireland seemed obvious.

The cult of Salazar in Ireland is a topic worthy of extended study in itself. As Great Britain's oldest foreign ally and itself a nakedly imperialist power, Portugal seemed an unlikely exemplar for the infant Irish state. Few connections existed between the two countries, in which mutual ignorance of the other ran deeply. This, though, worked to Salazar's advantage as he and his efficient network of propagandists set out Portugal's claims as the embodiment of the ideal Christian state. A talented self-publicist, Salazar depicted his *Estado Novo* of 1933 as the successful reconciliation of economic modernity and Catholic orthodoxy. The abolition of parliament, the establishment of an authoritarian one-party state and the reversal of the liberal Republic's anti-clerical legislation were represented as the political preconditions of the corporatist economic reforms that Salazar, a former Minister of Finance, proceeded to enact. Unlike the other three Catholic dictators, moreover, Salazar had accomplished his top-down revolution without bloodshed. For Irish enthusiasts unaware of, or willing to overlook, the regime's repression of trade unions and vigorous methods of dealing with clerical dissent, the Portuguese model provided a field-tested formula for the rectification of the country's structural problems.

A writer for *An tIolar/The Standard* drew the lesson for readers in a review of Salazar's *Doctrine and Action*:

> At the present time when intensive propaganda efforts are being concentrated on an attempt to persuade people that 'democracy' is the only system which will preserve civilisation, it is refreshing to find an intelligent critic of Dr. Salazar's calibre give his views on this subject. 'We are anti-parliamentarians, anti-democrats, anti-liberals', he boasts ...

93 A comprehensive account of the Irish Brigade is found in R. A. Stradling's *The Irish and the Spanish Civil War 1936–1939: Crusades in Conflict* (Manchester: Manchester University Press, 1999).

> There is scarcely a paragraph in the book which does not find a practical application in this country.[94]

In one vital respect, though, Salazar's Portugal was lacking. Because of its historic alignment with Great Britain, the Lisbon regime could hardly be looked to for assistance with Ireland's partition problem. To a young ex-civil servant of extremist views, Gearóid Ó Cuinneagáin, the solution lay in aligning Ireland with some country that was not only prepared to contest British international hegemony, but could be expected to translate its challenge into armed action within the foreseeable future. In an article for the republican *Wolfe Tone Weekly*, 'No Other Way: Italy and Éire as Allies in War', Ó Cuinneagáin called on the government to initiate a large-scale military expansion, including the creation of an air force capable of threatening British cities, so as to facilitate 'a Fascist link-up' with Rome: 'There is no need to doubt that Mussolini, did we show we meant business, meant to fight with all our available man power, all our economic power, all the power and influence of the Irish emigrant overseas … would with characteristic alacrity and thoroughness co-operate'.[95]

The growth of Irish anti-Semitism

In a country whose Jewish population was as microscopic as Ireland's, the idea of extensive anti-Semitism might be thought to present a somewhat ludicrous aspect. As late as 1881, fewer than five hundred Jews were living in Ireland, the majority of them in Dublin and Belfast. Although the number of Jewish immigrants increased in consequence of the programme of 'ethnic cleansing' unleashed in the Russian Empire by Konstantin Pobedonostsev that same year, the Jewish population in 1911 totalled a mere 5,148, a figure that remained virtually static throughout the following three decades.[96] Small in absolute terms as this influx was, the growth in the number of new arrivals, coupled with an upsurge of clerical bigotry sparked by the Dreyfus affair in France, was sufficient to spark a short-lived but highly-publicised boycott of Jewish tradespeople, the so-called 'Limerick Pogrom' of 1904.[97]

94 *An tIolar/The Standard*, 26 January 1940.
95 G. Ua Cuinneagáin, 'No Other Way: Italy and Éire as Allies in War', *Wolfe Tone Weekly*, 11 December 1937.
96 C. Ó Gráda, *Jewish Ireland in the Age of Joyce: A Socioeconomic History* (Princeton, NJ: Princeton University Press, 2006), p. 32, table 2.1.
97 The most detailed analysis of this episode is contained in T. J. Crain, 'The Triumph of Intolerance: Fr. John Creagh and the Limerick Pogrom of 1904', PhD diss., Arizona State University, 1998. A selection of relevant documents is provided in D. Keogh & A. McCarthy's *Limerick Boycott 1904: Anti-Semitism in Ireland* (Cork: Mercier, 2005).

Although the significance of this episode – which, notwithstanding the lurid name attached to it, bore no resemblance to the murderous campaign simultaneously under way against Jews in Eastern Europe – has been considerably exaggerated, there is no doubt that anti-Semitic sentiments were both flourishing and spreading at the beginning of the twentieth century. During the 1880s and 1890s Irish Judaeophobia had largely been the preserve of isolated figures like the Home Rule MP Frank Hugh O'Donnell (dubbed 'Crank Hugh' by T. M. Healy) whose periodic rants against the Judaeo-Masonic conspiracy and Jewish involvement in the white slave trade featured regularly in nationalist journals. By the turn of the century, however, such discourses were taken up and disseminated more broadly by leading figures in the advanced nationalist movement, like Arthur Griffith and D. P. Moran.[98] In Ireland, as elsewhere in Europe, the Great War contributed to the growth of anti-Jewish attitudes – as evidenced by the Irish Republican Brotherhood leader Thomas Ashe's belief that the war had been fomented by 'Jewish profiteers' – thereby providing an ironic counterpart to the popular belief among British ultra-rightists that the Easter Rising and the War of Independence had themselves been the work of 'the Irish section of Lenin's Jew Government, with Michael Collins and his murder gang – *i.e.* the Irish Republican army – acting directly under Lenin's orders'.[99]

The question of governmental responses to the 'Jewish question' in the two decades after the foundation of the State has been the subject of an important recent study by Dermot Keogh.[100] If anything, Keogh understates both the prevalence and virulence of popular anti-Semitism in Ireland during the same period. While physical attacks on Jews were comparatively infrequent, though by no means unknown,[101] lesser

---

98 B. Levitas, *The Theatre of Nation: Irish Drama and Cultural Nationalism 1890–1916* (Oxford: Clarendon Press, 2002), pp. 89–90.

99 B. Novick, *Conceiving Revolution: Irish Nationalist Propaganda during the First World War* (Dublin: Four Courts Press, 2001), p. 113; 'Ireland, the "Western Front" of Bolshevism', *The Hidden Hand*, December 1920.

100 D. Keogh, *Jews in Twentieth-Century Ireland: Refugees, Anti-Semitism and the Holocaust* (Cork: Cork University Press, 1998).

101 In a 1945 article for the literary journal *The Bell*, 'What It Means to be a Jew', A. J. (Con) Leventhal described the attitude of his Gentile neighbours in the Dublin inner-city district in which he grew up: 'we of Oakfield Place were regarded as strangers who, *as such*, ought to be liquidated'. However, '[t]hanks to a few hints in the science of fisticuffs which I received during a break in my evening Hebrew classes from a fellow co-religionist, who later became a distinguished Irish patriot, I was able to plunge boldly, and often successfully, into a physical demonstration of my right to use the pavement outside the ghetto'. Emphasis in original. The passages quoted here were deleted by the state censor from the version that appeared in print. G2/X/0040, Department of Defencee Military Archives (hereafter DDMA).

forms of intimidation – menacing graffiti, anonymous death threats, the daubing of Jewish-owned premises with offensive messages – were considerably more common.[102] Of greater significance even than these was the fact that the panoply of modern anti-Semitic attitudes, from assertions of the authenticity of the *Protocols of the Elders of Zion* and of various blood libels, to lurid exposés of the supposed 'links' between Judaism, Freemasonry and international Communism, constituted a regular and largely uncontroversial feature of Irish public and political discourse. Such allegations were in general relieved only by variations like that of the Bishop of Clonfert, Dr Dignan, who employed his 1933 Lenten pastoral to advertise his conviction that the forces behind capitalism rather than Communism were 'monied-vested interests chiefly in the hands of Jews and Freemasons'.[103]

In the Oireachtas, allegations that the Irish people and government were victims of a clandestine Jewish cabal, differing neither in phraseology nor malevolence from Oliver J. Flanagan's celebrated anti-Semitic broadside in 1943,[104] featured prominently from the body's earliest days. In August 1921 George Gavan Duffy, a member of the Treaty delegation and future Chief Justice of the Supreme Court, attributed the provisional government's difficulties in gaining favourable publicity overseas to the influence of a vindictive media 'octopus … all run by big Jew firms in London'.[105] Denis Gorey, Cumann na nGaedheal deputy from Kilkenny, sought on numerous occasions to alert the Dáil to the danger he perceived that the Irish people might 'be replaced absolutely by Jews' and 'driven out to starve and leave the country and allow it to become a Jewish colony'.[106] No less typical was the outburst of his party colleague, Captain Patrick Giles, in 1937: 'Who owns the wealth of Dublin? Is it the Irish volunteers or the Irish people? No, it is not, but the rotten old Jews'.[107] Anti-Jewish utterances were also common in the upper house of parliament, with Senator Oliver St John Gogarty being especially noteworthy in the vehemence of his attacks.[108]

With the accession to power of the Fianna Fáil government in 1932, and the subsequent rise of the Blueshirts and other right-wing leagues,

---

102 See, e.g., the anonymous letter addressed to Professor Guggenheim of the Banking Commission, c. 22 January 1935, JUS 8/417, NAI.
103 *Irish Press*, 27 February 1933.
104 See p. 135 below.
105 4 *DP–Dáil*, c. 10 (18 August 1921).
106 7 *DP–Dáil*, c. 281 (6 May 1924).
107 69 *DP–Dáil*, c. 1493 (1 December 1937).
108 See, e.g., 11 *Díospóireachtaí Páirliminte–Seanad Éireann* [hereafter *DP–Seanad*], c. 101 (13 December 1928); 20 *DP–Seanad* c. 2183 (11 March 1936).

the prevalence of anti-Semitic rhetoric increased markedly. As noted above, Cumann na nGaedheal's strategy in the 1932 general election had been to attempt to connect Fianna Fáil to forces in the pay of, or sympathetic to, Muscovite Bolshevism. Notwithstanding the failure of this 'Red scare' as an electoral strategy, in light of the supposed association of Jewry and international Communism – assiduously popularised in Ireland by such prolific anti-Semitic writers as Fathers Denis Fahey and Edward J. Cahill – it was but a short step to assert that the incoming Fianna Fáil administration was suspiciously solicitous of Jews, a complaint to which the presence on the Fianna Fáil benches in the Dáil of the most prominent Jewish politician in the country, Robert Briscoe, lent a veneer of credibility.[109] The allegation that de Valera was himself of Jewish parentage and that the country's affairs had fallen under the control of an alien clique of 'Spaniards, Jews and Manxmen',[110] first popularised by British ultra-right journals during the War of Independence and later taken up by the Nazi press in Germany, became a hardy perennial upon Cumann na nGaedheal and Blueshirt platforms in the mid-1930s.[111] So persistently reiterated was this allegation that a furious de Valera, in one of his least felicitous public interventions, denounced it from the floor of the Dáil in March 1934:

> There is not, as far as I know, a single drop of Jewish blood in my veins. I am not one of those who try to attack the Jews or want to make any use of the popular dislike of them. I know that originally they were God's people; that they turned against Him and that the punishment which their turning against God brought upon them made even Christ Himself weep.[112]

In spite of the impression conveyed by this unfortunately phrased disclaimer, the Fianna Fáil leader neither sympathised with nor lent

---

109 Fr Fahey, whose malign influence extended (and continues to extend) far beyond his native land, still lacks a biographer. A valuable short discussion of his life and work is contained in M. C. Athans' *The Coughlin-Fahey Connection: Father Charles E. Coughlin, Father Denis Fahey, C.S.Sp., and Religious Anti-Semitism in the United States, 1938–1954* (New York: Peter Lang, 1991). For examples of Fr Cahill's attitude toward Jews, see his *Framework of a Christian State: An Introduction to Social Science* (Dublin: M. H. Gill, 1932), pp. 144, 204–7, 240–1.

110 Speech by Denis Quish at Fedamore, Co. Limerick, 23 July 1934, quoted in 53 *DP–Dáil*, c. 2571 (10 August 1934).

111 See, e.g., *Plain English*, 9 July 1921; A. Roth, *Mr Bewley in Berlin: Aspects of the Career of an Irish Diplomat, 1933–1939* (Dublin: Four Courts Press, 2000), p. 52. An article in the Nazi newspaper by Alfred Rosenberg, citing the right-wing London *Morning Post* as its authority, alleged in 1921 that de Valera was a 'half-Jew' whose anti-British activities were financed by his supposed co-religionists in the United States. A. Rosenberg, 'Das Irische Problem', *Völkischer Beobachter*, 14 September 1921.

112 50 *DP–Dáil*, c. 2514 (2 March 1934).

encouragement to popular anti-Semitism.[113] It is not unfair to note, however, that he and his ministers were less than vocal in their condemnation of it, especially as the tide of anti-Jewish prejudice advanced both internationally and domestically in the second half of the 1930s. Although their intention may have been not to give further ammunition to their political opponents, the reticence of the country's leaders during these critical years allowed a barrage of anti-Semitic conspiracy theories and baseless apprehensions to go almost wholly uncontradicted in the public sphere. The result, predictably, was to add further fuel to the fire. One especially persistent myth was that Jewish refugees from Germany and elsewhere in Europe were arriving in Ireland in large numbers. A resolution passed by a co-operative society in Leitrim in September 1936, typical of many adopted during the late 1930s, demanded that the government 'cease immediately the introduction into the country of all foreigners of doubtful nationality, particularly hyphenated Jews from lands bordering on Russia'.[114] Another popular canard was that Ireland, along with Spain, constituted a 'Western Front' of Catholic states against which a 'triple alliance' of Communists, Jews and Masons had joined forces as part of a larger scheme of world domination. By the end of 1938 the German minister in Dublin, Eduard Hempel, could report to Berlin that the Irish people were 'beginning to recognise more than formerly a growth of Jewry within Ireland as well as the importance and necessity of a funda-mental solution to the Jewish question'.[115]

A favourable environment thus existed in Ireland, as elsewhere in Europe, for the rise of radical and anti-Jewish organisations, of a more extreme variety than even SPACL or the Irish Christian Front. The 1930s phenomenon of the right-wing anti-Semitic league, which on the Continent manifested itself in such bodies as the French *Jeunesses patriotes* or the early Rexist movement in Belgium, was replicated in Ireland on a smaller scale. Some of these entities had a relatively short existence and left little mark upon the political scene. Aontas Gaedheal ['Unity of the Gaels'], founded in Dublin by Patrick Smiddy and L. J. Ó Riain at the beginning of 1935 and said by the Gardaí to be composed of 'many well known business men in the City', proposed

113 De Valera's inclusion of state recognition of the 'Jewish Congregations' in Ireland in Article 41.1.3 of the 1937 Constitution is generally held to be an expression of his respect for and friendship with the Chief Rabbi of Ireland, Isaac Herzog. Whether or not this is the case, it was a gesture for which he could not have expected to be rewarded by the majority of Irish voters.

114 *Irish Independent*, 12 September 1936.

115 Quoted in H. Sturm, *Hakenkreuz und Kleeblatt: Irland, die Allierten, und das 'Dritte Reich', 1939–1945* (Frankfurt am Main: Peter Lang, 1984), p. 136.

to destroy the party political system and foil the machinations of international financiers as well as to curb the anti-social activities in Ireland of 'coons, Indians, foreign Jews, and various other types of bluffers'.[116] Its ten-point programme, which the organisation's weekly journal declared in so many words to be 'anti-Semitic' in character, consisted in essence of the tenfold reiteration of the need to recover the Irish economy from foreign and Jewish domination.[117] In a similar vein was An Córas Gaedhealach ['The Gaelic Network'], the brain-child of Hugh O'Neill and Father Alexander P. Carey, both of whom were to play prominent roles in Dublin's pro-Axis and anti-Jewish underground during the Emergency.[118] Other right-wing leagues, however, did succeed in attracting a nationwide following. The most significant of them was probably the Financial Freedom Federation (FFF). Headed by a former captain of the British Army, Henry Nevile Roberts, the Federation offered a potent combination of social credit economic doctrine and unrestrained abuse of Jews. Within two years of its formation in 1934, the FFF was claiming an implausibly high membership of 40,000 and proposing to put forward candidates of its own in municipal elections.[119] This political ambition did not prevent the movement from drawing supporters from other parties, notably Fianna Fáil, the secretary of whose Athboy, Co. Meath *cumann* [branch] doubled as the Federation's secretary.[120] Maud Gonne MacBride, whose unabashedly anti-Semitic views were frequently aired from FFF platforms, was perhaps the league's most prominent member.[121] By 1938 the FFF had metamorphosed into a fully-fledged electoral organisation, the Irish Social Credit Party. Its progress thereafter was hampered, firstly by the launch of a rival social credit movement, the League for Social Justice founded by Bulmer Hobson, and secondly by the misfortune of its having become confused in the public mind with the Communist Party of Ireland – a misapprehension resulting from the inability of many Irish people to distinguish its slogans of 'Social

116 Memorandum by Detective-Garda T. Keelan, Special Branch, 31 March 1935, DMD 3643/35, JUS 8/406, NAI; *Aontas Gaedheal Weekly Post*, 7 June 1935.
117 *Aontas Gaedheal Weekly Post*, 31 May 1935.
118 According to Fr Carey, the policies of the Fianna Fáil government were objectionable inasmuch as they had been 'based on a financial programme which was backed by International Jewish Bankers'. Memorandum by Detective-Sergeant L. Hannon, 6 July 1939, JUS 8/751, NAI.
119 Memorandum by Inspector J. Doody, Store Street Garda Station, 25 May 1936, JUS 8/409, NAI.
120 Memorandum by Station Sergeant D. E. McCarthy, Store Street Garda Station, 17 December 1934, JUS 8/341, NAI.
121 In an address at an FFF meeting at Clashganny, Co. Kilkenny, she opined that the banking system of the country 'was invented by the Jews and is controlled largely by them and the English'. *Kilkenny People*, 14 September 1935.

Justice' and 'Social Credit' from the advocacy of 'Socialism'. The mêlée that preceded a meeting of the movement in Dublin, in which 'the platform was overthrown and broken up, books and literature forcibly taken and torn up and missiles thrown at some of the Party's members by a gang of roughs of both sexes and all ages' proved to be a depressingly familiar overture to many of its subsequent public functions.[122]

By the time of the Second World War, as Marcus Tanner notes, 'shrill anti-Semitism remained politically respectable in Ireland',[123] and Judaeophobic discourse had become so widespread as to go unchallenged except by a few isolated voices. *An tIolar* exhorting the Jewish community in its own interests to deal with the 'parasites' in its midst, warned menacingly in 1940: 'Let the Jews make no mistake, anti-Semitism is growing in this country'.[124] While the journal did not go so far as to endorse the proposal of the pro-Nazi People's National Party to deprive Irish Jews of citizenship, civil rights and the protection of law,[125] some of its readers did not hesitate to draw their own conclusions as to the most appropriate solution to Ireland's – and the world's – Jewish problem. One correspondent writing after the fall of France to hail the imminent defeat of 'Jewish-Masonic finance', pointed out that

> Already a new Order in Europe is taking shape and great Catholic nations such as Italy, Hungary and Spain will have a big part to play. We should not forget that the great German nation is almost 50 per cent Catholic … And there is room within this new Order for an Irish Republic, founded on Christian Corporate lines.[126]

The prevalence of anti-Semitic, anti-parliamentary and anti-liberal ideas between 1919 and 1939 does not imply that the country was poised to follow in the wake of Germany and Italy – or even Portugal, Spain or Austria – had the Second World War not supervened. There was no general crisis of Irish democracy. Unlike these other countries, Ireland possessed throughout the period a broadly representative government that was determined to preserve the integrity of the state, if necessary by the most vigorous means. Emigration remained an important political safety valve. For those who stayed at home,

---

122 *Irish Press*, 22 April 1936. Social credit ideas also appealed to some members of the IRA, in which, as Brian Hanley observes, hostility to the 'pagan and unchristian' capitalist system was evident. B. Hanley, *The IRA, 1926–1936* (Dublin: Four Courts Press, 2002), p. 182.
123 M. Tanner, *Ireland's Holy Wars: The Search for a Nation's Soul, 1500–2000* (New Haven, CT: Yale University Press, 2001), p. 310.
124 *An tIolar/The Standard*, 23 August 1940.
125 *Ibid.*, 30 August 1940.
126 Letter by G. O'Doherty, *ibid.*, 6 December 1940.

unemployment was sufficiently high to exert a degree of 'social discipline', while remaining below the threshold that might produce a popular explosion. However deep its discontent with the status quo, no powerful or numerous interest group attempted to press its differences with the state to the point of a showdown. The Blueshirts came closest to doing so between 1933 and 1934, but even then drew back – or, more precisely, were pulled back by their conservative political collaborators – from the brink.[127] The nemesis of Blueshirtism came about not as a result of any action taken by the de Valera government, but because of Fine Gael leaders' realisation that the success of a quasi-legal paramilitary movement would inevitably render conventional politics and political parties, including their own, irrelevant.

By the same token, the mere absence of an imminent threat to the survival of the liberal democratic system cannot be taken as an indication that that system enjoyed general support. There is much justice in the complaints of historians like Fearghal McGarry and Kieran Allen that unwillingness to examine the popularity of anti-parliamentary and anti-democratic ideas between the wars represents a degree of 'ideological wishful thinking' on the part of many contemporary scholars.[128] In the specific circumstances of interwar Ireland, it was improbable that doctrines of this kind could have thrown down a successful challenge to the parliamentary regime. That does not mean a substantial constituency for those doctrines did not exist. While few Irish citizens were prepared to set their lives and liberties at hazard to overthrow the parliamentary system, a considerable number saw no particular merit in it and would have positively welcomed its departure. Even after the achievement of a relative degree of regime stabilisation, in other words, the market for political panaceas of an extremist type remained much larger than is generally supposed. Had some unforeseen set of circumstances led to the advent of an absolutist government, there is little to suggest that, provided the Catholic Church's position was respected, such a development would have encountered any more opposition in Ireland than in those Continental European countries in which it did take place.[129]

127 Cronin, *The Blueshirts and Irish Politics*, pp. 150–6.
128 K. Allen, *Fianna Fáil and Irish Labour: 1926 to the Present* (London: Pluto Press, 1997), p. 53. McGarry agrees that 'Arguably, Irish historiography has underestimated the potential for Irish fascism ... The role played by establishment figures in legitimizing anti-democratic views has not been sufficiently acknowledged by the many historians who draw a clear distinction between the support of Blueshirt intellectuals for the corporatist ideas associated with the Vatican and fascist ideology'. McGarry, *Eoin O'Duffy*, pp. 266–7.
129 For a thoughtful discussion of this aspect of the question, see P. Mair, 'De Valera and Democracy', in T. Garvin, M. A. Manning & R. Sinnott, eds, *Dissecting Irish Politics: Essays in Honour of Brian Farrell* (Dublin: University College Dublin Press, 2004).

At the close of the 1930s, moreover, two changes were occurring that made that scenario seem a great deal less abstract and remote. The first was the seemingly unstoppable momentum of the totalitarian powers in Europe, and the prospect of democracy disappearing from all but a handful of countries. Both defenders and opponents of the parliamentary system concurred in attributing Ireland's adoption of the 'Westminster model' of government to its historical roots as part of the British Empire. Whether Ireland should, or could, remain a democratic state if a defeated Britain were to be absorbed into an Axis-dominated European order was far from clear. The second change was the arrival to adulthood of the 'generation of 1939', the first cohort of Irishmen and women to have no personal memory of British rule and whose political frame of reference was defined wholly by the record of accomplishment – or lack of it – of their own independent government.[130] Impatient of their elders' shortcomings, disillusioned by the failure of the promise of Irish self-government to materialise in concrete achievements, possessing no stake in the existing order and envious of the apparent success of authoritarian and totalitarian systems elsewhere in Europe, representatives of this generation would prove their readiness to make a radical breach with conventional political traditions and pursue entirely new approaches to the problem of Irish national regeneration.

130 I use this term analogously with Robert Wohl's 'Generation of 1914', whose members' most distinctive intellectual characteristic was their conviction that 'they had the misfortune to be born into a dying world that lacked energy, vitality, and moral fiber'. R. Wohl, *The Generation of 1914* (Cambridge, MA: Harvard University Press, 1979), p. 215.

2

'New' and 'newer' orders

The outbreak of the Second World War – or, as it continues euphemistically to be referred to in Ireland, the Emergency – has traditionally been represented as a period in Irish history during which political life came virtually to a dead stop.[1] Historians have been impressed by the apparently massive national consensus that underlay the government's declaration in February 1939, reiterated on numerous occasions during the spring and summer of that year, that Ireland would remain neutral in the event of European hostilities. In light of the fierce political antipathies that marked the 1920s and 1930s, this coalescence around a single policy stance is indeed noteworthy. But neither, in a European context, is it in any respect unusual. Of the twenty-two self-governing states across the Continent when the Second World War began, only four – Germany, Poland, France and Great Britain – were directly involved in the conflict. The others stayed on the sidelines and, with the exception of Italy, Bulgaria and Hungary, were to remain there until themselves attacked or the end of the war supervened.[2]

The announcement of formal non-belligerency did not, however, mean that Irishmen and women bound themselves to be 'impartial in thought as well as in action', as Woodrow Wilson had optimistically but unavailingly demanded of his compatriots in August 1914.[3] The

1 Scholars' neglect of wartime politics in Ireland is extraordinary. In the course of a 475-page treatment of *Nationalism in Ireland*, D. George Boyce found so little of relevance to his topic during the years 1939–45 that the entire period is covered in a single paragraph; the full page assigned to the Emergency in Richard English's 625-page study devoted to the same subject seems expansive in comparison. See D. G. Boyce, *Nationalism in Ireland*, 3rd edn (London: Routledge, 1995); R. English, *Irish Freedom: The History of Nationalism in Ireland* (London: Macmillan, 2006).

2 The case of Romania is anomalous. Although she declared war on the USSR on the same day as the commencement of Operation Barbarossa, this may be regarded as a belated response to Soviet aggression the previous year, when Stalin demanded by ultimatum – and was ceded – Bessarabia and the northern part of Bukovina.

3 Presidential statement, 18 August 1914, quoted in J. W. Coogan, *The End of Neutrality: The United States, Britain, and Maritime Rights, 1899–1915* (Ithaca, NY: Cornell University Press, 1981), p. 172.

number of the truly neutral, in the sense of those who were personally indifferent to the prospect of either an Allied or an Axis victory,
must have been small indeed. Éamon de Valera's principal rationale
for neutrality, the force of which even his most stringent domestic and
foreign critics were compelled to concede, was that 'his country would
break apart in renewed civil war if the population was asked to choose
which of the belligerents it wished to support'.[4] That he had scarcely
overstated either the strength of feeling or the depth of division generated by the war was underlined by the proceedings during 1940 of the
Defence Conference, a governmental advisory body drawn from the
leadership of all three major parties, in which the Labour Party representative called for a policy of non-intervention if the Germans should
land in Northern Ireland and his Fine Gael counterparts warned that
they would not support the government in resisting a pre-emptive
British invasion of the twenty-six counties.[5] Even the rigours of what,
by common consent, was the most stringent censorship regime of
any of the European neutrals except Spain did not prevent ordinary
Irish citizens from closely following world events.[6] Elizabeth (Bowen)
Cameron, in the course of one of her wartime tours of Ireland on behalf
of the British Ministry of Information, reported 'the keen interest felt by
my rural South Irish people in the progress of the war. I have gathered
opinions on this from many people – employers of labour. All are
struck by the intelligence, the grip and the up-to-dateness shown, on
the subject of war news, by country working men. The interest would
appear to be greater than in many parts of rural England'.[7]

Nor were Irish people insensible of the fact that the course of the
conflict, whether Ireland participated as a belligerent or not, must
have profound ramifications for their own country. Brian Fallon recalls
that throughout the Emergency, 'the atmosphere of fear, menace and
foreboding was constant and almost tangible. Quite simply, one just
could not shut it out, at least for long'.[8] Clearly, for the large number

4 R. Fisk, *In Time of War: Ireland, Ulster and the Price of Neutrality 1939–1945* (London:
   André Deutsch, 1983), p. 415.
5 Untitled manuscript notes of Defence Conference proceedings, 25 July 1940, P7/a/212,
   Richard Mulcahy papers, University College, Dublin.
6 See S. G. Payne, *Franco and Hitler: Spain, Germany, and World War II* (New Haven, CT:
   Yale University Press, 2008), p. 122.
7 Elizabeth (Bowen) Cameron, 'Notes on Éire', 31 July 1942, The National Archive, Kew
   (hereafter TNA) DO 130/28. It is noteworthy in this context that 1941 saw the largest
   number of licences to own a radio receiver taken out in a single year. The figure, 183,000,
   was three times higher than the corresponding number five years previously. T. Brown,
   Ireland: A Social and Cultural History, 1922 to the Present (Ithaca, NY: Cornell University
   Press, 1985), p. 118.
8 B. Fallon, *An Age of Innocence: Irish Culture 1930–1960* (Dublin: Gill & Macmillan, 1998),
   p. 214.

who supported the Allies during the war and identified with their cause, the prospect of an Axis victory was deeply disturbing. But as de Valera himself acknowledged, 'Many people in Ireland were ready enough to acclaim a British defeat at any price',[9] and regarded the war as an opportunity to accomplish fundamental changes in both the national and international order that could not be achieved in any other way. He might have added that among them were a growing number of pro-Axis militants who were willing to take the initiative to bring those changes about.

By the end of the 1930s, both of the contending factions in the Irish Civil War had not only had an opportunity to assume control over the state, but even to compose and promulgate their own respective versions of its Constitution. Yet national reunification remained as far distant as ever; the economy had proven incapable of supplying the minimal requirements of the Irish people, as the disastrously high annual emigration figures attested; and the aspiration of creating an Ireland 'not free merely but Gaelic as well' was at best an unfulfilled ideal. These shortcomings appeared all the more starkly when set against the apparent ease with which the totalitarian states of Europe at precisely the same moment were recovering their territorial irredentae, revivifying their national cultures, and setting their peoples to work. To a significant number of Irishmen and women, the fault was traceable to the system of government established at the time of the creation of the state. By adopting wholesale a parliamentary liberal democracy on the Westminster model – and its accompanying mentality – complete with an elaborate bureaucratic apparatus, the new Irish polity had chained itself to an ideological corpse. The only hope seemed to be to begin again and reconstitute the state from its foundations, this time drawing upon those Continental European examples that were proving themselves by their effectiveness.

Pro-Axis sentiment in Ireland

It is no longer seriously questioned that the policy of the Irish government throughout the Emergency was supportive of the Allies as far as – and arguably a long way beyond – the point to which such a stance was consistent with the requirements of formal neutrality. Even when a comprehensive German victory in the summer of 1940 appeared a foregone conclusion, to the extent that – as a memorandum composed in the Department of External Affairs pointedly recorded – there did not seem to be 'a single organised State left in Europe or Asia which is

9 Sir J. Maffey, 'Conversation With Mr. De Valera', 21 October 1939, TNA CAB 66/2.

not ready to profit by what they regard to be the impending downfall of Britain',[10] de Valera's administration continued to hope for, if not entirely to believe in, the ultimate success of the Allied cause. In the military, economic and intelligence spheres, the Irish state co-operated closely with the British and later the United States governments to a degree that would almost certainly have led to unfortunate repercussions had it become known to the Axis powers. The nature of this collaboration has too often been described to require recapitulation here.[11]

So frequently reiterated, indeed, is the story of the Irish state's partiality towards the Allies during the war (which, to be sure, is to some extent necessary so as to correct the bizarre distortions of Irish wartime policy that continue to be disseminated by Hibernophobic commentators in Britain)[12] that the proposition that Irish opinion largely favoured the democracies has never been subjected to close scrutiny. Instead, it has been taken for granted that the accommodationist stance of the government, the true extent of which was largely concealed from the electorate, was generally reflective of public opinion as a whole. Certainly, in view of the all-embracing scope of official censorship and the fact that opinion-polling had yet to make an appearance on Irish shores, it is impossible to make any definitive statement about the degree to which Irish sympathies were engaged with one or other of the combatant blocs at any given moment. There is, however, ample evidence to suggest that pro-Axis sentiment, both north and south of the Border, was far more prevalent than is currently acknowledged.

In the first place, government policy cannot be taken as a proxy for public opinion. Undoubtedly Éamon de Valera himself and most, if not all, of his ministers were confirmed democrats and never doubted that Ireland's interests – and perhaps her survival as an independent state – were bound up with the success of the Allied cause. But the government's essentially pro-British stance was dictated as much by geographical propinquity as by ideological conviction. Like those other neutral democracies Switzerland and Sweden, whose wartime

10 Dermot Keogh, *Ireland and Europe 1919–1948* (Dublin: Gill & Macmillan, 1988), p. 138. The authorship of this unsigned and undated memorandum remains unclear; Keogh is most likely correct in attributing it to Joe Walshe.

11 See, e.g., Fisk, *In Time of War*; E. O'Halpin, *Defending Ireland: The Irish State and Its Enemies Since 1922* (Oxford: Oxford University Press, 1999), chs 5–6; J. P. Duggan, *A History of the Irish Army* (Dublin: Gill & Macmillan, 1989).

12 See, e.g., R. Body, *England for the English* (London: New European Publications, 2001), who claims *inter alia* that 'De Valera, Ireland's prime minister and a notorious anglophobe, preferred Hitler to Churchill' and that 'it was with his connivance that lights blazed along the Irish coast to guide the Luftwaffe on to Belfast to rain its bombs upon the shipyards' (p. 45).

demeanour vis-à-vis the *Reich* broadly mirrored that of the de Valera government with regard to Britain, Ireland could not hope to adopt a policy inimical to the belligerent with which she shared a land border and expect to remain unmolested. It was never a question, therefore, of whether the Irish government would take up a co-operative attitude with regard to the Allies – that much was given – but rather one of whether, through skill and good fortune, it might avoid being coerced into taking a position that could not be rationalised as falling within the bounds of 'friendly neutrality'.

Nor can the number of Irish citizens who gave concrete assistance to the Allied war effort, either by enlisting in the British armed forces or working in armaments factories, be interpreted as indicating the existence of a popular consensus in favour of the democracies. Apart from the obvious consideration that those who travelled overseas to offer their services to Britain can hardly be regarded as representative of the majority remaining at home, 'economic conscription' clearly played at least as great a part in the decision to emigrate as did pro-Allied sympathy. The United States' entry into the war in December 1941, to the surprise of many observers, had a very minor impact upon public sentiment, counterbalanced as it had been by the Soviet Union's inclusion within the Allied ranks six months previously and by unfavourable Irish reactions to the influx of American servicemen and civilian contractors into Northern Ireland (as one US intelligence agent recorded, 'It was being said "the Americans came to syphilize the country"').[13] On the merits of the conflict Irish opinion throughout the war appeared to be as deeply divided as it was on almost every other political controversy, neutrality alone excepted. Apart from the senior Fine Gael politician James Dillon, whose views evolved from support for the government's stance to active pro-interventionism, no national figure ever advocated joining the conflict on the Allied side. As one perceptive commentator recorded in April 1941:

> I take a mental census of my neighbours: say twenty or twentyfour [*sic*] households. Some there are who, in sympathy, are pro-English, as I know. Others are certainly anti-English and, in that sense, pro-German. But I know *not one* who would wish to see Éire in the war. If public controversy started, we would be at each other's throats. There is unity in neutrality: on nothing else.[14]

13 Martin Quigley, 'Notes on Éire', 27 August 1943, Office of Strategic Services (OSS) files, RG 226, Entry 210, Box 478, folder 1, US National Archives and Records Administration, College Park, Maryland (hereafter NARA).

14 Liam de Róiste diary, 4 April 1941, U 271/A56, Cork Archive Institute. Emphasis in original.

Lastly, Irish citizens' virtually unanimous protestations since 1945 that pro-Axis sentiment was unknown in Ireland need to be viewed in the same critical light as most Germans' equally vehement postwar disavowal of support for Nazism. Historians have far too readily taken at face value claims like those of Maureen Diskin, a Dublin bank clerk at the beginning of the war, that 'there was no sympathy for Germany at all. Nobody wanted them to win. Nobody had any use for Hitler or anything like that'.[15] Such retrospective self-justifications not only fly in the face of abundant contrary evidence, but are difficult to reconcile with the no less common claim among members of the Emergency generation that the Irish people's attitude with respect to the fascist powers would have been different had not wartime censorship prevented them from learning about the Holocaust. Leaving aside the logical contradiction between these two propositions, acceptance of the latter ignores the fact that Hitler's and Mussolini's persecution of the Jews did not commence on 1 September 1939.[16] Far from alienating Irish sympathies, however, it is clear that a broad consensus existed as to Hitler's handling of the Jewish question before the war, to wit: (i) the Jews were undoubtedly suffering at the Nazis' hands; (ii) some deplorable excesses notwithstanding, these misfortunes were often not unmerited; and (iii) the extent of Jewish suffering was exaggerated in media reports, and in any event much outweighed by the persecution of Catholics in Spain, Mexico, Northern Ireland and even Germany itself.[17]

Certainly it can be said that in the 1930s Irish enthusiasm for and sympathy with the fascist powers was held in check by the perception that the Nazi state was deeply hostile to Christianity in general and

15 B. Grob-Fitzgibbon, *The Irish Experience During the Second World War: An Oral History* (Dublin: Irish Academic Press, 2004), p. 136.

16 It also ignores the fact that BBC news broadcasts were not only received all over Ireland throughout the war but enjoyed a larger Irish audience than the less detailed and informative coverage of Raidió Éireann, whose first daily news bulletin was not transmitted until noon (18:40 on Sundays) and whose signals were often inaudible in many parts of the country, especially the southeast. Until 1946, moreover, Raidió Éireann had neither a paid news staff nor even a wire service subscription. Its 'journalists' obtained their foreign news by taking shorthand transcriptions of reports from the BBC and other international stations, the information from which – with scant regard for copyright law – was rebroadcast after token changes. D. Gageby, 'The Media, 1945–70', in J. J. Lee, ed., *Ireland 1945–70* (Dublin: Gill & Macmillan, 1979), pp. 124–5; 79 *DP–Dáil*, cols 2121–4 (1 May 1940); *ibid.*, vol. 83, cols 1517, 1531 (4 June 1941); *ibid.*, vol. 87, c. 1163 (17 June 1942).

17 See, e.g., *Catholic Mind*, July 1933; *Catholic Bulletin*, December 1939; editorial on *Kristallnacht* in *An tIolar/The Standard*, 18 November 1938; editorial in *ibid.*, 10 July 1940; de Róiste diary, 22 October 1940. See also M. Tanner, *Ireland's Holy Wars: The Struggle for a Nation's Soul, 1500–2000* (New Haven, CT: Yale University Press, 2001), pp. 305–6, 309–10.

Catholicism in particular. Journals like *An tIolar/The Standard* and the *Catholic Mind*, whose own views on such topics as the menace of Bolshevism and the Judæo-Masonic conspiracy often bore an uncomfortable resemblance to some forms of National Socialist rhetoric, nonetheless vigorously and repeatedly condemned the Hitler regime for waging a new *Kulturkampf* against the German Catholic Church. A firm anti-Nazi line was also taken by the *Irish Catholic* weekly, regarded as the unofficial voice of the Irish hierarchy; its Anglican counterpart, the *Church of Ireland Gazette*; de Valera's *Irish Press* newspaper; and, though somewhat more equivocally, the other Dublin dailies.[18] Much publicity was given to descriptions of 'Nazi Terror' and 'The New German Paganism', and denunciations by Pope Pius XI and the German episcopacy of the state's numerous violations of human rights and of the Concordat of 1934 received extensive coverage in the Irish print media.

Despite this, outside labour and trade union circles there was comparatively little criticism of fascism as an ideology. On the contrary, the Nazi state's Irish critics were often at pains to emphasise that the only genuinely objectionable aspect of National Socialism was its pretension to the status enjoyed by revealed religion. As *An tIolar* stated in a 1934 editorial commenting upon a papal condemnation of Nazi excesses, 'Against Hitlerism as a political system His Holiness makes no protest. Autocracy or democracy, dictatorship or constitutional rule, none concerns the guardian of the Christian tradition'.[19] The same distinction between the 'accidental' and 'essential' qualities of Nazism was drawn by the Bishop of Cork five years later. Praising the action of the Lord Mayor of the city in boycotting the official reception of a visiting *Kriegsmarine* training ship as a protest against offensive comments made by the German press about Pius XI, who had recently died, Dr Colahan went on to assure his listeners that 'we have no opposition to ... the great empire that is now Germany-Austria; none whatever. We have nothing at all to say in the way of criticism of Germany as a great political entity'.[20] For his part, Liam Ó Rinn of the *Catholic Bulletin* expressed positive enthusiasm in 1939 for the

18 The *Auswärtiges Amt* in Berlin had long noted what it considered the 'hostile attitude of the *Irish Press*'. From the summer of 1940, Eduard Hempel too complained repeatedly to the Department of Foreign Affairs of the 'pro-British' attitude of the *Press*, a stance which he considered was reflected even in 'the choice of letter-types'. It had not, he asserted, 'reached the level of objectivity attained in the "Irish Independent"'. Charles Bewley to Joe Walshe, 4 May 1939, *Documents on Irish Foreign Policy*, vol. V, *1937–1939* (Dublin: Royal Irish Academy, 2006), p. 463; P. 51, Department of External Affairs papers, NAI.
19 *An tIolar/The Standard*, 2 March 1934.
20 *Cork Examiner*, 27 February 1939.

New Order if it could only be divorced from its anti-Catholic excesses: 'If the national revival of great Germany were accomplished without a fresh *Kulturkampf* … there would be reason to rejoice in the new power that has come to the land that gave Christendom so many of its greatest souls and noblest works of art and letters'.[21]

Criticism of Nazi Germany, moreover, was by no means incompatible with enthusiastic support for its Axis partner. In Irish discussions of the fascist phenomenon, the German and Italian systems were often contrasted as representing respectively the 'irresponsible' and 'responsible' forms of the modern totalitarian state. As *An tIolar* put it, 'In Germany Catholicism is hounded, oppressed and held up as an enemy of the people. In Italy an astute leader envisages the Church as a friend and ally in making the country more prosperous and independent'.[22] A similar distinction was made by Dr Colahan, who commended Italian fascism as an ideology that 'pays homage to God and leaves the Church with a fair field for her sacred mission'.[23] The Jesuit essayist Stephen J. Brown concurred: wishing that 'the condition of the working classes and the poor in this country of ours were in every way as good as it is in Fascist Italy', Brown reminded his readers in 1938 that 'at least, in Italy, the worker is allowed to practise his religion, and it is possible for him to bring up his children in the fear and love of God'.[24] Mussolini was thus able to claim many prominent Irish admirers, among them Joe Walshe, Secretary of the Department of External Affairs, Canon John Hayes, founder of Muintir na Tíre, the prominent clerical commentator R. S. Devane, and a cross-section of Oireachtas members from all three major parties.[25] Even Italy's unprovoked invasion of Abyssinia did nothing to diminish the enthusiasms of Mussolini's retinue of supporters in the Dáil. Sir Osmond Esmonde of Fine Gael hailed him as the 'the Abraham Lincoln of Africa' waging a 'just war' on behalf of the Italian people, while the National Centre Party TD William Kent insisted that he would oppose any League of Nations sanctions against the *Duce*'s efforts 'to civilise and to Christianise a pagan race'.[26] Fascist

21 'Fear Faire' [Liam Ó Rinn], 'From the Hill Tops', *Catholic Bulletin* 29:3 (March 1939): 150.
22 *An tIolar/The Standard*, 14 January 1938.
23 *Catholic Herald*, 7 January 1938.
24 S. J. Brown, *Poison and Balm* (Dublin: Browne & Nolan, 1938), pp. 43–4.
25 C. C. O'Brien, 'The Roots of My Preoccupations', *Atlantic Monthly* 274:1 (July 1994): 73–81; D. O'Leary, *Vocationalism and Social Catholicism in Twentieth-Century Ireland: The Search for a Christian Social Order* (Dublin; Irish Academic Press, 2000), p. 44. For additional expressions of admiration for Mussolini and fascist Italy, see, e.g., the statements of Gogarty in 20 *DP–Seanad*, c. 1121 (13 November 1935) and James Coburn, 65 *DP–Dáil*, c. 710 (19 February 1937).
26 59 *DP–Dáil*, cols 530–1 (6 November 1935).

organisations elsewhere in Europe, like Jacques Doriot's *Parti Populaire Français* and Leon Degrelle's Rexist movement in Belgium, were held up for praise in Irish journals and their progress followed with keen interest.[27] Even Japanese racial expansionism was able to find champions in Ireland, notably the ex-Blueshirt senator Ernest Blythe, who spoke in 1935 in mitigation of Japan's forcible claims to *lebensraum* in China.[28]

This is not to suggest that the specifically German variant of fascism was lacking in supporters willing to overlook, or rationalise, its anti-Catholic excesses. Hitler's most assiduous Irish apologist, James Vincent Murphy, upbraided the German Church for having stood 'on the side of the enemies of religion' – the Social Democrats and Jews – in defence of the 'materialistic' Weimar Republic.[29] The Catholic Centre Party, he claimed, was the German analogue of the opportunistic Home Rulers in prewar Ireland, just as the Beer Hall Putsch had been Germany's 'Easter Rising' and the National Socialists 'Sinn Féin in Bavaria'.[30] Even before the Nazis gained power, the future President of Ireland, Cearbhall Ó Dálaigh, praised the party for its determination 'to smash forever the power of the Jews and [to make Germany] a stronghold and a beacon of knowledge between America and Asia'.[31] The *Irish Independent* columnist Gertrude Gaffney argued that 'Europe should be grateful to Hitler', warning that 'But for him even we here in Ireland might to-day be living under a Soviet flag'. Attacks on the churches, she suggested, were attributable to fanatics like Alfred Rosenberg, whom the *Führer* lacked the strength to restrain.[32] Writing in the *Irish Press* in 1936, Dr Liam Gogán of the National Museum of Ireland also assured readers that accounts of the Nazi regime's 'persecution' of Catholicism were greatly exaggerated: 'The ordinary work of the Church goes undisturbed [by Hitler], and in general the principles of Catholicism are the basic principles of the [Nazi] revolution'.[33]

27 See, e.g., *An tIolar's* editorial advocating co-operation between the PPF and Colonel de la Rocque's para-fascist *Parti Social Français*: 'The results of such an alliance would be tremendous'. *An tIolar/The Standard*, 4 June 1937. See also *Catholic Mind* 28:2 (February 1937): 98.

28 *Irish Press*, 20 March 1935.

29 J. V. Murphy, *Adolf Hitler: The Drama of His Career* (London: Chapman & Hall, 1934), p. 121.

30 *Ibid.*, pp. 120, 56, 46.

31 *Humanitas*, March 1930, quoted in P. O'Leary, *Gaelic Prose in the Irish Free State 1922–1939* (University Park, PA: Pennsylvania State University Press, 2004), p. 55.

32 *Irish Independent*, 14 August 1935.

33 L. Gogán, 'Nua-Chultúir na Gearmáine: Torthaí Reabhlóide Hitler', *Irish Press*, 2 January 1936. For a similar testimonial, see 'Osraidhe', 'Laethe Saoire sa Ghearmáin', *Irish Independent*, 30 August 1935.
   Gogán, who served at the National Museum under its Austrian director, Dr Adolf

Public expressions of approval of Hitler and National Socialism became more frequent as the 1930s progressed, arising from gratitude for the part played by German forces in Spain; the perception that the fascist states alone stood in the path of the Communist advance; admiration of Germanic efficiency and discipline; or sympathy for another state struggling to reverse its 'partition' twenty years previously.[34] Todd Andrews was typical of many Irish citizens who harboured 'a vague kind of sympathy for Germany and the Germans because they had been "our gallant allies" in 1916 and had been so badly treated at Versailles'.[35] Nazi Germany's absorption of Austria and the Sudetenland was appreciatively noted by numerous commentators, who saw in Hitler's solution of his 'partition problem' a lesson for Ireland.[36] The most outspokenly anti-fascist of the Irish bishops, Dr Michael Browne of Galway, was sufficiently concerned by the growing vogue in Ireland for extremist politics to devote his Lenten pastoral of February 1939 to a denunciation of totalitarian systems, warning that 'unfortunately there are in our midst some admirers of Nazi methods'.[37] Some of the pro-German partisans of whom the bishop spoke found an outlet for their enthusiasms in the correspondence columns of the *Irish Independent*, which by mid-1939 was featuring regular paeans of praise for the accomplishments of the German dictator and warnings of the danger of a war against him fomented by international financiers, Communists and Jews.[38] Several provincial papers were also noted for featuring stories of a marked pro-Axis slant. The *Bray Tribune*, for example, notified the German Embassy in London that it would be 'glad to receive propaganda literature issued by your Government in the English language' and offered its good offices in

Mahr – head of the NSDAP *Auslandsorganisation* in Ireland – remained resolutely pro-German in his sympathies throughout the Emergency, and later claimed to have conveyed vital information on British strategic deployments to the Germans in 1944. See J. P. Duggan, *Herr Hempel at the German Legation in Dublin, 1937–1945* (Dublin: Irish Academic Press, 2003), pp. 135, 215–16.

34 One such sympathiser – for a moment at any rate – may have been the Taoiseach himself. In 1936 the British Dominions Secretary, Malcolm MacDonald, reported in the context of a conversation with de Valera a fortnight after the reoccupation of the Rhineland: 'Naturally, he has keen sympathy with Germany in her struggle to establish equality with other nations'. Memorandum by MacDonald, 24 March 1936, TNA DO 35/399/3.

35 C. S. Andrews, *Autobiography*, vol II, *Man of No Property* (Dublin: Mercier, 1982), p. 138.

36 See, e.g., Maud Gonne MacBride's assertion during the Sudeten crisis that 'Czechoslovakia was not a nation, and the Czechs … had no more right to persecute Germans, Poles or Hungarians than Craigavon and England had to hold their Six Counties'. *Irish Press*, 26 September 1938.

37 *Cork Weekly Examiner*, 25 February 1939.

38 See, e.g., letters by 'Irishman', J. N. R. Macnamara, and 'J.C.M'., *Irish Independent*, 6 and 13 June, 3 July 1939.

printing and distributing copies of a letter by Joseph Goebbels.[39] Until it was eventually prevented from doing so by the censorship authorities, the *Kerryman*'s preferred method of elucidating for its readers the questions at issue in the Second World War consisted of reprinting on its front page, with approving commentaries, articles from the British Union of Fascists' journal *Action*.[40]

By no means should all Irish citizens who before the war expressed admiration for Hitler or defended the German regime against its critics be regarded as committed pro-Nazis, or for that matter be presumed to possess any very well-developed understanding of the ideology of National Socialism. Some at least of those giving vent to such opinions were motivated by frustration over the failure of their own government to deal effectively with the country's fundamental problems ('what we need is a Hitler here'), reflexive Anglophobia, anxiety over the growing power and prestige of Soviet Communism, and a variety of other extraneous factors. Nevertheless, by the beginning of the war a significant proportion of Irish men and women were clearly disposed, for whatever reason, to look favourably upon the Axis states and to entertain hopes for the success of their cause.

Among contemporary observers, opinions as to the precise extent of this pro-Axis sentiment varied. There is little question, however, that it grew rapidly both north and south of the Border in response to the advance of the German forces on the battlefield. The journalist George Douglas,[41] as a teenager in Derry, retained vivid memories of an atmosphere of 'barely-concealed jubilation' in the nationalist areas of the city as the *Wehrmacht* drove across Western Europe in the spring and summer of 1940. Similar reactions were observed in West Belfast, where a postal worker recorded in his diary that the nationalist Falls Road was 'delighted by every success on the part of Hitler', and where supporters of the Catholic-affiliated football team Belfast Celtic used to bait their Protestant Linfield rivals 'by giving them a Nazi-style salute'.[42] In the Belfast Christian Brothers' school attended by Tom Mageean, later to become an Ailtirí na hAiséirghe member, spontaneous cheering broke out whenever news was received of a German victory: 'Most of the nationalist population', Mageean believed, 'were pro-Axis – they used to like to see Britain getting it in the neck'.[43] This assessment was shared by Freddie Boland, Assistant Secretary at

39 *Bray Tribune* to the German Embassy, London, 16 August 1939, G2/X/0085, DDMA.
40 For examples of such articles appearing in a single month, see *Kerryman*, 4, 11 and 25 November 1939.
41 The present writer's father.
42 B. Barton, *The Blitz: Belfast in the War Years* (Belfast: Blackstaff, 1989), pp. 271–2.
43 Tom Mageean, author interview, 2 August 1999.

the Department of External Affairs, who recorded in April 1941 his conviction that 'the vast majority of Nationalists in the six-county area are absolutely pro-German on account of their unjustified treatment by the British government and its Belfast puppet'.[44]

In the twenty-six counties, too, well-placed observers were struck by the rising tide of pro-Axis sentiment in the early years of the war. Éamon de Valera admitted that 'the people were pro-German' in July 1940.[45] Early in 1941, the Fine Gael leader Richard Mulcahy also found that 'a number of quarters report mass opinion setting pro-German'.[46] A 'highly reliable' member of the Oireachtas expressed the same view to a representative of US military intelligence in May 1941, citing Irish ignorance of the harshness of German rule in the occupied countries as explanation for the fact that there was 'no anti-Nazism in Éire'.[47] In a confidential despatch to his superiors, the consul-general in Ireland of the Dutch government-in-exile, I. R. A. Weenick, reported that, 'The 94 per cent [Irish] Catholics are on the whole inclined to be pro-German. This means rather that they are anti-British rather than pro-German. Anything is better than the hated English who garrisoned and oppressed their country for 600 [sic] years'.[48] His Czech counterpart, D. K. Kostal, likewise recorded that the ordinary people and the educated classes alike were deeply sceptical of the 'ideological background of the European struggle', which they regarded as 'bluff … For the ordinary Irish person who does not know Germany it is sufficient that Germany is striking the English. Of anything further he does not meditate and does not wish to meditate'.[49] A journalist from

44 Quoted in H. Patterson, *Ireland Since 1939* (Oxford: Oxford University Press, 2002), p. 33. Patterson believes that Boland's perception of widespread pro-German sentiment was inaccurate.

45 De Valera interview with Patrick Herdman, July 5/6 1940, quoted by B. Girvin, 'The Republicanisation of Irish Society, 1932–48', in J. R. Hill, ed., *A New History of Ireland*, vol. VII: *Ireland 1921–84* (Oxford: Oxford University Press, 2003), p. 151. Eunan O'Halpin asserts that in his pro-Allied stance, 'the evidence suggests that de Valera was ahead of opinion within his own party in 1939–40, where many who had fought for independence against Britain hoped for her quick defeat and believed that a united Ireland would follow from a German victory'. E. O'Halpin, 'Irish Neutrality in the Second World War', in N. Wyllie, ed., *European Neutrals and Non-Belligerents During the Second World War* (Cambridge: Cambridge University Press, 2002), p. 290.

46 'Notes', 8 January 1941, P7/a/211, Mulcahy papers, University College, Dublin (hereafter UCD).

47 Military Intelligence Division Military Attaché Report no. 4101, 19 May 1941, OSS Research & Analysis Branch records, RG 226, Entry 16, reel 74, item 16785 C, NARA.

48 Transcript of an undated [c. 10 July 1941] and unsigned intercepted memorandum, 'The Political Situation', covered by a letter from Col. Dan Bryan, G2, to F. H. Boland, Department of External Affairs, 22 July 1941.

49 D. K. Kostal, 'Report on the Situation in Ireland', 31 May 1940, Department of External Affairs file A.8, NAI.

the *Yorkshire Post* who visited Dublin early in 1941 was 'amazed to find that a large section of the population was decidedly pro-German. Hailing with delight the Nazi victories … this anti-British element did little to hide its feelings of hatred for everything connected with the Crown. On walls and hoardings were chalked huge swastikas and anti-British slogans'.[50] John Betjeman, a press attaché serving with the British Ministry of Information in Dublin, was deeply concerned by this tendency: 'There is nothing succeeds like success and every German success means more pro-Germans'.[51]

After the fall of France, the widely held – and, in the circumstances, justifiable – perception that the final victory of the Axis was imminent lent further weight to the argument that Ireland in its own interests should adjust to the reality of an emerging post-democratic world order. According to the US minister in Dublin, David Gray, among those expressing such views was the Cardinal-Archbishop of Armagh and Primate of All Ireland, Cardinal Joseph McRory. Gray reported to Secretary of State Cordell Hull that McRory had said in a private conversation during the summer of 1940 'that he believed the Germans would win this war and that he was willing to take a chance on them'.[52] The US representative also recalled several talks with Joe Walshe of the Department of External Affairs immediately after the fall of France in which the latter 'discussed the "new order" that would follow the termination of the war … in which England would survive as a minor power analogous to Holland'.[53] Gray's testimony on such matters must always be treated with caution: but numerous other prominent figures in Irish life were recorded as expressing similar sentiments. Dan Bourke, for example, a Fianna Fáil TD and Lord Mayor of Limerick, remarked to another American diplomat that a German occupation of Ireland would not necessarily spell disaster: 'in fact, this country might even derive some "benefit" from the German

50 *Yorkshire Post*, 10 November 1944.
51 Betjeman to H. V. Hodson, Empire Division, Ministry of Information, 21 June 1940, TNA INF 1/528. For further details of Betjeman's work in Dublin, see R. Cole, '"Good Relations": Irish Neutrality and the Propaganda of John Betjeman, 1941–43', *Éire-Ireland* 30:4 (Winter 1996): 33–46.
52 Gray to Hull, no. 40. 'Irish Situation as of August 6, 1940', same date. Department of State records RG 84: Ireland: Dublin Legation: Security Segregated Records, 1936–49, Entry 2763, 350/61/29/07, Box 2, 800–711.1–824.2, NARA.
53 Gray added: 'On the occasion in late April 1940, when I lunched with the German Minister, Mr. Walshe was present and appeared to be on extremely intimate terms with the [Hempel] family, the children addressing him as Uncle Joe'. 'Memorandum on J.P. Walshe, Secretary, External Affairs, Dublin, and newly appointed Irish Ambassador to the Vatican', n.d. [c. April 1946], 'State Dept. Dispatches 2109–2199 Outgoing Mar.-Aug. 1946' file, Box 10, David Gray papers, Franklin D. Roosevelt Presidential Library, Hyde Park, New York.

way of life; German methods, in his [Bourke's] view, might provide the "starch" which this country needs'.[54]

Within some Catholic circles, the possibilities opened up by the Axis restructuring of the Continent seemed to quell lingering prewar doubts about National Socialism. Sylvia Couturié, a French teenager who spent the Emergency years in Dungarvan, Co. Waterford, recalls that local clergy often delivered pro-German sermons from the pulpit and that 'several times in church we were asked to pray for Hitler'. Her Irish neighbours, she noted, keenly anticipated a new era of Franco-German collaboration against the British Empire.[55] In the same vein, the supplanting of the 'decadent' Third Republic by the Vichy regime (whose programme 'must naturally be acclaimed by Catholics throughout the world'[56]), and the triumph of authoritarian Catholic leaders on the Iberian peninsula were hailed by *An tIolar*, which in an editorial of July 1940 looked forward to the place to be occupied by 'Ireland in the New Europe':

> Already we have seen the re-birth of Italy, Portugal and Spain … With the rapid changes now envisaged in Europe it will be possible for a resolute and far-seeing people to restore Ireland to Europe, to that group of Catholic peoples who have looked towards Rome for twenty centuries, but whose vision was blurred at the Reformation and distracted from its true object by the rise of liberalistic finance-capital.[57]

Such views were far from atypical during the early Emergency years. An illuminating perspective on Irish understandings of the meaning of the war can be gained from the writings of Liam de Róiste, whose diary is an invaluable document of Irish political history during the

54 Memorandum by Vinton Chapin, secretary of the Legation, 'Conversation with Mr. Dan Bourke, T.D., Mayor of Limerick', 14 June 1941, Department of State records, RG 84: Ireland: Dublin Legation: Security Segregated Records, 1936–49, Entry 2763, 350/61/29/07, Box 2, 800–711.1–824.2, NARA. Bourke's colleague in the Fianna Fáil Parliamentary Party, Martin Corry, TD for East Cork, had already expressed the hope that 'Hitler would blow the British to hell'. Corry was regarded as 'pro-German' by the British security service MI5. See B. Girvin, *The Emergency: Neutral Ireland, 1939–1945* (London: Macmillan, 2006), p. 93; 'Irish Affairs (The General Situation in Éire)', QRS/195, 1 May 1942, TNA DO 121/85.

55 S. Couturié, *No Tears in Ireland: A Memoir* (New York: Free Press, 2001), p. 130.

56 *An tIolar/The Standard*, 4 October 1940. John Charles McQuaid, Archbishop of Dublin, was another who expressed his satisfaction with the end of the Third Republic and support for the work of Pétain and Laval. Elizabeth (Bowen) Cameron, 'Notes from Éire', 10 February 1942, TNA DO 130/28.

57 *An tIolar/The Standard*, 12 July 1940. Some individuals in those countries were thinking in a similar vein. José Maria Doussinague, a senior official in the Spanish Ministry of Foreign Affairs, hatched a scheme early in 1943 for what Stanley Payne calls 'an entente of Catholic states such as Portugal, Ireland, Hungary, and Croatia' that would exercise a balance of power in a Europe divided between the Allies and the Axis. Payne, *Franco and Hitler*, p. 198.

state's early decades.[58] Fifty years of age when the Second World War began, de Róiste epitomised the newly emergent Irish political class. His national record was impeccable, including as it did membership of the Cork City battalion of the Irish Volunteers during the Easter Rising. A deputy in the first Dáil, he had spent part of the War of Independence on the run. Though he had taken the pro-Treaty side in the Civil War and served briefly as a Cumann na nGaedheal TD for Cork City, he had little sympathy with the economic conservatism and political sectarianism of the 'counter-revolutionary' wing of his own party. He was to abandon the Irish Christian Front, in whose foundation he had taken a leading part, in protest against Patrick Belton's attempt to turn it into a far-right political party. His own instincts, as a lifelong Irish-language activist and official of pre-1916 Sinn Féin, remained those of a committed Irish-Irelander.[59]

De Róiste, like many observers in Ireland and beyond, saw the fall of France in 1940 as marking the end of an epoch in European history:

> [T]he events of these past few weeks have been the death-knell of French Revolutionary tenets: nationalism, liberty, fraternity, equality, liberalism, democracy and such-like ideas that were sacrosanct in the 19th century and that seemed to have attained unshaken stability after the war of 1914–18. Communism, national-socialism, Fascism have brought men to more fundamental things: to clearer issues as to the purposes of life and living.[60]

Nazism's victories, he considered, were in large measure attributable to the fact that there was 'idealism, be it false or true, behind Hitler ... a something which the English have not now'.[61] Whereas the democracies could only offer a return to a discredited past, the totalitarian states, in however crude a fashion, were pointing the way toward the future.

> The possibility that England may be defeated and that, therefore, the old regime in politics, economics, social affairs, may disappear in that land, with repercussions here in Ireland, is agitating some minds at least. But only comparatively few, as yet ...
>   The obvious thing ... is to let and encourage Germany to expand to the east against Communist Russia: if the civilisation of Western Europe

---

58 Because the surviving version of the diary is a typewritten, and possibly edited, copy of the manuscript original produced by de Róiste between 1943 and 1946, it must be treated with a certain degree of caution. The fact that the author seems to have made no attempt to downplay his anti-Allied stance even after the defeat of Nazism, however, indicates that the passages quoted in this book may be taken as accurate reflections of his contemporaneous attitudes.
59 D. Ó Murchadha, *Liam de Róiste* (Dublin: An Clóchomhar, 1976).
60 Liam de Róiste diary, 28 June 1940, U 271/A56, Cork Archive Institute.
61 *Ibid.*, 10 September 1940.

that grew up out of Christianity is to be saved from Bolshevism.

But the politicians of England and the ex-politicians of France, with their backing of Jewish finance, are blinded, even to their own countries' interests, by their hatred of the regime in Germany and the rise to power of Germany.[62]

It was nonetheless scarcely conceivable that Ireland could remain indifferent to, or unaffected by, the direction in which world events were moving:

Those who still think in terms of pre-1914 'Democracy' are living in the past ... Or, is it that Éire will cling to 'parliamentary democracy' when all the world has abandoned it?[63]

De Róiste's interpretation of the issues at stake in the war is noteworthy because it expresses the viewpoint not of the political extremes but rather of a middle-aged, middle-class and – by contemporary Irish standards at least – well-informed observer. The disillusionment with parliamentarianism, casual anti-Semitism and reluctant admiration for the achievements of the totalitarian states that he expressed lay, as we have seen in Chapter 1, solidly within the mainstream of Irish political thought. While such men as de Róiste would not themselves take the initiative to set up a post-democratic system based on Continental examples, their belief that a shift toward authoritarianism was both inevitable and in many respects desirable created a political space that more resolute and determined movements would quickly seek to occupy.

Political extremism and the world war

From the late eighteenth century onwards, opponents of British rule in Ireland had sought to take advantage of occasions in which the attention of the government in London had been distracted, and its ability to enforce its will in Ireland diminished, by entanglements in conflicts overseas. The concession of the 'Constitution of 1782' had come about in large measure as a result of Westminster's recognition that it could not effectively resist demands for greater autonomy in Ireland while simultaneously conducting a far more extensive counter-insurgency operation in the American colonies. In December 1796, the Society of United Irishmen had attempted to exploit Britain's involvement in the Revolutionary War, when a powerful French invasion force accompanied by the SUI leader Theobald Wolfe Tone almost succeeded in making an unopposed landing at Bantry Bay. The extent of Britain's strategic overstretch, even with the benefit of the forewarning provided by this abortive assault, was emphasised still further by the initial success enjoyed by General Humbert's token force at Killala nineteen months later. The incursions by American-based Fenians into Canada in 1866 had been explicitly designed to provoke a war between the United States and Britain, which, it was hoped, would leave Ireland all but undefended against a rebellion at home. Likewise the Easter Rising in 1916, although obliged to proceed without the German assistance upon which its leaders had been counting, would almost certainly never have been contemplated had not the Great War given the insurgents reason to hope that the British government might choose to relax its grip upon Ireland rather than jeopardise its preparations for a major offensive on the Western Front and its efforts to secure a declaration of belligerency from the United States.

It was predictable, therefore, that the advent of the Second World War should have been accompanied by a revival of the traditional maxim that 'England's difficulty is Ireland's opportunity'. Although republicans were deeply divided by the Emergency, many going so far as to sink their differences with the de Valera government for the duration and enlist in the Irish defence forces for the purpose of resisting an attack by either belligerent,[64] elements of the IRA did see the war as providing scope for the final completion of the work left undone in 1919–21. To opponents not merely of British rule in the North but of the liberal-democratic system in the twenty-six counties, however, the war held out a more beguiling prospect still: that national unification *and* the displacement of the parliamentary regime in Dublin might be accomplished not as a result of revolutionary activity in Ireland itself, but as a by-product of a complete German victory in the West. For Irish ultra-rightists, the conclusion to be drawn was that political mobilisation, rather than paramilitary activity, was most urgently called for in the current situation. If the fascist powers were on the brink of overthrowing the existing power-structure in Britain and Ireland, it was of paramount importance that an alternative leadership cadre should be constituted in advance, ready to step forward to assume the duties of government in an Ireland whose future lay within an Axis-dominated European order.

---

64 O'Halpin, *Defending Ireland*, p. 166. At the other end of the political spectrum, not all Southern Unionists felt themselves able to follow suit. As Elizabeth Bowen recorded of the students of Trinity College, 'Many of them are not joining the L.S.F. [Local Security Force] as the fear of "having to fight England" still prevails'. Elizabeth (Bowen) Cameron, 'Notes on Éire', 9 November 1940, TNA FO 800/310/254.

One of the first to recognise the potential of the developing strategic situation on the Continent, and to begin working in anticipation of a German breakthrough, was a thirty-year-old tax consultant from Belfast, Gearóid Ó Cuinneagáin. Born in 1910 into a comfortable middle-class Catholic family living in the Protestant-dominated Stranmillis district of the city, the then Gerald Cunningham was educated at St Malachy's Christian Brothers' School, where his classmates included the future Cardinal-Archbishop of Armagh and Primate of All Ireland, William Conway. An intelligent and studious youth, Cunningham distinguished himself in the classroom,[65] gaining the third place nationwide in the Irish civil service examinations in 1927 and earning matriculation to Queen's University, Belfast. Rejecting an offer by his father, a restaurateur, to finance his university studies, Cunningham accepted an appointment as a tax clerk in the Irish Department of Finance and was posted to the Revenue Commissioners' office at Athlone. There, he renewed his acquaintance with one of his former teachers at St Malachy's, Patrick Lenihan,[66] who had also abandoned academia for a civil service career and now shared the same office with his former pupil. Inspired by Lenihan, an enthusiastic cultural nationalist, Cunningham began taking evening classes in Irish and adopted the Gaelic form of his name, by which he was to be known for the remainder of his life.[67] Ó Cuinneagáin continued to pursue his deepening interest in Irish language and culture following transfers to Castlebar in 1929 and Dublin in 1930, by which time he had attained the rank of Junior Executive Officer in the Department of Defence.[68] Shortly after the accession to power of the first Fianna Fáil administration in 1932,[69] Ó Cuinneagáin requested three months' unpaid leave to attend the Irish-language immersion programme in the Donegal Gaeltacht at the college of Rann na Féirste (Rannafast). His application was turned down, it being the policy of the civil service to grant such furloughs only to those officers who had demonstrated special promise by obtaining a scholarship to fund their studies. Ó Cuinneagáin's response was immediate and typical of his increas-

65 Ironically in light of his subsequent career, by far his weakest school subject was Irish.
66 Subsequently Fianna Fáil TD for Longford-Westmeath, 1965–70, and father of the politician Brian Lenihan. Patrick Lenihan's brother James, a resident in the Channel Islands when they were occupied by the Germans in June 1940, volunteered for service with the *Abwehr* and was parachuted into Ireland as an agent the following year before travelling to Belfast and surrendering himself to the Northern authorities.
67 Bernadette Cunningham, author interview, 21 October 1998.
68 Unsigned memorandum, 'Geroid' [sic] Ó Cuinneagáin', 27 April 1943, Military Intelligence records S. 231/40, DDMA, Cathal Brugha Barracks, Rathmines.
69 Radio interview of Ó Cuinneagáin by Prionsias Mac Aonghusa, Raidió na Gaeltachta, 11 August 1981.

ingly headstrong nature. He resigned abruptly from the service in July; proceeded independently to Rann na Féirste; and remained there for the following year, living amongst the villagers and perfecting his knowledge of the language. By the time he left the Gaeltacht he was no less at ease in Irish than in English and, although his speech in both tongues continued to be marked by a strong Belfast accent, developed an economical, forceful and effective writing style in Irish that contrasted markedly with the mannered and sometimes deliberately archaic modes of expression favoured by many turn-of-the-century Gaelic revivalists.[70] His commitment to the task of cultural revival, moreover, had been both deepened and narrowed by his association with the head of the Irish college at Rann na Féirste, Father Laurence Murray, described by the *Irish Press* as 'an implacable and relentless foe of all things opposed to Gaelic ideals'.[71]

Ó Cuinneagáin's command of the language gained him a position in 1933 as an editorial writer with the Republican weekly *An tÉireannach* ['The Irishman'], edited by the Protestant Irish-language activist Seán Beaumont. In light of his subsequent political evolution, this was a curious outlet for Ó Cuinneagáin's talents. Determinedly socialist in its orientation, *An tÉireannach* served as the 'house organ of the Republican Congress', the successor-body to Saor Éire; it was also noted for its strong anti-fascist stance. Nonetheless, the journal provided Ó Cuinneagáin with a forum for his first political articles, some of which were published under the pseudonym of 'Bruinneall Gan Smál' ['Immaculate Virgin'], and also with an entrée into republican circles which would later prove useful to him.[72] After some months, however, in need of a more reliable source of income and perhaps increasingly out of sympathy with the editorial stance of *An tÉireannach*, he resigned. By 1937, capitalising upon his civil service experience, he had become a partner in a small tax-consulting venture, Ó Cuinneagáin & Cooke, with offices at 55 Lower O'Connell Street, Dublin.

In early 1939, Ó Cuinneagáin took his first step into the political arena with the formation of An Cumann Díth-Shnadhmtha ['The Separatists' Society'], of which he styled himself the secretary. Little is known of this body, which left no records and appears to have engaged in no activities beyond the issuance of periodic press releases and the composition of letters on various topics to the Dublin newspapers. In

70 Risteárd Ó Glaisne has pointed out that Ó Cuinneagáin's Irish, while fluent and idiomatic, often contained a number of deviations from accepted orthographic and syntactical conventions. Author interview, 2 August 2003.
71 *Irish Press*, 25 August 1936.
72 One of his colleagues on the newspaper, for example, was the author and IRA member Mairtín Ó Cadhain.

view of the fact that its address was the same premises at 55 Lower
O'Connell Street at which Ó Cuinneagáin conducted his business, it
is an open question as to whether it ever possessed any membership
other than its secretary-founder. Whatever the case, the creation of
the Separatists' Society served to indicate Ó Cuinneagáin's departure
from commentary upon national affairs to taking an active part in
attempting to shape them.

As noted in Chapter 1,[73] as early as 1937 Ó Cuinneagáin was looking
to fascist Italy as a source of external support for a 'reconstructed' and
comprehensively militarised Irish state: 'Only as part of an alliance',
he declared the following year, 'will we be ... able to speak to the
English with a strong voice'. His choice of Mussolini as the most
suitable partner was predicated not only on the fact that a 'considerable
number of Catholic Churchmen ... [would] likely be disposed to view
an understanding with Italy with favour',[74] but that Italy's imperial
ambitions, in apparent contrast at the time to those of Germany,
conflicted directly with British interests in the Mediterranean and East
Africa. Whereas there was no reason to suppose that the relatively
amicable relations between Germany and Britain, underwritten by
the Anglo-German Naval Agreement of 1935 and the appeasement
policy of the Chamberlain government, were likely to deteriorate
in the near future, the Anglo-Italian relationship, aggravated by the
Abyssinian crisis and Mussolini's determination to make Italy a first-
rank naval power, could be relied upon to remain antagonistic. The
rapid deterioration of Anglo-German relations in the aftermath of
the Sudeten dispute, however, appeared to reveal the existence of
even more promising possibilities elsewhere. By the spring of 1939,
Ó Cuinneagáin had recognised that a major war between Britain and
Germany was imminent, and, on behalf of the Separatists' Society,
called on the Irish people to 'make use of this other great danger facing
England to benefit our country'.[75]

The outbreak of the Second World War, and the rapid triumph of
German arms in Poland, Denmark and Norway, were catalysts for
a dramatic advance in Gearóid Ó Cuinneagáin's political and philosophical development. In the new situation created by the conflict,
a more expansive and ambitious strategy now began to reveal itself
to him. No longer, he believed, was it possible to dispute that the
totalitarian countries of the European Continent had conclusively
established the superiority of their systems of government and admin-

73 See p. 34 above.
74 *Irish Press*, 25 August 1936.
75 *Ibid.*,17 March 1939.

istration. An equally evident corollary was that every modern state was destined to conform to the basic pattern these powers had laid down. But within the post-democratic world order in process of formation, a vital role might be found for a country capable, unlike the existing fascist states, of harnessing the potential of these new methods of political, economic and social mobilisation to some greater goal than mere territorial aggrandisement.

In an unpublished manifesto probably written in the spring of 1940, 'Ireland a Missionary-Ideological State?' Ó Cuinneagáin began to lay down the basic principles of his evolving political programme. It was first of all necessary, he argued, to reject the commonly held fallacy that the regimented pattern of life in the Continental fascist countries was in some way alien to the Irish mentality.

> If we in Ireland sincerely felt that the acceptance or institution of a strictly disciplinarian political and economic regime in this country even for a prolonged period would eventuate in great and memorable and worthy achievements in no other manner of government possibly obtainable, who can impute [sic] that we would not welcome regimentation or dragooning likewise?

The real question was not whether Ireland or any other country was amenable to 'discipline', but whether there existed 'a practicable Gaelic ideal, corresponding to the Nazi or Fascist ideal, which could rouse and inspire the whole people of the Ireland of 1940?' In Ó Cuinneagáin's view – picking up the baton from such figures as Aodh de Blacam and Father O'Leary – the only such objective that conformed to 'the requirements of the character of our racial genius' was the 'task of European and world re-Christianisation'. Among the Catholic countries, neither Mussolini's Italy, Franco's Spain nor even Salazar's Portugal – far less 'priest-impoverished France' – could provide 'a perfect example of Catholic national government'. Nor was the training and dispatch to foreign countries of missionaries sufficient to achieve this objective. 'The world requires to be shown in the twentieth century that Christianity can be practised in the world – not merely in the cloister!' Ireland's manifest destiny, then, was to prove by her example the compatibility of faith and modernity, and thus to provide a practical as well as an ethical alternative to the materialist heresies of capitalism and Communism. But it was futile to hope for any advance in this direction so long as the country retained its existing system of 'purely passive or administrative but non-directional government'.

> Our new Irish executive must become a living dynamic organism, maintaining intimate contact with every aspect of life within the national territory, directing it, informing and moulding it, infusing it with the

spirit which will constitute the nourishing substance of its life. In other words a corporative system of government, a quasi-totalitarian or disciplinarian form of government, is indicated for the new Ireland if our basic national twentieth century aspirations are to be achieved. We shall group ourselves inevitably with the [totalitarian] ideological bloc although it will not be necessary, as indeed it will be undesirable, for us to be as thoroughly totalitarian as certain of the other members of the bloc ... [But] if the whole object of our national being is to be the greater glory of God then our people will I believe recognise that to assure the achievement of that purpose there is adequate justification for small personal sacrifices, for acquiescence [sic] even in the adoption of a disciplinarian regime, and like the Italians even welcome its adoption.[76]

As already noted, Ó Cuinneagáin's vision of Ireland as an exemplary Christian state was by no means original. Éamon de Valera himself, in a speech at Athlone in 1933, had called upon the Irish people to take on 'the task – now a vital one – of helping to save Western civilization' through their commitment to 'spiritual and intellectual, rather than material, values'.[77] Similar appeals from the Catholic clergy for Ireland to dedicate herself to the re-evangelisation of a decadent modern world had been a pulpit commonplace throughout the 1930s. However, the assertion that the establishment of a palingenetic new order, aligned with the Axis, was a necessary precondition to this objective represented a marked advance in the radicalism of Ó Cuinneagáin's doctrines. When in December 1937 he had advocated a military alliance with Mussolini's Italy, he had been at pains to deny that 'a Fascist link-up' would require Ireland to become 'a Fascist State'. The regime he had then envisaged was to have been based on 'a democratic Republican Constitution more or less on the United States model with a Rooseveltean [sic] interpretation of the State's functions and responsibilities in the economic life of the nation. That is the sort of Republic I think most Irishmen want'.[78] Little more than two years later, Ó Cuinneagáin had come to reject not merely the concept of a democratic constitution, 'Rooseveltean' or otherwise, but even the idea that there was anything sacrosanct about 'the Republic' as the appropriate political embodiment of Irish self-determination. In doing so, he had turned his back upon the main current of Irish nationalist thought and set out upon a course fraught with potential hazards, of a personal as well as a political nature.

76 'Ireland a Missionary-Ideological State?', n.d., 10/2/11, Gearóid Ó Cuinneagáin papers (hereafter GÓCP), DDMA.
77 *Irish Press*, 7 February 1933.
78 G. Ua Cuinneagáin, 'No Other Way: Éire and Italy as Allies in War', *Wolfe Tone Weekly*, 11 December 1937.

   The beginning of the 1940s was an especially inauspicious moment to contemplate launching movements of a radical or extremist character. At the outbreak of war, the government had rushed through the Oireachtas an Emergency Powers Act that authorised the executive to issue such orders, having the force of law, as it considered 'necessary or expedient for securing the public safety or the preservation of the State'. Among the powers specifically enumerated in the Act was the ability to prohibit 'subversive statements or propaganda'; a later amendment enabled the government to issue orders of detention without warrant against Irish citizens.[79] When Gearóid Ó Cuinneagáin set out to turn his vision of a totalitarian reconstruction of Irish society into reality, therefore, he can have been under no illusion as to both the difficulty and danger of the task. Indeed, the care he took to conceal his activities from the authorities shows that he was keenly aware of the risk he was running. By the summer of 1940 those activities had already passed from political advocacy to efforts, by means of assistance to the Axis powers, to put an end to the Irish democratic experiment.

The pro-Axis underground

In so close-knit a political community as was Ireland during the Emergency, it was all but inevitable that Ó Cuinneagáin should soon have come into contact with others whose views ran parallel with his own. Among the earliest of these collaborators was a retired Commandant of the Free State Army from Gorey, Co. Wexford, W. J. Brennan-Whitmore. A veteran of the Easter Rising, Frongoch internee and former Blueshirt,[80] Brennan-Whitmore had long been convinced that Jews and Freemasons were engaged in a Machiavellian plot to achieve world domination over the Christian nations, and was outspoken in his condemnation of 'the disunion, intrigue and corruption that is the inevitable outcome of the parliamentary regime'.[81] In August 1939 he

---

79 For a discussion of the operation of the Act, see S. Ó Longaigh, 'Emergency Law in Action, 1939–1945', in D. Keogh & M. O'Driscoll, eds, *Ireland in World War Two: Diplomacy and Survival* (Dublin: Mercier, 2004), pp. 63–80.

80 According to the Stormfront White Nationalist Community website, Brennan-Whitmore concluded his political career in the 1970s as a member of 'Commander' Terry Byrne's tiny National Socialist Irish Workers' Party. See www.stormfront.org/forum/showthread.php/irish-neo-nazi-michael-j-186375p2.html (accessed 18 March 2008).

81 P. Maume, *The Long Gestation: Irish Nationalist Life 1891–1918* (New York: St Martin's Press, 1999), p. 165; letter by Brennan-Whitmore in *An tIolar/The Standard*, March 8, 1940. For particulars of Brennan-Whitmore's early career, see his unpublished autobiography, 'My Tempestuous Generation', W. J. Brennan-Whitmore papers, Acc. 5449, National Library of Ireland.

founded the 'Celtic Confederation of Occupational Guilds' (CCOG), a body characterised by one scholar of the Irish ultra-right as 'à la fois anti-parlementaire, anti-britannique, bilemment anti-bolchevique et légèrement anti-capitaliste'.[82] Despite modest subsidies from the *Abwehr*, the CCOG and its short-lived successor, Saoirse Gaedheal ['Freedom of the Gaels'], failed to thrive, and in the early months of 1940 Brennan-Whitmore turned his attention to the question of whether 'a sound political organisation could be formed to appeal to the people on corporative [*sic*] lines'.[83] As part of this effort, a meeting of former CCOG activists was convened at the Red Bank restaurant in Dublin, a well-known haunt of ultra-nationalist and extremist bodies owned by a German-born member of the Dublin Nazi Party, to discuss the adoption in Ireland of a corporate state on Portuguese lines. At this gathering it was proposed to form an organisation with the name Clann na Saoirse ['Tribe of Freedom']. A month later, again at Brennan-Whitmore's initiative, a similar meeting convened at 55 Lower O'Connell Street, in a third-floor room rented in the name of Ó Cuinneagáin & Cooke.[84]

The organisation and activities of Clann na Saoirse, and of the other small and shadowy pro-Axis groups with which it shared much of its membership, are not easy to reconstruct. Much of the information concerning these bodies has been obtained from official interrogations of its members, some of whom were interned in the summer and autumn of 1940 and whose testimony, intended as it was to exculpate them, is at best of dubious reliability. From such sources as are available, it appears that Clann na Saoirse was intended to function as a legal political party, and that two related bodies, the Irish Friends of Germany and Cumann Náisiúnta ['National Association'], were established both to identify and mobilise potential supporters and to engage in illegal subversive activities in support of the anticipated invasion.

Although principally involved with Clann na Saoirse, of which he had become *Stiúrthóir* [Director] by May 1940, Ó Cuinneagáin was an active participant in the underground branch of the movement. In both capacities he made clear his opposition to the democratic Irish state and his desire to emulate the approach and achievements of the totalitarian powers. An eight-point programme, of which he was almost

82 X. Audrain, 'Les milieux fascisants en Irlande du Sud durant la seconde guerre modiale', MA thesis, Université Pierre Mendès-France, Grenoble II, 1999, p. 22.
83 Unsigned memorandum of interrogation of Volunteer John R. Magee, 31 October 1940, G2/X/0253, DDMA.
84 Transcript of interrogation of Volunteer Joseph Leigh, 31 October 1940, G2/X/0311, DDMA.

certainly the author, described Clann na Saoirse as a 'Racial Resurgence Party' and declared that the existing political system 'must be replaced by the Irish principle of government by leadership'. Other points of the Clann na Saoirse manifesto included the mobilisation of 'the entire moral and material resources of the 26-county area' in preparation for 'a total effort' to recover the Northern irredenta; the augmentation of the population by means of a vigorous natalist policy and the banning of all emigration; the 'elimination' of the 'pernicious influence of aliens' from Irish economic life; and – presumably following the forcible dissolution by the Axis of the United Kingdom and the French Third Republic – the establishment of 'a Sovereign Federation of the Celtic peoples of Ireland, Scotland, Wales and Brittany'. Accompanying this last proposal was a demand for the complete and compulsory de-Anglicisation of Irish cultural life: 'The English language is the mortal enemy of Irish nationality and must therefore be ruthlessly extirpated by every means at the disposal of the State. As a preliminary measure its use must be unconditionally prohibited in every sphere of public life including all governmental, educational, and other public institutions'.[85]

Ó Cuinneagáin's tenure at the head of Clann na Saoirse was brought to an abrupt halt by a general round-up of Axis sympathisers by the authorities at the beginning of June. The arrest on 23 May of Stephen Carroll Held, a republican emissary to the *Abwehr*, led to the discovery of an IRA-drafted blueprint, the so-called 'Plan Kathleen', for joint operations between a German invasion force and republican paramilitaries against the British army.[86] Although in reality the Germans were neither responsible for, nor particularly interested in, this amateurishly-conceived scheme, the government reacted swiftly to what appeared to be a significant threat to the state by taking the principal members of Clann na Saoirse and the Irish Friends of Germany/Cumann Náisiúnta (IFG/CN) into custody. Perhaps because his connection

85 Clann na Saoirse, *Programme* (n.d.). In the possession of Aindrias Ó Scolaidhe, Dublin.
86 As early as 1938, Held's pro-Nazi activities had come to the attention of MI5. It is a measure, though, of the poor performance of the wartime British intelligence services in Ireland that for two years, MI5 laboured under the misapprehension that Held's sister was the wife of the Minister for Co-Ordination of Defensive Services, Frank Aiken. British ministers' belief that Aiken was 'prepared to assist the Germans whenever and wherever he could do so without prejudice to his present position' stemmed largely from this erroneous assumption. It is yet to be determined whether Aiken's hostile reception by President Roosevelt when he visited Washington in the spring of 1941 might have been influenced in part by the communication of such misinformation to the American government. See Held's personal file, TNA KV 2/1443; unsigned and undated 'Note on Stephen Carroll Held Case' [c. December 1941], TNA KV 2/1450; telegram from Sir Alexander Cadogan, Foreign Office, to Lord Halifax, British Ambassador, Washington, 2 April 1941, TNA FO 371/29108.

with the former movement had not become public knowledge until three days after Held's arrest, Ó Cuinneagáin was not caught up in the dragnet. Within days, moreover, most of the detainees were released after the Irish military intelligence service, G2, decided that the organisation in Ireland of the pro-Axis underground was too rudimentary and the intellectual calibre of its members too low to pose any serious threat to the state.

Such a judgement was in fact premature. One of the first IFG/CN suspects to be set at liberty because he was believed to be an insignificant ordinary member was Maurice O'Connor, a pro-Nazi railway clerk from Dublin who had visited Germany before the war. A founder-member of both Clann na Saoirse and IFG/CN, O'Connor set to work to rebuild the shattered infrastructure of the Friends of Germany in anticipation of what he believed, in the wake of the collapse of the Allied armies on the Continent, to be an imminent invasion of Ireland and Britain by the *Wehrmacht*. After holding several meetings in Dublin restaurants, the reconstituted IFG/CN – which had lost its use of the premises at 55 Lower O'Connell Street as a result of a rent dispute between Ó Cuinneagáin and his landlord – transferred operations to the Gardiner Street home of Reginald Eager, a former Blueshirt and British Army veteran who eighteen months previously had been dismissed for embezzlement from his position as a cartographer in the Ordnance Survey.[87] During the following three months a series of meetings was held which combined an Irish language class conducted by Ó Cuinneagáin, partly to provide cover, and the planning of subversive activities intended to assist the expected German invasion and establish the pro-Nazi credentials of IFG/CN's membership. While many of these schemes were fanciful – for example, O'Connor's announcement at a gathering on 17 September of a plan 'to organise in groups of 50 in readiness for taking over different buildings of importance in the city as soon as the Germans landed in this country',[88] participants at the Gardiner Street meetings did engage in definitely treasonable activity, notably the circulation of pro-German leaflets and attempts to persuade serving members of the armed forces to refuse orders to resist a landing by German troops.[89] IFG/CN activists' practice of exchanging Nazi salutes at the gatherings, and

87 Garda Síochána Dublin Metropolitan District weekly reports for weeks ending 8 July and 24 July 1940; report by Sergeant M. J. Wymes, Garda Síochána Special Branch, '"Cumann Náisiúnta" or "Irish Friends of Germany"', 1 August 1940, G2/2571, DDMA.

88 O'Connor added that 'all those who took an active part in assisting Germany would be assured of good positions when the occupation of the country was completed'. Wymes, '"Cumann Náisiúnta" or "Irish Friends of Germany"', 19 September 1940, *ibid*.

89 Wymes, '"Cumann Náisiúnta" or "Irish Friends of Germany,"', 30 September 1940, *ibid*.

the declaration by a number of servicemen within the organisation of their intention to turn their weapons against the government when the Germans landed, provides further confirmation of the extremism, if not the sophistication, of the organisation of which Ó Cuinneagáin had become a part.[90]

Unhappily for Maurice O'Connor and his associates, ever since the June arrests the inner circle of IFG/CN had been thoroughly penetrated by the security services, which received detailed reports of all of its meetings and activities. Rather than proceed to an immediate round-up, the deputy head of G2, the efficient Colonel Dan Bryan, chose to leave its members at liberty to see how many pro-Axis activists might be drawn into the net. This period of grace was to prove crucial for Gearóid Ó Cuinneagáin's subsequent career. In the last week of September 1940, he declared his intention to break away from his former associates and launch an organisation of his own. As he explained to his IFG/CN colleagues, his aim was to form 'a Hitler Youth Movement ... under the guise of an Irish Class and if possible he intended giving Nazi lectures through the medium of Irish'.[91] Ó Cuinneagáin's new society was to be a branch of the respected Irish-language body Conradh na Gaeilge ['Gaelic League'] and would adopt the name of 'Craobh na hAiséirghe' [the 'Branch of the Resurrection']. Two days after this announcement, the security forces raided the homes of Maurice O'Connor and Reginald Eager, taking both into custody along with a number of smaller IFG/CN fry. Once again Ó Cuinneagáin escaped arrest, becoming the most significant member of the pro-Axis underground to remain at liberty in the autumn of 1940. That he was able to do so is explained in part by his use of several aliases and a rare lapse on the part of the intelligence services. Not until April 1941, by which time the danger of imminent invasion and, hence, the need for additional round-ups had passed, did the authorities at last realise that 'Séamus Cunningham', 'Jerry Cunningham' and Gearóid Ó Cuinneagáin were in fact the same person.[92]

The reasons behind Ó Cuinneagáin's decision at this critical time to strike out on his own remain shrouded in mystery. It is unlikely that he had any foreknowledge of the authorities' impending round-up: if he had done, he would hardly have courted additional scrutiny by inviting the other members of IFG/CN to attend Craobh na hAiséirghe's

90 Garda Síochána Dublin Metropolitan Division report, 6 September 1940; Wymes, '"Cumann Náisiúnta" or "Irish Friends of Germany"', 30 September 1940, *ibid.*
91 Wymes, '"Cumann Náisiúnta" or "Irish Friends of Germany"', 30 September 1940, *ibid.*
92 Wymes to Superintendent S. Gantly, Garda Síochána Special Branch, 18 April 1941, G2/2988, DDMA.

lectures.[93] Whereas Ó Cuinneagáin did not share the outspokenly anti-clerical views of the IFG/CN leader, and although his personality was not of the cast that readily accepted the authority of others, neither is there anything to indicate that he departed on other than cordial terms with O'Connor.[94] He supported the latter's proposal on 27 September to reconstitute Clann na Saoirse, and even after leaving IFG/CN promised to do 'all in his power to assist' in this endeavour. The simplest and most straightforward explanation appears to be that by September 1940 Ó Cuinneagáin no longer considered membership of O'Connor's organisation a productive use of his time and talents, which were suited to a much larger stage. While he shared IFG/CN's enthusiasm for the totalitarian state and undoubtedly desired to see a German victory in the war, Ó Cuinneagáin stood head and shoulders above the other members both in intellectual capacity and breadth of vision. As Colonel Bryan later noted, one of the principal *raisons d'être* of the organisation had been to establish its members as 'good friends and emulators of the expected invaders before their arrival ... thereby obtaining influential positions in the creation of the expected new order in Ireland'.[95] Ó Cuinneagáin harboured no such petty ambitions. For him a German victory was desirable not as an end in itself, but merely as the precondition for the revolutionary reconstitution of Irish politics and society that he wished to accomplish. Inasmuch as it had become clear by the autumn of 1940 that such an objective would hardly be significantly advanced by the kind of pinprick activities in which the Friends of Germany were engaged, the strong likelihood is that Ó Cuinneagáin desired to seek a more expansive field for the exercise of his abilities.

Craobh na hAiséirghe

A long-standing legend asserts that the launch of Craobh na hAiséirghe took place in response to a confrontation between Gearóid Ó Cuinneagáin and Éamon de Valera at a meeting of the Cumann Gaelach ['The Gaelic Society'] at Trinity College, Dublin in the early days of the Emergency. According to one published version of the story, while the Taoiseach was delivering a lecture 'a man began barracking him [*ag tógáil challáin*]. That man was Gearóid Ó Cuinneagáin. Craobh na hAiséirghe was founded shortly thereafter as a result of the events

93 Wymes, '"Cumann Náisiúnta" or "Irish Friends of Germany"', 30 September 1940, G2/2571, DDMA.
94 Garda Síochána Dublin Metropolitan District report for week ending 8 July 1940, G2/X/0253, DDMA.
95 'Irish Born Groups', n.d. [c. December 1940], P 71/30 (ii), Dan Bryan papers, University College, Dublin.

of that evening in the house of Seán [Ó hÉigeartaigh]', the Auditor of the Society.[96] Appropriately symbolic though this account of Craobh na hAiséirghe's emergence through a clash between the representatives of the old Gaelic establishment and the new militant generation may be – a quality that no doubt accounts for its persistence – in reality there was no connection whatever between the two events. Ó Cuinneagáin's run-in with de Valera at TCD occurred in October 1939; Craobh na hAiséirghe's inaugural meeting took place eleven months later on 25 September 1940 – not at Seán Ó hÉigeartaigh's house but at an O'Connell Street café owned by Ó Cuinneagáin's landlord, a prominent Dublin anti-Semite. The mythical version does contain one element of truth, however, inasmuch as it was at the Cumann Gaelach in Trinity that Ó Cuinneagáin first encountered Craobh na hAiséirghe's co-founder, Ciarán Ó Seachnasaigh.[97] Little is known of Ó Seachnasaigh, a student of French at the College, and efforts by G2 to discover more about him yielded no more information than that he was believed to have studied in Germany and spoke with a 'pronounced Oxford accent'.[98]

Craobh na hAiséirghe was a very different organisation, in style and composition, to the societies with which Ó Cuinneagáin had previously been associated. In the first place, notwithstanding his shorthand characterisation of the body to his IFG/CN colleagues as a 'Hitler Youth Movement', Craobh na hAiséirghe was much more than a pro-Axis ginger group. The branch did evince a keen interest in German culture, offering classes in the language and adopting songs like the *Wacht am Rhein* as its own.[99] Many of its leading members, like Proinsias Mac an Bheatha, a Belfast-born civil servant and editor of a small Irish-language periodical, *An Fánaí* ['The Wanderer'], made no secret of their desire to see Nazi Germany prevail in the war.[100] Through one of its instructors, Dr Heinrich Becker – an expatriate folklorist resident in Dublin, Nazi Party member, veteran of the *Sturmabteilungen* (SA) and close friend of Maurice O'Connor – the personnel of Craobh na hAiséirghe maintained sufficiently close links with the German Legation to cause much anxiety to G2, the detectives of the

---

96 *Indiú*, 5 January 1951. A similar version of events is contained in Risteárd Ó Glaisne's *Gaeilge i gColáiste na Tríonóide 1592–1992* (Dublin: Preas Choláiste na Tríonóide, 1992), p. 70.
97 Or Ó Seachnasa.
98 Unsigned G2 memorandum, 23 November 1940, G2/2988, DDMA. Proinsias Mac an Bheatha describes Ó Seachnasaigh as 'an energetic cheerful man, well-fed in appearance and with a musical tone to his voice'. P. Mac an Bheatha, *Téid Focal le Gaoith* (Dublin: Foilseacháin Náisiúnta, 1967), p. 93.
99 Proinsias Ó Conluain, author interview, 25 January 2006; *Irish Times*, 16 August 1941.
100 Mac an Bheatha, *Téid Focal le Gaoith*, p. 84.

Special Branch, and the British security service MI5.[101] It also attracted a considerable, and with the passage of time an increasing, number of self-declared fascist supporters. Nevertheless Ó Cuinneagáin's new society was never merely an Axis front, and many of its members had little interest in totalitarian ideology in either its Continental or domestic manifestations.[102] Like Conradh na Gaeilge, the larger body of which it was a part, Craobh na hAiséirghe claimed to be a non-political, non-ideological organisation dedicated exclusively to the preservation and dissemination of the Irish language and culture.

On the surface, Ó Cuinneagáin's decision to launch his new organisation as a branch of Conradh na Gaeilge appeared a paradoxical one. Since its formation by Douglas Hyde, Eoin MacNeill and Eugene O'Growney in 1893, Conradh had passed through several stages of development. Conceived originally as a body within which Irish Catholics and Protestants alike could rediscover and celebrate their common Celtic heritage, by the early years of the twentieth century it had become one of the most powerful pressure groups in the country and, alongside the Gaelic Athletic Association, the principal agency of the cultural-nationalist revival in Ireland. During these heroic early days, squads of *timirí*, or organisers, had fanned out into the countryside by bicycle to bring the movement's message directly to the people; almost every town and village had its Irish-language study group; and the nationwide membership of the organisation surpassed six figures. By the time the Great War approached, however, Conradh's leadership had been infiltrated by members of the paramilitary Irish Republican Brotherhood (IRB), a development that famously led to the resignation in 1915 of Dr Hyde in protest against the politicisation of the movement he had helped to create. As political and military activism increasingly supplanted cultural nationalism in the Ireland of the post-Rising era, Conradh's initial dynamism had continued to wane, until by the 1930s it had become a mature – or, in the eyes of many, a geriatric – organisation, whose leadership was dominated by elderly notables from both the main political parties and whose crusading zeal had been replaced by a genteel atmosphere reminiscent of a Gaelicised Rotary Club. The two dozen or so associates of Ó Cuinneagáin and Ó Seachnasaigh who attended the formative meeting of the new branch were at least

101 For particulars of Becker's activities, see C. Molohan, *Germany and Ireland 1945–1955: Two Nations' Friendship* (Dublin: Irish Academic Press, 1999), pp. 78–9, 83–4.
102 Proinsias Ó Conluain observes that in the depiction of Proinsias Mac Aonghusa, 'Craobh na hAiséirghe was the fascist wing of the Gaelic League movement. I myself thought that was very unfair to those people in Craobh na hAiséirghe who didn't go along with what Ó Cuinneagáin was saying politically'. Proinsias Ó Conluain, author interview, 25 January 2006.

impatient with, and more often contemptuous of, what Conradh had become. The majority were in their early twenties, much younger than the typical member of the League; many of them were not native speakers, but recent converts to the Gaelic ideal, in the full flush of enthusiasm; and a high proportion, like Ó Cuinneagáin himself, were or had been employed in the public sector – as civil servants, teachers, librarians, lecturers or servicemen – and their advancement in their professions derived in part from their mastery of Irish. There seemed little, then, to attract them to so establishment-dominated a movement as Conradh na Gaeilge, nor was their presence likely to be welcomed by the existing conservative leadership.

Association with Conradh nonetheless served a variety of immediate and long-term objectives. Membership of so well-regarded an organisation provided an element of protection from the attentions of the security forces, a circumstance of which other vulnerable entities, notably the IRA, had already taken advantage.[103] The decentralised structure of Conradh, on the other hand – individual branches owed few obligations to the parent organisation beyond the payment of an annual affiliation fee – meant that Ó Cuinneagáin would be able to direct the affairs of his group virtually without interference from above. Conradh's extensive social programme, ranging from the organisation of *céilithe*, or traditional Irish dance sessions, to the holding of classes and the production of books and periodicals, offered the potential of a steady stream of revenue for the new branch that might be applied to purposes beyond the promotion of the language.

Ó Cuinneagáin's characteristically ambitious objective in joining Conradh, though, was not merely to obtain shelter for the new branch under its umbrella, but to reprise the tactic of the IRB a quarter of a century earlier and capture the entire organisation for his own purposes. Intimately familiar with the recent history of the Irish struggle for independence, he drew inspiration from the use that republican infiltrators had made of both Conradh and Sinn Féin prior to the War of Independence to awaken a spirit of popular resistance to British rule. As the most celebrated of these IRB 'moles', Pádraig Pearse, had stated in 1913, 'the vital work to be done in the new Ireland will be done not so much by the Gaelic League as by men and movements that have sprung from the Gaelic League'.[104] Ó Cuinneagáin's vision of Conradh's part in his political strategy was identical. Craobh na hAiséirghe's first order of business would be to revivify the parent

---

103 Some branches of Conradh – for example, Craobh na bhFiann and Craobh an Chéitin-nigh – had so high a proportion of republican members as to be virtual IRA adjuncts in the early 1940s.

104 P. H. Pearse, 'The Coming Revolution', *An Claidheamh Soluis*, 8 November 1913.

body and rejuvenate its membership. The second would be to gain control over it. The third, as in the revolutionary era, would be to send those who had received through Conradh a thorough ideological preparation into the political arena to carry out the task of national mobilisation. It was unimportant whether the vehicle for achieving this political goal would be an entirely new party or, as in 1917, an existing one. What mattered, rather, was that the elements responsible for the stultification and ossification of Irish society since 1922 should be driven out and the leadership of the national struggle assumed by a generation of young, uncompromising idealists, prepared to dedicate themselves totally to the establishment of a radical new order in cultural and political life. The intentionally ambiguous name Ó Cuinneagáin and Ó Seachnasaigh chose for the branch spoke to this sense of mission: a crusade to accomplish the resurrection not of the language alone, but the Irish nation and the Christian faith.[105] As Conradh na Gaeilge's historian and future president, Proinsias Mac Aonghusa, remarked of the new organisation, 'A kind of revolution was in the air from the beginning'.[106]

Other than their personal dedication, the pioneers of Craobh na hAiséirghe had few resources to bring to bear upon the task of rekindling the country's enthusiasm for the ideal of Irish-Ireland. Their first public meeting, in Foster Place at the corner of College Green in Dublin, involved no more elaborate preparation than the construction by a founder-member of a crude wooden structure upon which Ó Cuinneagáin and his associates could stand to harangue passers-by. He did, nevertheless, display the rudiments of administrative acumen: when Proinsias Mac an Bheatha handed Ó Cuinneagáin his hat while he held forth upon the makeshift platform, the latter immediately circulated it among the audience and raised the branch's first funds, a total of three shillings and threepence.[107]

The organisation's early days continued to test the commitment of the membership. Meetings were held in two fourth-floor rooms at a premises in Dawson Street which initially lacked electricity and consequently took place in virtual darkness, the speaker being furnished with the single oil lamp available to enable him to squint at his notes. Proinsias Mac an Bheatha recalled spending his first Christmas Eve after joining the branch stringing wires along the stairwell of the building,

---

105 Some rather more pedestrian titles were considered by the pair, including Craobh Lár na hÉireann and the less geographically misleading Craobh Lár na Cathrach. Mac an Bheatha, *Téid Focal Le Gaoith*, p. 99.
106 P. Mac Aonghusa, *Ar Son na Gaeilge: Conradh na Gaeilge 1893–1993* (Dublin: Conradh na Gaeilge, 1993), p. 277.
107 Mac an Bheatha, *Téid Focal le Gaoith*, pp. 95, 97.

and the New Year in painting benches in preparation for the Irish-language classes Craobh na hAiséirghe began to hold. Such dedication, however, was characteristic of the organisation as a whole, whose sternest critics acknowledged the tireless energy and zeal the membership of Craobh na hAiséirghe brought to their task. The extraordinarily high calibre of the volunteers who responded to Ó Cuinneagáin's call was the principal factor making for the success of the movement. At the outset, he stated in August 1941, 'our crowd was composed mainly of T.C.D., U.C.D. and U.C.G.' students, but it soon attracted representatives of 'almost every trade and profession'.[108] Those joining during the branch's first year included individuals who would later rise to positions of considerable eminence in Irish life, among them Séamus Ó hInnse [Henchy], the future Chief Justice of the Supreme Court; Pádraig Ó hUiginn, who concluded his distinguished civil service career as Secretary of the Department of the Taoiseach, the country's highest administrative post; Stiofán Ó Cearnaigh, his counterpart at the Department of Defence; the architect Aodhagán Brioscú; the author Cathal Ó Sandair; the journalists Ciarán Ó Nualláin, Annraoí Ó Liatháin and Prionsias Ó Conluain; and the film-maker and future head of the Irish Film Institute, Liam Ó Laoghaire.

That membership, moreover, was growing with remarkable speed. Within little more than a year the branch had enrolled between 1,200 and 1,500 adherents around the country. It was also engaged in a wide range of activities. In addition to its twice-weekly public meetings, which usually featured a mobile platform bedecked with tricolours and a banner bearing the branch's strikingly inappropriate motto, *Téid Focal Le Gaoith Acht Téid Buille le Cnáimh* ['Words fly away with the wind, but blows strike home to the bone'], Craobh na hAiséirghe organised countless Irish-language classes, study circles, dances, lectures, debates, theatrical performances, street meetings and demonstrations. A twenty-minute 'propaganda film' of the branch's work, directed by Ó Laoghaire and patterned upon Leni Riefenstahl's *Triumph of the Will*, became one of the most widely shown domestic productions of the Emergency years; the premiere was attended by Eoin O'Duffy.[109]

---

108 *Irish Times*, 16 August 1941. The students were from Trinity College, Dublin, University College, Dublin and University College, Galway.

109 *Irish Independent*, 21 January 1941; H. O'Brien, *The Real Ireland: The Evolution of Ireland in Documentary Film* (Manchester: Manchester University Press, 2004), p. 68; *Irish Times*, 11 November 1941. Regrettably, no copy of this film, *Aiséirghe*, appears to have survived; a brief description of its theme and composition can be found in L. Ó Laoghaire, *Invitation to the Film* (Tralee: The Kerryman, 1945), pp. 95–6.

  Craobh na hAiséirghe was particularly noted for its members' interest in the potential of motion pictures. One of its publications, *The Film*, was to have included contributions from the director Michael Powell (*The Life and Death of Colonel Blimp* and *The Red*

Many of the branch's initiatives were consciously designed to attract public attention, and often succeeded in doing so with well-crafted displays of wit or irreverence – qualities for which Irish public life in the 1940s was hardly noted. Craobh na hAiséirghe's 'Orange Céilí' of 1941, a celebration held on the anniversary of the defeat of the Catholic Irish at the Battle of the Boyne in 1690 that featured an address by Captain Denis Ireland of the Ulster Union Club[110] and concluded with a rendition by those present of the loyalist anthem 'The Sash My Father Wore', was a typical example of the spectacles in which the branch specialised, combining defiance of traditional orthodoxies with a well-marked political subtext – in this instance a tongue-in-cheek appeal to the non-Catholic population of the island. The function, which was broadcast nationally by Raidió Éireann, the state radio service, gained Craobh na hAiséirghe valuable publicity. Although not all such events were equally successful – Ó Cuinneagáin's idea for a mock funeral in which an effigy representing the Irish language, pierced by symbolic spears representing foreign newspapers, films and radio transmissions, would be conducted in solemn procession to Glasnevin cemetery, failed to get off the ground – Craobh na hAiséirghe quickly gained a reputation as the most enthusiastic, innovative and effective cultural-nationalist movement in the country.

The branch provided fertile ground for authoritarianism, both in its internal organisation and, increasingly, its ideology. Composed almost exclusively of the young and impatient – Gearóid Ó Cuinneagain, who had recently celebrated his thirtieth birthday, was to be found well to the geriatric end of the society's age-distribution – the membership of Craobh na hAiséirghe had little interest in or tolerance for bureau-cratic procedure of any kind, or even for internal debate. When Ó Cuinneagáin moved to establish the principle of leadership throughout the organisation, therefore, he found himself pushing at an open door. At the movement's second meeting in the offices of Ó Cuinneagáin & Cooke, he took the chair and was duly elected President [*Uachtarán*], Ó Seachnasaigh filling the post of Secretary. Within a few weeks, Ó Cuinneagáin substituted for his original title that of *Ceannaire*, a word literally meaning 'Leader' that, in its capitalised form, carried unmistakable overtones in the context of the early 1940s.[111] At Craobh

---

Shoes), as well as Ernest Blythe, Liam Gogán, Ó Laoghaire, Fr S. J. Devane and Patricia Hutchins. The organisation was dissolved before work could be completed. *Irish Times*, 13 March 1942.
110 Founded in March 1941, the Ulster Union Club was an association of Northern Protes-tants who supported the abolition of the Border and the creation of a thirty-two-county independent Irish state.
111 The term 'taoiseach', literally 'chieftain', was the more common title of the head of an

na hAiséirghe's first annual meeting, Ó Cuinneagáin moved to copper-fasten his authority, demanding and receiving from the member-ship absolute powers of direction over the branch. Proinsias Mac an Bheatha, between whom and the *Ceannaire* serious differences were later to emerge, makes clear that in this respect at least, Ó Cuinneagáin was acting in accordance with the expectations of most members.

> People perhaps may consider it strange that we were willing to grant [Ó Cuinneagáin] the power he called for at the first annual meeting ... One needs to remember that our entire focus in Craobh na hAiséirí was on saving the Irish language. We were ready to do anything at all that appeared reasonable for the furtherance of our objective. We were prepared on that account to yield up absolute powers of control to the man in command – the man on whom the responsibility and duty to push the work forward weighed most heavily – so long as it seemed to us he was guiding us along the path towards the Revival.[112]

If Ó Cuinneagáin bore a disproportionate burden of responsibility, to him also belongs much of the credit for the branch's success. Without his inspiration and drive, Craobh na hAiséirghe could never have attained the prominence it did by the end of 1941. Mac an Bheatha, although no friend of Ó Cuinneagáin's in later years, never lost his admiration for the *Ceannaire*'s leadership qualities. 'Ó Cuinneagáin reawakened our fervour, gave us a plan of action and drove our work forward. He himself was full of life. He was courageous, fearless, enterprising, imaginative'.[113] Mac an Bheatha did note that he made no close friends, had little understanding of how to deal with people and often gave unnecessary offence. Notwithstanding these shortcomings, within little more than a year of its establishment Ó Cuinneagáin had built Craobh na hAiséirghe up to the point where it had become not so much a component of Conradh na Gaeilge as its rival. The *Ceannaire* himself made no secret of the fact, announcing at its first annual meeting in October 1941 that 'Craobh na hAiséirghe had ceased to be a branch and had become a movement'.[114] Like the parent organisation, Craobh na hAiséirghe boasted its own network of sub-branches in Blanchards-town, Clontarf, Dalkey, Glasnevin, Inchicore, Rathfarnham, Rathmines and Terenure in the greater Dublin area; and others in Cork city and county, Dundalk, Waterford town and Sligo. Unlike other components of Conradh, however, these were not quasi-autonomous bodies, but carried out their tasks in strict compliance with the directives of the *Ceannaire*. With the exception of two 'auditors', Mac an Bheatha and

organisation; in its capitalised form, it refers to the prime minister of the Irish state.
112 Mac an Bheatha, *Téid Focal le Gaoith*, p. 110.
113 *Ibid.*
114 *Irish Independent*, 4 October 1941.

Micheál Ó Fearghail, all officers and members were personally responsible to Ó Cuinneagáin and at his discretion might be dismissed from their posts or expelled from the movement itself. Under the branch's constitution adopted at the first annual meeting, even the members of the elected *Comhairle*, or executive committee, served at his pleasure. Craobh na hAiséirghe thus constituted a highly responsive instrument for the promotion of the *Ceannaire*'s political agenda.

It was not, however, the only such instrument. In the spring of 1940 a new political movement called Córas na Poblachta ['The Republican System'] emerged, whose leading lights were prominent members or supporters of the Irish Republican Army. The most notable of these were Roger McCorley, former commanding officer of the IRA's Third Northern Division; Roger McHugh, a lecturer in English at University College, Dublin; Simon Donnelly, head of the National Association of Old (i.e. pre-Civil War) IRA; and Michael O'Mullane, formerly an associate of Éamon de Valera. Although Donnelly had publicly declared, 'We want to see the enemy that saddled our people for 700 years crushed in this war', Córas na Poblachta's principal objective, as explained in a manifesto originally drafted in March 1940, was to organise a truce between the IRA and the de Valera government so as to form a united republican front and 'avail of the opportunity which the international situation promises for the establishment of the Irish Republic'.[115] Efforts to arrange such an alliance, in which O'Mullane tried unsuccessfully to obtain the assistance of the American minister, David Gray, were temporarily shelved at the beginning of September when the government executed two IRA members, Patrick McGrath and Thomas Harte, for the shooting dead of police officers.[116] Thereafter Córas na Poblachta relaunched itself as a political party in opposition to Fianna Fáil, aiming in the first instance at the capture of power in the twenty-six counties. In the course of this redefinition of priorities the movement acquired an esoteric set of objectives, of which the 'first step' was to be 'the destruction of the Masonic Order in Ireland'. The party also called for the reversal of 'the cultural conquest of our country by England' and announced that it did not 'exclude the employment of compulsion' towards that end.[117]

A movement of this kind could not long escape the attention of the pro-Axis underground and its numerous fellow-travellers. By the

115 *New York Times*, 12 February 1940; undated Córas na Poblachta pamphlet, G2/X/0251, DDMA.
116 O'Mullane to Gray, 23 August 1940, Department of State records RG 84: Ireland: Dublin Legation: Security Segregated Records, 1936–49, Entry 2763, 350/61/29/07, Box 2, 800–711.1–824.2, NARA.
117 Undated Córas na Poblachta pamphlet, G2/X/0251, DDMA.

end of 1940, when Córas na Poblachta began to hold its first public meetings, its members included such luminaries of the Irish ultra-right as Maurice O'Connor, Alec McCabe and Reginald Eager from the Irish Friends of Germany, each of whom had recently been released from internment; George Griffin, the brothers Patrick and John Moylett, and Joseph Andrews of the minute pro-Nazi People's National Party; Dermot Brennan of Saoirse Gaedheal; and Hugh O'Neill and Fr Alexander Carey of the prewar Córas Gaedhealach. James O'Donovan, the IRA's principal liaison with the *Abwehr*, was also associated with the movement. With the influx of these elements, Córas na Poblachta assumed a more overtly pro-German and anti-Semitic character. The incorrigible O'Connor, at a meeting of the party in November 1940, announced his undiminished faith in an Axis victory and 'advocated the handing over to Germany of Foynes Airport after the war had been won'.[118] Another Córas representative, according to a police report, invited Dr C. H. Petersen, press attaché at the German Legation, to address the party on the subject of 'National Socialism' and informed him that 'the policy of his organisation was like the German policy'.[119] Members of Córas were also believed by the Gardaí to have been behind the daubing of anti-Semitic slogans on the walls of Trinity College, Dublin, in August 1941, seemingly in response to a visit to Ireland by the British politician Leslie Hore-Belisha, a Jew.[120] A police record of proceedings at the weekly meeting of the organisation on 17 June 1941 gives the flavour of a typical Córas function:

> Joseph Andrews spoke on the Jewish-Masonic grip on this country, and referred to the international control which was exercised by Jews ... He referred to the influence which was exercised by Deputy Briscoe, and to the small wages paid by Jews in this country.
>
> Mr Quinn supported Andrews, and said that all aliens should be driven out of this country.
>
> Mr [Séamus] Dobbyn stated that Córas na Poblachta had adopted in their policy the remedy suggested by Andrews [recte: Quinn].
>
> The Chairman [Hugh O'Neill] did not agree with the remarks of Andrews, and maintained that Christians in this country were worse than Jews.[121]

118 Report by Wymes, 7 December 1940, *ibid.*
119 Petersen declined to appear personally, but provided Córas na Poblachta with the text of a lecture which was read by Joseph Andrews at a meeting of the party on 6 May 1941. Extract from Garda Síochána Dublin Metropolitan District report for week ending 7 April 1941; report by Wymes, 13 May 1941, *ibid.*
120 Memorandum by Inspector Patrick Breen, Special Branch, 18 August 1941; Chief Superintendent Carroll to Bryan, 19 August 1941, *ibid.*
121 Report by Wymes, 25 June 1941, *ibid.*

It would be incorrect to view Córas na Poblachta as simply the Irish Friends of Germany on a larger scale. Despite the considerable number of ultra-right extremists who found a congenial home within the party organisation, many prominent republicans – the 1916 veterans Dr Kathleen Lynn and Helena Moloney, the future Clann na Poblachta TD Con Lehane, and James Connolly's daughter Nora Connolly O'Brien – were also drawn to the movement.[122] Reflecting divisions within the IRA itself, a minority of Córas' leaders sympathised with Communism rather than fascism. Though it was to remain throughout its history an ideologically incoherent body, Córas na Poblachta was nonetheless substantial enough, and sufficiently well-associated with the pro-Axis cause, to be of interest to Ó Cuinneagáin.

It is unclear precisely when, and by what means, he became involved with the party. One possibility is that he was introduced to it by his former IFG/CN colleague, Maurice O'Connor. Another is that an approach was made by one or other of Córas' leaders, for whom Craobh na hAiséirge would have appeared as a natural component of their mooted republican popular front. What can be stated with certainty is that by May 1941, when he is first recorded as having spoken on Córas' behalf, Ó Cuinneagáin had unambiguously identified himself with the movement. At a 'monster meeting' in Dublin, following a pro-German speech by Hugh O'Neill, Ó Cuinneagáin ascended the platform and 'called on the young men to flock into Córas na Poblachta'.[123] While he was to give several other such addresses in the following months, most of his work on behalf of Córas was carried out after he assumed the leadership of its youth wing, Aicéin ['Action'].[124] For Ó Cuinneagáin, this association carried several benefits. The membership of Aicéin constituted a fresh reservoir of potential recruits for his own organisation; it was probably not a coincidence that the news-sheet of Córas na Poblachta's Dublin party organisation, launched in July 1941, bore the title *Aiséirighe*.[125] Involvement with the party also enabled

122 In the cases of Moloney and Lynn, the relative attractions of republicanism and pro-Germanism as factors underlying their association with Córas remains an open question. The former was one of the many republican activists involved in sheltering the fugitive *Abwehr* agent Hermann Goertz in 1940; the latter took a leading role after the war in the Save the German Children Society, a body in which Dublin pro-Nazis were especially prominent.

123 Report by Wymes, 26 May 1941, G2/X/0251, DDMA.

124 Though its adherents claimed it to have this meaning, the accepted Irish word for 'action' is 'gníomhaíocht'. During a period when the pronunciation, spelling and even existence of Irish terms was fluid and uncodified (an official Irish dictionary, compiled under the auspices of the Government of Ireland, was not completed until 1977) such variations were by no means uncommon.

125 The word 'Aiséirghe' has several variants of spelling, among them the archaic 'aiséirighe' and the more modern 'aiséirí'.

Ó Cuinneagáin to make connections to the IRA and its affiliates, a relationship that might prove advantageous in the future, without exposing him to political or personal risk. Lastly, an alliance offered the possibility of influencing Córas' policy in directions favoured by the *Ceannaire*. A bilingual party circular of May 1941, almost certainly drafted by Ó Cuinneagáin, drew its readers' attention to 'the constitutional system the Saxons gave us, a system that confers power and wealth on a small group of people and denies the bare necessities of subsistence to the majority'.

Nonetheless, Ó Cuinneagáin's dalliance with Córas na Poblachta, and with another anti-Semitic and pro-Axis organisation, the Young Ireland Association,[126] was never intended to be more than an adjunct to the larger task of making Craobh na hAiséirghe into an organisation carrying real influence. The latter continued to be the principal vehicle through which he pursued his ideological agenda. With the passage of time, moreover, it was Craobh na hAiséirghe rather than Córas na Poblachta that took the lead in drawing up policies for a post-democratic Irish state. By the summer of 1941 Ó Cuinneagáin had substituted for the branch's original cultural goals the explicitly political objective of working for 'the establishment of a State which, in the Christian perfection of its social and economic systems, will be a model for the whole world'. The shift in emphasis was accompanied by a public call for workers to join a Craobh na hAiséirghe 'Propaganda Squad', and by the issuance of a series of 'Current Pamphlets' on social and economic questions.[127] In these, Craobh na hAiséirghe authors contended that the objective of language revival could not be achieved by educational means alone. The cause of Irish and the condition of the Irish nation were indivisible. Unless a spirit of unyielding dedication to the completion of the national mission could be inculcated among the people, it was unrealistic to hope for the restoration of the language, or of any other aspect of Irish culture. But it was equally naive to suppose that the bulk of ordinary men and women would voluntarily make the sacrifices required by such an ideal. The task of a genuinely national organisation, therefore, was to create the political and economic conditions under which patriotism would be neither optional nor negotiable.

Writers for Craobh na hAiséirghe rang the changes on the cultural

---

126 The YIA was founded in December 1941 as the 'Anti-British Propaganda Committee' by Séamus G. ('the Cripple') Ó Ceallaigh, an IRA activist who also held a prominent position in Craobh na hAiséirghe. Its supporters included J. J. Walsh, Maud Gonne and Brendan Behan. For further particulars, see R. M. Douglas, 'The Pro-Axis Underground in Ireland, 1939–1942', *Historical Journal* 49:4 (December 2006): 1176–7.
127 *Irish Independent*, 28 January 1941.

and spiritual decadence of contemporary Irish society: 'We are not a nation', the pro-Axis republican activist Séamus G. Ó Ceallaigh declared, 'no matter how much we try to humbug ourselves that we are'.[128] According to Pádraig Ó Fiannghusa, the country was 'full of foulness and cowardice'.[129] Riobárd Breathnach accused his compatriots of 'toleration gone mad, the toleration of national degeneration'.[130] Nor could any improvement be expected from an Anglophone generation, for 'the English language corrupts the mind to the extent of feeding it on foreign ideas'.[131]

Craobh na hAiséirghe's mission, therefore – and that of Conradh na Gaeilge also – should be to constitute a revolutionary vanguard to accomplish the task of national regeneration. They were 'willing to make a sacrifice of our lives in the nation's interest as no other race has ever done, [not] even the people of Sparta. Conradh na Gaeilge promises the people neither butter nor guns nor houses, but rather to instill in them a manly patriotic spirit'.[132] Spokesmen for Craobh na hAiséirghe laid stress upon the degree of commitment that would be required of each volunteer:

> [Y]ou must be prepared to be personally active, to give service and to make sacrifices. You are to be prepared to work day and night for the restoration of the Gaelic tongue, of the Gaelic culture, of complete political and economic as well as cultural independence ... Constant labour, self-sacrifice, discipline, great courage and a readiness to face death if necessary are the essentials for our young 1942 manhood, so that Ireland may again shine forth as the Christian beacon light in a pagan world.[133]

Evidence suggests that early as the beginning of 1942, Ó Cuinneagáin had resolved to use Craobh na hAiséirghe as a launching-pad for a new political movement. He may have been encouraged to take this step by Córas na Poblachta's decision in February to terminate the independent existence of Aicéin, which would henceforth become nothing more than an 'Organising Committee' of its parent.[134] Whether or not this action was intended to bring Ó Cuinneagáin to heel, it served

128 P. Ó Fiannghusa & S. G. Ó Ceallaigh, *Aiséirghe 1842, nó Young Ireland Spoke Out* (Dublin: Craobh na hAiséirghe, 1942), p. 14.
129 *Ibid.*, p. 5.
130 R. Breathnach, *An Dá Shruth–The Two Currents* (Cork: Glún na h-Aiséirghe, 1943), p. 18.
131 S. Ó Ceallaigh in *Aiséirghe 1842*, p. 14.
132 G. Ó Cuinneagáin, 'Oileán na Sagart agus na Saighdeoirí', *An tIolar/The Standard*, 11 July 1941.
133 Mathúin Ó Gráda & S. Ó Ceallaigh, *Náire Náisiúnta, nó Seán Treacy's Shame* (Dublin: Craobh na hAiséirghe, 1942), pp. 10–11.
134 Aicéin press-release, February 1942, 93/1/152, no. 139, Office of the Controller of Censorship files, NAI.

to confirm that his political objectives could only be accomplished by means of an organisation under his own direct control. It was probably not coincidental, then, that within a couple of weeks of the termination of Aicéin an associate offered the *Ceannaire* his congratulations on learning of 'your intention to extend your organisation … The news is of course going to be very distasteful to that bunch of futile old women who dominate the moribund [Gaelic] League, but that is all to the good'.[135] After Ó Cuinneagáin's announcement in early 1942 of a 'Spring Offensive' of public campaigning for the exemplary Christian state, Craobh na hAiséirghe dropped all further pretence of confining its ambitions to the cultural sphere. 'For what purpose are the members of Craobh na hAiséirghe in such a fever of activity?' the *Ceannaire* rhetorically asked in a Galway address:

> To gain the upper hand over Conradh na Gaeilge? … We are sweating to gain the upper hand indeed, and soon – but the upper hand over all of Ireland! … For the people who are not swayed by our words will be tamed and silenced by our blows …
>
> Adolf Hitler said that he aimed to arrange the history of Europe for 1,000 years. But [for] we Irish, it is fated for us to co-operate with arranging the affairs of the world for all eternity![136]

The politicisation of Craobh na hAiséirghe both contributed to and was accelerated by Ó Cuinneagáin's lack of success in his effort to secure the leadership of the organisation of which it was nominally a part. Both the *Ceannaire* and Proinsias Mac an Bheatha had represented the branch at the *Ard-Fheis* [Annual Convention] of Conradh in 1940. Although neither had thought it necessary to conceal, in Mac an Bheatha's words, how 'fed up to the back teeth [we were] with the ineffectuality of Conradh na Gaeilge',[137] the credibility Craobh na hAiséirghe had already earned, combined with some initial indulgence on the part of Conradh's leadership for the natural impetuosity of youth, led to Ó Cuinneagáin's election as a member of the organisation's national executive, the Coiste Gnótha, for 1941. Much of this initial goodwill dissipated when Ó Cuinneagáin became embroiled in a prolonged wrangle with the other members of the Coiste Gnótha over publicity. Shortly after joining the executive, Ó Cuinneagáin secured from the anti-Semitic and pro-Axis industrialist J. J. Walsh[138] a personal guarantee of supplies of paper for a proposed Conradh publication commemorating the twenty-fifth anniversary of the Easter

135 É. Ó Murchadha, Waterford, to Ó Cuinneagáin, 24 February 1942, G2/ 2988, DDMA.
136 Quoted in *Aiséirí*, November 1969.
137 Mac an Bheatha, *Téid Focal le Gaoith*, p. 110.
138 See p. 000 below.

Rising. In light of the acute nationwide shortage of newsprint, Ó Cuinneagáin felt justified in insisting that Ciarán Ó Nualláin of Craobh na hAiséirghe be appointed editor of the commemorative issue. The Coiste Gnótha, suspecting that the reason behind this demand was to have a publication containing the agenda of Craobh na hAiséirghe appear with Conradh's seeming endorsement, in turn specifed that a three-person editorial board be formed, with Ó Nualláin joined by two of the Coiste's own nominees.[139] Ó Cuinneagáin rejected this condition, with the result that the paper supplies originally promised to Conradh wound up being diverted to Craobh na hAiséirghe's own publications.

Relations deteriorated rapidly from that point onward. Ó Cuinneagáin attempted to appeal to the branches of Conradh na Gaeilge over the heads of his colleagues by issuing a circular letter that referred, according to Proinsias Mac Aonghusa, to the Coiste Gnótha in 'insulting [and] impolite' terms.[140] The Coiste responded in kind. Ó Cuinneagáin also suffered repeated setbacks in his attempts to pack the leadership of Conradh with members of his own branch. Of Craobh na hAiséirghe's panel of six candidates for the Coiste Gnótha in 1941, only Ó Cuinneagáin and Mac an Bheatha were elected. The *Ceannaire's* personal bid for the presidency of the organisation likewise was to prove premature. Despite the energetic lobbying of Mac an Bheatha and of Ciarán Ó Nualláin, who warned ominously in a newspaper article that Ó Cuinneagáin's election as its leader represented 'the last chance Conradh na Gaeilge will get to reform itself',[141] the *Ceannaire* came under strong pressure from republican members to withdraw his candidacy so that Seán Ó Tuama, a mathematics lecturer interned in the Curragh for suspected IRA activities, could be elected instead.[142] Although he refused to do so, Ó Cuinneagáin received just 13 votes of a total of 113 in the first round of balloting, and was eliminated from the contest. (He did, however, mend bridges with the republicans by swinging his support to Ó Tuama in the subsequent round, thereby securing the latter's election.) A second presidential campaign the following year proved still less fruitful, yielding the *Ceannaire* only ten votes. The effect of these setbacks appears to have been to convince Ó Cuinneagáin that, as had been the case with IFG/CN, his association with Conradh had outlived its usefulness. From that

139 Mac an Bheatha, *Téid Focal le Gaoith*, p. 112.
140 Mac Aonghusa, *Ar Son na Gaeilge*, p. 283.
141 C. Ó Nualláin, 'Togachán an Chonnartha: Cé Bhéas 'na Uachtarán?' *An tIolar/The Standard*, 17 October 1941.
142 Copy of an intercepted letter from 'Seán' [Mac Bride] to Roger McHugh, 28 October 1941, G2/X/0251, DDMA.

point onward, Ó Cuinneagáin commenced a virtual boycott of the parent organisation, prohibiting Craobh na hAiséirghe delegates from participating in the Coiste Gnótha and withholding the annual fee due from the branch. Seosamh Ó Duibhginn, a sympathiser who would later become one of Ó Cuinneagáin's salaried officials, considered that he was foolish to have done so and that if he had bided his time 'Gearóid Ó Cuinneagáin would certainly have been elected President of Conradh'.[143] But by mid-1942 it had become apparent that an Axis victory in the war could not be expected at least in the short term. As a young man in a hurry, Ó Cuinneagáin was unwilling to wait upon events either domestically or internationally. Rather than waste further time and effort upon the 'old men, or even the middle-aged men' who dominated both Conradh and the chambers of government alike, he resolved to appeal over their heads directly to the Irish people.

The division between the 'political' and 'cultural' factions of the movement was brought into the open during the Whit weekend of 1942. A commemorative convention to mark the centenary of the founding of the *Nation* newspaper by Young Ireland was organised at Domhnach Phádraig [Donaghpatrick] in the Meath Gaeltacht. Ó Cuinneagáin was invited to give the keynote address, in recognition both of the work that he had done on behalf of the Irish-language movement and the recent publication by Craobh na hAiséirghe of a bilingual pamphlet entitled *Aiséirghe 1842, or Young Ireland Spoke Out*. Before a crowded hall of youthful activists 'eager to hear the gospel of Craobh na hAiséirghe', the *Ceannaire* for the first time laid out explicitly the ideas he had been germinating since 1940. In a speech lasting over two hours, he accused the Irish people of laziness, softness, snobbishness, avarice and cowardice: '[O]f the white peoples of the universe the Irish are very much the most backward in many respects'. These failings Ó Cuinneagáin attributed to his compatriots' affinity for idle talk rather than action; a lack of leadership on the part of the 'word-spinners and old men' who controlled Irish society; and, above all, the enervating influence of a party-political system that set groups of Irish citizens at odds with each other. The picture he painted, though, was not uniformly negative. The forces unleashed by the Second World War had compelled every Western country, Ireland included, to proceed to a comprehensive mobilisation of the nation's resources. Facing the danger of invasion, the government had assumed extensive powers of control; demonstrated its unwillingness to be frustrated by parliamentary obstructionism; and built up a mass army to protect the state against external and internal enemies. In so doing, it had not only

143 S. Ó Duibhginn, *Ag Scaoileadh Sceoil* (Dublin: An Clóchomhar, 1962), p. 58.

demonstrated what could be accomplished even by so unsatisfactory a system as the twenty-six-county democratic regime, but psychologically prepared the Irish people to accept national discipline and rule by decree. What the de Valera government had done ad hoc as an emergency measure, Ó Cuinneagáin argued, needed to be systematised and made the basis of the future Irish state. He accordingly called for the creation of a totalitarian government under a single all-powerful leader, and announced the formation of a new political movement named Ailtirí na hAiséirghe ['Architects of the Resurrection'] alongside the existing Craobh na hAiséirghe to work for its establishment. The relationship between the two, he proposed, should be analogous to that prevailing between Sinn Féin and Conradh na Gaeilge in the period immediately before the War of Independence. It was, however, vital to act quickly, for the opportunity the Emergency offered Ireland to achieve her manifest destiny would soon disappear.

> If we had had 100,000 men in readiness at the time of the Abyssinian, Austrian, or Sudeten crises; the King of England's Abdication crisis [or] the day of Dunkirk; 100,000 trained men and a national leader at any of those moments, we would today be free of the disgrace of English subjection. How many chances are required by Irishmen today before they will seize one of them?
>
> ... Let us place our trust in God and in our own destiny, and whether America or Germany should gain the upper hand in the war will be of no concern to us.[144]

Parting of the ways

According to Prionsias Mac an Bheatha, Ó Cuinneagáin's Domhnach Phádraig address came as a thunderbolt to those members of the organisation who wished to maintain its focus upon the language and cultural questions exclusively. This is clearly not the case. Apart from the explicitly political rhetoric which had marked Craobh na hAiséirghe's public statements throughout the previous year, its change in orientation had already given rise to significant internal dissension. In March 1942, for example, Pádraig Ó Casáide, a serving soldier, resigned as a member of the Craobh na hAiséirghe Comhairle to protest against the movement's new approach: 'I am not satisfied', he told the *Ceannaire*, 'with the direction in which Aiséirghe is going ... Lately, as you know, the Branch has been engaged in a great deal

144 Transcript of speech by Ó Cuinneagáin, 'Cinneamháin Nua-Aoiseach Éireann', 1 June 1942, 93/1/171, no. 158, Office of the Controller of Censorship files, NAI. The passage quoted here was suppressed by the censor.

more than the promotion of Irish culture'.[145] Ó Cuinneagáin, in his reply, declared that he had never attempted to conceal the organisation's political objectives, and reminded Ó Casáide of what Pearse had famously said on the subject of Conradh na Gaeilge and philology.[146] 'If you wish to work for the language alone', he advised, 'I agree that you ought to stand down'.[147]

The public announcement that Craobh na hAiséirghe was henceforth to sponsor a political movement aiming at a totalitarian regime nonetheless created an acute dilemma for those members who derived their livelihood from the very state for whose overthrow Ó Cuinneagáin was now openly agitating. The *Ceannaire* himself was a former government official and a disproportionate number of his supporters drew their salaries from the same source, as civil servants, teachers or members of the armed forces. As Proinsias Mac Aonghusa noted, 'it did not appear that any important person held any standing in the Craobh who was not working for the State'.[148] Even before then, Craobh na hAiséirghe's increasing outspokenness on matters of public controversy had caused embarrassment to some of its members. Pádraig Ó hUiginn, at that time a junior official in the Department of the Taoiseach, recalls: 'I was actually interviewed by Mr de Valera, who asked me bluntly, "Is this a political organisation?" I assured him that it wasn't'.[149] Proinsias Mac an Bheatha was sufficiently concerned as to 'make clear to Ó Cuinneagáin where I stood with regard to the new movement'.[150] He particularly impressed upon the *Ceannaire* that photographs taken of him for the Craobh na hAiséirghe yearbook – to be entitled *Aiséirghe 1942* – should not be used to suggest that he was in any way connected with Ailtirí na hAiséirghe.

Events were to show that Mac an Bheatha's apprehensions were by no means misplaced. Thanks to the good offices of J. J. Walsh, *Aiséirghe 1942* was published in September. To the horror of the branch's cultural nationalists it contained no mention of Craobh na hAiséirghe's activities, but was rather an 18,000-word manifesto for the new party, expressed in the most uncompromising terms. Ó Cuinneagáin's Domhnach Phádraig speech was reproduced almost

---

145 P. Ó Casaide to Ó Cuinneagáin, 25 March 1942, 1/1/12, GÓCP.

146 '[A]nyone who has been working for the language merely ... has never had the true Gaelic League spirit at all ... it was not philology, not folklore, not literature, we went into the Gaelic League to serve, but: Ireland a Nation'. P. H. Pearse, 'The Psychology of a Volunteer', in *Political Writings and Speeches* (Dublin: Phoenix, 1924), p. 107.

147 Ó Cuinneagáin to Ó Casaide, 31 March 1942, 1/1/12, GÓCP.

148 Mac Aonghusa, *Ar Son na Gaeilge*, p. 282.

149 Pádraig Ó hUiginn, author interview, 27 July 1999.

150 Mac an Bheatha, *Téid Focal le Gaoith*, p. 125.

in full, accompanied by articles containing blueprints for the revolutionary reconstruction of Irish political, economic and intellectual
life. Still more disturbing, from Mac an Bheatha's point of view,
was the reproduction on the pamphlet's cover of a photograph of
Ó Cuinneagáin and himself flanking an Aiséirghe banner. This and
other images of the Craobh na hAiséirghe hierarchy within the pages
of *Aiséirghe 1942*, Mac an Bheatha believed, had been included for
the express purpose of conveying the misleading impression that the
officers of the branch identified themselves with the political agenda
contained therein.

A confrontation between the *Ceannaire* and many of his subordinates thus began to loom as Craobh na hAiséirghe's annual meeting
approached in November. Internal tensions were exacerbated by the
fact that it proved impossible in practice to preserve even a nominal
distinction between the cultural and political wings of the movement.
At the beginning of September, Craobh na hAiséirghe abandoned its
cramped headquarters in Dawson Street for more spacious premises
nearby, at 27 South Frederick Street. Although in theory Ailtirí na
hAiséirghe was to occupy parts of the new building as Craobh na
hAiséirghe's tenant, Ó Cuinneagáin's dual róle as leader of both
organisations meant that disputes over the allocation of rooms and
resources were invariably settled in favour of the former.

In the late autumn of 1942, consequently, Craobh na hAiséirghe
slowly drew apart into two camps. A significant proportion of its
members had no desire to be caught up in party politics, a stance
that had been deepened rather than diminished by their involvement in the movement. Others concurred with Ó Cuinneagáin that
grass-roots activism of the kind Craobh na hAiséirghe had practised
for the previous two years in itself could never save the language,
but disagreed with the authoritarian policies Ailtirí na hAiséirghe
proposed to adopt. Others again approved of Ailtirí na hAiséirghe's
outline programme, but feared victimisation by employers or the state
if they joined the new party. In the circumstances, it was unsurprising
that a number of leading members should have vacillated between
the alternatives facing them. Annraoí Ó Liatháin, for example, initially
became a member of the Ailtirí, but had second thoughts as he began
to contemplate, seemingly for the first time, what an Ireland under the
absolute control of the *Ceannaire* might actually be like:

> You are the kind of person who cannot tolerate any restraint whatever.
> You would not be willing to accept the authority of anyone; you could
> not work under the direction of anyone; you would not agree to give up
> your personal freedom under any circumstances ... From what I have

seen, a year spent working under you is a lot worse than the novice year in a monastic order ...

I heard you say one night at the Executive that we ought to accept your direction as we would a direction from God ... The greatest fear I have about you, [an individual] possessing neither reliability nor prudence nor sense, if he were leader of the country, is that your power would go to your head, you would believe you had a divine right to interfere in every single aspect of the lives of the people, and impose your will upon them ...

[A]s bad as it is I respect my country, and greatly respect the people of my country – my own people – because I understand them and I understand how it is that they are as wretched as they are, and I will never do them harm; and that is what I would do, I firmly believe, if I were to help you any more.[151]

For most dissentients, however, the formation of Ailtirí na hAiséirghe did not lead to any such anguished soul-searching: 'It wasn't a situation', Proinsias Ó Conluain recalls, 'where one side walked out and left the other. It was a gradual thing – people just became disillusioned with Ó Cuinneagáin and decided they were not going with him. There certainly wasn't any concerted action with people saying "We're not having this," though they may have arrived at that conclusion on an individual basis'.[152] Pádraig Ó hUiginn likewise remembers the bifurcation of the movement as having occurred by tacit consent of the membership rather than as a result of any open breach. With the formation of Ailtirí na hAiséirghe, Ó Cuinneagáin 'tried to make himself this Hitlerite, Messianic figure'.[153] Those like Ó Conluain or Ciarán Ó Nualláin who could not envisage him in such a role, or were unwilling to stake their professional future on his achieving it, gave notice that they would not be following him into any new party.

The separation of the two wings of Craobh na hAiséirghe was formalised at its annual meeting on 6 November 1942. Though his priorities were now invested in Ailtirí na hAiséirghe, Ó Cuinneagáin still hoped to maintain some degree of control over the 'cultural' wing of the movement. He therefore proposed at the meeting that an entirely

151 In a letter to *Indiú*, Ó Liatháin declared that he had never taken out membership of Ailtirí na hAiséirghe, and that he had sent a letter to Ó Cuinneagáin setting out his disagreement with the party's objectives before its first public meeting. Ó Cuinneagáin replied that Ó Liatháin was registered as a member; that Ailtirí na hAiséirghe's inaugural meeting had been on 22 June 1942 and its first public event the following 24 September; and that Ó Liatháin's letter of resignation – which the *Ceannaire* acknowledged receiving – was dated 1 October of that year. *Indiú*, 16 March 1951; Ó Cuinneagáin to the Editor, *Indiú*, 16 March 1951. Ó Liatháin's letter is in 1/1/6, GÓCP.
152 Proinsias Ó Conluain, author interview, 25 January 2006.
153 Pádraig Ó hUiginn, author interview, 27 July 1999.

new language organisation, independent both of Ailtirí na hAiséirghe and of Conradh na Gaeilge, be created with his nominee Peadar Ó Ceallaigh, a teacher from the Meath Gaeltacht, at its head. While all agreed that the shackles of Conradh should be cast off – a decision facilitated by that body's vote the previous month to withdraw recognistion from Craobh na hAiséirghe and other branches that had not paid their affiliation fee[154] – there was little enthusiasm for electing Ó Cuinneagáin's chosen candidate in his stead. To do so would only have perpetuated the fundamental problem of confusion between the two movements that had made separation necessary in the first place. Accordingly, the meeting elected Mac an Bheatha as leader of an independent organisation to continue the work originally set in train by Craobh na hAiséirghe.[155] The following month the 'culturalists' adopted the new name of Glún na Buaidhe ['Generation of Victory'] and agreed to assume Craobh na hAiséirghe's outstanding debts, leaving Ó Cuinneagáin and Ailtirí na hAiséirghe free of financial encumbrances.

The division of the movement was made easier by Ó Cuinneagáin and Mac an Bheatha's tacit agreement that it should take place as amicably as possible. Each had compelling reasons for doing so. If Glún na Buaidhe was to maintain the momentum built up by its parent, a public squabble over the finances of Craobh na hAiséirghe needed to be avoided at all costs. Ó Cuinneagáin, too, had no desire to bring about the destruction of the sociey he had laboured to build during the previous two years. It was clearly in his interest that it should continue to thrive, inasmuch as the more people were drawn into the Gaelic-revival movement, the larger the pool of potential Ailtirí na hAiséirghe voters and supporters would be. In his final address as head of Craobh na hAiséirghe, Ó Cuinneagáin pledged his continued co-operation with its objectives and asked members to assist Mac an Bheatha in the immense tasks that lay before Glún na Buaidhe in the future. For his part, Mac an Bheatha in a subsequent interview – though once again disclaiming responsibility for any of the opinions expressed in Aiséirghe 1942 – emphasised that his new organisation harboured no enmity towards anyone, and would willingly assist any work tending to benefit the language.[156]

For the second time in two years, Ó Cuinneagáin had split a movement he had helped to create. Neither IFG/CN nor Craobh na hAiséirghe had proven capable of acting as a springboard to enable the

154　*Irish Times*, 5 October 1942.
155　Mac an Bheatha, *Téid Focal le Gaoith*, pp. 133–6.
156　*Comhar*, December 1942.

Ceannaire to exercise power on a national scale. Ailtirí na hAiséirghe was designed for this very purpose. At the time of its formation, however, Ó Cuinneagáin himself was the party's principal *raison d'être*, and its only real asset. Important though the personality of the leader within any authoritarian movement may be, he appears to have been under no illusions as to how far an approach to the Irish people based on his own charismatic appeal was likely to carry him. If Ailtirí na hAiséirghe was to gain popular support, it would have to do so based on the persuasiveness of its ideas. It was to that problem that Gearóid Ó Cuinneagáin now turned.

3

The ideology of Aiséirghe

Gearóid Ó Cuinneagáin's Domhnach Phádraig speech of June 1942 represented the mature form of the political philosophy that he had been developing during the previous two and a half years. Throughout the remainder of his long life he was to add little to the principles elaborated in this address and to amend nothing – a factor that in itself goes far to explain Ailtirí na hAiséirghe's ultimate decline. The many policy statements and pamphlets issued by the movement – the most important of which, *Aiséirghe Says …* (1943) openly proclaimed its ideological lineage with the subtitle *The New Order in the New Ireland* – consisted largely of clarifications or elaborations of Ó Cuinneagáin's original formulae. Despite the rigidity and inflexibility of thought that this eventually produced, it constituted in the short term a source of doctrinal consistency and stability that most rival movements lacked. Indeed, it is arguable that with the possible exception of its political antithesis, the Communist Party of Ireland, Aiséirghe was the first Irish party to take ideology seriously; that is, to attempt to base its policies upon first principles. Its ideas, and the manner in which it proposed to give practical expression to them, are thus worthy of detailed attention.

Aiséirghe, totalitarianism and Christianity

The first point to be noted about Ailtirí na hAiséirghe's emergence as a totalitarian movement is that, contrary to the claims of its opponents, the organisation did not represent an attempt slavishly to apply in Ireland the formulae first elaborated by similar movements on the European Continent. Unlike Doriot and Brasillach in France, de Man in Belgium or Quisling in Norway, Ó Cuinneagáin neither held the doctrines preached by Hitler or Mussolini in any particular reverence nor viewed Aiséirghe as the northwesternmost branch of a constellation of co-operating fascist parties. The success of right-wing totalitarianism in Europe during the late 1930s and early 1940s held significance for him principally as confirmation of the direction in which world history was unfolding, and an indication of the boundaries of the possible. Many characteristics of German and Italian fascism, on the other hand, left him unmoved. Although he could, when it suited his purposes, dilate luridly upon the hidden menace of socialism, Ó Cuinneagáin did not share Hitler's anti-Marxist mania and occasionally surprised his listeners by speaking in terms of praise – albeit heavily qualified – of the USSR's economic achievements under Stalin.[1] While taking a keen interest in foreign affairs, he was not attracted to martial adventure or visions of conquest in the conventional sense. Ireland's natural boundary was the sea surrounding all of its thirty-two counties; that it should seek additional territorial expansion seemed to him both impractical and undesirable.[2] Even Aiséirghe's anti-Semitism – as will be discussed in greater detail below – was much more the product of domestic influences than a pastiche of National Socialism.

Ó Cuinneagáin's ambitions by mid-1942 for an Aiséirghe-governed Ireland, moreover, were beginning to extend far beyond passive membership in an Axis-dominated world order. In his unpublished paper of more than two years previously, 'Ireland a Missionary-Ideological State', he had described 'the task of European and world re-Christianisation' as an agenda 'corresponding to the Nazi or Fascist ideal'. With the entire world now at war and the victory of Nazism and Italian fascism seriously in question, the more likely outcome appeared to him to be a peace of exhaustion in which no visible ideals of any kind would be found to prevail. It was more than ever apparent, Ó Cuinneagáin believed, that Anglo-American 'civilisation' had nothing to offer the postwar world beyond a restoration of the bankrupt liberal and capitalist formulae of the past. Soviet Communism was a doctrine born of desperation, attractive only to those who were denied anything more inspiring in which to believe. Hitler and Mussolini, by seeking to ground their respective revolutions essentially, and in Nazi Germany's case, exclusively, upon materialist principles and for no higher purpose than national aggrandisement, had built upon sand and confined the potential influence of their leadership to the territories they directly controlled. Regardless of whoever 'won' the war, therefore, the peoples of Europe and the world could expect to find themselves confronted by an undisguised moral vacuum, bereft of any source of inspiration or hope for the future. 'Dreadful were the fruits of the rotten [*lobhthach*]

1 Nor were these the only qualities to recommend the Soviet Union in the party's eyes. 'Even the Communists', one Aiséirghe publication observed, 'are realistic enough to have no time for effete liberalistic parliamentarianism'. Ailtirí na hAiséirghe, *Aiséirghe for the Worker* (Dublin: Ailtirí na hAiséirghe, 1946), p. 18.
2 Ailtirí na hAiséirghe, *Partition: A Positive Policy* (Dublin: Ailtirí na hAiséirghe, 1946), p. 28.

Conference of Versailles. The new European settlement after the war will be far more terrible and frightful than that.'[3]

Only a single European nation, one of the handful that had success-fully maintained their neutrality and avoided being tainted by associ-ation with either power bloc, possessed the ability to light a beacon for a Continent plunged into a second Dark Age: 'As no other people has, we Irish have racially inherited a true knowledge of temporal or world affairs, of the real meaning of creation'.[4] Because of the antiquity of their Christian faith and the peculiarities of their history, the Irish people had escaped falling under the sway of the Godless and worldly philosophies that since 1789 had infected to a greater or lesser degree every other developed country. As Ó Cuinneagáin saw it, this providential exemption from secularist contamination, like Ireland's preservation from involvement in the world war, was by no means accidental, but rather evidence of an unfolding divine plan: 'Even did we will it, it would be virtually impossible for us to avoid the fulfil-ment of our modern racial destiny'.[5]

As the chosen instrument of the Almighty in the modern age, Aiséirghe had been charged with the duty 'ultimately to subject the whole world to the spiritual influence of a reinvigorated and vitally Christian Ireland'. The island's very location, positioned athwart the maritime and aerial crossroads connecting Europe and North America, seemed to have been selected with such a purpose in mind. After the war, Ireland's mission would be not only to re-Christianise a Europe and a world over which the darkness of paganism had fallen, just as it had done after the fall of the Roman Empire, but eventually itself to assume the leadership of a new global Christendom. If this divine mandate were accepted and carried out to the full, Ó Cuinneagáin was convinced that Ireland would receive her reward in gratifyingly tangible, as well as spiritual, forms:

> To make Ireland mistress of the Atlantic as it is the wish of Japan to become mistress of the Pacific. With the difference that we shall be masters in the Pacific Ocean also. Dictators are fairly plentiful both in the eastern and western worlds in 1942. Should we play our cards carefully and cleverly it will be possible for us from the capital of Ireland to dictate to the dictators themselves. In any event in co-operation with Divine Providence we can give a new twist to the destiny of the modern world. Yes, settle the affairs of the universe for another 2,000 years!'[6]

3 G. Ó Cuinneagáin, 'Má Chailltear Éire Caillfear an Eoraip', *An t-Ultach*, February 1942.
4 G. Ó Cuinneagáin, *Ireland's Twentieth Century Destiny* (Dublin: Ailtirí na hAiséirghe, n.d. [1942]), p. 3.
5 *Ibid.*, p. 5.
6 *Ibid.*

It was not to be supposed that power of this kind, far surpassing that wielded by the rulers of mere ideological blocs, would be granted to a people who shrank from imposing upon themselves the sacrifices that such a leadership role entailed. On the contrary, Ireland's expanded national mission made the reorganisation of the state on authoritarian lines and a permanent breach with 'the hackneyed "will of the people" dictum' more, not less, necessary. The Axis powers had shown what could be achieved in this regard by governments seeking no more exalted goal than territorial expansion and military conquest. But 'If we as a race are in an exemplary fashion Christian we shall create a civilisation never known before in the whole world – and possess influence and power internationally accordingly'.[7]

To realise this vision would require 'extraordinary courage and moral qualities' from the leadership cadre, to a far greater extent than had been demanded of any national movement of the past. Lacking, as they had done, the fullest expression of integral nationalism or a sufficient number of committed activists willing to dedicate their whole lives to the cause regardless of discouragements or setbacks, all of Aiséirghe's predecessors since the Conquest of 1169 had been virtually preordained to fail.[8] Only if 'one thousand young men with one hundred thousand associate Aiséirghe patriots co-operating' could be mustered, would 'our historic international mission' become a reality. To these, however, would belong the imperishable glory not only of succeeding where twenty-five previous generations had fallen short, but of transforming Ireland from an international irrelevance to a country at the forefront of the newly emerging post-democratic world order. In the most expansive passage of his Domhnach Phádraig speech, Ó Cuinneagáin rhapsodised about the characteristics his followers would embody and the prize that lay within their grasp.

> These new youthful Ailtirí, architects of our new destiny, to work incessantly, ever organising, ever preaching acceptance of our three great national objectives of to-day, freedom, Gaelicisation, the establishment of the exemplary Christian state. These apostolic, architects of the resorgimiento, seeking nothing in reward for their services, merely sufficient to provide the ordinary necessities of life. Adequate the recompense in their eyes assured final conclusion in our time of the war of Gael and Gall [foreigner], and the Gael as victor … We shall obtain a hold on the mind and ears and heart of the public as no national movement

7 Ó Cuinneagáin, *Ireland's Twentieth Century Destiny*, p. 6.
8 In 1964 Ó Cuinneagáin declared his belief that these earlier movements had been 'providentially frustrated' because of their leaders' having based their claim to national independence 'on the will of the people' rather than 'the will of God'. *Aiséirí*, June 1964.

ever yet had in any country. Our strenuous unremitting labour in the national interest, our lofty idealism will assure us of that. We Ailtirí, shall be given power to do as we deem right, as we know to be right, with the wealth and manhood of Ireland ultimately and that precisely is what we seek. Mussolini, Hitler, Roosevelt, Stalin, these we shall leave a thousand miles behind in the matter of personal influence through the depth and strength and wisdom of our personal sincerity.[9]

The extent to which the grandiosity and extravagance of Ó Cuinneagáin's vision in 1942 was shared by activists and ordinary members who joined the Aiséirghe movement remains debatable. All indications, however, suggest that those following him into the farther realms of geopolitical fantasy were in a distinct minority. Some of his most loyal lieutenants, most notably Seán Ó hUrmoltaigh, did indeed firmly believe that the Irish people had been 'providentially preserved through an era of oppression, so that we may continue and expand our great Christianising influence'.[10] First-person testimonies by other former adherents, on the other hand, make clear that most were drawn to Aiséirghe by more down-to-earth considerations: its credentials as a fascist party; its promise of an end to partition, unemployment and emigration; and its repudiation of the inefficiency, division and corruption associated with parliamentary democracy. While many were deeply impressed by Ó Cuinneagáin's personal dedication, often describing his unwavering conviction and sense of mission as more characteristic of a spiritual than a political leader, their conception of the rôle of the 'exemplary Christian state' was on a considerably more modest scale than his. The establishment of a revolutionary political, social and economic order in Ireland alone would be a more-than-sufficient challenge for the 'generation of 1939', without entering into the question of how that revolution might be exported overseas. Ó Cuinneagáin's messianic excursions, consequently, were echoed in few of the reported speeches delivered by other Aiséirghe leaders, who preferred to concentrate on matters of more immediate concern to their audiences. Even many of his senior associates were apt reflexively to discount Ó Cuinneagáin's more effusive pronouncements as so much leaderly grandiloquence, and viewed him as prone to being

9 Ó Cuinneagáin, *Ireland's Twentieth Century Destiny*, p. 12 (orthography, grammar and punctuation as in original). A few of these flourishes (e.g. 'These apostolic, architects of the resorgimiento ...') were subsequent additions, absent from the original Irish-language text of the address. See G. Ó Cuinneagáin, 'Cinneamhain Nua-Aoiseach Éireann', in Croabh na hAiséirghe, *Aiséirghe 1942* (Dublin: Craobh na hAiséirghe, 1942), p. 13.
10 S. G. Ó hUrmoltaigh, 'Ireland and Israel', unpublished and undated article [c. 1944], Seán Ó hUrmoltaigh papers (in the possession of Hugo Hamilton, Dún Laoghaire).

carried away by his own rhetoric. In this they made a serious error. Although with the passage of time Ó Cuinneagáin learned to express himself publicly with more caution and reserve, he made no secret of his continued adherence to the belief that both he and the organisation he headed had been chosen to fulfil a great historic purpose. As events years later were to show, the principal fault-line within Ailtirí na hAiséirghe lay in fact between those who considered themselves members of a political movement, albeit a revolutionary one, and a man who – while not regarding himself as inerrant – never doubted that he had been providentially entrusted with the mission of leading into a new epoch both his party and his country.

The 'Governmental Plan'

Ó Cuinneagáin's scheme for a new system of government in an Aiséirghe Ireland was in essence a transposition of the party's structure to a larger field. As in the case of Ailtirí na hAiséirghe itself, the central component of the 'New Order' was to be a *Ceannaire Stáit*, or 'State Leader', in whose hands all legislative and executive power was to be reposed. The *Ceannaire Stáit*, who would serve for a term of seven years in the first instance, was to be indirectly elected by a *Comhairle Náisiúnta* [National Council] composed of fifty representatives elected by vocational bodies, and thirty-five more nominated by the 'National Party', which would be the only legal political body in the state.[11] Once elected, the *Ceannaire Stáit* would bring the membership of the National Council up to its full complement of one hundred by appointing fifteen 'men of outstanding merit not otherwise selected' of his own choosing. In this manner, Ó Cuinneagáin declared, the *Ceannaire Stáit*'s 'independence of all parties and vested interests will be emphasised'.[12]

Other than to serve as a sounding board for the leader, the National Council does not appear to have had any practical function. In his Domhnach Phádraig speech, Ó Cuinneagáin specified that it would be allowed to convene for only three months each year so as to limit the amount of 'talk' in which it engaged.[13] Its members would be 'permitted to offer advice, praise and criticism' to the *Ceannaire Stáit* (*Aiséirghe Says* … introduced the qualification that it would do so only

11 'Cinneamhain Nua-Aoiseach Éireann', p. 11.
12 Ailtirí na hAiséirghe, *For National Government and Action* (Dublin: Ailtirí na hAiséirghe, n.d. [c. 1943]).
13 'Cinneamhain Nua-Aoiseach Éireann', p. 11; Ó Cuinneagáin, *Ireland's Twentieth Century Destiny*, p. 9. The clarification appeared only in the published English-language version.

'if considered by him desirable'), but it was repeatedly specified that the National Council was not to vote on any matter other than the election of a leader every seven years.[14] *Aiséirghe Says ...* did state that the council, by a two-thirds vote, might remove a leader 'for grave cause', a provision added to the final draft on the recommendation of the onetime Craobh na hAiséirghe member Ernest Blythe.[15] However, in light of the fact that the leader as head of the party possessed the power to nominate more than a third of that body, and an additional fifteen members in his capacity as *Ceannaire Stáit*, it is difficult to imagine how such a super-majority could have been assembled – especially inasmuch as there was nothing to prevent him from removing dissentients from the council at any time and replacing them with more tractable appointees. As Pádraig Ó Fiannghusa explained, moreover, the Aiséirghe state would not shrink from taking measures to ensure that 'those elected to the National Council by vocational bodies can be prevented from becoming small unfriendly groups with a vocational bias or ... creat[ing] a second or opposition party in reality'.[16] Like its Italian counterpart the Fascist Grand Council, therefore, the National Council seems to have been included in the scheme to provide the appearance rather than the substance of a genuinely representative body.

Local government was likewise to be reorganised by the abolition of the 'effete imposed corrupt uneconomic County Councils' and their replacement by four *Comhairleacha Conndaethe* [Provincial Assemblies].[17] These were to be elected triennially by the vocational organisations, and to assume the functions of the old local government system 'and some others'.[18] As with national administration, however, executive power in each district would be exercised by a provincial governor or *Ceannasaidhe Cúige*, appointed by and responsible only to the *Ceannaire Stáit*. Additional governers would be appointed for the cities of Dublin, Belfast and Cork. All *Ceannasaidheanna Cúige* would

14 Ó Cuinneagáin was more explicit still in his Domhnach Phádraig speech: other than the septennial elections, the National Council was to be 'powerless' [*gan cumhacht*]. 'Cinneamhain Nua-Aoiseach Éireann', p. 11; Ailtirí na hAiséirghe, *Aiséirghe Says ... The New Order in the New Ireland* (Dublin: Ailtirí na hAiséirghe, 1943), p. 8.

15 *Aiséirghe Says ...*, pp. 8–9; 'An Phaimpléid Molta', n.d., P/24/970, Ernest Blythe papers, University College, Dublin.
   Several published sources assert that Blythe was a member of Ailtirí na hAiséirighe as well as its predecessor. No evidence has come to light to support such a contention. Blythe's Craobh na hAiséirghe membership-card is to be found (at reference P/24/966) in his papers at UCD.

16 *Dungarvan Observer*, 11 March 1944.

17 Ailtirí na hAiséirghe election handbill, 'Partition', summer 1943, 4/1/12, GÓCP.

18 'Cinneamhain Nua-Aoiseach Éireann', p. 11.

be equipped with the power to veto measures not supported by a two-thirds majority of their respective assemblies.[19] At the base of the governmental pyramid lay the vocational corporations, which would 'administer the affairs of and legislate for the industry concerned, after the manner of borough councils'; and a nationwide network of *Comhairleacha Paróiste* [Parish Councils]. These last appear to have been envisioned by Ó Cuinneagáin as a sort of Gaelicised *kolkhoz*: in addition to exercising the 'usual functions' of such bodies, they would provide farmers with agricultural machinery and arrange for the purchase of seeds and tools and the marketing of farm produce. Curiously, they were to be detached from the rest of the local government framework and placed under the exclusive control of the *Ceannaire Stáit*, in what may have been intended as a safeguard against the emergence of an excessively popular *Ceannasaidhe Cúige*. Their members were to be elected every three years by 'heads of families', a provision evidently intended to ensure an all-male electorate.

Ó Cuinneagáin had little to say about the judicial branch of government, and it clearly did not figure highly in his list of priorities. *Aiséirghe Says* ... did include a commitment to draft 'a new democratic constitution for a Christian Vocational State based on the proclamation of the Provisional Government of the Republic, 1916'; but, other than asserting that the legal code would be revised by a commission charged with replacing English statutes and precedents with the best features of European, American and Brehon law, offered no specific commitments in this area.[20] Ó Cuinneagáin's insistence that 'the head of state [was] to be the supreme authority during his seven years of office' indicates that the new regime did not intend to be hamstrung in its actions by purely legalistic obstacles.[21] Nor would any lukewarmness on the part of public servants be tolerated: 'Keymen of the civil services will be replaced where necessary by men of the Aiséirghe outlook. We shall ensure militant, patriotic and Christian leadership in every department of national activity'.[22]

Aiséirghe Says ... described the movement's proposed scheme of government as 'functional democracy combined with the principle of leadership characteristic of the Gaelic state'. In reality it contained little that could be described as 'democratic' in any meaningful sense

19 In the original text of the Domhnach Phádraig speech, the threshold given for a veto-proof majority was 60%, before being revised upward in the English translation. See 'Cinneamhain Nua-Aoiseach Éireann', p. 11; Ó Cuinneagáin, *Ireland's Twentieth Century Destiny*, p. 9.
20 *Aiséirghe Says* ..., p. 18.
21 Ó Cuinneagáin, *Ireland's Twentieth Century Destiny*, p. 9.
22 *Aiséirghe Says* ..., p. 9.

of the word.[23] The outlawing of rival political movements, the purging of the civil service, the restriction of the franchise for the office of head of state to a body half of whose members would be his own unelected appointees, and the subordination of the legislative and judicial branches of government to an all-powerful executive ensured that effective decision-making power would pass from the formal institutions of state to the party and, within the party, to its leader. In the Aiséirghe schema, in neither the party nor the state did there exist any genuine possibility of countermanding the dictates of the *Ceannaire* or of compelling him to yield up power at the end of his term of office should he prove unwilling to do so. There can be no doubt that Ó Cuinneagáin himself recognised the rhetorical character of his invocations of 'functional democracy', and that he was fully conscious of the extent of his indebtedness to totalitarian precedents overseas. In the peroration to his Domhnach Phádraig address, published in pamphlet form in both Irish and English and elaborated on in a host of subsequent statements and publications, he spelt this out in terms of unmistakable clarity.

> There is a section in Ireland who never weary proclaiming: 'The people of Ireland cannot be driven' … I assert that loyalty to a leader, fidelity to the noblest ideals, faithfulness to death are the true Celtic characteristics … I assert the people of Ireland will accept leadership, vigorous, courageous, decisive, genuinely national leadership. National enthusiasm has always been at peak when the national leadership was in the hands of a single, strong personality …
>
> Observe how already … the youth of Ireland is being trained to accept leadership in the new emergency forces which have arisen in the south. Soon these will have little or no patience with the cumbersome indirect methods of our imposed corrupt, unchristian, Godless, inefficient brand of parliamentary democracy. They will appreciate the value of national discipline. As a result of the war we are, all of us, becoming very much accustomed to government by state decree, the legislative method which will be practiced hereafter … The young men of the new national resurgence will be impregnated with the Aiséirghe spirit and faith and the public will eventually appreciate that and act accordingly.[24]

---

23 Aiséirghe's invocation of the term is perhaps best viewed in the same light as Mussolini's similar description of Italian fascism as representing 'organised centralised, state democracy'. Quoted in R. Conquest, *The Dragons of Expectation: Reality and Delusion in the Course of History* (New York: Norton, 2005), p. 25.
24 Ó Cuinneagáin, *Ireland's Twentieth Century Destiny*, p. 12.

Economic and social policy

Ailtirí na hAiséirghe was founded as, and frankly declared itself to be, a revolutionary movement.[25] In the same way as it was intended to eradicate all traces of the existing political system and replace it with an entirely new regime, so Aiséirghe aimed at a radical breach with the economic and social precedents established by the mainstream parties since independence. In their stead the party proposed to inaugurate a massive programme of state-sponsored initiatives with the twin aims of creating an ultra-modern autarkic economy and binding together the people of Ireland into a single organic entity, from which every vestige of sectarian, social or ideological division would be eliminated.

Aiséirghe perceived the failure of successive Cumann na nGaedheal and Fianna Fáil administrations to solve the country's persistent economic difficulties as the democratic system's greatest point of weakness. Few of the party's publications or platform addresses were free of scathing, and often exhaustive, denunciations of continuing high levels of emigration, unemployment and social inequality, two decades after the achievement of self-government. Aiséirghe propagandists acknowledged no historical disadvantages or external constraints as contributing to, or tending to mitigate, this dismal record. If Ireland was underdeveloped, its workers idle, its resources untapped, the responsibility lay exclusively with those 'slaves of political expediency, corrupt, incompetent and vacillating, the professional party politicians'[26] who had betrayed the sacrifices made by the revolutionary generation of 1916:

> In Ireland, in political affairs at any rate, we have the identically same national leaders we had twenty-four years ago in 1918. I am unaware of any other country of which that can be said. In virtually every other country youth is urged on to action. In Ireland youth is held in check and prevented from advancing. Our duty [is] to listen eternally to sermonising by the old and inactive and too often times nationally corrupt.[27]

Only in a few isolated instances – the Ardnacrusha hydroelectric scheme, the development of air facilities at Collinstown (Dublin) and Foynes, the import substitution programme of the 1930s – could any partial credit be given to previous administrations. Even these projects, though, had been unadventurously conceived, and their potential allowed to go to waste. In every other aspect of economic

---

25 An admission requirement was that 'Members must realise the revolutionary significance of the movement with which they are associated'. *For National Government and Action*, p. 7.

26 *Aiséirghe Says …*, p. 8.

27 Ó Cuinneagáin, *Ireland's Twentieth Century Destiny*, p. 13.

life, governments of both parties, reflexively duplicating the policies of their counterparts in London, had set in place a system that only benefited 'anti-national' elements at home and alien finance capitalists overseas.

In Aiséirghe's view, the solution to all of these problems lay readily to hand, requiring no additional resources or outside assistance. The first requisite was to make a clean sweep of the 'parasitic politicians' and 'Rip Van Winkles' who had presided over the country's economic ruin. Once this had been accomplished, the way would be clear for a revolutionary reorganisation of credit, agriculture, manufacturing industry and transport, under the leadership of, and if necessary through the assumption of direct ownership by, the state. 'Germany's six millions of supposedly docile unemployed', an Aiséirghe speaker pointed out, had only found work by 'stand[ing] firm as a rock and demand[ing] ... the replacement of an incompetent by a competent Government'.[28] It was incumbent upon Irish workers to do likewise.

The foundation of a healthy economy, Aiséirghe averred, was a system of credit and finance that was firmly under the control of the national government. To that end, it was necessary to break the link between the Irish currency and the pound sterling; adopt a decimal currency (and substitute 'for the coinage imposed on the long-suffering Irish people in the south by the Cumann na nGael government ... a set of coins really representative of Irish life, history and culture'); assume state control of foreign trade; and apply to government spending priorities the £500 million of capital invested by Irish citizens overseas and the 'tens of millions of pounds of "dead" unused money on deposit' in the country's commercial banks.[29] The movement warned that wherever urgent national tasks lay ahead, 'camouflaged short supply of money will not be permitted to constitute itself an insurmountable obstacle ... Facetiously speaking, should we establish a banking commission it will be to try bankers for crimes against society, not to write the epitaph of social and economic reconstruction in Ireland'.[30]

The sinews of economic development having been secured, an Aiséirghe government would proceed to eliminate unemployment, relieve social distress and modernise productive capacity by means of an unprecedented programme of public works. These were to include the construction of 100,000 houses, the electrification of the

28 Notes of Aiséirghe speech, n.d. [c. winter 1942], 10/2/8, GÓCP.
29 'The successful repatriation and protection' of these overseas assets, Aiséirghe observed in a masterpiece of understatement, would be 'one of the most difficult problems facing the reconstituted national monetary authority.' *Aiséirghe Says ...*, p. 16.
30 *Ibid.*, pp. 15–16, 19–20.

railways (and – bizarrely – the canals); the completion of a network of motorways modelled on the German *autobahnen*; the laying-down of 500,000 tons of naval and mercantile vessels; the building of regional airports; and the exploitation of the country's mineral assets. A binding guarantee of work 'at fair and Christian rates of remuneration' would be extended to every physically and mentally capable adult, with the state serving as employer of last resort should that become necessary. Aiséirghe was confident, however, that such expedients would not in fact be required: 'For decades to come there should be no question of unemployment in undeveloped, underpopulated Ireland'.[31]

Some of the movement's proposed schemes were on an even more monumental scale. *Aiséirghe 1942* contained an article by the architect Daithí Ó hÁinle, who would later achieve prominence for designing the Garden of Remembrance in Dublin and the Basilica at Knock, reviving Ó Cuinneagáin's suggestion eight years previously of removing the capital city of an Aiséirghe Ireland from its existing location in Dublin and constructing an entirely new capital – a kind of Hibernian Brasilia – on the Hill of Tara.[32] To restore the seat of government to the historic locale of the High Kings of Ireland, Ó hÁinle asserted, would 'break the alien influence exercised by the denizens of Rathmines, Rathgar and the Royal Irish Academy over the Government of Ireland', and serve as 'a highly visible symbol that we had bade farewell to the old, bad life we had experienced during the seven hundred years we were under the oppressive yoke of England; that we were in earnest in our intention to create for ourselves a fresh new world in Ireland'.[33] The new city, for which Ó hÁinle provided a preliminary sketch, was to be on a heroic scale, including a broad, sweeping 'Great National Avenue'; a cathedral; a 'Garden of Heroes' with the *Columhan na hAiséirghe* ['Column of the Resurrection'] as its centrepiece; and a new national university, theatre and stadium. Elaborate though this scheme may have been, it was at all events within the bounds of physical achievement, which Aiséirghe's further proposals for the cultivation in Ireland on a commercial scale of soya beans and tobacco plants almost certainly were not.[34]

Agriculture in general was an area in which Aiséirghe appeared less than sure of itself. Beyond invocations of the need to modernise Irish

---

31 *Ibid.*, p. 26.
32 Ó Cuinneagáin in his turn may have derived this idea from the Blueshirts, who advocated it in early 1934. See F. McGarry, *Eoin O'Duffy: A Self-Made Hero* (Oxford: Oxford University Press, 2005), p. 249.
33 D. P. Ó hÁinle, MRIA, 'Maoidheamh ar Árd-Chathair Stáit i dTeamhair', in *Aiséirghe 1942*, p. 43.
34 *Aiséirghe*, May 1945; *Aiséirghe Says ...*, p. 28.

farm methods on the lines established in Denmark, the Netherlands and Italy – a suggestion that had been reiterated by so many commentators on agricultural policy over the previous half-century as to become the rankest of clichés – the movement seemed to believe that the principal reason a larger market for agricultural produce was not forthcoming was an excessively high level of exports. The complaint that too much of Ireland's food was crossing the sea 'for John Bull's dinner table' in all likelihood stemmed from the commonly held belief, familiar to every Irish schoolchild, that the Great Famine of 1845–51 had been due largely to the continued export of food to Britain while those at home were left to starve.[35] At all events, Aiséirghe policymakers took for granted that to retain these supplies in Ireland would automatically bring about a higher rate of consumption, thereby improving the health of the population and putting an end to malnutrition. The movement did not exclude the possibility *à tout jamais* of exporting food, although its mention of Argentina as a possible customer for Irish meat after the war serves to indicate the general level of its expertise in agricultural matters.[36] The same observation applies in respect of its plans to launch a range of protected industries based on agricultural by-products, including such unlikely schemes as the production of glassware from milk.[37] But in return for its renewed commitment to the agricultural sector, including the establishment of a network of state farms, the government of an Aiséirghe Ireland expected to enforce its will in the countryside as well as the towns. As *Aiséirghe 1942* warned, 'The State will exercise power over the farmers through the parish councils', and might 'compel them to give up their land if that is necessary'.[38]

In the sphere of industrial policy, Aiséirghe declared its intention to subject 'the establishment and development of industry ... to state control'. Although it accorded some grudging praise to the Fianna Fáil administration for its Control of Manufactures Acts in the 1930s, which required the majority interest in all new manufacturing enterprises to be held by Irish nationals, these laws, it claimed, had been honoured

---

35 Scandalous though the export of food in the midst of famine undoubtedly was, Margaret Crawford has calculated that the retention of all food within Ireland would still have left a net caloric deficit of 12%. Of course, there was no shortage of foodstuffs on the world market; the Great Famine was the consequence of the inability of Irish peasants to pay for them. E. M. Crawford, 'Food and Famine', in C. Póirtéir, ed., *The Great Irish Famine* (Dublin: Mercier, 1995), p. 65.

36 Argentina was the world's largest single exporter of beef in the mid- twentieth century; to hope to export meat there constituted optimism on the same scale as aspiring to sell coals to Newcastle, ice-cream to Italians, or sand to Arabs.

37 A. Ó Liatháin, 'Talmhaíocht ins an Nua-Éirinn', in *Aiséirghe 1942*, p. 24.

38 *Ibid.*, p. 23.

more in the breach than the observance. 'Aliens and masonic elements were permitted to secure control of industries in a number of instances, however cleverly camouflaged'. Health and safety regulations were also being evaded, although 'unhygenic workshops are usually found to be under the control of aliens of an undesirable type'.[39] Such abuses, and the system of free enterprise from which they derived, would no longer be allowed to occur.

> [I]n a Christian corporate state unbridled competition in industry is prohibited. Under the Ailtirí na hAiséirghe regime, licences for the operation of industrial concerns will be issued only to persons of the highest integrity and Irish nationals and with due regard to the amount of competition already in the particular industry or, if a new industry, whether it is genuinely valuable from the community's standpoint … Likewise the prices of manufactured products must be fixed on a just basis, to assure the manufacturer and his employee of a fair return for their labour and capital, and at the same time safeguard the public against exploitation in point of price or quality.[40]

The degree of *dirigisme* inherent in Aiséirghe's economic policy raised awkward questions about the coherence of its ideology. The advantage of vocationalism over state socialism, the party maintained, was that whereas the latter led to 'a centralised administration ruled by a soulless arrogant caste', the former was 'a complete realisation of Pius XI's famous principle of subsidiary function. This asserts that what can be done by subsidiary groups should not be undertaken by a higher one'.[41] Despite this pious aspiration, under Aiséirghe's scheme of administration the economic life of the country was to be subject to a degree of centralisation almost as great as in the field of politics. State control of banking and commerce, the export trade, prices and wages, and new investment – to say nothing of those industries, like transport and fisheries, which it was proposed to take into direct state ownership – appeared to leave open relatively few outlets in the economic sphere for the operation of subsidiarity. Nor was it clear how the principle of vocational control of industry by the producers themselves was to operate when the industries concerned had already been nationalised, or how the workers in those sectors could be represented within the corporatist framework when the only 'corporation' of which they could claim membership was the government that paid their wages. It is, of course, possible that like the Italian corporate structure from which it drew inspiration, Aiséirghe's version of the vocational system was never

39 *Aiséirghe Says* …, pp. 32–3.
40 *Ibid.*, pp. 31–2, 34.
41 R. Breathnach, 'The Philosophy of Aiséirghe', p. 8, 8/7/1, GÓCP.

intended to do more than provide a public facade with which to conceal the reality of a state-directed command economy. That is certainly the impression conveyed by Pádraig Ó Fiannghusa's declaration that even after the Aiséirghe revolution, the government would take whatever action was necessary to ensure the predominance of 'the more patriotic-minded and idealist members of the National Party' over 'those representing vocations'.[42] But the prominence accorded to 'Christian corporatism' in the movement's propaganda as the panacea for the country's economic problems would have made a mere token effort of this kind extremely difficult to disguise, in the event of Aiséirghe ever being called upon to put its policies into effect.

Northern and security policy

Well before the outbreak of the Second World War, Gearóid Ó Cuinneagáin had concluded that the Irish state he desired to create was hardly likely to come into existence through peaceful means alone. It was, he believed, a permanent British strategic and economic interest that Ireland should remain divided and underdeveloped. The emergence of a united, commercially aggressive country on her western flank, owing no allegiance to the Crown and from which all trace of the British military presence had been removed, was so obviously disadvantageous to imperial power and prestige that any government in London was certain to go to great lengths to prevent it.

> A strong Ireland would be a menace to England in time of war, and wars occur at regular intervals, particularly in the history of Empires. Therefore, it must ever be an aim of English foreign policy to keep Ireland weak, always economically and militarily comparatively powerless ... In the circumstances isn't it absurd to approach England with a view to securing the abolition of Partition? Why should England facilitate Ireland in this regard for a mere verbal or paper promise that the use of Irish territory as a base of attack on England will not be permitted by any Irish Government? Isn't England's best guarantee her military occupation of the six Northern Irish Counties, wih an air base in Ireland's most important industrial centre, Belfast?
> ... What I mean is that clearly in the matter of securing national sovereignty, we are not going to get anywhere by purely constitutional means.[43]

Between 1937 and 1941 Ó Cuinneagáin had believed that Irish unity and national renewal could only be achieved with external assist-

42 *Dungarvan Observer*, 11 March 1944.
43 *Labour News*, 5 February 1938.

ance, either through an anti-British alliance with Mussolini's Italy or as the logical consequence of Britain's defeat and occupation by Nazi Germany. By early 1942, however, he was beginning to have second thoughts. The entry of the United States and the Soviet Union into the war, he recognised, had created an entirely new strategic situation, in which an Axis victory could no longer be taken for granted. With the benefit of recent experience, furthermore, it was naive to assume that the interests of small nations, even those prepared to adapt themselves fully to the German *gleichschaltung* of Western Europe, would necessarily be advanced by the appearance of Axis troops on their borders. An Axis victory was still the most desirable outcome of the war, inasmuch as 'in my view we can say that the peoples of Germany and Italy and Japan are not as worldly in their outlook and temperament as those of the other lot'. Nevertheless, it was clear that, as in the conflict of 1914–18, 'every one of [these] countries is fighting or will fight for its own interests'.[44] It followed that Ireland, in the postwar world, should expect to have to rely largely upon its own resources.

In one vital respect the Emergency had brought about a considerable augmentation of national strength: '[T]o-day, in 1942, there are more Irishmen in Ireland trained as soldiers than at any period in our history – 200,000 men with guns in their hands. We are aware that 200,000 more could be made available in the morning if the right clarion call for national action were issued'.[45] This wartime enhancement of the country's military potential needed not merely to be maintained after the conclusion of the Emergency, but built upon still further: '100,000 men, 200,000 men, 300,000 men if possible. Train every available man. Muster *all our* strength'.[46] The permanent militarisation of Irish society, Ó Cuinneagáin declared, would be an indispensable feature of the Aiséirghe governmental system. The Ireland of the future was no longer to be 'the island of saints and scholars' but an 'island of priests, scholars and soldiers. God has ordered that it be so'.[47]

> Ailtirí na hAiséirghe will not merely build up a large national army that will provide for us national security and win for us national freedom. It will ensure that that army is made independent of foreign supplies to

44 Ó Cuinneagáin, 'Má Chailltear Éire Caillfear an Eoraip'.
45 Ó Cuinneagáin, *Ireland's Twentieth Century Destiny*, p. 3.
46 *Partition: A Positive Policy*, p. 24. Emphasis in original. Elsewhere, Ó Cuinneagáin suggested that a force of '500,000 trained soldiers' would be required to accomplish the tasks required of it, although 'I do not envisage that all of these will be in the army at the same time'. 'Comh-Bhráithreachas: Cosaint: Obair do Chách', in *Aiséirghe 1942*, p. 28.
47 Ó Cuinneagáin, 'Oileán na Sagart agus na Saighdeóirí', *An tIolar/The Standard*, 11 July 1941.

the greatest possible extent in regard to munitions and equipment ...

Apart from those in religion the soldier in the Aiséirghe Ireland will be the most respected citizen – and not merely during a war-time emergency period.

He must be given his due honoured privileged place in the national life.[48]

To create and sustain this vast standing army – a force which on the scale envisaged by Aiséirghe would have necessitated the recruitment of up to one in every three adult males[49] – compulsory military service would be introduced. The armed forces' duty would be twofold: to regain the Northern irredenta by means of 'a just war of aggression',[50] and thereafter to stand on constant guard against any countermeasures attempted by Ireland's hostile and resentful neighbour to the east: 'When finally we secure complete national freedom we must take steps to ensure that we do not easily and quickly lose it again through military negligence'.[51] Aiséirghe was undeterred by the challenge of building up a military-industrial complex with which to equip the new garrison state: 'It is true that we do not possess in Ireland such modern military essentials as steel mills, oil wells, rubber plantations. Well, then so much the better shall we be in a position to display our ultra-modernity through the development and improvement of our ersatz industries!'[52]

Aiséirghe's attitude to the problem of integrating a million Unionists into its Gaelicised state of the future, once the Border had been erased, was a curious mixture of recognition of the difficulties involved and wishful thinking as to the ease of their solution. As a Belfast-born Catholic, brought up in a predominantly Unionist area, Ó Cuinneagáin was aware that few Northern Protestants had material or other reasons actively to desire Irish unity. A letter he published in February 1938 in the *Irish Times*, a paper read largely by the Anglophile and Protestant communities in the twenty-six counties, was remarkable for its acknowledgement of the economic disruption to which any attempt at abolishing the Border would inevitably lead, and which even the most strenuous efforts could only partly alleviate. 'Perfervid Southern or Northern unity advocates', he charged, had made no attempt whatsoever to view the question from the perspective of 'the Orange householder in the North of Ireland ... Maybe more than those incorrigible Orangemen are narrow-minded and selfishly self-centred

48 *Aiséirghe Says ...*, p. 39. Emphasis in original.
49 According to the 1936 census, the number of men aged between 20 and 44 residing in the twenty-six counties was 522,604.
50 S. Glanbhille, 'An Teorann', 23 June 1945, 8/5/7, GÓCP.
51 *Aiséirghe Says ...*, p. 38.
52 Ó Cuinneagáin, *Ireland's Twentieth Century Destiny*, p. 6.

in Ireland!'[53] The same sympathetic note was struck in Aiséirghe's most detailed statement on the question, *Partition: A Positive Policy*, published in 1946. In the field of shipbuilding, for example 'virtually every order for Béal Feirste [Belfast] is placed by England. If we cannot assure the shipbuilding workers of continual employment it is stupid to denounce them *all* as *bigots* because they won't vote themselves into an Irish Republican state'.[54]

On the other hand, a majority of Northern Protestants could be expected to respond positively to a movement that aimed seriously at the creation of that *civitas Dei* on earth that the Puritans in their day had sought to establish. His own unconcealed Catholic devotionalism notwithstanding, Ó Cuinneagáin never made the error of equating 'Christianity' with Catholicism alone: according to Risteárd Ó Glaisne, a committed Methodist, 'his attitude to Protestantism was not only unsectarian but unpatronising'.[55] As fellow Christians, Ó Cuinneagáin believed, the Protestants of the North would be no less amenable to a call to translate their religious convictions into social policy than their Catholic counterparts south of the Border.

> The average non-Catholic in Ireland does not deem himself a Gael; but he does consider himself both an Irishman and a Christian. The combined ideals of political liberty and Gaelicisation leave him as they have left him unaffected. But freedom and the establishment of a realistically Christian social and economic system in Ireland would definitely arouse and whet his interest. Gaelicisation and freedom as essential preliminaries for the guaranteeing of the proper organising of the state to provide Christian standards of living for every Irish citizen, that certainly would secure his sympathetic and indeed enthusiastic support. 'Christianity' will solve all the most difficult national problems for us! A magic word![56]

For those whose Christian fervour was insufficient to induce them to swallow the pill of the Gaelic totalitarian state, the expedient of ethnic cleansing remained. An indeterminate number of Northern Protestants, though 'surely not more than 250,000', would resist all inducements to join in the task of building an exemplary Christian order: 'In the last analysis Ailtirí na hAiséirghe can offer these the alternative of residing physically as well as spiritually in the England they so dearly love, they to be replaced by a like number of our exiled Irish kith and kin'.[57] But the remainder, and especially the young,

---

53 *Irish Times*, 10 February 1938.
54 *Partition: A Positive Policy*, pp. 15–16. Emphases in original.
55 Ristéard Ó Glaisne, author interview, 2 August 2003.
56 Ó Cuinneagáin, *Ireland's Twentieth Century Destiny*, p. 8.
57 *Partition: A Positive Policy*, p. 18.

would be attracted to Aiséirghe's 'revolutionary financial and industrial policies', while majority-Protestant educational institutions like Trinity College, Dublin, suitably reconstituted, could be used as 'an effective instrument towards winning the loyalty of the descendants of that section of our countrymen … whose eyes have traditionally been turned away from their own country. For them it can be made the gateway to the hidden Ireland'.[58]

Aiséirghe's failure throughout its history to make any serious attempt to engage in dialogue with Northern Protestants, and its constant reiteration that partition would come to an end only as a result of military confrontation, suggests that Ó Cuinneagáin was less confident than he professed to be that his programme would appeal to a significant number of non-Catholics. Like the IRA, Aiséirghe had no real formula for the achievement of Irish unity other than the application of physical force; and despite Ó Cuinneagáin's claim to empathise with the concerns of 'Orange householders', its expectation that the majority of Unionists would acquiesce in its new order was no less blinkered and unrealistic. Where the two differed most markedly, though, was in Aiséirghe's disdain for paramilitarism as a means of achieving national unity. Such activity was not only ineffective, Ó Cuinneagáin believed, but objectionable in principle. It was no part of the duty of any private group or body of Irishmen to take upon itself a task that ought properly to be discharged by the state. Once the levers of political power had been captured by the Aiséirghe revolution, the solution not only to partition but all outstanding national problems would lie readily to hand.

Language, education and culture

The launch of Ailtirí na hAiséirghe did not imply any de-emphasis of the work of language revival taken up by its predecessor in 1940. Rather, it heralded a new resolve to complete the task of Gaelicisation as a matter of urgency and by whatever means might prove necessary. Shortly before the public announcement of the new movement, Séamus G. Ó Ceallaigh had declared uncompromisingly on behalf of Craobh na hAiséirghe, '*The time has passed for people to say they do not understand Irish; they will have to understand it*'.[59] His rationale was

58 *Aiséirghe Says …*, p. 47. 'The hidden Ireland', a term coined by the literary scholar Daniel Corkery, was a reference to the Irish-speaking nation that typically was ignored by Anglophone historians. See D. Corkery, *The Hidden Ireland: A Study of Gaelic Munster in the Eighteenth Century* (Dublin: M. H. Gill, 1925).

59 M. Ó Gráda and S. G. Ó Ceallaigh, *Náire Náisiúnta, nó Seán Treacy's Shame* (Dublin: Craobh na hAiséirghe, 1942), p. 8. Emphasis in original.

not that of earlier Gaelic revivalists like Pádraig Pearse, *Ní tír gan teanga* ['without a language there's no country'], but rather that only a monoglot Irish nation would be insulated sufficiently from corrupting cultural influences. In the blunt formulation of Tomás Ó Dochartaigh, Aiséirghe's National Organiser, 'We reject Anglo-Ireland as a mongrel, illegitimate offspring of the foreign conquest'.[60]

In *Aiséirghe 1942*, Risteárd Mac Maghnusa described how 'the battle of Irish' would be won. 'Compulsion in the use of the language in ordinary life', he asserted, was essential. The 'slavery' of an alien tongue was to be eradicated 'with or witbout the consent of the people'.[61] A five-year plan to achieve the complete Gaelicisation of the country would be the most imperative task of an Aiséirghe administration. From the first day of its accession to power, all official business would be conducted in Irish, and no civil servant under the age of thirty retained who was not fluent in the language. Irish was to be substituted for English in every form of printed writing. Lawyers, accountants and others making representations to the government were to be denied a hearing unless they pleaded their case in the official language. A register of households using Irish as their ordinary tongue was to be compiled, with members of such households accorded positive discrimination in employment, the purchase of houses and farms, the award of grants, and student loans. A heavy stamp duty was to be imposed on all notices in English, 'from film posters to the labels on sauce bottles'. Nor was even the Church to be exempted. Although sermons, bishops' pastoral letters and other such communications in English were to be tolerated 'for a reasonable time', these too would be required to make a start by incorporating short passages in Irish. By the end of the five-year transition period, except in institutes of higher education where it might be studied on the same basis as other modern European language, 'English was to be entirely prohibited'.

> No letters or parcels of domestic origin or destination to be accepted or delivered unless the address is in Irish. The names of shops, hotels, streets, towns, transport networks, neon signs in cities [to be] in Irish alone. All the foreign monuments and memorials to be eradicated without delay. Associations, etc., to be forbidden to make use of the title 'Royal'[62] or individuals to use titles conferred by the King of England. Every citizen henceforth to make use of the correct Irish form of his or her name.[63]

60 'An Fiolar' [T. Ó Dochartaigh], *Dungarvan Observer*, 23 October 1943.
61 R. Mac Maghnusa, 'Seo Mar Bhainfimíd Cath na Gaedhilge', in *Aiséirghe 1942*, p. 16.
62 In the course of Gaelicising the education system, Mac Maghnusa observed, the name of Queen's University, Belfast would have to be altered.
63 'Seo Mar Bhainfimíd Cath na Gaedhilge', p. 19.

As elsewhere in Aiséirghe's explication of its doctrine, the version of the Gaelicisation programme set out in *Aiséirghe Says ...* was couched in more emollient terms. The document contained a noteworthy concession, absent from *Aiséirghe 1942*, in its undertaking to adjust the pace of change in Northern Ireland to local conditions, 'so that no one will justifiably nourish a feeling of being wronged'. The essence of the policy, however, remained unchanged. Aiséirghe rejected 'the heresy that Ireland can or should become bilingual'. The Irish language stood as 'a shield against modern material and atheistic cultural influences'; its restoration was both symbol and instrument of a revival of national morale.[64]

The massive emphasis placed by Aiséirghe on the language question, almost to the exclusion of all other aspects of Irish culture,[65] is not easily explained. Unquestionably Aiséirghe was not the only nationalist movement to pursue language revival with a single-mindedness bordering on obsession – one that in the party's case impelled it to disseminate the bulk of its propaganda and election literature in a language that it was fully aware most of its target audience could not understand. Like these other organisations, Aiséirghe believed that the essential, if not the sole, requirement to save Irish was an inflexible determination to use it in all circumstances, no matter how unpromising. The movement's cultural-nationalist credentials, moreover, derived largely from its championing of the language. Yet it appears that Ó Cuinneagáin and his colleagues viewed Irish not merely as a repository of national values or an expression of cultural distinctiveness, but as an instrument through which Aiséirghe ideals could be communicated to and inculcated in an unwilling populace. The identification of Aiséirghe as the only party truly dedicated to the cause of Irish – indeed, the virtual equation of the party and the medium – meant that Gaelicisation would take place not in an atmosphere of ideological neutrality, but rather within a highly politicised context. Victor Klemperer, Simonetta Falasca-Zamponi and other scholars have noted how Continental fascist movements sought to circumscribe the limits of the thinkable or expressible by substituting for everyday language their own distinctive locutions, vocabularies and even grammatical structures.[66] Aiséirghe, for its part, aimed at something more ambitious still: the intellectual 'reprogramming'

64 *Aiséirghe Says ...*, pp. 3–4.
65 A notable exception was the promise that 'Instruction in traditional dancing in the primary schools will be compulsory'. *Ibid.*, p. 43.
66 V. Klemperer, *LTI–Lingua Tertii Imperii: The Language of the Third Reich*, trans. M. Brady (London: Continuum, 2000); S. Falasca-Zamponi, *Fascist Spectacle: The Aesthetics of Power in Mussolini's Italy* (Berkeley, CA: University of California Press, 2000).

of an entire people.[67] To say this is not in any way to imply that the adoption by a society of another language than the one it had been accustomed to use – a process that was accomplished by many of the countries of central and southeastern Europe in the nineteenth century and by Israel in the second half of the twentieth – is in itself part of a totalitarian programme. Nevertheless, the opportunity offered by a government-directed and -enforced language campaign to extend the reach of the state deeply into individual consciousness and to collapse the boundaries between the public and private spheres was by no means lost on Aiséirghe activists. Whether, in the event of such an opportunity actually materialising, the Aiséirghe-approved version of the Irish language to be instilled in all citizens would in the course of time have given rise to a Hibernian analogue of Klemperer's *Lingua Tertii Imperii* must remain a matter for speculation.

Educational policy was presented largely in instrumental and voca-tional terms. Aiséirghe regarded the schools and universities as agencies for reviving the language, training future workers and producing 'loyal citizens of a Christian Gaelic and independent Ireland'.[68] Liberal ideals of education came in for much caustic commentary in party publica-tions. The curriculum, in Aiséirghe's view, had been based on 'the apparent presumption that the bulk of the nation's school-going youth are either going to take holy orders or enter the learned professions'. Instead of 'compelling students with no mathematical gift to bewilder themselves with the differential calculus', post-primary education (i.e. that offered to students above the age of twelve) was to be reorganised on a vocational basis. Pupils in the countryside would receive training in 'rural science' and farm management; in the towns 'boys will be induced to take up those handicrafts which may become the basis of their future trade'. Girls, on the other hand, would be steered firmly away from the paid workforce: 'The school curriculum now in force may aid them towards becoming competent shop assistants and short-hand typists, but it in no way makes provision for the possibility of their someday becoming wives and mothers'. To rectify this deficiency, 'housecraft in the widest sense of the word will form an integral part of the curriculum, and it will be seen to that every school is provided with adequate cooking appliances'.[69] The universities, too, were valued principally as a source of technically qualified personnel: 'The time is past when they can function merely as repositories of learning'.[70]

67 See untitled typescript by Riobárd Breathnach, c. August 1944, 9/2/32, GÓCP.
68 *Aiséirghe Says* …, p. 43.
69 *Ibid.*, pp. 44–5.
70 *Ibid.*, p. 47.

The task of social and political formation in the Aiséirghe state was to be left to the end of the educational process. A network of continuation schools, catering to those aged between sixteen and eighteen, would provide 320 hours per year of instruction in technical subjects accompanied by obligatory 'moral and cultural' education. In the country areas, residential *ard-scoileanna tuaithe*, or rural high schools, would fulfil a similar function, offering courses of three months' duration. In addition to imparting instruction in up-to-date agricultural methods, these were to be 'schools of patriotism and spiritual development in which the sons and daughters of farmers would by association learn the inestimable wisdom of comradeship and co-operation'.[71] The crown jewel of Aiséirghe's educational restructuring, however, was the 'Labour Comradeship Corps', which seems to have been modelled directly on the Nazi *Reichsarbeitsdienst*.[72] Like its German counterpart, service in residential camps for a period of six months was to be compulsory for all young men attaining the age of eighteen. Manual labour was emphasised, as a means of physically hardening the country's youth. The principal objective of the corps was to be the eradication of class and sectarian differences and the cultivation of 'a young Irish manhood ... of national and Aiséirghe morale, a manhood that may be depended upon in the most arduous tests'.[73]

Aiséirghe and women

The question of European fascist movements' attitudes to and appeal among women has become the focus of a growing volume of scholarly attention in recent years.[74] In place of the once-dominant perception of fascist ideology with regard to women as consisting exclusively of *kinder, kirche, küche*, it is now apparent that fascist parties embraced a wide range of policies extending from the near-complete exclusion of women from the public sphere at one end of the spectrum to explicit forms of 'fascist feminism' at the other – and that some

---

71 *Ibid.*, p. 48.
72 See H. Heyck, 'The Reich Labour Service in Peace and War: A Survey of the *Reichsarbeits-dienst* and its Predecessors 1920–1945', MA thesis, Carleton University, Ottawa, 1997.
73 *Aiséirghe Says* ..., p. 40. Curiously, Aiséirghe appeared to ignore the failure of de Valera's own pilot scheme for a Construction Corps of unemployed workers in October 1940. Unlike the mooted Labour Comradeship Corps, however, participation in this experiment had been voluntary. See K. Allen, *Fianna Fáil and Irish Labour: 1926 to the Present* (London: Pluto Press, 1997), p. 68.
74 See especially M. Durham, *Women and Fascism* (New York: Routledge, 1998); J. V. Gottlieb, *Feminine Fascism: Women in Britain's Fascist Movement, 1923–1945* (New York: I. B. Tauris, 2000); and K. Passmore, ed., *Women, Gender and Fascism in Europe, 1919–45* (Manchester: Manchester University Press, 2003).

movements contrived at various times to stand for both of these desid-
erata simultaneously. Along this continuum, Aiséirghe was normally
to be found supporting a traditionalist view of women's place in
society. This stance was often contradicted in practice, on the other
hand, by the active roles played by many female members within the
movement.

So far as the male leadership is concerned, it would be misleading
to suggest that the 'woman question' was ever close to the forefront
of Aiséirghe's thought. A promised policy document on the subject
never materialised, and to judge by some of the statements made by
Ó Cuinneagáin's associates, it is hard to imagine that a great deal of
mental effort was expended by the party's leading ideologues in this
area.[75] Nevertheless, over the course of the early 1940s a distinctive,
and strongly pro-natalist, policy with respect to women did emerge.
The twelfth point of Aiséirghe's programme advocated that 'measures
… be taken for race preservation through the prohibition of emigration and the introduction of a scheme of State marriage grants and
family allowances'.[76] The rationale behind this policy was set forth in
frankly social-Darwinian terms. A rapid increase in Ireland's population from 4,000,000 to 15,000,000 was, according to *Aiséirghe Says …*,
the movement's single most imperative goal in social policy: 'The
blunt truth is that if we do not populate the country ourselves … some
other more progressive race will take over the national territory and
do it for us'. The principal duty of women under an Aiséirghe regime,
therefore, would be to supply the human stock for the achievement
of the state's various objectives, and above all for the vastly enhanced
national army the movement proposed to create: 'We cannot expect to
hold Ireland militarily without a much larger population in the years
that lie ahead'.[77]

The means by which the party proposed to achieve this objective
was the encouragement of early marriages: 'In the Aiséirghe Ireland
we shall provide that woman can follow normally her normal vocation.
We shall stress and emphasise that the marriage period for Irish girls is
18 to 22, not 26 to 36. As for men … !' In contrast to many other aspects
of its social policy, and despite its promise of 'radical measures' to
address the population problem, Aiséirghe's specific proposals in this

---

75 One may cite as an example Seán Mac Mathúna's assertion in 1942 that women could
materially contribute to the national cause by refusing to accept love letters that were
not composed in the Irish language.

76 In an article the previous year, Ó Cuinneagáin had expressed the hope that 'the day will
soon come upon us when permission will not be granted to any Irishman to leave the
country'. G. Ó Cuinneagáin, 'Fíor-Oideachas do Chách', *An Glór*, 13 September 1941.

77 *Aiséirghe Says …*, p. 41.

area were both few and uncharacteristically unambitious. An undertaking to introduce 'family allowances payable for every child after the third', however desirable in itself, was unlikely if implemented to have had a major impact upon the country's demographic profile. The movement instead appeared to be confident, in light of Ireland's success in avoiding 'the racial suicide and immoral practices popularised in certain other countries', that to make young people economically self-sufficient at an early age through the provision of full employment and publicly funded housing would provide as much encouragement to marry and procreate as was required.

When addressing potential women supporters, Aiséirghe took care not to appear to speak the language of compulsion alone. A policy statement on *Aiséirghe for the Worker*, issued in 1944, asserted that 'We do not intend to hinder the participation of Irishwomen in industry in suitable employments, but rather to eliminate the necessity of their lingering there over long periods, even during married life'. The party promised that *'low rates of pay for female workers, not in proportion to the value of their output, will be prohibited'* and condemned the government of the day for failing properly to compensate junior-grade women civil servants – although this stance may have been influenced by the pragmatic consideration that such individuals made up a significant proportion of Aiséirghe's membership.[78] On the other hand, Ó Cuinneagáin regarded a proposal in an early draft of *Aiséirghe Says* ... to establish a system of 'state-sponsored kindergartens for the care and education during the day of the infants of mothers with large young families and of widows who find it necessary to work outside the home in order to supplement their frequently pitiably inadequate incomes' as much too radical, and ordered its deletion from the final version.[79] But the party also offered a back-handed acknowledgement of the burdensome element of women's domestic role, promising that in an Aiséirghe Ireland the worker's wife, as well as the female wage-earner, would receive an annual holiday from her duties at state expense.[80]

Women Aiséirghe activists, for their part, professed themselves enthusiastic proponents of early marriage and liberation from wage-slavery. As one of them, Máire Ní Dhubhshláine, declared in 1942, 'It is a strange fact that for contentment and peace of mind and natural charm and beauty, the women who marry young (from 18 to 22)

78 *Aiséirghe for the Worker*, p. 9. Emphasis in original.
79 Draft of education section of *Aiséirghe Says* ... with manuscript corrections by Ó Cuinneagáin, 8/3/3, GÓCP.
80 *Aiséirghe for the Worker*, p. 9.

compare more than favourably with the votaries of "our fling first"!'
In reality, relatively few of Aiséirghe's female adherents themselves
appear to have conformed to this ideal, being like their male counterparts disproportionately represented among the ranks of unmarried
clerical and secretarial workers, secondary-school and university
students, and primary schoolteachers. This was not the only area
where a distinct gap appeared between prescription and performance.
While Aiséirghe may have asserted its adhesion to 'that mediaeval
if Christian notion, that woman's place is in the home' and its confidence that '99% of the women of Ireland' thought likewise, the variety
of roles female members were called upon to play made such rigid
formulations impossible to adhere to.[81]

Some of Aiséirghe's precepts for its female members could undoubtedly appear, if not mediaeval, then at least distinctly Victorian. A case
in point was Ó Cuinneagáin's ordinance in March 1944 that Aiséirghe
women should refrain from the use of either tobacco or cosmetics,
lipstick being considered especially objectionable on the ground that,
'being red, [it] should be as un-Aiséirghe as Communism itself!'[82] His
deputy, Tomás Ó Dochartaigh, likewise condemned the 'wine sipping,
whiskey drinking young women' of Ireland as representatives of the
new 'soft, pleasure-loving' generation who were eroding national
morale from within.[83] But in spite of periodic eruptions of leaderly
puritanism, female members not only succeeded in occupying, but were
encouraged to assume, positions of responsibility within the movement
– a trend to which Ó Cuinneagáin, in spite of himself, occasionally
lent support. Contradicting his own rhetoric of 'separate spheres', he
held up Jeanne d'Arc – for Aiséirghe a potent icon combining images
of militarism, martyrdom, Catholicity and Anglophobia – as a model
for emulation, and declared that contemporary Ireland needed 'a
thousand and twenty brave, super-dedicated heroines' like Jeanne to
join the national struggle.[84] On various occasions, the organisation's

81 *Ibid.*, pp. 12–13.
82 Ó Cuinneagáin, 'Litir Pearsanta', March 29, 1944, 6/2/21, GÓCP. A definite ascetic tradi-
    tion, it should be noted, had long existed in Irish nationalist circles. As Todd Andrews
    recorded of the women's auxiliary of the IRA, Cumann na mBan, in the 1920s: 'Among
    the Cumann women fashionable clothes were despised. Any form of personal embel-
    lishment was avoided. Make-up was not commonly used by Irish women in those days
    but it was unknown among the Cumann na mBan'. C. S. Andrews, *Autobiography*, vol.
    II, *Man of No Property* (Dublin: Mercier, 1982), p. 50.
83 *Tipperary Star*, 28 June 1945.
84 Introduction by Ó Cuinneagáin to R. Ní Sheaghdha, *Jeanne d'Arc (Eisiompláir Tír-Ghrádha)*
    (Dublin: Craobh na hAiséirghe, 1942). As Pádraig Pearse had previously observed, 'The
    story of Joan of Arc … means more for boys and girls than all the algebra in all the
    books'. P. H. Pearse, 'The Murder Machine', in *The Murder Machine and Other Essays*
    (Cork: Mercier, 1986), p. 21.

need for female members' talents was allowed to override doctrinal consistency, as in 1945 when Ó Cuinneagáin solicited a married woman activist to stand as an Aiséirghe candidate. As the party grew increasingly militant in the late 1940s, officials like Denise Nic Réamoinn could even find themselves engaging in physical skirmishes, during its occasional forays across the Border into Northern Ireland, with the Royal Ulster Constabulary.

The absence of any substantial theoretical elaborations of Aiséirghe doctrine produced by female activists greatly complicates the task of determining to what degree the appeal of the movement to its women members diverged from that of the men. Some pointers, however, may be offered by a pair of articles written by leading ideologues of Craobh na hAiséirghe in 1942 shortly before the formation of the party, both of which were published by the movement in pamphlet form. If these can be taken as indicative of the thinking of those who joined Ailtirí na hAiséirghe in the following months, it would appear that the cultural struggle in which they believed Ireland to be engaged assumed a much higher priority for Aiséirghe women than purely material or economic interests. Both writers, Moinice Ní Mhurchadha and Máire Ní Dhubhshláine, perceived the war between the Christian and Gaelic ideal and the way of life embodied in the 'pagan countries like England and America' as a contest in which women's interests in particular were heavily invested.[85] 'The first "Ave Maria"', Ní Dhubhshláine declared in *A Cailíní, Éistighidh!* ['Listen, Girls!'], 'was woman's Magna Charta. All other religions degraded us … The stronghold which Christianity gave to woman to defend her dignity and her rights was her kingdom, the Christian home. And it is not surprising that it is against this unit-foundation of Christian society that the fiercest attacks of materialistic paganism are directed.' The battle for the survival of the Irish language, driven to the brink of extinction by centuries of Anglicisation, was viewed as a vital element in this campaign against the corrosive influence of Anglo-American cultural norms. With the hegemony of the English language Ireland had been laid open to all the baneful elements of an alien mass culture with its relativism, its consumerism, and its obliteration of everything that was local and particular.

Both Ní Dhubhshláine, *ceannasaidhe* of the newly formed Waterford City branch of Craobh na hAiséirghe in August 1942, and Ní Mhurchadha, whose address on 'The Young Women of Ireland' immediately preceded that of Gearóid Ó Cuinneagáin at the Domhnach Phádraig meeting, heavily emphasised the failure of Irishwomen, most

---

85 Moinice Ní Mhurchadha, 'Mná Óga na hÉireann: An Obair Atá le Déanamh Acú', in *Aiséirghe 1942*, p. 38.

notably those of the previous generation, to discharge the responsi-
bilites laid upon them. Not only had women not vigorously enough
opposed the spread of Anglo-American cultural influence, they had
actively collaborated in it as 'fifth columnists in the ranks of Gaeldom'.
In their capacity as arbiters of fashion; consumers of books, films and
magazines; and above all as transmitters of authentically Irish values
to the next generation, women since independence had failed in their
duty to a nation that had entrusted them with full political rights. Such
an indictment could not be levelled at all Irishwomen, and Moinice Ní
Mhurchadha in particular chided her peers for lacking in knowledge
and appreciation of 'the women who did exceptional work for Irish
freedom in times past'. Nevertheless, as Ní Dhubhshláine declared, 'a
fundamental change of mentality and outlook amongst the women of
Ireland must be resolutely effected in our time'.

If attitudes like these were representative of the ideas of female
Aiséirghe supporters, then a definite distinction does indeed appear
to have existed between the agendas and priorities of men and
women members respectively. For male adherents, the revolutionary
and dynamic character of Aiséirghe was most often stressed as the
principal reason for supporting the movement. What it offered them
was a radical breach with the past, and unlimited opportunities for
innovation and initiative in a wholly new political and economic
system. Women supporters, on the other hand, appear to have been
drawn to Aiséirghe less as a harbinger of ultra-modernity than as a
bastion against it. Though it may seem paradoxical that so conservative
a society as mid-twentieth-century Ireland could be perceived by any
section of the population as moving too far or too fast in the direction
of its more highly developed neighbours, female Aiséirghe members
were deeply disturbed by the inroads of a consumerist, secular and
cosmopolitan ethos which the independent Irish state, its lofty aspirations as expressed in the 1937 Constitution notwithstanding, seemed
unwilling or unable to resist. In the absence of a sustained counter-
offensive, they believed, the erosion of the nation's cultural distinctiveness that had already occurred would proceed to undermine its
political independence as well. Nor were they alone in that perception. James Donnelly Jr, has noted the degree to which Catholics in
mid-twentieth-Ireland 'saw themselves as gravely menaced above all
by communism and by moral pollution, particularly in the form of
the new modern sexuality. In the way that Irish Catholics perceived
their world, there was a widespread and persistent tendency to fuse
or elide these two great threats'.[86] The very seductiveness of many of

---

86 J. S. Donnelly Jr, 'The Peak of Marianism in Ireland, 1930–1960', in S. J. Brown & D. W.

these external influences, and their evident appeal to large numbers of women, was further proof of the gravity of the danger. As Ní Dhubhshláine angrily declared, 'it is our right to cry shame on those, who misnaming themselves Irishwomen and Christians, elect to join ranks with the pagan materialists who to-day spit in the face of God's Son as surely as did the mockers in the court of Caphais [*sic*]!'[87]

In opposition to a regime that left both the nation and Irish womanhood exposed to the caprices of powerful and uncontrollable external forces, Aiséirghe offered its female supporters the vision of an 'ethical' or 'normative' state – one that was explicitly Gaelic, Christian, and resistant to the undermining of women's traditional sphere of authority. Such a polity, however desirable for men, was a vital necessity for women who, 'being highly strung temperamentally … have more need of a spiritual background'. To Aiséirghe women who had attained young adulthood in the early 1940s, moreover, the duty of national regeneration was itself a feminist imperative. 'Now that we have an opportunity, unparalleled in history, to prove that we are not what it is said we are – pleasure-loving, empty, without ideals, shall we fail Ireland? We the emancipated, the capable and the self-reliant!'[88]

A second factor underlying the scale of Aiséirghe's female support – and one that has been treated somewhat casually by scholars – was the reality of emigration as the ultimate destiny of most young women during this period. As J. J. Lee has pointed out, 'Irish emigration was, to an extent unusual in Europe, female emigration'.[89] By mid-century the scale of emigration had reached socially catastrophic proportions: four of every five children born in the twenty-six counties between 1931 and 1941 would eventually seek their living overseas. What is frequently overlooked is how heavily this bore upon young Irishwomen in particular. As early as the 1920s, the ratio of female to male emigrants had approached 1.3:1, a pattern that continued unchanged throughout the following decade. In some areas the haemorrhage abroad was on an even more pathological scale: of every hundred girls aged between 15 and 19 living in the western province of Connacht in 1946, forty-two had emigrated by 1951.[90] There is a tendency greatly to underes-

      Miller, eds, *Piety and Power in Ireland 1760–1960: Essays in Honour of Emmet Larkin* (South Bend, IN: University of Notre Dame Press, 2000), p. 266.
87 M. Ní Dhubhshláine, *A Cailíní, Éistighidh! no, For Girls Only* (Dublin: Craobh na hAiséirghe, 1942), p. 11.
88 *Ibid.*, p. 4.
89 J. J. Lee, *Ireland 1912–1985: Politics and Society* (Cambridge: Cambridge University Press, 1989), p. 376.
90 *Ibid.*, p. 377.

timate how traumatic many young Irishwomen found this prospect. Whereas the departure of male emigrants has often been represented as at the very least a regrettable necessity and more commonly as a personal and national tragedy, a marked historiographical divergence has arisen with regard to female migration. In some treatments of the subject, descriptions of these population movements take on virtually a celebratory tone, with women's emigration being depicted as an escape from oppressive familial and clerical structures and an opportunity to achieve personal and financial independence in the more unfettered environment of the British or American city.[91] While this may reflect the view of women's emigration held by modern scholars, and even how many of the emigrants themselves came in retrospect to view their own experience, it is very different from the way in which young Aiséirghe women regarded the prospect of exile in the 1940s. Although a large proportion did eventually leave the country, a factor that in itself is a significant part of the explanation for the movement's loss of support in the late 1940s, there is much evidence to suggest that many Irish girls and young women, to a greater extent than their male counterparts, were deeply apprehensive over the likelihood of being compelled not merely to leave their home and familiar surroundings, but to fend for themselves abroad in a paid workforce for which neither their upbringing nor their education had adequately prepared them. For such members of the Aiséirghe movement, debates over whether women's proper sphere lay in the world of paid employment or in the household must have appeared at best academic and at worst bitterly ironic in a country that could offer them little assurance of being able to participate in either.

'The Philosophy of Aiséirghe'

As is true of most European fascist movements, Aiséirghe's effort to devise a credible philosophical basis for its ideology was largely an afterthought. Though Ó Cuinneagáin admitted that '[m]any of the failures in our past ... have been largely due to the absence of a

---

91 See, e.g., C. Clear, '"Too Fond of Going": Female Emigration and Change for Women in Ireland, 1946–1961', in D. Keogh, F. O'Shea & C. Quinlan, eds, *The Lost Decade: Ireland in the 1950s* (Cork: Mercier, 2004); H. R. Diner, *Erin's Daughters in America: Irish Immigrant Women in the Nineteenth Century* (Baltimore, MD: Johns Hopkins University Press, 1983); J. A. Nolan, *Ourselves Alone: Women's Emigration from Ireland, 1885–1920* (Lexington, KY: University Press of Kentucky, 1989); D. Fitzpatrick, 'A Share of the Honeycomb: Education, Emigration and Irishwomen', *Continuity and Change* 1:2 (1986): 217–34; P. Travers, '"There Was Nothing For Me There": Irish Female Emigration, 1922–71', in P. O'Sullivan, ed., *Irish Women and Irish Migration* (London: Leicester University Press, 1995).

philosophical background',[92] it was not until the spring of 1945, three years after the *Ceannaire*'s Domhnach Phádraig speech, that Riobárd Breathnach, a junior lecturer in English at University College, Cork and the acknowledged 'intellectual' of the movement, attempted to position Aiséirghe within the larger framework of European thought. His task was greatly complicated by the fact that – the war being by then in its final days – reference to the supposed anti-democratic trend of world politics, which had formed a mainstay of Aiséirghe's distinctive appeal in the early 1940s, was no longer available to him. Instead, Breathnach elected to justify the one-party state as being not merely consistent with, but the inescapable political expression of, Catholic social teaching. Such an undertaking would have posed a formidable challenge to a theorist with a thorough command of political science, theology and European intellectual history. Inasmuch as Breathnach possessed no specialised training in any of these areas, it was unsurprising that the manuscript he produced, a 4,500-word draft pamphlet entitled 'The Philosophy of Aiséirghe', should have been an unsophisticated and sometimes incoherent piece of work, bespeaking above all its author's relative youth.

Because Breathnach resigned from the Ard-Chomhairle, or National Executive, and from the party itself within a few months of the draft's completion, 'The Philosophy of Aiséirghe' was never published.[93] From the movement's own standpoint this was perhaps fortunate, inasmuch as the tone and phraseology of the pamphlet seemed likely to win Aiséirghe few friends. Breathnach's reference to 'the thick and unwholesome minds of our people' and his description of his fellow-citizens as 'the degraded voting-machines which are modern depersonalised Irishmen' revealed what would become a growing propensity within the movement to address its audience in terms bespeaking an element of contempt. The document's attempt to trace an intellectual lineage for Aiséirghe in Catholic social doctrine was unpersuasive, resting as it did largely upon quotations wrenched from their original contexts in the writings of such figures as Jacques Maritain, Emmanuel Mounier and Vladimir Solove'ev. So too was its repudiation of 'Imperialism, Socialism, Communism and Totalitarianism' as representing 'the negation of nationality'. Elsewhere in the draft, however, Breathnach reiterated Aiséirghe's repugnance for parliamentary democracy and its continued adherence to the 'leadership' principle. Irish civilisation, he declared, was 'at the mercy of parasitic forces such as are generally found in any democracy'; their

92 *Aiséirghe Says* ..., p. 5.
93 See ch. 6 below.

most insidious and 'audacious' strategem was to seek to 'canonise this [democratic] system itself, to make loyalty to our country and our state synonymous with the belief in or defense of existing institutions in the political, economic or social orders'.

Aiséirghe (or, as Breathnach styled it, the 'National Movement') was by contrast 'consistently anti-individualist and anti-liberal'. It aimed at 'the rousing of the only spirit with which we ever made any advance – national enthusiasm' and the development of an integral state charac- terised by 'great uniformity of principles and thought'. It would not shy away from 'enforcing patriotism as a necessity where it does not exist as a self-acknowledged duty', but in so doing would restore man to 'his true significance as the member of some group in a hierarchical system of orders'. Only as part of an 'organic entity', Breathnach claimed in an unconscious echo of Giovanni Gentile, could humans find meaning in the modern world, and that entity was and could only be the wholly integrated nation. 'Humanity without nationality is empty, and the national plan is the human plan, and is the best plan for the life and interests of mankind.' In the specific circumstances in which Ireland found herself in the middle of the twentieth century, there was no reason to fear what 'imitative cliché-mongers might call "agressive [*sic*] nationalism"'.

> When we have a normal nation really free, really sovereign, and really Irish, it will be time enough to fear agressive nationalism but not till then. And not even then if we realise that ours is a 'land apostolic', and the Irish a missionary people ... seeking a new convergence of wills around a nucleus of unchallangeable [*sic*] principles regarding the reali- ties of our life on the national and spiritual planes.[94]

Aiséirghe ideologues' efforts to locate the movement philosophi- cally within the framework of Catholic social teaching provided the basis for its claim to constitute a 'third way' between the Godless extremes represented by the materialist doctrines of Communism and capitalism. The assertion that the Aiséirghe programme was wholly in accord with the papal encyclicals was also intended to reassure those whose enthusiasm for fascist and totalitarian doctrines had been dimmed by the scarcely concealed secularism of Mussolini's Italy and the aggressively anti-Christian ethos of Hitler's Germany – although it was hardly consistent with the frequently reiterated declaration that Aiséirghe was not a confessional party. Such a stance, however, was complicated by the arm's-length relationship which the Catholic Church and the party leadership maintained with respect to each other.

94 Breathnach, 'The Philosophy of Aiséirghe'.

Despite the centrality of vocationalism and other aspects of Catholic social doctrine to Aiséirghe's ideology, Ó Cuinneagáin made even less effort to enlist the support of Catholic clerics than that of Northern Protestants. While the co-operation of individual priests was welcomed on the comparatively few occasions when it was volunteered, there is no record of the *Ceannaire* setting out to attract the public endorsement of any minister of religion.[95] No clergyman held a position in the movement higher than that of ordinary member, although a member of the Christian Brothers briefly directed the Monaghan branch sub rosa.[96] The standard method of fundraising for Irish political parties – the weekly churchgate collection – was deliberately forgone in favour of the more laborious method of house-to-house solicitation. It is, indeed, a richly ironic circumstance that in its day-to-day operations Aiséirghe maintained a more rigorous separation between the political and clerical spheres than any Irish party other than the Communists.

For its part, the institutional Catholic Church likewise found it expedient not to take official notice of Aiséirghe's existence. There are several indications that, behind the scenes, the movement was quietly discouraged. Canon John Hayes, founder of the vocationalist rural self-help organisation Macra na Feirme, once apologetically declined an invitation from Ó Cuinneagáin to deliver a lecture before an Aiséirghe audience on the ground that such an engagement would not be well-received by his clerical superiors.[97] Members of Aiséirghe in Holy Orders displayed much reluctance to advertise their political enthusiasms from the pulpit, a highly un-Irish reticence that is most unlikely to have been accidental.[98] But neither did any prominent member of the clergy ever take a public stance against the party, or propose modifications to its ideology.

It seems clear that the position adopted by both parties reflected a calculated decision as to where their respective interests lay. From Ó Cuinneagáin's point of view, in spite of his own rigorous Catholic orthodoxy – the sincerity of which cannot be questioned – there was little to be gained, and much to be lost, by involving the Church in his political activities. The Irish hierarchy's profound conservatism and

---

95 The most prominent clerical contributor to the party was Dr Cornelius Lucey, the future Bishop of Cork, who sent Ó Cuinneagáin a donation of £1.1.0 'for language revival'. Lucey to Ó Cuinneagáin, 16 December 1942, G2/2988, DDMA.

96 Aindrias Ó Scolaidhe, author interview, 22 July 1999. The individual in question subsequently left the society in order to marry.

97 J. M. Hayes to Ó Cuinneagáin, 15 February 1944, G2/2988, DDMA.

98 For an extensive discussion of the party-political activities of the Irish Catholic clergy during the interwar years, see P. Murray, *Oracles of God: The Roman Catholic Church and Irish Politics, 1922–37* (Dublin: University College Dublin Press, 2000).

hostility to revolutionary movements of whatever stripe was too well known to admit of any doubt as to the futility of seeking support from that quarter.[99] Had Ó Cuinneagáin harboured any illusions on the subject, the example of the extremist movement Maria Duce would have provided a salutary object-lesson. Founded about the year 1942 by Fr Denis Fahey, Maria Duce, an organisation with a demographic profile not dissimilar to that of Aiséirghe, regarded the Irish Constitution as illegitimate because of its affirmation of the legality of sects other than the Catholic Church, and because it failed explicitly to acknowledge the kingship of Christ over the island of Ireland. Nothwithstanding the movement's perfervid declarations of loyalty to the Church and of its readiness to render implicit obedience to the guidance of the hierarchy, it was regarded as an embarrassment and in 1955, the year after Fahey's death, peremptorily directed to cease its activities by the Archbishop of Dublin, John Charles McQuaid.[100] Ó Cuinneagáin's distancing of the Catholic clergy is best explained by his desire to avoid courting a similar fate, as well as his publicly ventilated conviction that the Church had yet to 'appreciate the magnitude of her blunder in co-operating in the destruction of our national language and culture in the nineteenth century'.[101] For its part, the hierarchy can have had little interest in promoting any movement seeking to weaken the existing political structure, far less one that was as radical in its ideology and difficult to control as Ailtirí na hAiséirghe. The Irish Catholic Church was so well-served in mid-century by the Irish state, and accorded such deference by the mainstream political parties, that any interference with the status quo could only have served to undermine its position. The single serious clash to arise in Church–state relations, the controversy over the 'Mother and Child' scheme in 1951, provided a vivid illustration of the point when the government of the day declined to support a public health measure proposed by its own Minister of Health, Dr Noël Browne, rather than engage in a showdown with the bishops.[102] To the Irish hierarchy, therefore,

---

99 See especially D. Keogh, *The Vatican, the Bishops and Irish Politics 1919–39* (Cambridge: Cambridge University Press, 1986), and *Ireland and the Vatican: The Politics and Diplomacy of Church–State Relations, 1922–1960* (Cork: Cork University Press, 1995).

100 E. Delaney, 'Political Catholicism in Post-War Ireland: The Revd. Denis Fahey and *Maria Duce*, 1945–54', *Journal of Ecclesiastical History* 52:3 (July 2001): 487–511.

101 Ó Cuinneagáin, *Ireland's Twentieth Century Destiny*, p. 7.

102 It should, however, be borne in mind that notwithstanding Browne's tireless efforts during the following decades to depict his Cabinet colleagues as having cravenly journeyed to Canossa, their stance owed at least as much to their resentment over his prima donna-like behaviour and his involvement of the government in what they regarded as a wholly unnecessary public wrangle, as to their desire not to antagonise the Catholic episcopacy. See N. Browne, *Against the Tide* (Dublin: Gill & Macmillan,

Aiséirghe represented not so much the shining promise of a militantly Christian social order, as the cure to no known disease.

Aiséirghe and the 'Jewish question'

The Irish political environment has historically provided few opportunities to movements whose appeal is based on racial doctrines. Although there is no reason to suppose that Irish culture is more resistant than others to popular prejudice, the course of Irish nationalism placed formidable obstacles in the way of those who might seek to ground their definition of Irishness in blood or biology. A nationalist pantheon that included John Mitchel and Pádraig Pearse – both of whose fathers were British – as well as such figures as Lord Edward Fitzgerald, Thomas Davis and Charles Stewart Parnell, raised obvious difficulties for any equation of 'Celtic' lineage and membership of the national community. So too did the growth of republicanism, a secular and self-consciously inclusive ideology, as the characteristic form of Irish nationalism. Whether its aspiration to 'substitute the common name of Irishman in place of the denominations of Protestant, Catholic, and Dissenter' had been in practice even partially achieved was beside the point. Rather, the achievement of independence, and still more so the ending of partition, required at least an implicit acknowledgement that a united Ireland must be ethnically heterogeneous. To insist that 'nation' and 'race' must be identical, on the other hand, was to concede the argument of Unionists that Ireland's divided population necessitated a 'two-state' solution. It was for this reason that Riobárd Breathnach, a self-professed 'Norman', maintained on behalf of Aiséirghe that 'uniformity of race, religion, character and ideals is found in no modern nation whatever ... Clearly, a nation is the reconciliation of differences, not the assertion of uniformity and if North-East Ulster has qualities and aptitudes different from the rest of Ireland, these qualities and aptitudes *must be developed within the national organism and not outside of it*'.[103] Ó Cuinneagáin himself would later declare that in Aiséirghe 'the main emphasis is on Christianity, not racialism'.[104]

1986); D. McCullagh, *A Makeshift Majority: The First Inter-Party Government, 1948–51* (Dublin: Institute of Public Administration, 1998), pp. 202–32. For a discussion of the 'Mother and Child' controversy, see E. McKee, 'Church–State Relations and the Development of Irish Health Policy: the Mother and Child Scheme, 1944–53', *Irish Historical Studies* 25:98 (November 1986): 159–94.

103 *Aiséirghe*, July 1945; R. Breathnach, 'Aiséirghe and Partition: A Positive Policy', 8/5/3, GÓCP. Emphasis in original.

104 *Irish Times*, 3 September 1954.

In the case of one particular 'race', however, this tolerant stance was not to apply. As noted in Chapter 1, a powerful undercurrent of anti-Semitism was plainly visible in Irish political and social life decades before the emergence of Nazism as a significant force. While it is undoubtedly true that the right-wing leagues of the 1930s derived both encouragement and a degree of inspiration from the rise of fascism on the European Continent, the anti-Jewish invective of these organisations for their part drew in the main upon domestic sources of prejudice rather than those fed from overseas. Scientific racism had few followers in Ireland during the mid-twentieth century. The works of de Gobineau, Chamberlain, Günther or Madison Grant were virtually unknown; nor would their apotheosis of 'Nordics' or Anglo-Saxons have been well-received if they had succeeded in achieving a wider circulation.[105] Even the canonical texts of European anti-Semitic literature like the *Protocols of the Elders of Zion* – no Irish edition of which was ever published – were accessible only to a comparative few who made it their business to obtain copies from overseas. Irish adherents to these ideas were thus constrained to gain their information about them at second hand, through such sources as the books of the clerical anti-Semites Frs Denis Fahey and Edward J. Cahill.

There is nothing to suggest that the anti-Semitism of Ailtirí na hAiséirghe differed from this general pattern. Some members, it is true, had been in receipt of anti-Jewish propaganda from Germany – notably the productions of the *Deutscher Fichte-Bund* – before the onset of the Emergency, but this appears to have left no lasting impression on them. According to the Ard-Chomhairle member Dónall Ó Maolalaí, anti-Semitism occupied so inconspicuous a position in Aiséirghe's early doctrine that the owner of the first premises occupied by the movement was a Jewish solicitor – a circumstance that provoked the resignation of one outraged anti-Jewish stalwart.[106] In the later stages of the war, however, hostility to Ireland's Jewish minority became an increasingly overt feature of Aiséirghe discourse. The reason that it should have done so is unclear, but one possibility is that it was at least in part a local manifestation of a broader wave of popular anti-

105 De Gobineau included 'Celts' – a linguistic category rather than a racial one – in his enumeration of those peoples 'whose inferiority is not only manifested in their defeat, but also in the absence of the qualities to be seen in their conquerors'. Chamberlain rated what he called 'the still-unmixed Celts' more highly; unhappily for his Irish followers, his test for racial purity consisted of loyalty to the British Crown and hostility to the 'anti-Germanic' Catholic Church. J. A. de Gobineau, *Essai sur l'inégalité des races humaines*, vol. I (Paris: Firmin Didot, 1853), p. 49; H. S. Chamberlain, *Die Grundlagen des 19. Jahrhunderts* (10th edn) (Munich: Bruckmann, 1912), p. 470.
106 Dónall Ó Maolalaí, author interview, 15 July 1999.

Semitism, perhaps fuelled to some degree by disappointment over the declining fortunes of the Nazi cause on the battlefield.

Much evidence exists to indicate that expressions of anti-Jewish feeling increased markedly in frequency and virulence during the second half of the Emergency, particularly in 'respectable' middle-class circles. Archbishop McQuaid, in a memorandum for the Sacred Congregation of the Holy Office, observed that 'Irish Catholics frequently feel justified in resenting the number of Jews who have come to this country and the wealth they have amassed'.[107] The practice of Jews legally changing their names for ones less suggestive of Eastern European origins – doubtless for the very purpose of reducing their vulnerability to anti-Semitic attacks – was a fruitful source of local animosity at this time, especially when the new names chosen were those of Irish patriots. In the autumn of 1943, both the Longford and Tipperary (South Riding) County Councils passed by unanimous votes identically-worded resolutions expressing their 'protest against this practice being permitted to continue in the interest [*sic*] of the community'.[108] Anti-Semitic sentiments also figured prominently at the 1943 annual convention of the National Agricultural and Industrial Development Association, which adopted a motion calling for action to counter what its proposer described as 'an invasion of aliens for the purpose of sabotaging Irish national assets'. In the ensuing debate, Jack O'Sheehan, a director of the Irish Hospitals' Trust, described Irish Jews as a 'gang of parasites … I doubt very much if they are human'. Another speaker, the outgoing president of the organisation, rhetorically enquired '[w]hat was the use of talking about Irish culture when all the time these people were sneering at us', and undertook to start a 'campaign' against them. A third called for the compilation and publication of a list of recently arrived aliens including their addresses, promising ominously that '[p]ublic opinion would do the rest'.[109]

On the national political scene, too, anti-Semitism was openly and

107 Quoted in J. Cooney, *John Charles McQuaid: Ruler of Catholic Ireland* (Dublin: O'Brien Press, 1999), p. 185. McQuaid, a former student of and member of the same congregation as Fr Denis Fahey, had publicly expressed views on Jews as 'allies' of Satan not dissimilar to those of his brother priest and provided an approving foreword for the latter's 1931 work *The Kingship of Christ*. By 1942, however, the Archbishop had come to regard with disapproval Fahey's propensity 'where Jews are concerned' for making 'remarks capable of rousing the ignorant or malevolent'.

108 J. Smyth, Assistant Secretary, Longford County Council, to the 'Secretary to the Government', 6 August 1943; L. Ó Riain, Secretary, Tipperary County Council, South Riding, to the Secretary to the Department of the Taoiseach, 8 October 1943. Department of the Taoiseach files, S 13310A, NAI.

109 *Irish Times* report, 15 March 1943, G2/X/0040, DDMA. Publication of the report was prohibited by the censor.

unapologetically ventilated. At its chaotic first convention in March 1943, the recently-founded farmers' party Clann na Talmhan ['Tribe of the Land'] staked its claim to a share of the prejudiced vote when its leader, Michael Donnellan – who three months later would compare his political mission to that of Adolf Hitler – announced that the party's five-point programme had been framed to 'break the stranglehold of the money grubbers and Jews'.[110] The January 1944 Fine Gael Ard-Fheis was likewise marked by overt anti-Semitism, with one delegate complaining in a platform speech about an influx of 'aliens fleeing from justice in Central Europe' and establishing businesses employing 'slave labour' in Ireland. It seemed, he said, 'impossible to get Jews convicted in court'.[111] The following month, a number of shops in the exclusive Grafton Street area of Dublin 'were daubed with two-foot squares of yellow paint, and the word "Jews" written across them'. Several shop windows were defaced with 'stickyback' adhesive labels bearing the words 'Perish Judah'.[112] By the beginning of 1945, Colonel Dan Bryan of G2, never prone to invest excessive significance in casual displays of anti-Semitic sentiment, had become sufficiently concerned about the situation to warn Joe Walshe of the Department of External Affairs that 'the extent to which Dublin has become what may be described as Jew-conscious is frequently coming to the notice of this Branch'.[113]

Aiséirghe's own 'Jew-consciousness' began to manifest itself at the same time, although the vigilance of the censorship authorities ensured that a considerable proportion of the movement's anti-Semitic propaganda never found its way into the public domain. In the first draft of *Aiséirghe Says …*, an elaboration of the fifteenth point of the party programme – which undertook to bring about 'the elimination of the controlling influence of aliens and freemasons' – accused 'Jewish speculatives' of buying up land in Ireland. The draft went on to declare that 'Jews never would or could become genuinely patriotic'. These allegations never saw print, the censor's office substituting the word 'alien' for 'Jewish' in the first sentence, and deleting the second entirely. The same procedure was adopted the following year in the preliminary draft of *Aiséirghe for the Worker*, which deplored the practice of

---

110 *Irish Press*, 15 March 1943. In a speech at Creggs, Co. Galway, in June 1943, Donnellan said: 'I have been called a Hitler. I accept the name because I intend to drive the professional politicians out of Ireland, just as Hitler drove the Jews out of his country'. *Ibid.*, 25 May 1944.
111 Report of speech by delegate O'Driscoll, 27 January 1944, G2/X/0040, DDMA. Publication of the report was suppressed by the censor.
112 *Ibid.*, 27 February 1944. Reporting of these incidents was suppressed.
113 Bryan to Walshe, 6 January 1945, Department of External Affairs files, P. 90, NAI.

Irish hire-purchase customers being 'reduced to the mercy of Jews Englishmen and Scotchmen'. On this occasion the authorities obliterated the reference to all three groups, replacing it with the anodyne term 'foreigners'.[114] At approximately the same time the party received a formal warning from the Office of the Controller of Censorship that no anti-Semitic material of any kind would be approved for publication. To Gearóid Ó Cuinneagáin, whose views on the subject were identical to, and probably derived from, those of Fr Fahey,[115] these excisions, and the official policy they reflected, served only to confirm the strength of the foothold that world Jewry had succeeded in establishing in Ireland. 'Through the censorship merely', he warned the party's assistant National Treasurer Seán Ó hUrmoltaigh, 'we know definitely the Jew has already extraordinary influence (of course unscrupulously achieved and exercised) in 26 County gov[ernmen]t circles'.[116]

An examination of the views of other leading party activists makes clear that the *Ceannaire*'s ideas on the Jewish question represented the outlook of Aiséirghe as a whole. Riobárd Breathnach, in a pamphlet that succeeded in escaping the attention of the censors, complained in 1943 of the 'Judaeo-Masonic control of [Press] Agencies' in Ireland.[117] Tomás Ó Dochartaigh was another who frequently ventilated the opinion that 'Jews and Freemasons controlled [Ireland's] money while want stalked the land'.[118] A full-blown exposition of Aiséirghe's paranoiac fantasies was offered nine months later by Pádraig Ó Fiannghusa [Patrick Fennessy], in the course of a lengthy published gloss upon the party's platform. Pointing out that the true menace to Irish civilisation derived not from external aggression but 'peaceful penetration', he explained that

> There is a certain race of people who are expert at this vile method of breaking down the spiritual barriers of nations, thus endeavouring to make all people cosmopolitan in the worst sense, thereby preparing world domination for themselves. We know the methods these sly boys employ to subjugate the nation under the guise of international peace and goodwill ... Those parasites have already dominated most of the Anglo-Saxon countries ... It is sheer nonsense to endeavour to Gaelicise Eire and yet not to strike at these sources of foreign power ... The point I wish to stress most in this article is that Ailtirí na hAiséirighe are fully conscious of the methods by which our freedom is assailed and have a plan to combat the assault successfully.[119]

114 Department of Justice: Office of the Controller of Censorship files, 4/45, R. 42, NAI.
115 See D. Fahey, *The Kingship of Christ and Organized Naturalism* (Cork: Forum, 1943).
116 Ó Cuinneagáin to Ó hUrmoltaigh, n.d., Ó hUrmoltaigh papers.
117 R. Breathnach, *An Dá Shruth–The Two Currents* (Cork: Glún na h-Aiséirghe, 1943), p. 15.
118 *Dungarvan Observer*, 5 June 1943.
119 *Ibid.*, 25 March 1944.

Ó Fiannghusa spoke too soon, for at the time of his article's appearance – as Aiséirghe activists impatiently pointed out – no such plan existed. At the party *Comhdháil* [convention] six months later, Gearóid Ó Broin demanded that 'the outlook and stance of Aiséirghe concerning the question of aliens and Masons be clearly publicised, especially [the policy] to be applied by an Aiséirghe government'. For the Cork branch, Seán Ó hÉanraic presented a motion prohibiting members from engaging in any form of transaction with alien-owned businesses, or 'patronising any doctor or lawyer or dentist who is not an Irishman and a Christian'.[120]

Possibly responding to such pressure from below – although there can be no question that in this area party members were pushing at an open door – Ó Cuinneagáin decided that Aiséirghe required a definitive statement of policy on the Jewish question. The task was entrusted to Ó hUrmoltaigh, an engineer from Cork who had ascended rapidly through the movement's ranks since joining in the spring of 1944. Ó hUrmoltaigh's first effort, a 4,000-word handwritten manuscript entitled 'Ireland and Israel', is noteworthy for its comparative sophistication and repudiation of the more hackneyed anti-Jewish themes: measured against the admittedly undemanding standard set by the majority of such productions, it may be the most technically-accomplished piece of Irish anti-Semitic literature ever written. Ó hUrmoltaigh began by dismissing a priori the overheated claims of his party colleagues that 'the Jews are pledged in long-standing conspiracy to destroy our civilisation, that the Jew is the sworn enemy of Christianity'.[121] As history demonstrated, it was not Judaism but the Reformation that had 'led Europe to the perdition she faces today … She was not tricked by any infiltration of Jews into surrendering her treasures. It was German heresy and English debauch and pillage that robbed the people of Christ's Sacrifice'. The worst charge that might be levelled against the Jews was that they had taken advantage of the chaos produced by the centuries-long civil war of Western Christendom to advance their own interests, but that war had not been of their making.

For that reason ignorant anti-Semitism, motivated by hatred and bitterness, was not only immoral, but condemned to defeat its own purposes. The same could be said of the various expedients popularly canvassed as solutions to the Jewish problem. Proposals for 'the elimination of the Jewish minority by destruction' were 'quite unthinkable', whereas mass expulsions or the creation of a Zionist homeland could

120 Minutes of second Comhdháil, 28 October 1944, 5/2/2, GÓCP.
121 Ó hUrmoltaigh, 'Ireland and Israel', n.d., Ó hUrmoltaigh papers.

be ruled out on the grounds of impracticality or, in the case of the former, moral indefensibility. On the other hand, pious liberal hopes that the problem could be dealt with by ignoring it or denying its existence were equally futile. 'Assimilation ... would indeed be completely satisfactory if it could be applied. The lesson of history is however quite decisive. The Jews alone are unique in this respect that they cannot be absorbed by their hosts.'

The essence of the matter, according to Ó hUrmoltaigh, was that 'the problem is one of race and not of religion'. There was nothing inherent in the Jewish creed that made co-existence with Gentiles an impossibility; indeed, weighty Jewish authorities in every era had preached the brotherhood of man and the rule of universal justice as duties binding upon all who followed the law of Moses. The difficulty lay rather with the distinctive characteristic of the race: its extraordinary singlemindedness and determination in the pursuit of its goals.

> What we regard as *avarice* in the Jew is not avarice at all in the sense that we conceive it. We are thinking of the tight-fisted gombeen, whereas it is something quite different. The Jew has in his make-up an almost fanatical tenacity of purpose, so that he directs all his efforts to the accomplishment of his end whether that end be science, art, medicine, or business. When it is money he seeks, his method of achievement frequently involves shady dealing, heartless extortion, usury and the whole gamut of trickery.

Inasmuch as these Jewish tendencies were innate, and hence immutable, the most rational and Christian response was to take such action as was required to curb their evil effects. Because Ireland was faced with 'the inevitable prospect of the continuance of a Jewish minority in our midst', Aiséirghe must resist the temptation 'to use popular feeling in a muddle-headed opportunism'. The way forward, instead, was to 'ensure, in our re-building of society, that it is going to be impossible for anybody Jew or Gentile, by his financial power, to direct our lives to his own ends'. This did not mean that the state must adopt a policy of impartiality or neutrality between Jew and non-Jew. On the contrary:

> [O]ur own people must be made as independent as far as possible of the influence of the Jews in the international press, international finance, and the films. We must build up a film industry of our own. We must employ Irish news correspondents in the great cities of the world who will give us undistorted reports of international events. Our people must be weaned away from the deleterious influence of those so-called popular songs, Jewish mass-produced sensual slime, foisted on us and boosted by the Jewish dance-bands of New York. Few, I am afraid, realise the harmful effect of these voluptuous ravings.

Ó hUrmoltaigh offered other examples of the measures an Aiséirghe government might choose to adopt to deal with the Jewish question. The practice of 'concealment' by the adoption of non-Jewish names was one 'intolerable habit' to which an end would definitely be put. Striking a note of thinly veiled menace, Ó hUrmoltaigh warned that 'if the Jew wishes to be at peace with his hosts he must abandon this foolhardy policy, which serves no useful purpose and exposes him to extreme danger'. The logic of Ó hUrmoltaigh's condemnation of 'Jewish monopoly' as a 'colossal evil which has to be reckoned with' implied, at a minimum, the imposition of severe disabilities affecting Jews in commercial life, the media and the professions. The paper hinted that an Aiséirghe regime would find it necessary to 'curb immigration, [and] restrict [Jewish] political activity … by unilateral action or by agreement'. Ó hUrmoltaigh's repeated insistence upon the inassimilability of the Jewish people, and the hereditary rather than religious basis of the threat that they posed to their Gaelic neighbours, further suggested the inauguration of a system of racial classification and of sustained discrimination even against those Jews who might seek in the future to convert to Christianity. For all its apparent recognition of 'the complex human factors involved' and its aspiration 'in our dealings with the Jews [to] preserve the traditions of the past and lead the world in Christian treatment of this historic race', then, Ó hUrmoltaigh's paper revealed a deeply prejudicial mindset that differed less from the practitioners of traditional anti-Semitism than he may himself have recognised.

Regardless, Ó hUrmoltaigh's stance was considerably more tolerant than that of his *Ceannaire*. In a sharply-worded commentary on the draft, Ó Cuinneagáin dismissively referred to the 'very fair-minded' approach taken by his subordinate, but took him to task for omitting any positive statement of Aiséirghe policy and for prioritising educational rather than legislative measures as the preferred response to be taken. The correct line for the party to follow, Ó Cuinneagáin specified, was one that dealt directly and unambiguously with the problem.

> Our policy permissive plus *control* of ordinary social and economic activities of Jews, requiring them to conform to Christian standards in business. *Never* permitting them to attain or retain a dominant position in any branch of industry or finance, or in any sphere of activity outside the practice of their religion. The historically sinful immorality of the Jew not sufficiently stressed. No good in gainsaying that Jewry is the antithesis of Christianity – its arch-enemy. The Jew looks for a *worldly Messiah*. Emphasise that in fact the problem in Ireland *is* an urgent one.[122]

122 Untitled and undated Ó Cuinneagáin minute, *ibid*. Emphases in original.

His dissatisfaction with Ó hUrmoltaigh's work notwithstanding, Ó Cuinneagáin agreed to allow a condensed version of the paper to be prepared for public distribution. Five weeks before the end of the war, he submitted an 800-word draft, prepared by Ó hUrmoltaigh, to the censor for permission to issue as a party handbill. Although 'Aiséirghe and the Jewish Question' drew heavily on its predecessor, the new leaflet contained a number of significant differences. Reflecting a growing public awareness of the scale of Nazi atrocities, the document disavowed any intention on Aiséirghe's part 'to attack or make a holocaust of any section of the community', or to 'exclude' Jews from any occupational field – a formula which did not, however, rule out of court the application of discriminatory measures against them. In other respects, the revision took a more uncompromising stance than had Ó hUrmoltaigh's earlier work. Asserting the need for an end to immigration and to 'the anonymous press agencies … the unseen hand in politics and finance … and the subterfuge of the false name', the draft promised 'legislation, much of it of a very urgent nature', so as to ensure that no section of the community regardless of its creed might undermine the common good. 'Aiséirghe and the Jewish Question' was at pains to stress, however, that these measures alone could not address the 'real Jewish problem – the problem of an alien body within the nation'. While it forbore to specify how that difficulty would ultimately be overcome, the document congratulated itself on the 'Christian charity and justice' of its approach. This, it asserted, was 'the best answer we can give to those dishonest propagandists who call us Facists [*sic*] … [while] our determination to tackle the matter vigorously and courageously should dispose of those who are inclined to classify Ailtirí na h-Aiséirghe as merely another political party with new personnel'.[123]

Despite the prevalence of anti-Semitism in Irish political life in the 1940s, Aiséirghe's growing preoccupation with the Jewish question did distinguish it in important ways from mainstream political parties. Their comfort with and occasional exploitation of popular Judaeo-phobia notwithstanding, no attempt was ever made by Fine Gael, Fianna Fáil, Labour or even the unreconstructed founders of Clann na Talmhan to deprive Irish Jews of their status as acknowledged, if rarely valued, members of the national community. Certainly none of these parties considered it necessary to emulate the extreme-right movements of the Continent in adopting a statement of policy dealing with the 'Jewish question'. Though a high degree of imperviousness to insult was always necessary, individual Jews might ascend to prominent positions in Irish political life, as the careers of such

123 Ó hUrmoltaigh, 'Aiséirghe and the Jewish Question', n.d. [c. March 1945], *ibid*.

figures as Robert Briscoe and Gerald Goldberg attested. There were, moreover, unspoken but definite limits of acceptability applicable to the public expression of anti-Jewish sentiments by mainstream politicians. The criticism, muted though it was, that greeted the statement in the Dáil by a youthful TD, Oliver J. Flanagan, that there was 'one thing that Germany did, and that was to rout the Jews out of their country',[124] may have been directed as much against the appalling crudity of his rhetoric as against the intolerance that underlay it. Nevertheless, coming as it did at a moment when news of the Nazi extermination programme against the Jews was already a matter of public knowledge,[125] Flanagan's attack marked a point beyond which 'respectable' parties were unwilling to go. Aiséirghe's readiness to advance still further, at little cost to its political standing, showed that for thousands of young Irishmen and women in the 1940s respectability was at a considerable discount.

Aiséirghe: fascist innovator?

Ailtirí na hAiséirghe aspired to a unique position in Irish politics: author of a comprehensive ideological programme drawn from and sustaining the native culture. As such it sought to differentiate itself from every previously existing political movement. Neither Fianna Fáil, Fine Gael nor the Labour Party was able to lay claim to anything remotely resembling a fully-formed philosophical or theoretical framework for their policies. The single organisation that could, the Communist Party of Ireland, was able to do so only by importing from overseas a doctrine far better adapted – and even then inadequately – to the Germany of the mid-nineteenth century than to the Ireland of the twentieth, complete with an inappropriate and mystifying vocabulary that rang false to the vast majority of its Irish hearers. (Aiséirghe activists noted wryly that the Irish language contained no Gaelic equivalent for 'proletariat'.) Attempts by a pair of University College, Cork academics, Michael Tierney and James Hogan, to devise a theoretical basis for Blueshirtism grounded in an amalgam of the 'liturgical' elements of Mussolinian fascism and of the Papal encyclicals had died stillborn after the fading-away of O'Duffy's populist movement. There was some basis, therefore, to Aiséirghe's claim to be the sole Irish party to have approached the problem of governance systematically and worked out its proposals from first principles.

124 91 *DP–Dáil*, c. 572 (9 July 1943).
125 D. Keogh, *Jews in Twentieth-Century Ireland: Refugees, Anti-Semitism and the Holocaust* (Cork: Cork University Press, 1998), p. 173; B. Wasserstein, *Britain and the Jews of Europe 1939–1945* (Oxford: Oxford University Press, 1988), pp. 172–4.

Viewed in retrospect, however, it appears that Aiséirghe's ideological apparatus was at least as much a hindrance as a help. This was partly the result of its own parochialism and lack of sophistication. For all their claims to have taken ideas seriously, Aiséirghe's leaders were philosophical and political dilettantes. Victims of the contemporary Irish education system's indifference to modern languages and positive hostility to the social sciences,[126] they possessed an inadequate knowledge of the main currents of Continental European thought since 1789 – an era whose intellectual fruits, they considered, were in any event too debased to merit serious scrutiny. As a result, there was little in Aiséirghe's ideology to attract, or to satisfy, those seeking a systematic and rigorously thought-out political system. The quasi-religious intrinsic appeal of Marxism, embodying as it did 'an unbroken line of descent from the founding fathers, [and] claiming scriptural precedent for [its] policies',[127] found no echo in Ó Cuinneagáin's organisation. Few disputes within the movement were ever settled by the recitation by one of the contending parties of an apposite extract from *Aiséirghe Says ...*, nor was it common for members to apply to the *Ceannaire* for guidance as to the correct 'line' to be followed in any given political situation.

In economic policy too, there was less to Aiséirghe's doctrine than met the eye. Some observers have seen in Ó Cuinneagáin's *étatisme* a quasi-socialist commitment to economic egalitarianism and the promotion of the interests of the working class. Such an interpretation is unwarranted. There was undoubtedly a strong bias towards asceticism in the movement's ethos: the fact that no Aiséirghe official received a wage exceeding £2.10.0 for a work-week averaging seventy-two hours was aired prominently in party publications.[128] But with the exception of the mooted Labour Comradeship Corps, the ideal of social levelling was conspicuous by its absence from Aiséirghe policy statements. Rather than seek a classless society, the party promised to include within its ranks elements 'from every class in the state' and explicitly repudiated the suggestion that Irish business-owners were *ipso facto* 'ruthless exploiting capitalists'.[129] The right to own private property, it maintained, was as fundamental a principle as 'that a man shall own his own soul'.[130] Like Fianna Fáil, although to a far greater degree, its economic radicalism 'was not socialist or left-wing, but

126 See D. H. Akenson, *A Mirror to Kathleen's Face: Education in Independent Ireland 1922–1960* (Montreal: McGill-Queen's University Press, 1975), pp. 74, 76.
127 R. Samuel, *The Lost World of British Communism* (London: Verso, 2006), p. 58.
128 See, e.g., *Aiséirghe for the Worker*, p. 19.
129 *Aiséirghe Says ...*, p. 10; *Aiséirghe for the Worker*, p. 6.
130 *Aiséirghe for the Worker*, p. 16.

rested on the view that it was necessary to generate socio-economic development for inclusive nationalist ends'.[131]

Lastly, Aiséirghe's ideological sclerosis proved a formidable handicap to a party which claimed to base its appeal on the strength of its ideas. The almost obsessive degree of centralisation maintained by Ó Cuinneagáin meant that there was no other source of new thinking within the movement, while the *Ceannaire's* reluctance to delegate even comparatively trivial responsibilities to his subordinates left him with little time and less energy for policy formation. Even had Ó Cuinneagáin enjoyed more leisure, however, it is most unlikely that he would have taken advantage of it to revise or modernise Aiséirghe's ideology. The dogmatism that prevented him throughout his lifetime from acknowledging personal errors or faults was not conducive to reappraisal of fundamental tenets. This resistance to new ideas was to be especially problematical in light of the pace at which world events were occurring, leaving Aiséirghe after the Emergency to confront a post-fascist world with doctrines that had been conceived during totalitarianism's high tide. It was scarcely to be wondered at that so many of the movement's adherents confessed to supporting it despite, rather than because of, its detailed policies.

The foregoing considerations raise the question of whether a party afflicted by so many ideological limitations can be acknowledged as having made any distinctive contribution to the corpus of fascist thought. Some observers, indeed, have gone so far as to question whether it ought to be accommodated within this category at all. John A. Murphy, for example, has maintained that though Aiséirghe 'was sometimes accused of anti-semitism, to describe it as fascist would be both facile and unhelpful'.[132] Such a view, however, is impossible to sustain. In the first place, Ailtirí na hAiséirghe members at all levels never questioned that they belonged to an organisation drawing from the same wellsprings as other extreme right-wing totalitarian movements in Europe. While Aiséirghe activists occasionally disclaimed 'Fascist' or 'Nazi' affiliations – although the frequency of such disavowals increased notably from 1944, when the tide of battle had turned decisively against the Axis[133] – they did so on the narrow semantic ground of repudiating allegiance to Mussolini or Hitler respectively rather than the broad doctrines with

131 B. Girvin, *From Union to Union: Nationalism, Democracy and Religion in Ireland – Act of Union to EU* (Dublin: Gill & Macmillan, 2002), p. 73.

132 J. A. Murphy, 'The Irish Party System, 1938–51', in K. B. Nowlan & T. Desmond Williams, eds, *Ireland in the War Years and After 1939–51* (Dublin: Gill & Macmillan, 1969), p. 157.

133 An MI5 report noted that 'at their meetings there is less reference to Nazi ideals. The organisation seems to be finding an intellectual refuge in Dr. Salazar'. 'Irish Affairs (The General Situation in Éire)', 1 January 1944, QRS/206, TNA DO 121/85.

which both dictators were associated. Both at the time and in retrospect, members of the leadership cadre made no secret of their recognition of Aiséirghe as an explicitly fascist movement. Dónall Ó Maolalaí, who rose from membership in Craobh na hAiséirghe to a position on the Ard-Chomhairle of the Ailtirí, acknowledged: 'Gearóid was a fascist ... He was influenced by Hitler, Mussolini, by Salazar and by Perón in Argentina – even though Perón was left-wing ... I accepted Gearóid's fascism because that was a means to an end'.[134] His Ard-Chomhairle colleague Aindrias Ó Scolaidhe concurs: 'I wouldn't protest if somebody said, "You were all Fascists" ... I had great respect for Mussolini'.[135] The same is equally true of ordinary members and supporters. Deasún Breathnach, later to become film critic for the movement's newspaper, recalls among his Aiséirghe acquaintances 'a lot of admiration for Hitler and Mussolini', though he adds in justification that '[a]t that time we didn't know anything about what fascism really was'.[136] Others appear to have been better informed. One adherent, a teacher from Kiltimagh, Co. Mayo, in the course of a 1943 letter, intercepted by the postal censorship, that expressed regret over the fall of Mussolini, informed her correspondent: 'I joined "Ailtirí na hAiséirighe" this year. All my friends in it are very pro-Axis. The party has a Fascist programme also'.[137] Another, a serving soldier who joined the movement in 1945, reported that the Dublin branch of which he was briefly a member consisted entirely of 'Nazis and people who were in the I.R.A'., and that its songs consisted of the *Horst Wessel Lied*, the *Wacht am Rhein* and similar anthems.[138] A third gave as his reason for adhering to Aiséirghe his conviction that its 'totalitarian Fascism' stood as the only viable alternative to 'totalitarian Bolshevism' or 'totalitarian Bureaucracy'.[139] A fourth, who had initially volunteered to assist Ó Cuinneagáin when the latter was involved with Córas na Poblachta, described himself as 'a National Socialist [who favours] a totalitarian state organised on corporate lines'; wrote poetry in praise of Hitler; and was in the habit of closing his correspondence with the expression 'Sieg Heil!'[140] It is clear, therefore, that those who joined Aiséirghe were under no illusions whatever as to the nature of the organisation of which they were a part.

Nor can there be any question – setting to one side the ongoing lively controversy as to the existence and nature of the so-called 'fascist

134 Dónall Ó Maolalaí, author interview, 16 July 1999.
135 Aindrias Ó Scolaidhe, author interview, 22 July 1999.
136 Deasún Breathnach, author interview, 31 July 2005.
137 M. Carney to R. Stiano, n.d. [letter intercepted 28 July 1943], G2/2988, DDMA.
138 Liam Mac Domhnaill to Ó Cuinneagáin, dated 'September, 1945', 9/2/18, GÓCP.
139 Torlach de Grae [Terence Gray] to Ó Cuinneagáin, 19 December [1942], 9/2/32, *ibid.*
140 J. N. R. Macnamara to Ó Cuinneagáin, 29 October 1941, G2/0298, DDMA.

minimum'[141] – that Ailtirí na hAiséirghe conforms as faithfully to the emerging consensual scholarly models of 'generic fascism' as do its better-known Continental counterparts. Roger Griffin's definition of fascism as 'a genus of modern, revolutionary, "mass" politics which ... draws its internal cohesion and driving force from a core myth that a period of perceived national decline and decadence is giving way to one of rebirth and renewal in a post-liberal new order'[142] is as applicable to Aiséirghe as Emilio Gentile's more lengthy taxonomic classification:

> [Fascism is] a modern political phenomenon, which is nationalistic and revolutionary, anti-liberal and anti-Marxist, organised in the form of a militia party, with a totalitarian conception of politics and the State, with an ideology based on myth; virile and anti-hedonistic, it is sacralised in a political religion affirming the absolute primacy of the nation under-stood as an ethnically homogeneous organic community, hierarchically organised into a corporative State, with a bellicose mission to achieve grandeur, power and conquest with the ultimate aim of creating a new order and a new civilisation.[143]

It is, in fact, precisely in the context of Gentile's discussion of the fascist 'sacralisation of politics' that Aiséirghe's ideological distinctiveness can most clearly be perceived.[144] During much of the twentieth century, the assumption by many commentators that Christianity, and especially Catholicism, was compatible with fascism seemed too obvious to require analysis, the connection between them being expressed by the portmanteau term 'clerico-fascism'. Subsequent scholarship has largely discredited this association, recognising that the authoritarian right-wing movements which gained the most enthusiastic support from elements of the Christian churches – those of Franco, Salazar, Pétain and even O'Duffy – were conservative, backward-looking and anti-modern, having little in common with fascism beyond external appearance and 'liturgical' practice. While noting the extent to which Christian clergymen and members of the faithful, individually or in groups, participated in or collaborated with fascist movements, researchers like Juan Linz have emphasised the essential incompatibility between fully realised fascism and 'all

141 See, e.g., R. Eatwell, 'On Defining the Fascist Minimum: The Centrality of Ideology', *Journal of Political Ideologies* 1:3 (October 1996); R. O. Paxton, *The Anatomy of Fascism* (New York: Knopf, 2004).

142 R. Griffin, *International Fascism: Theories, Causes and the New Consensus* (London: Arnold, 1998), p. 14.

143 E. Gentile, 'Fascism, Totalitarianism and Political Religion: Definitions and Critical Reflections on Criticism of an Interpretation', *Totalitarian Movements and Political Religions* 5:3 (Winter 2004): 329.

144 See especially his *Il culto del littorio: la sacralizzazione della politica nell'Italia fascista* (Bari: Laterza, 1993).

organizations and movements that can be conceived as international in character', including the Catholic Church.[145]

More recently, however, scholars have begun to re-examine the complex relationship between modern political ideologies that purport to provide – or claim the authority to impose – a 'total' philosophy of life, and the network of symbols, rituals and myths that are conventionally associated with religious practice. This interaction, whose outlines are only beginning to be delineated, extends far beyond the simple (and cynical) manipulation of mystical elements for political ends. Rather, it suggests that the appearance of fascism marks the point of breakdown between the sacred and secular spheres in face of the crisis of modernity, a challenge to which in the early twentieth century neither traditional political parties nor the Churches were able adequately to respond. The dynamic element of fascism that serves to explain the extraordinary range of its appeal despite the cultural and historical particularities of the various societies in which it emerged, therefore, may indeed be that 'palingenetic' character identified by Griffin – but one that is to be interpreted as representing a personal and collective spiritual experience as well as a political metaphor.[146]

It is in this respect that a study of Ailtirí na hAiséirghe holds particular significance beyond its purely domestic context. Aiséirghe's principal *raison d'être* was to assert and to provide a practical demonstration not merely of the possibility of coexistence between theocentric and totalitarian philosophies, but of the complete realisation of Christianity within the technologically liberated integral state. In so doing it distinguished itself from traditional conceptions of theocratic rule – although Ó Cuinneagáin once idiosyncratically (and doubtless ignorantly) cited the short-lived Ecuadorian 'Theocratic Republic' (1869–75) of Gabriel Garcia Moreno as a potential role-model[147] – as well as from those totalitarian systems like Mussolini's that, as Gentile asserts, 'did not attempt to hijack traditional institutionalised religion, but, on the contrary, attempted to establish a form of symbiotic relationship with it, with the aim of incorporating it into the movement's own mythical and symbolic universe, thereby making it a component of

145 J. J. Linz, 'Some Notes Toward a Comparative Study of Fascism in Sociological Historical Perspective', in W. Laqueur, ed., *Fascism: A Reader's Guide* (Harmondsworth, Middlesex: Penguin, 1982), p. 26.
146 See R. Griffin, *The Nature of Fascism* (London: Routledge, 1993), pp. 32–40. In this earlier work, Griffin sought to establish a sharp distinction between 'political ideology' and what he regarded as the unhelpful concept of 'political religion'. He has since retreated from this position.
147 'Ireland a Missionary-Ideological State', 10/2/11, GÓCP.

secular religion'.[148] Such a conception also differs significantly from what at first glance might be considered Aiséirghe's closest European counterpart, the Romanian Legion of the Archangel Michael (or 'Iron Guard'), headed by Corneliu Z. Codreanu. This movement too, in the words of one of its principal ideologues, Mircea Eliade, had 'a spiritual and Christian meaning ... the reconciliation of the Romanian nation with God'.[149] In the Legion's case, however, this seems not to have gone far beyond the recruitment (or dragooning) of elements of the Romanian Orthodox clergy in its own cause and the exploitation of some of the more primitive aspects of peasant spirituality. It did not preclude the wholesale adoption from German National Socialism of explicitly pagan, *völkisch* and eugenicist doctrines.[150] Nor did it prevent the Legion from engaging in actions that, as Codreanu himself was to acknowledge, were 'incompatible with Christianity, even his form of militant Orthodoxy'.[151] Lastly, the extremely strong anti-modernist bias of the Legion, represented most visibly in its monarchism, its valorisation of the rural smallholder and its hostility to industrialisation and urbanisation, at the least leaves open to question its categorisation as a genuine fascist movement.[152]

Aiséirghe, in contrast, not only foregrounded its 'ultra-modernity' but sought to show that Christianity could be fully reconciled with the demands of an advanced industrial civilisation. The rationally organised totalitarian state would function as the linch-pin connecting, and directing, the two. This in turn was to form the basis of a unique concept: a fascism designed explicitly for export. Throughout the

148 E. Gentile, 'The Sacralisation of Politics: Definitions, Interpretations and Reflections on the Question of Secular Religion and Totalitarianism', *Totalitarian Movements and Popular Religions* 1:1 (Summer 2000): 23.

149 Quoted in R. Ioanid, *The Sword of the Archangel: Fascist Ideology in Rumania* (Boulder, CO: East European Monographs, 1990), p. 146.

150 An additional complication was the insistence of leading Legion ideologues like Nae Ionescu, professor of logic and metaphysics at the University of Bucharest, that Catholics and other non-Orthodox Christians could never be part of the Romanian nation. 'Catholicism and Orthodoxy are not simply religions that have some differences of dogma and culture, but two fundamentally different understandings of existence in general.' Such formulations called into question the relevance of Legionary principles beyond Romania's borders. Quoted in P. A. Shapiro, 'Faith, Murder, Resurrection: The Iron Guard and the Romanian Orthodox Church', in K. P. Spicer, ed., *Antisemitism, Christian Ambivalence, and the Holocaust* (Bloomington, IN: Indiana University Press, 2007), p. 154.

151 S. M. Cullen, 'Leaders and Martyrs: Codreanu, Mosley and José Antonio', *History* 71:233 (October 1986): 426.

152 For these reasons, Alain Colignon classifies the Legion as a movement of the 'radical right'. Roger Griffin, for his part, sees it as a 'para-fascist' movement, by which he means one that co-opts the 'externals' of fascist organisations as 'a cosmetic ploy to retain hegemony, to manipulate rather than to awaken genuine populist energies'. See A. Colignon, 'Les droites radicales en Roumanie: 1918–1941', *Transitions* 34:1 (1993): 145–71; Griffin, *The Nature of Fascism*, p. 121.

1920s and 1930s, European fascist leaders had uniformly denied that their movements could be recapitulated or recreated overseas. Rooted in the specific circumstances of its own national – or racial – history, fascism needed to develop organically in each country and reflect the distinctive culture from which it emerged. Efforts by members of the short-lived *Centre internationale d'études sur le fascisme* and similar organisations to articulate some set of general principles produced nothing more substantial than vapid invocations of the 'spirit of youth' and violent disagreements about whether National Socialism was to be regarded as a perfected form of fascism or a deviation from it.[153] Though fascist movements might share a basic world-view and co-operate from time to time in their own mutual interest, the notion of 'fascist internationalism' as a universalist doctrine was a contradiction in terms. Any attempt to transplant the Mussolinian version of fascism, say, to France or Great Britain was thus doomed to failure. Aiséirghe, on the other hand, saw the universal forces of Christianity and modernity under totalitarian direction as combining not to weaken, far less replace, but to transcend the nationalist essences from which cultures and civilisations derived their vitality. Freed of unnecessary social-Darwinian accretions, the 'ideological' and the 'missionary' elements of New Order politics need not be in tension. Instead they might constitute twin pillars of strength.

It should of course be acknowledged that Aiséirghe's attempted reconciliation of Christianity and the needs of a 'holistic-national radical Third Way' state[154] represented the assertion of an idea, not the working-out of a fully-fledged philosophy. Ó Cuinneagáin gave no indication that he recognised even as a possibility that the respective views of the 'National Movement' and of the Church as to what constituted the appropriately Christian course of action in any given circumstance might sometimes differ. In light of Aiséirghe's internal dynamic, it seems improbable that the *Ceannaire* in such an eventuality would be willing to permit the scope of action and the pace of development of a government headed by him to be defined by a hierarchy of which some members regarded the 1937 Constitution as dangerously advanced in its conception. It was in some respects fortunate for the party he headed, therefore, that his assumptions remained untested by experience. As with all other fascist movements, the credibility and consistency of Aiséirghe's ideology stood in direct proportion to its success in evading confrontation with reality.

153 For a discussion of these failed initiatives, see M. A. Ledeen, *Universal Fascism: The Theory and Practice of the Fascist International, 1928–1936* (New York: Howard Fertig, 1972).
154 R. Eatwell, *Fascism: A History* (London: Chatto & Windus, 1995), p. xxi.

1 Gearoid Ó Cuinneagáin (left) and Proinsias Mac an Bheatha (second from right) lead a Craobh na hAiséirghe parade.

2 Craobh na hAiséirghe publicity poster.

144

3 Ailtirí na hAiséirghe meeting in Dublin, 1943.

4 The Aiséirghe cartoonist Seán Ó Riain comments
on Irish democracy's achievements.

5 Aiséirghe youth on the march.

6 Aiséirghe's approach to the partition problem.

7 Tomás Ó Dochartaigh (left) and Gearóid Ó Broin (right).

8 The Jewish menace: a constant theme in Aiséirghe propaganda.

4

The green totalitarian band

If one of the preconditions of political success is good timing, Ailtirí na hAiséirghe began its career at a highly propitious moment. By the Emergency's mid-point, the de Valera government's popularity had diminished sharply. Wartime shortages of fuel, clothing, fertiliser and other necessities were beginning to bite hard. Industrial output had fallen by a quarter from its prewar level; and real wages by about a third. The situation was exacerbated, as Dónal Ó Drisceoil notes, by the imposition in 1941 of coercive economic measures by the British government in an effort to induce the de Valera administration to abandon neutrality.[1] By 1943 the country was being forced to make do with '25 per cent of its normal requirements of tea, 20 per cent of its requirements of petrol, less than 15 per cent of its paraffin [kerosene], 16 per cent of its gas coal, no domestic coal whatever and 22 per cent of its textiles'.[2] A mismanaged rationing and price controls system, the imposition of a wage freeze in 1941, and a ban on strikes the following year gave rise to widespread popular discontent, demonstrations and acts of disorder.[3] Even the traditional safety-valve of emigration was partially blocked, as the government took measures to prevent essential workers, especially agricultural labourers, from leaving the country. While Fianna Fáil was the object of widespread criticism for the inadequacy of its response to these difficulties, its chief rival, Fine Gael, was disorganised and demoralised, seemingly unable to offer a credible alternative to voters. The holding of nationwide local government elections in August 1942, just nine weeks after Gearóid

1 D. Ó Drisceoil, '"Whose Emergency Is It?" Wartime Politics and the Irish Working Class, 1939–45', in F. Lane & D. Ó Drisceoil, eds, *Politics and the Irish Working Class, 1830–1945* (Basingstoke, Hampshire: Palgrave Macmillan, 2005), p. 266.
2 J. F. Meenan, 'The Irish Economy During the War', in K. B. Nowlan & T. D. Williams, eds, *Ireland in the War Years and After, 1939–51* (Dublin: Gill & Macmillan, 1969), p. 36.
3 D. Ó Drisceoil, 'Keeping the Temperature Down: Domestic Politics in Emergency Ireland', in D. Keogh & M. O'Driscoll, *Ireland in World War Two: Diplomacy and Survival* (Dublin: Mercier, 2004), pp. 176–7.

Ó Cuinneagáin's Domhnach Phádraig address, thus represented a golden opportunity for a new and untainted political movement to capitalise upon popular discontent with the mainstream parties. It was, however, one Ó Cuinneagáin was unable to seize. Even if the *Ceannaire* had been willing to allow Ailtirí na hAiséirghe to take part in twenty-six-county electoral politics, a question that as yet remained unresolved, he had made no preparations that would have enabled his fledgling movement to contest an early election. Instead the benefits were reaped by other small parties and independent candidates. Both the Labour Party, which doubled its vote over the previous election, and the farmers' party Clann na Talmhan made major inroads into the support of the two leading parties, leaving them well positioned to translate their gains into Dáil seats in the general elections of the following year.

A second self-inflicted handicap was the movement's failure to issue a detailed statement of principles in English until the spring of 1943. The seriousness of this omission was underlined by the publication in December 1942 of a pamphlet issued under the auspices of the Gaelic Athletic Association entitled *National Action*. Its pseudonymous author, the retired schools inspector Joseph Hanly, was almost certainly familiar with *Aiséirghe 1942*; his work can be regarded in part as an attempt to pre-empt the more extreme elements of that document. Like Ó Cuinneagáin, Hanly called for the abolition of 'Party Politics' and the creation of a national government to implement an agreed programme of economic and social development. Social evils were to be dealt with by 'penal servitude, expulsion of aliens, and the lash'.[4] A network of parish guilds and councils would provide the government with any necessary advice or criticism in lieu of parliamentary opposition. The Irish language would be restored by every available means. Hanly rejected, however, proposals for the establishment of a dictatorship, a corporate state or a large-scale military apparatus. Dictators 'are not found or selected. They usually find and select themselves. They then impose their will on a country for better or worse'.[5] His recommended models were the right-wing personalist and paternalist regimes of Salazar and Pétain, which, he maintained, by the force of personal example rather than despotism had inculcated in their peoples a spirit of 'simplicity, honesty and Christian social teaching'.[6] Despite its relatively high cover price of one shilling, *National Action* enjoyed an extraordinary vogue, with more than 100,000 copies being sold in

---

4 'Josephus Anelius' [Joseph Hanly], *National Action: A Plan for the National Recovery of Ireland* (Dublin: Gaelic Athletic Association, 1942), p. 112.

5 *Ibid.*, p. 28.

6 *Ibid.*, p. 33.

its first year of publication. The expression 'national action' quickly became part of the contemporary political vocabulary, being applied generically to any scheme of state-directed mobilisation and regimentation along extra-parliamentary lines. In the face of this evidence of the vitality of the market for authoritarian ideas, Ailtirí na hAiséirghe chose to ignore rather than attempt to co-opt Hanly's largely monoglot Anglophone supporters. Beyond hastily retitling a broadsheet of his own 'For National Government and National Action',[7] Ó Cuinneagáin took little note of the phenomenon. Fortunately for him, Hanly's marked preference, notwithstanding the title of his manifesto, for words rather than deeds – a 'Provisional Council of National Action' was not established until 1944, while the 'National Action Party' made its belated and ignominious appearance a full decade later – meant that Aiséirghe at least did not face serious competition on the far right wing of Irish politics.[8] But Ó Cuinneagáin's lack of agility in recognising and taking advantage of such opportunities when they presented themselves was to bedevil his own movement and lead to growing tensions from within.

This does not mean that Ailtirí na hAiséirghe was foredoomed to failure. In many respects the party enjoyed significant advantages over other contemporary political movements at home and abroad. Its lack of a prewar pedigree and its isolation, both physical and intellectual, from extremist organisations on the European continent meant that its fate did not need to be determined by the outcome of the war. Aiséirghe leaders could invoke, or distance themselves from, the record of other fascist movements as tactical requirements dictated. As the party with by far the youngest age-profile in Irish politics, Aiséirghe could legitimately disclaim any responsibility for the existing condition of the country while distinguishing itself from more hidebound bodies by its youthful vigour and idealism. Repudiating the poisonous legacy of the Civil War, it was able to appeal to those who had grown weary of the bitter and futile divisions of the past while pointing the way forward to a holistic Third Way style of activism. The political environment in which Aiséirghe emerged, in short, was sufficiently favourable as to enable it to make significant progress notwithstanding the *Ceannaire's* early tactical missteps. A leadership organisation, however, ultimately stands or falls by the character and ability of its leader. Upon Ó Cuinneagáin's shoulders would rest the fortunes of his movement. The challenge was greater than any he had yet faced.

7 Its previous title had been 'For National Government and Action'.
8 Chief Insp. P. Carroll to the Secretary, Department of Justice, 14 May 1954, JUS 8/1020, NAI.

Initial reactions

Early media responses to the launch of Ailtirí na hAiséirghe and the publication of its first policy statements were mixed, if not openly conflicted. In the Irish-language reviews, the characteristic pattern was to praise Aiséirghe for its evident determination to bring about the restoration of Irish as the national vernacular, but to question the realism of its political programme. In a tongue-in-cheek 'Open Letter to Gearóid Ó Cuinneagáin' in the monthly journal *Comhar*, 'Sáirséal', a writer identifying himself as a founder-member of Craobh na hAiséirghe who had declined to follow Ó Cuinneagáin into the Ailtirí (and who most likely was Seán Ó hÉigeartaigh, director of the Irish-language publishing house Sáirséal agus Dill) gently mocked the *Ceannaire*'s aspirations to unlimited power: 'I don't know whether you believe in dictatorship *per se* or whether it's simply that because you ran Craobh na hAiséirghe as a dictator, you think that's the way to go'. He was equally unimpressed by Aiséirghe's fulminations against Freemasons: 'Why didn't you toss in the Jews while you were about it? Break their power if necessary, and to the extent that it's necessary, but don't make a meal of it [*ná déin rosc catha de*]. All of the human race are our brothers'.[9]

A somewhat kindlier stance was taken by the *Irish Catholic*. While expressing some reservations as to the practicality of many Aiséirghe proposals, the anonymous reviewer went on to add: 'For myself I prefer the person who sets a broad expanse before us to the individual lacking any ideals at all beyond constantly obstructing and mocking the efforts of others. Even if not every objective is achieved, it is better for the country and the people to have them set in motion'.[10] *An tIolar*, too, commended the movement's founders for their dedication and 'passion for the welfare of the nation', even as it deprecated the 'cheap theatricality' of their claims to 'dictatorship and even world dominion'. Oliver Cromwell, it recalled pointedly, had been the last figure in Irish history to attempt to establish a Christian state based on his personal interpretation of God's will.[11]

In the Anglophone and political press, as might be expected, opinion was a great deal more polarised. The once-supportive Ulster Union Club, before which Ó Cuinneagáin had once spoken at the invitation of its founder, Denis Ireland, now regretfully but firmly closed the door

9 'Sáirséal', 'Litir Oscailte Chuig Gearóid Ó Cuinneagáin', *Comhar*, November 1942.
10 *Irish Catholic*, 3 September 1942.
11 'F. Mac M'., 'Young Men Plan for a New Ireland', *An tIolar/The Standard*, 28 August 1942.

upon the prospect of friendly co-existence between the two bodies. An Aiséirghe Ireland, Seán Ó Baoghill declared in a review of *Aiséirghe Says* …, would be 'The Ireland of My Nightmares … Not since the early Nazi and Fascist days has such a programme of sheer dishonesty and trickery been offered as a policy'.[12] The journalist Myles na gCopaleen/Flann O'Brien [Brian O'Nolan], began the first of a lengthy series of scathing bilingual satires in his 'Cruiskeen Lawn' column in the *Irish Times* against Aiséirghe, a stance that was fuelled both by his own disdain for what he regarded as the excesses and absurdities of language revivalists and the fact that he was the elder brother of Ciarán Ó Nualláin.[13] The *Midland Tribune*, a newspaper traditionally sympathetic to the Labour Party, was still more hostile. In an article entitled 'Our New Fuehrer', the paper summarised Ó Cuinneagáin's objective as being the creation of 'a one-party Dáil where everyone will say "yes" to himself … There will, however, be a national collection, and that is about the only appeal to the people which the new party intends to make'.[14]

Ó Cuinneagáin responded to the various criticisms with characteristic pugnacity. He did not, he told *Comhar*'s pseudonymous author in a published reply, believe in dictatorship *'per se'*, although the argument he advanced in justification – that he sought to become 'virtually all-powerful' for a period of only seven years rather than for life – was far from reassuring.[15] (His assertion at an Aiséirghe meeting in September 1942 that 'there would be no room for debate in Ailtirí na hAiséirghe … and the leader would be supreme' also tended to underline the accuracy of Seán Ó hÉigeartaigh's characterisation of his previous leadership style.[16]) He dismissed *An tIolar*'s review of *Aiséirghe 1942* as an example of the 'reactionary opposition' he and his colleagues had always expected to encounter.[17] As for the Ulster Union Club's treatment of *Aiséirghe Says* …, Ó Cuinneagáin regretted that 'it would appear to be fruitless to endeavour to explain anything at all to an individual of the seemingly blunted intelligence of Seán Ó Baoghill. One can only pray for him'.[18]

Aiséirghe's policies, however, attracted enthusiastic praise as well as criticism in the mainstream press. In its review of *Aiséirghe Says* …,

12 S. Ó Baoighill, 'The Ireland of My Nightmares', *Club News*, March 1943.
13 The younger Ó Nualláin had been dismissed by Ó Cuinneagáin from his position as a paid official of Craobh na hAiséirghe in the summer of 1942; the belief that he had been treated shabbily by the *Ceannaire* was mentioned by several members as their reason for refusing to proceed into the Ailtirí.
14 *Midland Tribune*, 18 October 1942.
15 *Comhar*, January 1943.
16 *Irish Press*, 26 September 1942.
17 *An tIolar/The Standard*, 11 September 1942.
18 Ó Cuinneagáin to S. Ó Cinnéide, editor, *Club News*, 5 April 1943, 7/6/10, GÓCP.

Ernest Blythe's *Leader* defended Ó Cuinneagáin against the charges of dictatorship levelled against him: 'A Head of State elected for seven years and given the widest powers during his period of office might well be better able to interpret and implement the will of the people than a council in which conflicting elements would go far to neutralise one another and so render the Government incapable of prompt and effective action'. In principle, moreover, 'we see nothing wrong or repulsive in the idea of a [single] National Party', which might fill the gap in Irish public life caused by the disappearance of the old Gaelic aristocracy.[19]

The appearance of Aiséirghe was also noted with interest by the German Minister, Eduard Hempel. In a secret despatch of October 1942 to the *Auswärtiges Amt* in Berlin, he observed that despite Ireland's fundamentally Catholic and nationalist orientation, a left-wing reaction based on growing social discontent could not be ruled out: 'Whether such a tendency obtains the upper hand, or whether the apparently promising beginnings of a certain recent movement seeking a new order based on the principles of National Socialism or Fascism will gain general acceptance, cannot yet be foreseen'.[20]

Ailtirí na hAiséirghe's public launch caused G2 to refocus its attention upon Ó Cuinneagáin, who had ceased to be a target of interest since his defection from IFG/CN. His involvement with Córas na Poblachta and with the leader of the Young Ireland Association had kept him in Colonel Bryan's sights to the extent of the latter ordering the postal censorship periodically to intercept and open his incoming correspondence, but otherwise he had not been the subject of detailed scrutiny. This now changed. Aiséirghe's postal and telephonic communications were monitored; contacts within the new party were cultivated; and inquires were set in train to determine whether Ó Cuinneagáin was in contact with fascist movements overseas. No very alarming information came to light as a result of these efforts, but G2 decided nonetheless to maintain Aiséirghe and its leader under a continuous watching brief. An appreciation of Ó Cuinneagáin, probably written by Bryan in November 1942, set forth the official estimation of the *Ceannaire's* character and capabilities:

Ó Cuinneagáin is:
(1) Ambitious and fanatical in his plans – he can endure hardship and has apparently an abundance of moral courage – but he is too immature to make a good Dictator and lacks the requisite personality at present.

19 *The Leader*, 6 March 1943.
20 Telegram no. 536 from Hempel to Otto Köcher, German Minister at Berne, 22 October 1942, TNA GFM 33/99.

(2) He is anti-British and pro-German if his associates are to be regarded as a guide to his outlook.

(3) Any tendency manifested up to the present on internal politics is towards the Republican Groups but his new Dictatorship Scheme may cause complications for him.

(4) In the event of a German victory in the present war Ó Cuinneagáin would very likely be one of a number of groups [*sic*] who would embrace the New Order if he thought he could gain political power by means other than through the electorate – that he now desires political power is evident from the objects of his new organisation.[21]

The sinews of war

If state interference with Aiséirghe's propaganda effort constituted the greatest obstacle faced by the movement during the Emergency, the parlous state of its finances ran it a close second. As a youth-oriented party, Aiséirghe was never likely to be able to generate large sums of money from within its own ranks. This fact, though, was generally lost sight of as a result of the aura of secrecy surrounding the movement. Instead, foreign and domestic intelligence agencies, the police, journalists and political commentators alike speculated ceaselessly about Ó Cuinneagáin's supposedly abundant sources of money. The leading theory canvassed during the Emergency was that Aiséirghe was either the political instrument of, or heavily subsidised by, J. J. Walsh.[22] A Córas na Poblachta informant told a representative of G2 in November 1942 that Ó Cuinneagáin 'had the financial backing of J. J. Walsh who dictated certain reservations re this policy. Córas had got the offer of this support but declined owing to the effect of the stipulated ties on their policy'. The reliability of this source is open to question,[23] but Walsh's name continued to surface in connection with that of Ó Cuinneagáin. An Aiséirghe member suggested in 1944 that Walsh had supplied some or all of the large sum of money required for election deposits in the general election of that year, and a G2 minute added: 'Recent reports repeat the suggestion that a well known wealthy industrialist is financing Ailtirí na h-Aiséirghe & is in

---

21 Unsigned memorandum, 'Ó Cuinneagáin', 11 November 1942, G2/2988, DDMA.
22 See, e.g., 'Dublin Letter', *Tipperary Star*, 2 September 1944.
23 The same source also claimed that William Norton, leader of the Labour Party, was providing Córas na Poblachta with 'every support', and that the party 'had the support of Cardinal McRory and Fr. Senan, O.F.M. Cap'. All these allegations are highly improbable. Minute by Lieut. H. P. Carrick, Eastern Command, 8 November 1942, G2/X/0251, DDMA.

a position to control policy'.[24] The usually well-informed Detective-Garda Thomas Boyle of Special Branch added the names of Ernest Blythe and Nora Ashe, sister of the 1916 leader Thomas Ashe, to the list of those who had made generous contributions. Boyle cautioned, however, 'from my personal knowledge of Cunningham that he is not likely to confide in any of his friends on such matters as the identity of his hidden financial backers. In this respect it is noteworthy that Cunningham in addition to appointing himself *Ceannaire* also assumed the position of Finance Officer as provided for in the programme of the organisation'.[25] Both the American Minister, David Gray, and the British security service concurred in identifying Walsh and Blythe as Aiséirghe's principal backers, although it is probable that their information in each case derived from Irish security sources at second- or third-hand.[26]

Unusually, Gray's suspicions on this occasion proved correct. The deeply paranoid minister's record in such matters was normally extremely poor. Even after the end of the war he was to remain convinced that Irish government ministers had secretly been collaborating with Berlin and was to continue to seek evidence to bear out his suspicions. While the conflict was still under way, Gray drove almost to distraction the London bureau of the Office of Strategic Services (OSS), the US overseas intelligence agency, much of whose time was wasted chasing down the vague and implausible rumours of Nazi activity in Ireland which he collected with an avidity bordering on the obsessive.[27] Nevertheless, at a conference with OSS officers in June 1944 Dan Bryan confirmed that Walsh was indeed a financial supporter of Ailtirí na hAiséirghe.[28] He was, however, by no means the only one. In addition to those already mentioned, Ó Cuinneagáin was assisted by prosperous associates from his IFG/CN days like the pro-Nazi J. J. O'Kelly of Dalkey. Others, including wealthy Britons like Terence Gray,

24 Capt. G. C. Ryan, G2, 'Note on Craobh na h-Aiséirighe and its Offshoots Ailtire [*sic*] na h-Aiséirighe & Glún na Buaidhe', 19 May 1944; unsigned and undated G2 minute, G2/0162, DDMA.
25 Det.-Garda T. Boyle to Superintendent S. Gantly, 29 May 1943, G2/2988, DDMA.
26 D. Gray, dispatch no. 2037, 18 October 1945, 'State Dept. Dispatches 2004–2096 Outgoing Aug. 1945–Feb. 46' file, Box 10, David Gray papers, Franklin D. Roosevelt Presidential Library, Hyde Park, New York; 'Irish Affairs (The General Situation in Éire)', QRS /201, 1 March 1943, TNA DO 121/85.
27 The OSS found it expedient to pursue such fables so as to 'discourage the independent investigation of rumors by Mr. Gray'. See memorandum from SAINT, London (Puritan) to SAINT, Washington (DH001), 28 September 1944; SAINT (BB027) to SAINT (Washington), 8 June 1945, Office of Strategic Services, Record Group 226, Entry 210, box 299, 'Éire' file, NARA.
28 Memorandum from Lieut. Edward J. Lawler Jr, to Norman H. Pearson, Chief, X-2 Branch, OSS, 26 September 1944, *ibid*.

a well-connected *littérateur*; Maurice Cadell, a decorated British Army commando; and Raymond Moulton O'Brien, an oil company executive and self-styled 'Prince of Thomond', seem to have been impelled to aid Ó Cuinneagáin as much from complicated psychological motives as from their abhorrence of liberal democracy.[29] Unsolicited donations were received from enthusiasts at home and in Great Britain.[30] It is far from clear, therefore, that Walsh ever 'ran' Aiséirghe in any meaningful sense, while some indications suggest that his interest in the movement may have been episodic and short-lived. Several months before its launch, Walsh had rejected an approach by Ó Cuinneagáin for corporate assistance from Clondalkin Paper Mills and the Solus electrical company, firms of which he was a director.[31] A year later, he was publicly to call for the creation of 'a new national party of all the best elements of full-blooded nationalism outside the Fianna Fáil Party' whose mission would be to 'eliminate the half breeds and cross breeds'.[32] In light of Ó Cuinneagáin's marked aversion to any kind of external restraint, as well as his probable reaction to suggestions that he permit his own movement to be submerged within some far-right Popular Front, the notion that Walsh would ever have been accorded a position from which to dictate Aiséirghe policy seems unlikely.

The sheer ineptitude of the movement's subsequent approaches to the propertied classes lends further support to the inference that Walsh did not feature as prominently within its financial apparatus as Dublin gossip suggested. Walsh was, if nothing else, an astute and successful businessman who knew how to appeal to others of his kind. Aiséirghe's fundraising efforts during these years, in contrast, were carried out with the same combination of youthful naivety and arrogance that was later to characterise its election campaigns. A typical example was a circular letter addressed to influential members of the Dublin business community by Tomás Ó Dochartaigh in April 1944. Inviting them to a private meeting 'with a view to discussing the

---

29 Founder of the Cambridge Festival Theatre and son of the Conservative MP for Cambridgeshire, Gray produced eight books on Zen Buddhism after the war under the pseudonym of 'Wei Wu Wei'. His three-year involvement in Aiséirghe (and, indeed, his activities during the whole of the Second World War) goes unmentioned in his biography. See P. Cornwell, *Only By Failure: The Many Faces of the Impossible Life of Terence Gray* (Cambridge: Salt, 2004). Some biographical details of Cadell are given in R. de Róiste, 'An Irishman's Diary', *Irish Times*, 25 August 1999. For additional particulars of O'Brien's political activities, see pp. 281–2 below.
30 A postal censorship report noted that one well-wisher from Sheffield had sent Ó Cuinneagáin a cheque for £50 in November 1942. Undated and untitled memorandum, G2/2988, DDMA.
31 Walsh to Ó Cuinneagáin, 1 May 1942, *ibid*.
32 *Sunday Independent*, 4 July 1943.

situation and seeing in what way you can assist us', the letter pointed out that in view of 'the greatness, the sublimity and the nobility of our objective ... we feel that we have a right to any help and advice you can give us'.[33] Predictably, few of the recipients perceived their obligation to Aiséirghe in the same light. Even if they had been disposed to do so, there was little in the party's ideology to attract the well-to-do. Not many would have welcomed the prospect of a massive extension of state control of the economy, far less the commercial implications of Aiséirghe's plan for a 'just war of aggression' against the British Empire. As Ernest Blythe noted at the outset, Ó Cuinneagáin's fundraising programme had to confront the fact that 'the wealthier sections of the community are unlikely to have anything to do with him'.[34] Aiséirghe's public appeal in March 1943 for contributions to a 'war chest' of £100,000, consequently, appears to have gone largely unanswered.

For these reasons, there seems little reason to doubt the assertion of Aindrias Ó Scolaidhe, Aiséirghe's bookkeeper from 1943, that the bulk of the movement's funds were generated by its own efforts. Senior Aiséirghe officials were encouraged to make loans, some of them quite substantial, to the movement.[35] There is no record of these debts having been repaid. An enormous variety of fundraising initiatives was set in train by local branches, ranging from patriotic exhibitions, dances and athletic contests to such culturally questionable activities as whist drives. As will be discussed in greater detail below, the distribution of the proceeds remained a bone of contention throughout Aiséirghe's history.

If the financial position at the turn of the year 1944–45 was typical, it is clear that the movement operated on a shoestring budget, at least at the centre. For the last week of October 1944, the Dublin headquarters was in receipt of £30 in income from all sources and ended the period with just £5 in liquid funds on hand. Although cash flow improved somewhat with the launch of the Aiséirghe monthly paper, which yielded a modest profit on sales as well as advertising revenue, the organisation's expenses, and overdraft, rapidly increased. By the early summer of 1945 the debts incurred by party headquarters at Harcourt Street amounted to £650, causing one Ard-Chomhairle member to propose in the interest of economy that an Aiséirghe communal

33 Circular letter by Tomás Ó Dochartaigh, 14 April 1944, 6/2/22, GÓCP.
34 *The Leader*, 27 March 1943.
35 Seán Ó hUrmoltaigh, who joined Aiséirghe early in 1944, had lent the movement a total of £110 by September that year. Ó hUrmoltaigh to Ó Cuinneagáin, 18 September 1944; Ó Cuinneagáin to Ó hUrmoltaigh, 24 September 1944, 9/2/17, GÓCP.

residence be established in Dublin for all full-time party workers.[36] The vociferous protests of the organisation's married officials led to the swift rejection of this scheme. By far the heaviest strain on the movement's finances, however, were the costs associated with elections. As part of a deliberate strategy to restrict participation in the political process to the affluent classes, the Cumann na nGaedheal government had introduced an Elections Act in 1923 requiring each Dáil candidate to lodge with the Returning Officer at the time of nomination a cash deposit of £100 – a sum equivalent to four or five months' wages for the average worker. This deposit was forfeited to the state in the event of the candidate failing to obtain one-third of the 'quota' of votes required for election.[37] Once established in office, Fianna Fáil found this provision no less useful than their predecessors had done in reducing the likelihood of a challenge from the 'men of no property'. As its authors had intended, the effect of this law was to compel upstart movements either to stake their financial future upon the unlikely prospect of achieving a first-time electoral breakthrough, or to conserve their resources and confine their campaign to a small number of constituencies. The strategy succeeded admirably in Ailtirí na hAiséirghe's case. In none of the party's Dáil contests did the amount of money spent in each constituency equal, or even approach, the sum it was compelled to raise for electoral deposits.

Membership and organisation

Although Ailtirí na hAiséirghe's central membership ledgers for the period 1942–47 have survived, it is impossible to state with any certainty how many members the movement had at any given time. Five surviving Ard-Chomhairle veterans acknowledge that the names of the great majority of those who took out party cards were never recorded by, or reported to, national headquarters. By far the most important reason for this was the financial structure Ó Cuinneagáin imposed on the organisation.

Under the Aiséirghe organisational scheme, local branches, or *cumainn*, were to be ruthlessly squeezed of funds to the benefit of the national headquarters. Article 9 of the constitution provided that the Dublin leadership was to receive 75% of the membership fees paid by individual members. That, however, was only the beginning. Because

---

36 Ard-Chomhairle minutes, 29 October 1944; 6 January 1945; 30 June 1945, 5/12/1, GÓCP.
37 The requirement for electoral deposits to be lodged was struck down as unconstitutional by the Supreme Court in 1994.

Ó Cuinneagáin expected Aiséirghe's public relations effort to be not merely a self-financing but a profit-generating enterprise, branches were required to purchase from head office on a 'cost-plus' basis all the propaganda material they used, including posters, handbills, calendars, Christmas cards and anti-partition stamps. They were allowed to retain only 20% of the takings from sales of Aiséirghe publications, a theoretical profit that was usually wiped out by Ó Cuinneagáin's insistence that full payment also be made for any unsold copies.[38] The Aiséirghe badge, a small chrome lapel-pin featuring the party symbol, yielded branches a mere 10% on sales. A weekly collection, the *bailiúcháin seachtniúil*, was to be taken among all members, and two-thirds of the proceeds remitted to Dublin. Local organisations were also expected to provide workers for the yearly door-to-door national collection, of which headquarters retained 75% of donations; to sell advertising space in Aiséirghe publications and tickets for the headquarters' (often illegal) raffles and sweepstakes; and to pay a 'tax' on the profits from local fundraising activities like flag days, dances and exhibitions.

These exactions, had they been complied with, would swiftly have rendered the countrywide organisation unviable. Ó Cuinneagáin's unremitting efforts to enforce them resulted in little more than pervading the internal operations of Ailtirí na hAiséirghe with a culture of concealment and sharp practice. The most common expedient – resorted to, according to Aindreas Ó Scolaidhe and Dónall Ó Maolalaí, by almost every branch leader throughout the country – was to maintain a separate set of local membership records rather than forwarding completed application forms to Dublin. By doing so, branches were able not only to retain for themselves the whole of their members' affiliation fees, but to count on a reliable flow of income from the weekly in-house collection. The number of these 'off-the-books' members could be significant. While on a tour of inspection in 1945, Ó Scolaidhe was particularly impressed by a 'most magnificent branch' he observed in Co. Monaghan, some 150 strong.[39] Only thirteen of these members had been reported to head office.[40] While a similar multiplier is unlikely to apply across the entire movement, there is no question that concealment of members from national headquarters was systematic and pervasive. This helps to explain the persistent failure of branches to submit the mandatory monthly reports – the

38 For this reason, Ó Cuinneagáin later found it necessary to increase the sellers' commission to 25–30%. Branches that were persistently in arrears, however, were required to pay for their materials in advance.
39 Aindreas Ó Scolaidhe, author interview, 22 July 1999.
40 Register of members, 2/1/4, GÓCP.

Ceannaire's greatest ongoing cause of complaint – and the wild fluctuations that occurred in recorded membership and income. The Cork City branch, for example, reported to Harcourt Street a membership of 127 and an income of less than £7 for the month of October 1944, but only 56 members and receipts in excess of £48 two months later. In reality, the Cork organisation was growing in numbers and financial strength throughout this period. As a general rule, the greater the physical distance separating a given branch and head office the more flagrant was the concealment of members and income: but even Dónall Ó Maolalaí, who headed a northside Dublin city branch while serving on the Ard-Chomhairle, found it necessary to resort to subterfuges of this sort to preserve his own organisation in being.[41]

Often, it was the members themselves rather than the branches who insisted that no written record of their involvement be kept. Caoimhín de Eiteagáin recalls the case of a member who was dismissed from his job after speaking from an Aiséirghe platform, and believes that many others feared similar victimisation.[42] So long as the Emergency lasted, the possibility that association with Aiséirghe might lead to arrest and internment could never be entirely excluded. While some branch leaders regarded prospective members' readiness to identify themselves openly with the movement as a test of commitment, many others were willing to accommodate the more timid by selling them an Aiséirghe badge as a token of de facto membership and permitting them to take part in activities on the same basis as those properly enrolled. So widespread did this practice become that at the end of 1943 Ó Cuinneagáin forbade *cumainn* to have emblems manufactured independently, later adding a rule to exclude all but properly registered members from branch meetings.[43] Both provisions were widely ignored. So great, indeed, was the number of sympathisers 'who do not wish to be associated openly with us yet' that in a partial reversal of his previous ruling the *Ceannaire* ordered in June 1944 that weekly collection cards be issued to these persons also.[44]

In view of these considerations, it is necessary to distinguish between three categories of 'member': those duly reported to national headquarters; those who, despite paying annual fees and receiving a party card, were recorded only on the books of their local branch; and those who, having received an emblem, regarded themselves and in turn were regarded by their branch leader as belonging to the

41 Dónall Ó Maolalaí, author interview, 15 July 1999.
42 Caoimhín de Eiteagáin, author interview, 29 July 1999.
43 Circular letter to members, 15 December 1943, 6/2/13, GÓCP.
44 Circular letter to *ceannasaidheanna*, 28 June 1944, 6/2/23, *ibid*.

movement notwithstanding their lack of formal documentation. In the peak year of 1945, only 612 members were listed in the first category. This undoubtedly understates the true number considerably. The national register contains no mention of any members at all in places like Youghal, Co. Cork, where active branches existed; in others, only the names of one or two of the officers are listed. It was even possible for Aiséirghe's elected representatives themselves never to be card-carrying members of the party, as Ó Cuinneagáin discovered when his effort in 1950 to expel Caoimhín Ó Coigligh for insubordination was stymied by the discovery that the latter had represented the party on Drogheda Corporation for the previous five years without having been formally enrolled in it. Even the national headquarters itself was compelled to confess its ignorance as to the geographical distribution, far less the approximate membership, of the movement. A meeting of the Ard-Chomhairle in June 1945 inquired whether it would be possible to find out '(1) how many branches we have at present (2) the number of members (roughly) there are in the movement (3) how many counties there are in which not a trace of Aiséirghe is to be seen'.[45] It seems that Harcourt Street never succeeded in obtaining answers to any of these questions.

How many adherents the movement could claim at any given time, therefore, can only be a matter for informed speculation even among its own leaders. Ard-Chomhairle members Dónall Ó Maolalaí, Aindreas Ó Scolaidhe and Risteárd de Róiste each consider that the number of those paying some kind of affiliation fee to Aiséirghe rose to as many as 4,000 in the summer of 1945. Estimates in this range, though at the high end of the spectrum, are not beyond the realm of possibility. The very considerable sales figures for Aiséirghe manifestos – nearly 30,000 copies of *Aiséirghe Says* ... alone had been sold by the end of 1945 – suggests that a substantial number of people were sufficiently interested in the movement as to give its policy statements a serious reception. The largest Aiséirghe meetings in 1944 and 1945 attracted audiences in the four-figure range, although Ó Cuinneagáin was compelled to admit that attendances did not necessarily translate into votes. On the other side of the equation, though, a peak membership of 4,000 means that the average size of each Aiséirghe branch must have been between 60 and 70. This figure seems improbably high, in view of the preponderance of small rural branches within the movement. Although the question is unlikely ever to be definitively resolved, a

---

45 Extract from minutes of Ard-Chomhairle meeting, 30 June 1945, 5/12/1, GÓCP. A 'back of the envelope' calculation by officials in 1945 showed the number of branches in operation at that time to have been sixty-one. For their distribution, see map, p. viii.

thirty-two-county total of about 2,000 'self-identified' members in the late summer of 1945 seems most consistent with the evidence.

As a 'leadership' movement, Ailtirí na hAiséirghe sought to differentiate itself from conventional political parties by its internal organisation no less than its policies. Debates, motions, amendments, rules of order and the petty-bourgeois paraphernalia of 'club' life were to have no place in its operations. Rather, the Aiséirghe branch was to be 'a kind of Flying Column ... ever-enthusing the people, ever-preaching the Aiséirghe gospel to them'. In a circular letter of January 1944, Ó Cuinneagáin laid down the procedure to be followed by local branches at their weekly meetings:

> Long discussions are not to be permitted at *cumann* meetings. The person in authority will answer any questions that may be put to him, if he considers it appropriate. It is unnecessary to answer every question. Ailtirí na hAiséirghe is not a society for debating and squabbling. Nevertheless, it is a recommended practice to read an extract from *Aiséirghe Says* ... at each meeting and to explain it more fully to the membership.
>
> All meetings to be concluded with the singing of *Amhrán na bhFiann* [the national anthem].[46]

The Ard-Chomhairle amplified this message, reminding officers that their role was to 'give orders' to members rather than allow 'disputation to arise through talking and voting'.[47] The peremptory leadership style of the headquarters staff in Dublin was thus emulated by the rural organisations, sometimes with unfortunate results. The head of the Clonmel branch, for example, expressed his frustration in November 1944 with the inadequacies of his local membership by expelling them en masse from the movement, only to be relieved of office in his turn ten months later for his inability to discharge the organisation's accumulated debts.[48] Aiséirghe activists' self-perception as a *corps d'élite*, sacrificing all they possessed on the altar of Irish integral nationalism, also earned them a reputation for self-righteousness that often manifested itself in personalised commentaries upon the mental and moral shortcomings not only of their political opponents but even of their own audiences.[49] Ó Cuinneagáin found it necessary to remind officials of the necessity of avoiding 'insulting "personal" speech at meetings ... It's incumbent on us to do our utmost to unify the people. Insulting speech will help little in that'.[50]

---

46 Circular letter to organisers, 28 January 1944, 6/2/20, GÓCP.
47 Ard-Chomhairle minutes, 6 January 1945, *ibid.*
48 Tomás de Léis to Ó Dochartaigh, 11 November 1944; Ó Cuinneagáin to de Léis, 25 September 1945, 7/8/4, *ibid.*
49 See, e.g., *The Leader*, 10 July 1943.
50 Circular letter to organisers, 28 January 1944, 6/2/20, GÓCP.

Other expedients to set Aiséirghe apart from politics-as-usual, however well-intended, were probably ineffective at best. The *Ceannaire's* demand that members distinguish themselves by their ascetic zeal was often seen as excessive even by well-wishers. The normally supportive *Leader*, for example, derided the proposal to forbid Aiséirghe women to use tobacco or cosmetics. The spectacle of 'a Branch Secretary with a pipe in his mouth reproving or expelling a girl member because it had been reported by credible witnesses that they had seen a cigarette case fall out of her handbag' would be deeply damaging to the movement's morale and cohesion. 'As to cosmetics the suggestion that a political organisation seeking mass support and having a serious social and economic programme ... should give up time and energy to attempt to ban the use of lipstick is really only material for the comic cartoonist'.[51] The journal was more sympathetic to Ó Cuinneagáin's rule not only that meetings should not be held in licensed premises, but that all members avoid bars both before and after meetings.[52] In rural localities, though, public houses were often the only venues large enough to accommodate branch meetings. Once again, this regulation would have caused much inconvenience had *cumainn* attempted to abide by it.

It should not be supposed that casual insubordination was rife throughout the movement. Ó Cuinneagáin intended Aiséirghe to be a Christian vanguard party, and set high standards for his followers at all levels. While the almost uninterrupted stream of written exhortations and complaints that he addressed to them might lead On the contrary impression, officials and ordinary members alike went astonishingly far to meet the requirements the *Ceannaire* laid down. Few joined Aiséirghe, and even fewer remained within the movement for long, who did not share his vision of a disciplined national organisation. If his subordinates honoured the more rigorous of his edicts more in the breach than the observance, it was less because they disagreed with his objectives than with the methods he advocated of achieving them.

Those drawn to the party tended to share from the outset its fundamental value system. Some members had backgrounds in other right-wing organisations like the Blueshirts; a very few, including the *Ceannaire's* brother, Seosamh Ó Cuinneagáin (Joseph Cunningham), had served as members of O'Duffy's pro-Franco Irish Brigade in the Spanish Civil War. The typical recruit, however, was in his or her late teens or early twenties, in keeping with Ó Cuinneagáin's conviction that it was easier to politicise the formerly apolitical than to entice

51 *The Leader*, 15 April 1944.
52 'Leitir Phearsanta', 29 March 1944, 6/2/21, GÓCP.

supporters of mainstream parties away from their existing allegiances. Anecdotal evidence, reinforced by data yielded by the surviving membership application forms, suggests that most members had had the benefit of at least some secondary education, and that the proportion of university graduates was higher than in the population at large. Students, junior-grade public servants and white-collar employees were disproportionately represented in the movement; relatively few farmers, manual workers or members of the *haute bourgeoisie* were to be found within its ranks. As the appearance of such figures as Breandán Ó hEithir and Brian Cleeve indicates, the movement was not without appeal to talented individuals in the arts. Nevertheless, Aiséirghe's social backbone was to be found among what Eric Hobsbawm calls 'the lesser examination-passing classes'. For them – as *mutatis mutandis* for their counterparts elsewhere in Europe – not the least of the attractions of 'the return of Ireland to its native language' was that 'it would become the qualification for all but the most subaltern civil service jobs and passing examinations in Irish would therefore be the criterion of belonging to the professional and intellectual classes'.[53]

According to the schedule issued by the *Ceannaire* in 1944, each Aiséirghe branch was to have a minimum of ten active members and at least five officers: a *ceannasaidhe cumainn* or branch leader, a secretary, a local organiser, a treasurer and a propagandist. Collectively these constituted the council of the branch. Although full decision-making authority was vested in the *ceannasaidhe cumainn*, his was an unenviable position. He not only was answerable to the *Ceannaire* – and the first target for the latter's wrath – but to the *Ard-Cheannasaidhe* of the district, the District Organiser, the National Organiser, and his own council. The secretary's duties were limited to record-keeping; Ó Cuinneagáin specified that the branch leader personally was to sign every item of outgoing correspondence. The local organiser's position guaranteed its holder unpopularity, involving as it did responsibility for ensuring that the leader's instructions were implemented and that every active member devoted two evenings a week to the affairs of the movement. Devising revenue-generating schemes as well as maintaining the accounts was the job of the treasurer. The propaganda officer, likewise, was expected to secure coverage for Aiséirghe in the local newspapers as well as to generate the 'ultra-modern publicity that, after prayer and self-sacrifice, distinguishes Aiséirghe's style of combat'.[54]

53 E. J. Hobsbawm, *Nations and Nationalism Since 1780: Programme, Myth, Reality* (2nd edn) (Cambridge: Cambridge University Press, 1992), pp. 118, 122.
54 'Dualgasaí Oifigeach Cumainn', 31 July 1944, 6/2/25, GÓCP.

Aiséirghe's internal ethos was strongly masculine, although individual female members could rise rapidly through the ranks. In the beginning Ó Cuinneagáin does appear to have envisaged women serving largely in a supportive capacity. Early in 1943 he invited Mairéad Brewster, the movement's most prominent Protestant member, to organise Cumann na gCailíní [the 'Girls' Club'], which he described as a service organisation for the 'girls or women or womanhood of Aiséirghe'.[55] According to the rules laid down by the *Ceannaire*, a section of Cumann na gCailíní was to be formed whenever a branch included five or more female members; the section was always to be headed by a woman. The duties of Cumann na gCailíní, several sections of which were formed in the larger urban centres as well as such lesser towns as Navan, Drogheda, and Ballina, included assisting with the activities of Óige na hAiséirghe ['Aiséirghe Youth'], arranging in each locality a weekly Irish-language party for poor children [*Fleadh na bPáistí*], providing catering at meetings and raising money on behalf of the movement.[56] No attempt, however, was made to compel female members to join Cumann na gCailíní, something that in light of the small size of some rural Aiséirghe branches would have been impracticable in any event. As the movement spread, moreover, women filled an increasing number of positions at branch level and ultimately were represented on the Ard-Chomhairle itself. The *Drogheda Independent* considered on the basis of its observation of party meetings that Aiséirghe could boast 'a bigger percentage of young women enthusiasts than that actively associated with any other political group', although in the Ireland of the mid-twentieth century this was not a difficult distinction to achieve.[57]

Geographically, Aiséirghe's centre of gravity lay along the Leinster coast and in Munster. Contrary to expectations, the movement gained few converts in the surviving *gaeltachtaí*, or Irish-speaking areas, of Connacht, west Kerry and Meath. Nor, in proportion to population, did it make great headway in Dublin city. Though Aiséirghe was never formally proscribed in the Six Counties, a combination of threats of internment, confiscation of publications and property, and suppression of meetings by police ensured that it remained in Northern Ireland an underground fringe movement. The highest concentration of branches and active members was to be found in Cork, Tipperary and Wexford. Although these areas were traditional republican heartlands, they were also sufficiently far removed from Harcourt Street

---

55 Ó Cuinneagáin to Mairéad Brewster, 22 January 1943, 7/11/2, *ibid.*
56 Minutes of Comhairle Laighean, 17 March, 12 August 1943, 5/14/1, *ibid.*
57 *Drogheda Independent*, 23 June 1945.

for branch leaders to be able to exercise a degree of local initiative. Moreover, they were among the comparatively few regions in which Aiséirghe was able to attract members disproportionately from the more educated end of the social spectrum. In contrast to the Dublin *cumainn*, whose membership was predominantly working class, Cork city and county branches included manual workers; a cadre which was 'more or less on the literary side'; and a significant number of people with university education.[58] This mixture of practical and intellectual talent, added to its financial self-sufficiency, elevated the Cork organisation above its counterparts in other regions. By 1944 its status as *primus inter pares* had been broadly acknowledged within the party. Though this was initially to be a source of strength, the southerners' growing habit of independence of mind, added to the traditional resistance of what many Dubliners exasperatedly refer to as the 'Republic of Cork' to anything smacking of dictation from the capital, was a harbinger of trouble for a movement that placed as much emphasis on the *führerprinzip* as did Ailtirí na hAiséirghe.

A slightly unconstitutional party?

For almost a year after Aiséirghe's launch, Gearóid Ó Cuinneagáin remained studiously vague as to whether his movement sought power by lawful means or was aiming at the forcible overthrow of the state. While it is possible that he had not yet resolved this matter for himself, his ambiguous stance may also have stemmed from a desire not to give his many ex-IRA recruits reason to question his militancy. Even after Aiséirghe had participated in its first election campaign in the twenty-six counties, the *Ceannaire* continued to speak of 'fighting and bloodshed' in the movement's future.[59] This deliberate obfuscation did not escape the attention of his leading supporters. As Ernest Blythe pointed out in *The Leader* during the 1943 election campaign, 'Unless he [Ó Cuinneagáin] desires to get into government at some future point, he shouldn't bother with electioneering at all. But if, however, he does want to get into government he should understand by now that there are only two roads to office, by means of the Dáil chamber or of the shedding of blood'.[60]

There are indications that Ó Cuinneagáin did briefly flirt with the idea of taking an extra-constitutional short-cut along the road to power, and may have done so even before the launch of Ailtirí na

58 Síle Bean Uí Chuinneagáin, author interview, 24 July 1999.
59 Minutes of Comhdháil Náisiúnta, 30 October 1943, 5/1/1, GÓCP.
60 *The Leader*, 12 June 1943.

hAiséirghe. A letter from Séamus G. Ó Ceallaigh to Ó Cuinneagáin intercepted by G2 in January 1942 raised questions about the latter's continuing subversive associations and aims. Ó Ceallaigh, a prominent member of both Craobh na hAiséirghe and the IRA, had recently founded a new pro-Axis republican splinter, the Anti-British Propaganda Committee, which he soon renamed the Young Ireland Association. Credibly suspected of being behind several violent attacks, including the shooting of an opponent on Eden Quay in the centre of Dublin in March 1942, the organisation engaged in a number of seditious activities. Its attempts to recruit among members of the armed forces were a cause of particular concern.[61] Ó Ceallaigh's letter referred to a suggestion Ó Cuinneagáin had apparently made that the Young Ireland Association should come 'under the leadership of Craobh na hAiséirghe'. Though Ó Ceallaigh considered such a subordinate role 'impossible', he expressed his earnest desire for co-operation with the *Ceannaire* and Craobh na hAiséirghe, and his belief that 'we could work together'.[62] Although the threat from the YIA, which was not taken very seriously in view of the body's diminutive size, was snuffed out altogether by Ó Ceallaigh's internment the following autumn, G2 remained troubled by the connection with Ó Cuinneagáin and especially disturbed by the number of active-duty servicemen and reservists who were becoming members of Ailtirí na hAiséirghe. That concern was considerably heightened the following year when information was conveyed to military intelligence of an 'alleged plot' to suborn certain officers from their loyalty to the state. According to information provided to G2 by an army lieutenant, an infantry captain from the 6th Motor Squadron had met at the Red Bank restaurant in August 1943 with some Aiséirghe friends. The Aiséirghe representatives broached with the captain the question of forming 'an armed wing to the Ailtire na h-Aiseirighe movement'; expressed interest in recruiting 'army officers like himself'; and 'offered him 2nd i[n] c[ommand of] the proposed body, if he was interested'. The lieutenant who recounted this story added that he himself had been approached by Ó Cuinneagáin the previous spring and that the *Ceannaire* had 'made similar suggestions' to him on that occasion. When intelligence officers questioned the captain at the centre of the story, the latter denied participating in any meeting at the Red Bank. He had, he said, merely had a chance encounter with a girl friend from Aiséirghe who had mentioned to him a remark by Ó Cuinneagáin that the movement

---

61 N. C. Harrington, G2 Eastern Command, to Dan Bryan, 16 April 1942; memorandum by
    Sergeant M. J. Wymes, Special Branch, 19 November 1942, G2/X/0946, DDMA.
62 Ó Ceallaigh to Ó Cuinneagáin, 29 January 1942, G2/2988, DDMA.

could not achieve its objectives except by violent means. G2 remained dissatisfied with this explanation, and recommended further investigation into the matter.[63] Other rumours of active collaboration between Aiséirghe and the IRA continued to reach G2's ears as late as 1945.[64] The authorities were unable to substantiate – nor, in most cases, to disprove – these various reports.

The security services' apprehensions about the intimacy of the relationship between Ó Cuinneagáin and leading republican militants were well-founded. Since the collapse of Saor Éire and the stagnation of Córas na Poblachta, politically conscious IRA members had been seeking a suitable outlet for their energies. To a significant number of them, especially those who were already participants in the language revival movement, Ailtirí na hAiséirghe's rhetoric of cultural renewal and completion of the 'resurrection of 1916' made a powerful appeal. So too did its uncompromising rejection of party politics. Though by no means all of those thus drawn to the new organisation were pro-Axis in their sympathies, neither were they deterred by Ó Cuinneagáin's aspirations to dictatorial power. As Todd Andrews noted of the political culture of the time, republicans 'shared the tradition of Jacobinism. It was this Jacobin streak, always present in Irish Republicanism, that so frightened our bourgeoisie'.[65] The IRA's own dismal record of internal divisions, splits, expulsions and betrayal by informants underlined, in the view of many activists, the need for discipline, unchallenged authority and unity of purpose that Ailtirí na hAiséirghe appeared to exemplify.

Ó Cuinneagáin, for his part, cultivated republican support assiduously. From his writings for *An tÉireannach* and the *Wolfe Tone Weekly* in the 1930s, he could plausibly claim membership of the broad republican community. As leader of Craobh na hAiséirghe he had developed personal relationships with many influential republican members of Conradh na Gaeilge, who respected his work on behalf of the language and had not forgotten the part he had played, however reluctantly, in securing the leadership of the organisation for the imprisoned Seán Ó Tuama in 1941. He had been prominent

---

63 Capt. G. C. Ryan, G2, 'Memo on the Alleged Plot', 28 September 1943; Ryan to Bryan, 26 October 1943, G2/X/1320, SI/256, DDMA.

64 In February that year, for example, Mairtín Ó Cadhain, then a republican internee in the Curragh, reportedly advised that 'all arms remaining in the possession of the I.R.A. should be handed over to hAiseirge [*sic*]'. Though Ó Cadhain was never a member of Aiséirghe, his literary work was published in the party's newspaper. Unsigned MI5 minute no. 1863, 26 February 1945, 'Miscellaneous Enquiries' file, part II, 474, G2/X/1091, DDMA.

65 C. S. Andrews, *Autobiography*, vol. I, *Dublin Made Me* (Dublin: Mercier, 1979), p. 230.

nationally in the activities of the Green Cross Fund, which provided inancial assistance to the families of republican internees on both sides of the Border. With the foundation of Ailtirí na hAiséirghe, he began his own outreach programme to IRA members in the Curragh and other internment camps. Under Aiséirghe's auspices, film screenings were arranged for prisoners; books and gramophone records lent; and copious quantities of Aiséirghe literature and posters provided without charge.

The effort soon began to bear fruit. A recently released Curragh internee informed Roger McHugh that 'the best of the lads below [i.e. in the camp] think that Ó Cuinneagáin seems to fit the bill', although he added that 'we don't know very much about him and I would like to get a bit of dope on him'.[66] Tarlach Ó hUid [Terence Wood], editor of the IRA newspaper *War News* and co-founder of the pirate 'Irish Republican Radio' station, was untroubled by Aiséirghe's reputation as a 'fascist organisation' and became an active member upon his release.[67] In a January 1943 letter to Ó Cuinneagáin, the IRA's Adjutant-General, Tomás Ó Dubhghaill, gave the party his broad approval.[68] As a result, republicans became leading figures in the organisation, with at least one – Gearóid Ó Broin – combining membership of the Aiséirghe Ard-Chomhairle with that of the Army Council of the IRA. Others like Seosamh Ó Duibhginn [Joe Deegan], another Curragh ex-internee who had become disillusioned with the ineffectuality of militant republicanism, were drawn to Aiséirghe because '[n]o other group was putting forth in Ireland so important a compendium of ideas in an era in which intellectual rebirth and upheaval was occurring across the world'.[69]

The prominence of republican elements within Ailtirí na hAiséirghe gave G2 valid grounds for concern, as did the suggestion that Ó Cuinneagáin was attracted by the potential of an Aiséirghe-orchestrated military *coup*. At the outset, he does indeed seem to have given consideration to the possibilities of physical force. During his IFG/CN days he had been implicated in activities very similar to those alleged against him in the August 1943 'plot'. His widow confirms that for a time 'he thought we [Ailtirí na hAiséirghe] should take up arms', though she adds that 'when he realised that nobody was interested, he

---

66 Extract from letter by ex-internee named Canty (Cregan Avenue, Limerick), to McHugh, n.d. [c. May 1943], G2/2988, DDMA.
67 T. Ó hUid, *Faoi Ghlas* (Dublin: Foilseacháin Náisiúnta, 1985), p. 198. See also A. Mac Póilin, 'Irish in Belfast, 1892–1960: From the Gaelic League to Cumann Chluain Ard', in F. de Brún, ed., *Belfast and the Irish Language* (Dublin: Four Courts Press, 2006), pp. 133–4.
68 Ó Dubhghaill to Ó Cuinneagáin, 26 January 1943, 12/1/6, GÓCP.
69 S. Ó Duibhginn, *Ag Scaoileadh Sceoil* (Dublin: An Clóchomhar, 1962), p. 63.

dropped it'.[70] If the *Ceannaire* did briefly entertain such ideas, however, he does not appear to have pursued them very far. That any concerted effort aimed at overthrowing the state could have been maintained without the knowledge of the security forces, or that Ó Cuinneagáin would long have remained at liberty in such circumstances, is equally improbable. Aiséirghe's careful avoidance of the grosser illegalities that might provoke a full-blooded repressive response from the authorities also indicates a keen awareness on the *Ceannaire*'s part of where the boundaries of permissible conduct lay.

One example of this was the question of an Aiséirghe uniform. In 1934, when confronting the threat of Blueshirtism, the de Valera government had introduced a Wearing of Uniform (Restriction) Bill that made the public display of uniform connected with a political party an offence punishable on summary conviction by three months' imprisonment. Although the measure failed in the Seanad and was not revived even in the wartime emergency legislation, it was clearly understood that the adoption of any distinctive form of attire by a political body represented a gesture of defiance that the government would certainly not ignore.[71] For this reason, Ó Cuinneagáin consist-ently resisted pressure from his subordinates to make Aiséirghe a 'shirted' movement. Within the prescribed limits, though, a good deal could be done in a similar vein. By 1944 it had become common for male Aiséirghe members to advertise their loyalties by wearing an informal attire consisting of a green shirt, an Aran belt and a yellow tie.[72] The de facto prohibition on uniform could also be circumvented to a degree by including in Aiséirghe parades a contingent of Irish dancers in traditional dress.

The measure of Aiséirghe's respect for bourgeois legality, however, was the point at which official counter-measures could be expected. As will be shown below, activists did not shy away from significant public order offences so long as the likelihood of detection and punish-ment was not high. During 1943, the movement earned a reputation for physically disrupting meetings of Dublin Corporation, the local authority for the capital, as part of its campaign to rename city streets after revolutionary heroes.[73] Although these intimidatory tactics failed to bear fruit, similar methods continued to be employed by Aiséirghe's younger and more irresponsible elements. The national leadership, for its part, generally avoided direct confrontations with the authorities.

70 Síle Bean Uí Chuinneagáin, author interview, 24 July 1999.
71 Section 15 (1) of the Offences Against the State Act, 1939, made it an offence for any unauthorised person to drill or practise 'military exercises, manœuvres or evolutions'.
72 Aindrias Ó Scolaidhe, author interview, 22 July 1999.
73 See, e.g., *Tipperary Star*, 6 November 1943.

Nevertheless, Aiséirghe members were expected to place themselves on the wrong side of the law when the interests of the movement demanded it. In the spring of 1945, for example, the Gardaí shut down one of Aiséirghe's unauthorised sweepstakes in Co. Tipperary. The Ard-Chomhairle ordered that it was to be restarted in defiance of the authorities and, when the responsible official, Muiris Mac Gearailt, proved reluctant to run the risk of prosecution, threatened him with deprivation of office unless he complied with their instruction.[74]

The balance of probabilities, therefore, suggests that Ó Cuinneagáin did not plan for the acquisition of power by unlawful means in any serious or sustained fashion. Initially, the possibility that a wave of popular support combined with military or paramilitary assistance might enable him to bypass the electoral process altogether, as Mussolini had successfully done and O'Duffy had once contemplated, no doubt seemed beguiling. But once it became clear that nothing of the kind was going to occur, he appears to have rejected any kind of *putschist* scenario and focused exclusively upon the political process. The degree to which he was dependent on republican support, however, inhibited him from openly acknowledging the fact. Instead he continued to draw comparisons between his own movement and the Sinn Féin party of 1917–19, and to demand the 'restoration' of the Republic of Pearse and Connolly notwithstanding the obvious contradictions between the aspirations of the 1916 Proclamation and those of Aiséirghe.[75]

With the passage of time, though, this balancing act became increasingly difficult to sustain. Republicans within Aiséirghe expected the party to hew to the IRA's larger agenda, and were prone to defect en masse when it did not. Tomás Óg Ó Murchadha reported to Ó Cuinneagáin in February 1944 that the members of the Balbriggan, Co. Dublin branch had announced that they were 'leaving the movement because I said ... not to go around extolling the Republican Army. I believe that they are all in that organisation, which is why the youth of the town aren't helping us'.[76] Aiséirghe activists like Caoimhín de Eiteagáin, for their part, 'resented' the IRA 'because they didn't do a damn thing about the revival of the language'.[77] Within the organisation, complaints that Ó Cuinneagáin was allowing the misleading impression to prevail that Ailtirí na hAiséirghe was a mere 'appendix'

74 Ard-Chomhairle minutes, 17 March 1945, 5/12/1, GÓCP.
75 E.g. the former's guarantee of 'religious and civil liberty' and its promise of a government 'representative of the whole people of Ireland and elected by the suffrages of all her men and women'.
76 Ó Murchadha to Ó Cuinneagáin, 10 February 1944, G2/2988, DDMA.
77 Caoimhín de Eiteagáin, author interview, 29 July 1999.

of the republican movement grew steadily more insistent. Divisions over the question of Aiséirghe's stance vis-à-vis armed republicanism would ultimately become so deep as to threaten the survival of the party itself.

Inter-party relations

In view of Gearóid Ó Cuinneagáin's record of splitting or abandoning movements with whose direction he had come to disagree, it was to be expected that Ailtirí na hAiséirghe would jealously guard its independence. According to his sister Bernadette, the *Ceannaire* on numerous occasions spurned offers of financial aid that he thought might compromise his freedom of action.[78] Nonetheless, such a stance did not necessarily preclude tactical co-operation or local understandings with other political movements. During the Emergency Aiséirghe was to engage in both.

The existing party with which Aiséirghe possessed the closest affinities was of course Córas na Poblachta. Less sectarian than Ó Cuinneagáin's movement, Córas seems to have welcomed the advent of the new body and to have volunteered its assistance. Aindrias Ó Scolaidhe's first speech upon an Aiséirghe platform was a lightly modified version of a previously delivered address by a Córas na Poblachta speaker, the text of which the latter provided him.[79] Domestic and foreign intelligence agencies also noted the seemingly co-operative relationship between the two parties. A minute by G2's Eastern Command of November 1943 claimed that Ó Cuinneagáin and the Aiséirghe Ard-Chomhairle desired 'fusion with Córas but owing to the strength of J. J. Walsh's financial backing they could not take the chance at present'. The accuracy of this statement is highly questionable: but despite the ideological similarities between the two movements the likelihood of their combining forces was at best slim. Ó Cuinneagáin was dismissive of Córas' prospects, informing a clerical supporter that 'they are not in any respect better than was Fianna Fáil 10 years ago'.[80] As the Eastern Command intelligence report recognised, moreover, a serious obstacle to any coalition was Córas na Poblachta's lack of internal cohesion. Its executive committee, G2 noted, was made up of 'four ex-Army men, old [pre-Civil War] I.R.A., ex-Blue Shirts, and a number of I.R.A. who had been active up to comparatively recently'. While a majority desired a combination

78　Bernadette (Bernie) Cunningham, author interview, 21 October 1998.
79　Aindrias Ó Scolaidhe, author interview, 22 July 1999.
80　Ó Cuinneagáin to Fr D. Mac Eochagáin, 22 August 1949, 7/6//26, GÓCP.

of the principal extreme nationalist movements including Aiséirghe, the three most prominent leaders – Roger McCorley, Simon Donnelly and Seán Dowling – 'did not favour fusion with the other organisations as they believed Córas would be submerged'.[81] Exploratory discussions with Ó Cuinneagáin on the possibility of collaboration reinforced Córas na Poblachta's fears that the *Ceannaire* desired not an alliance of equals but an outright takeover by Aiséirghe under his own leadership. Accordingly, proposals for a merger were dropped, though the two organisations continued to maintain cordial relations. British observers, however, remained anxious about the formation of an extremist popular front. In a 1943 report, John Betjeman offered as an explanation for the Irish government's unwillingness to adopt a more overtly pro-British stance de Valera's supposed anxiety that the 'small totalitarian parties, the I.R.A., Glún na Buaidhe ... Ailtirí na hAiséirghe, Clann na Talman [as well as] the less totalitarian but equally anti-British sections – the old I.R.A., Córas na Phoblachta ... the Gaelic League' might amalgamate into 'one formidable combine of Gaelic speaking Republican-totalitarian-democrats far more formidable than Fine Gael for they will stand for removal of partition, social amelioration schemes, extreme nationalism (whether Republican or totalitarian) and everything that Dev stands for himself'.[82] MI5 too expressed concern that 'the rise of Ailtirí na hAiséirghe, Córas na Poblachta and other small subversive organisations is symptomatic of disintegration in the main national movement [Fianna Fáil]'.[83]

At the other end of the political spectrum, the Labour Party perceived Aiséirghe as a serious menace to democracy in general and to itself in particular. At the outset, Labourites did not know what to make of the movement, initially taking it for a revival of the Blueshirts.[84] Later, Labour spokesmen typically depicted Aiséirghe as a local manifestation of Continental fascism, often dropping dark hints that the party was funded by Hitler, Mussolini or both. James O'Connor, a Labour member of Waterford City Council, asserted in 1944 that Aiséirghe was 'just one of those imitating parties that has crushed the freedom of other peoples'.[85] When Ó Cuinneagáin sought to initiate legal action against the councillor and a newspaper that had reported the comments, his solicitors advised him that the

---

81 'Extract from Minute of Eastern Command Dated 15th November 1943', G2/2777; same title, G2/3261, DDMA.
82 Betjeman to W. C. Hankinson, 21 March 1943, TNA DO 130/33. Orthography as in original.
83 'Irish Affairs (The General Situation in Éire)', QRS/202, 1 May 1943, TNA DO 121/85.
84 *Torch*, 3 April 1943.
85 *Waterford News*, 12 October 1944.

reputation of political parties enjoyed no protection in law and that, in any event, it could hardly be considered defamatory 'to say that someone is a "Fascist" or even a "Nazi" in a country that is neutral in the current European war'.[86] Aiséirghe responded instead by painting Labourites as crypto-Communists, philo-Semites or both. Before long, unmodulated exchanges of abuse, and occasionally of fisticuffs, enlivened relations between the two parties. At a pair of Waterford meetings in 1943, Tomás Ó Dochartaigh described members of the Labour Party as 'political reptiles' and alleged that one of its more prominent spokesmen, Owen Sheehy Skeffington, had demonstrated the spuriousness of its patriotic professions by giving a lecture under the party's auspices entitled 'In Defence of Jews'. 'That inconsistency might be explained', said Mr Ó Dochartaigh, 'when we remember that Karl Marx, Lenin, Trotsky and Molotoff were all Jews'.[87] Labour activists replied in kind, referring to Ó Cuinneagáin's movement as 'Ailteóirí na hAiséirghe' ['Clowns of the Resurrection'], 'apes' and 'bedraggled Napoleons'.[88]

The special rancour that characterised relations between the two parties reflected their awareness that each was the other's most serious competitor for the youth vote. Labour assertions that 'the Ailtirí fascists … are so un-Irish in their outlook, so obviously copied from a foreign fashion that is getting out of date already, that they are not likely to win a single seat'[89] were belied by the party's apprehension that young Irishmen and women would be beguiled by the superficial appeal of Aiséirghe's radicalism. Writing in the Labour weekly *Torch*, the political economist Arnold Marsh compained that 'whole slabs' of *Aiséirghe Says* … had been 'lifted out of the Labour Party's programme, or out of the writings of Labour's individual supporters but they are served up with such an air of originality that to many readers they seem fresh and new'.[90] A similar danger was perceived by his party colleague Harry Ryan, who warned against taking the advent of Aiséirghe lightly: 'If Labour does not bestir itself in the interest of youth and its problems others will exploit youth's resentment against the injustices and inequalities of present day conditions … we are tending to ignore the growth of this allegedly new political system, which is really as old

86 Little, Ó hUadhaigh & Proud, solicitors, to Ó Cuinneagáin, 30 October 1944, 11/4/6, GÓCP.
87 *Munster News*, 11 and 18 June 1943.
88 *Torch*, 17 April 1943.
89 *Ibid.*, 19 June 1943.
90 *Ibid.*, 5 June 1943. There was some justification for Marsh's complaint, in light of the fact that his own *Ireland's New Foundations* was one of the required 'Standard Works on Irish Nationalism' to be read by all Aiséirghe speakers.

as tyranny itself'.[91] British commentators interpreted the subsequent launch of Labour Youth as the party's effort to 'attract the youth of Ireland away from Ailtirí na hAiséirghe'.[92]

Both G2 and MI5 looked warily upon Aiséirghe's contacts with Sinn Féin, noting that members often were to be found attending the latter's meetings and even speaking from its platforms.[93] Several Aiséirghe officials, among them Seósamh Ó Ceallaigh of Ballaghaderreen and Liam Breathnach [Willie Walsh] of Waterford had Sinn Féin pedigrees. This led MI5 to apprehend that 'Ailtirí na hAiséirghe is being used as a breeding ground for the IRA, and that membership of the one may in a number of cases lead to membership of the other organisation'.[94] As noted above, a significant degree of overlap between the two did exist, something that disturbed many Aiséirghe activists also. Nevertheless, in an attempt to reassure his supporters, Ó Cuinneagáin promised officials in a February 1944 letter that Aiséirghe meant to plough its own furrow rather than follow in the tracks of either Sinn Féin or Fianna Fáil.[95] The *Ceannaire*'s sincerity in this matter need not be doubted, inasmuch as the successful achievement of an Aiséirghe regime would necessarily have involved a breach with his republican associates.

Between Aiséirghe and the two leading parties no formal relationship existed. Both Fianna Fáil and Fine Gael correctly calculated that the best way of inhibiting Aiséirghe's growth was to deny it the oxygen of publicity, even that provided in the form of denunciation. Public references to the movement by national politicians were, in consequence, few and indirect. James Dillon may have had Craobh na hAiséirghe as well as his own Blueshirts in mind when at the 1942 Fine Gael Ard-Fheis he warned delegates against youth movements: 'For God's sake look out for them'. He had never, he went on, 'known a youth movement started with the highest possible motives that did not end by being used by the most unscrupulous elements for their own rotten ends'.[96] Éamon de Valera is known to have mentioned Aiséirghe in public only once, describing it in the course of a platform address as a body that was 'crazy politically, but there were at least some ideals behind it'.[97] Behind the scenes, though, Aiséirghe was scrutinised far

91 *Ibid.*
92 'Irish Affairs (The General Situation in Ireland)', 1 January 1944, QRS/206, TNA DO 121/85.
93 *Ibid.*
94 *Ibid.*, QRS/212, 31 December 1944.
95 'Leitir Phearsanta', 1 February 1944, 6/2/19, GÓCP.
96 *Irish Press*, 21 March 1942.
97 *Irish Times*, 4 February 1948.

more assiduously. As Caoimhín de Eiteagáin recalls, the Fianna Fáil government carefully monitored the movement's growth and development: 'They had their G-men about the place. Every meeting you could spot the Special Branch men within the crowd listening for subversive statements'.[98] Aiséirghe publications also received the personal attention of the Minister for Co-Ordination of Defensive Measures, Frank Aiken, who included among his responsibilities supervision of the censorship system. The fact that few surviving Aiséirghe drafts in the Office of the Controller of Censorship files are free of caustic ministerial marginalia in blue pencil attests to the seriousness with which the movement was taken at the highest governmental levels.

Aiséirghe's determination to maintain its independence and distinctiveness from all other movements was the logical consequence of its radical critique of the Irish political system. As an 'anti-party', it had no option other than formally to distance itself from existing organisations. The result, however, was to narrow its potential sources of support dramatically. Having already written off the 'middle-aged' cohort of society as too timid and hidebound, Fine Gael as too reactionary and pro-British, Fianna Fáil as too self-serving and the Labour Party as too socialist, Aiséirghe found itself directing its appeal to that section of the population that was least politically conscious and amenable to mobilisation. To be sure, most fascist organisations faced the dilemma of maintaining the appearance of 'outsiders' while trying to forge tactical alliances with other movements or institutions. By 1944, some prominent Aiséirghe leaders had come to recognise that they, too, would have to do likewise if they were to gain power. For them, the aim of political mobilisation was to obtain for Aiséirghe a seat at the bargaining-table. They reckoned, though, without their *Ceannaire*. Gearóid Ó Cuinneagáin was not seeking any such mundane objective. His goal was to transform the very basis of Irish national consciousness, without which a change of regime would mean nothing more than the substitution of one failed philosophy for another.

Political activity

The characteristic form of Aiséirghe activity during the Emergency years was the public meeting. Rejecting as excessively gradualist and tending to corrupt by association the failed Craobh na hAiséirghe strategy of permeating existing organisations, Ailtirí na hAiséirghe's leaders resolved to take their message directly to the people. Through personal exhortation, the movement aimed not merely at spreading

98 Caoimhín de Eiteagáin, author interview, 29 July 1999.

the Aiséirghe gospel, but instilling a spirit of daring and national-mindedness in the people. Each branch was expected to organise at least one public address or function per week, and senior Aiséirghe members and paid officials crisscrossed the country – often travelling astonishingly long distances by bicycle, boat or even on foot – to help establish local organisations and speak at meetings.

Though varying widely in size and sophistication, Aiséirghe events normally followed a set pattern. A suitable location was chosen where a ready-made crowd might be found – the immediate vicinity of pubs and cinemas, sporting events or churches were favourite venues. The organisers were responsible for providing a platform, upon which the Irish tricolour and a banner depicting the Aiséirghe symbol – a super-imposition of the Christian cross upon the lower-case letter 'E', for Éire[99] – would be displayed. The speakers would be introduced by a chairman, a role often assigned to neophytes who needed to gain experience in addressing the public. Each speaker would deliver an oration in Irish before switching to English. This preliminary address was much more substantial than the pro forma exercise which in Ireland is cynically known as the *cúpla focail* ['a couple of words'] – the custom by Irish politicians of commencing their discourses with a few short sentences in the first official language as a genuflection before the ideal of cultural nationalism. According to Aindrias Ó Scolaidhe, he and other Aiséirghe orators might speak in Irish to their largely uncomprehending audiences for as long as fifteen minutes before turning to English. To his surprise, he found that far from causing them to drift away in boredom, this practice often whetted their curiosity and swelled their numbers.[100] While the speeches were in progress, Aiséirghe activists would filter through the crowd selling party litera-ture and soliciting recruits. The meeting would close with the singing of the national anthem.

In their addresses to the public, Aiséirghe speakers frequently drew upon the motif of 'cultural despair' to illustrate the depths to which the country had fallen.[101] Tomás Ó Dochartaigh, in particular, made the 'scepticism, inertia or despondency' of Ireland's 'lost genera-tion' a favourite platform theme: 'It is only when one has travelled throughout the twenty-six counties, contacting the people, that one fully realises the awful depths of degradation to which the children of the Gael have been dragged by the wily alien'.[102] But Aiséirghe orators

99 See frontispiece.
100 Aindrias Ó Scolaidhe, author interview, 22 July 1999.
101 See F. Stern, *The Politics of Cultural Despair: A Study in the Rise of the Germanic Ideology* (Berkeley, CA: University of California Press, 1961).
102 *Dungarvan Observer*, 6 November 1943.

by no means attributed the state of Ireland to foreign scapegoats alone, or absolved the citizenry from responsibility for their own plight. On the contrary, one of the most characteristic elements of an Aiséirghe speech was a frank exposition of the personal and civic shortcomings of those listening to it. As Tomás Ó Sleibhín declared uncompromisingly at Nobber in 1943, 'The Irish people had degenerated into a backward race of miserable crawlers who buy foreign goods, read foreign trash, ape English ways and wallow in slushy jungle rhythm'.[103] Gearóid Ó Broin, similarly, advised his audience that 'they had lost their courage and will-power....The people could thank themselves for this state of affairs....Instead of being men and demanding that a halt be called to all this national back-sliding, they took the easy road and let the politicians play havoc with the country'.[104] Although Aiséirghe speakers saw it as their duty to speak uncomfortable truths regardless of the consequences, many of their hearers resented being made the targets of a tirade of abuse from party spokesmen, a significant proportion of whom had but recently found it necessary to shave. Scarcely less objectionable to some observers – though by no means to all – was the party's self-perception as a vanguard elite with the right and duty to reshape the country according to its own standards. Pointing out the contrast with the 'shoneens and traitors who can find space in the daily papers to voice their contempt of everything national', Ó Dochartaigh lauded Aiséirghe activists for their 'moral courage, their devotion, their discipline, their love for the language of the Gael, their iron determination to conquer'.[105] Drawing the obvious conclusion from this polarity, party leaders did not hesitate to stake their claim not merely to represent the Irish nation, but themselves to constitute it. In the words of Eoin Ó Coigligh, 'We are the new Ireland and we will make and mould this new Ireland to our liking'.[106]

Aiséirghe's appearance on the streets did not go uncontested by either the authorities or rival political parties. For its largest meetings in the Dublin and Cork city centres, where attendance might run into the thousands, a police permit was required. This was given only with the attachment of stringent conditions. As Aiséirghe grew in strength, it became increasingly common for the Gardaí to withdraw official sanction for these meetings with minimal notice or none at all, or to require them to be held in some distant or unsuitable location. So preva-

---

103 *Meath Chronicle*, 4 September 1943.
104 *Ibid.*, 11 March 1944.
105 *Dungarvan Observer*, 6 November 1943. The word *seóinín* ['shoneen'] means 'toady' or 'lickspittle', and was customarily applied to those Irishmen who curried favour with their British masters.
106 *Meath Chronicle*, 21 August 1943.

lent was this practice that it is hard to contradict Aiséirghe's assertion that the police were engaging in an officially-sanctioned policy of petty harassment aimed at weakening the movement. Speakers also ran the risk of organised interference or even physical attack by members of other parties. Aiséirghe's regular meetings at Cathal Brugha Street in Dublin were frequently disrupted by squads of Labour or Communist opponents, to which Aiséirghe members replied in kind. Street clashes between bands of youths from all three parties were not uncommon in the capital. Elsewere, Derry Kelleher, a member of the Communist-front Cork Socialist Party, would later recall with pride his participation in a squad that ambushed and beat Aiséirghe activists on their way to and from meetings in the city as part of a 'no free speech for fascists' campaign.[107]

In addition to the ubiquitous street meetings, Aiséirghe engaged in an immense variety of public spectacles and cultural offerings. The most impressive were the periodic *aeridheachtaí*, or day-long open-air functions, usually held on St Patrick's Day and during the weekend of the All-Ireland hurling and football finals. These events generally commenced with a parade including massed bands (some hired for the occasion), banners, posters and often a retinue of Irish dancers. Such marches offered a suitable occasion for the rendition of the Aiséirghe anthem, set to the tune of *Funiculì, funiculà*:

There are Irishmen in Ireland alive with native hope
Rising [*ag aiséirghe*] again, rising again,
Eagerly bursting the alien enemy's bonds
Unceasingly, tirelessly,
Secretly the bonds of affectionate trust the youth of Fál
Are building, are building.
Forging ahead under full sail with the controlling guidance
Of Aiséirghe, of Aiséirghe.

    Bestir yourselves, bestir yourselves vigorously, Irish masses.
    Bestir yourselves, bestir yourselves, marching in unison ahead.
    Strongly vigorously vivaciously ahead
    Subduing every enemy of our entire little land,
    Irish masses, seed of heroes,
    Forward with Aiséirghe.

The entire little land of Ireland will be free without borders
Without division without strife; without division without strife.
Flourishing lyrical poetry speaks to us in Gaelic
Alive as it once was, alive as it once was.
And the culture of the Gael will yet be free of foreign perversion

---

107 Derry Kelleher, author interview, April 14, 2000.

In spite of West Britons [*seoiníní*], in spite of West Britons.
The stalwart descendants of the Gael ever united
Will rise again, will rise again.[108]

The procession would terminate at a gathering-place at which spectators would be regaled with games, children's entertainments and free refreshments, interspersed with addresses by Aiséirghe notables. An evening *céilidhe*, or traditional Irish dancing session, at the local Aiséirghe headquarters would round out the day's programme.

The day-to-day missionary work of the movement, however, was carried on through a constellation of ancillary bodies. The most important of these was Cumann Cultúrdha na hAiséirghe ['Aiséirghe Cultural Society'], organised by the future *Ceann Comhairle* [Speaker] of Dáil Éireann, Seán Treacy. Cumann Cultúrdha's original mission was to continue the educational activities begun by Craobh na hAiséirghe in 1940. Though theoretically independent and non-partisan, by 1944 it had assumed a wide variety of propaganda activities on behalf of its parent. Among its more important functions was the direction and supervision of Óige na hAiséirghe ['Aiséirghe Youth'], an organisation formally established in July 1943 to train boys aged between ten and eighteen 'properly to carry out their duties and display their loyalty to the nation in a Christian and Gaelic manner'.[109] Originally named Gasraí na hAiséirghe ['Aiséirghe Warriors'], Óige na hAiséirghe adopted as its slogan the watchwords 'Discipline, Work, Joy'. Its charges were prepared for eventual active membership in the adult movement by means of a highly regimented training schedule. According to the scheme of organisation, weekly meetings commenced with prayers for Aiséirghe and the unity of Ireland, followed by instruction in party doctrine and Irish history. To instill 'strength of mind and body', drilling, hiking and participation in competitive games were emphasised.[110] British observers viewed this development with considerable alarm, with MI5 reporting that in the spring of 1943 Aiséirghe had established twenty-three such branches in private houses in the Dublin area alone. In addition to physical exercise, '[l]ectures are given to the youths on Nazi lines'. Though it is doubtful that Aiséirghe's youth wing by this time had progressed quite as rapidly as MI5 suggested, it is quite likely that the security service's account of Catholic priests visiting Dublin schools to warn teachers not to permit their students to join Óige na hAiséirghe had a basis in fact.[111]

108 Lyrics of 'Aiséirghe', 11/4/1, GÓCP.
109 Provisional constitution of Óige na hAiséirghe, n.d., 7/12/1, *ibid.*
110 Minute by Conchubhar Ó Laoghaire, superintendent of Óige na hAiséirghe, 22 January 1944, 7/12/5; organisational scheme of 'Buachaillí na hAiséirghe', n.d., 7/12/7, *ibid.*
111 'Irish Affairs (The General Situation in Ireland)', 1 May 1943, QRS/202, TNA DO 121/85.

In addition to the task of forming the next generation of activists, the cultural section was responsible for disseminating the Aiséirghe version of Irish history by means of a series of public exhibitions and displays. Ostensibly intended to celebrate notable moments in the struggle for Irish independence, these depictions of the nation's past contained a subtle but unmistakable Aiséirghe slant, laying stress upon the disastrous consequences of internal division and noting how much could be achieved when, as in 1916–21, the country was united behind a single movement that stood above party and faction. Cumann Cultúrdha's historical exhibitions generated much public interest and were among the most effective forms of Aiséirghe propaganda; by the summer of 1945 they had been staged in most cities and large towns. So successful were these financially as well as politically that plans were laid for an Aiséirghe historical roadshow to tour the United States at the end of the war.

Smaller constitiencies were by no means neglected. Aiséirghe attached considerable importance to cultivating future leaders, and established dedicated branches for each of the country's three university colleges. The *Ceannaire* was a frequent speaker at campus events, regularly proselytising the Aiséirghe doctrine even in the seemingly inveterately Anglophilic milieu of Trinity College. Lecture series and study circles devoted to topics of contemporary interest – industrial development, social policy, the cinema – catered to the requirements of the urban intelligentsia. For the less sedentary, a wide range of athletic teams, cycling clubs and swimming parties beckoned.

The net effect of these multifarious activities is difficult to gauge, but it does not seem that the results achieved were in proportion to the efforts invested in them. Despite Ó Cuinneagáin's efforts to induce his subordinates to take seriously the tedious business of maintaining adequate records and answering correspondence promptly, few did so who did not, like him, possess some civil service training. Such exhortations were in any event contradicted to some degree by the *Ceannaire*'s insistence that Aiséirghe members show themselves to be actively engaging the people at all times, and his demands upon their time for the purpose of selling literature, conducting house-to-house collections and other revenue-generating operations. In the absence of paid full-time officials, organisation was left in the hands of enthusiastic youthful amateurs, a large proportion of whom proved better at initiating ambitious schemes than following-up effectively upon them. *An tIolar*'s initial reaction to Ailtirí na hAiséirghe – 'one takes away an impression of very energetic folk behaving with cheap theatricality' – was to be echoed by many others in the years ahead.[112]

112 'F. Mac M'., 'Young Men Plan For a New Ireland'.

'The Year of Victory'?

Gearóid Ó Cuinneagáin made no secret of his conviction that Aiséirghe's triumph would be achieved in the near rather than the distant future, and did not hesitate to offer several public hostages to fortune in testimony to that belief. The year 1945 was invested with a special significance in his vision of Aiséirghe's political progress. In the revised English-language edition of his Domhnach Phádraig address, he inserted the promise that 'Around the year 1945 consciousness of England's military and political power, of British tyranny in Ireland, will be like a bad memory or a bad dream'.[113] Nor did he retreat from that prediction, notwithstanding the party's halting first steps. 'We have said', he reminded officials in a 'Personal Letter' of April 1943, 'that all Ireland will be mobilised behind Aiséirghe within 24 months. *We repeat that.*'[114] He continued to commit himself to the same timeframe during the 1943 general election campaign, explaining in a letter to the *Dublin Evening Mail* that he would not take his Dáil seat 'until we are sufficiently strong, as after the next general election anticipated within the next 24 months, to replace constitutionally the government then in office'.[115] Tomás Óg Ó Murchadha, the then Dublin County organiser, also recollected Ó Cuinneagáin in 1943 'telling the people he would be in power in 1945'.[116]

Claims of this sort were not entirely the product of leaderly bravado. Though MI5 initially drew comfort from its perception that 'Ailtirí na hAiséirghe is making headway only with the very young', by the end of 1944 it noted that the movement was 'making a big drive among young people all over Ireland'.[117] An indication closer to home of the movement's progress was provided by the response of Brian O'Nolan ['Myles na gCopaleen'], Aiséirghe's most persistent gadfly. In December 1944 O'Nolan wrote a one-act sketch, *An Sgian* ['The Knife'], that was staged as part of the Gate Theatre's Christmas programme.[118] The theme of this drama concerns a fierce political dispute between a splenetic Aiséirghe official named Tadhg Mac Phearsan and his wife Peig, an adherent of Glún na Buaidhe. Infuriated by the latter's derision of his manhood, his movement and his efforts to revive the

113 G. Ó Cuinneagáin, *Ireland's Twentieth Century Destiny* (Dublin: Ailtirí na hAiséirghe, n.d. [1942]), p. 11.
114 'Litir Phearsanta', 12 April 1943, 6/2/5, GÓCP. Emphasis in original.
115 Ó Cuinneagáin to editor, *Dublin Evening Mail*, 1 June 1943.
116 Tomás Óg Ó Murchadha to Eoin Ó Coigligh, 19 June 1945, 5/3/11, GÓCP.
117 'Irish Affairs (The General Situation in Éire)', QRS/202, 1 May 1943; QRS/212, 31 December 1944, TNA DO 121/85.
118 *Irish Times*, 29 March 2002.

Irish language, Mac Phearsan responds by stabbing her to death with a kitchen knife presented as a wedding-gift to the couple by Conradh na Gaeilge.[119] One of O'Nolan's least-successful literary efforts, substituting strident agitprop for his usual deft wordplay, *An Sgian* failed even to provoke any response from the notoriously thin-skinned Ó Cuinneagáin, of whom the character of Mac Phearsan was a barely-disguised caricature.[120] That the author should have felt compelled to escalate his anti-Aiséirghe campaign from raillery to undisguised vilification, however, serves as a measure of his alarm at the ground Ó Cuinneagáin had succeeded in gaining. Part of the explanation for that progress is suggested by Liam de Róiste, who was keenly observing Aiséirghe's rise in Cork. Musing over the fall of Mussolini's regime, de Róiste recalled that in its national aspect, Italian fascism 'was comparable to our Sinn Féin movement in Ireland. And, in Sinn Féin there was also the strain of thought that would have only one party in the State and have the State direct all activities. That strain of thought is not dead in Ireland by any means'. Thus de Róiste found himself increasingly drawn to Aiséirghe. 'I sympathise very much with them', he recorded in his diary in 1944; 'may indeed, though unasked, give their candidate my first preference. They are young: they have much to learn; but they have ideals'.[121]

Aiséirghe would, however, require to pose a much more potent threat before official counter-measures became likely. Mere fascist alignment or sympathy for the Axis cause was not sufficient to bring down the repressive hand of the government. In the absence of evidence of overt subversive activity, the de Valera administration, in contrast to its more panicky counterparts elsewhere in Europe, was content to let the combination of a rigorous censorship regime and petty official harassment keep the growth of Aiséirghe in check.[122] The only eventu-

---

119 B. O'Nolan, 'An Sgian', MS 97–27, section 2, item 54, Flann O'Brien papers, Burns Library, Boston College, Chestnut Hill, Massachusetts.

120 Ó Cuinneagáin's son Fionán recalls that his father invariably spoke of Myles na gCopaleen in complimentary terms and with amusement, bearing out Risteárd Ó Glaisne's observation that it was impossible to insult the *Ceannaire* so long as the aspersion was delivered in the first official language. Fionán Ó Cuinneagáin to author, 9 November 2007; Risteárd Ó Glaisne, author interview, 2 August 2003.

121 Liam de Róiste diary, U 271/A56, Cork Archive Institute (entries of 15 September 1943 and 22 May 1944).

122 For treatments of governmental over-reactions to the perceived 'Fifth Column' threat, see L. DeJong, *The German Fifth Column in the Second World War* (Chicago, IL: University of Chicago Press, 1956); R. M. Delacor, 'From Potential Friends to Potential Enemies: The Internment of "Hostile Foreigners" in France at the Beginning of the Second World War', *Journal of Contemporary History* 35:3 (July 2000): 361–8; A. Grynberg, '1939–40: l'internement en temps de guerre: les politiques de France et de la Grande Bretagne', *XXe Siècle* 54 (April–June 1997): 24–33; S. Hurlburt, 'Enemy Within Our Gates: The National Press and the Fifth Column Scare in Britain, April–June 1940', BA thesis,

ality that might have impelled it to adopt a more assertive stance was a demonstration by Ó Cuinneagáin's movement of an ability to garner significant electoral support. As the Tenth Dáil's term of office drew to its close, Aiséirghe would be given an early opportunity to do so.

Colgate University, 2001; A. W. B. Simpson, *In the Highest Degree Odious: Detention Without Trial in Wartime Britain* (Oxford: Clarendon Press, 1992).

5

Democratic deficit

As Roger Griffin has observed, electoral failure is the normal fate of European fascist movements.[1] Beyond the obvious paradox of anti-parliamentary organisations seeking representation in bodies whose destruction is one of their principal *raisons d'être*, fascist parties rarely contain significant reservoirs of political expertise. Appealing as they do to the young, the alienated, the previously apolitical and those who have failed to find a home in more conventional movements, such parties usually lack members who possess the experience and skill required to build up an effective political structure from scratch. An ideology that emphasises spontaneous action as against bureaucratic procedures and word-spinning does not easily adapt itself to the patient, unheroic work of organisation and administration. In normal times, moreover, voters even in imperfect parliamentary systems are highly resistant to appeals from movements perceived to be radical or extremist in character. Notwithstanding the turmoil into which Italy was plunged after the Great War, Mussolini's *Fasci Italiani di Combattimento* gained just 36 parliamentary seats in the election that preceded the March on Rome – probably an accurate reflection of the extent of its popular support at the time. The NSDAP was an even more marginal phenomenon, winning a mere 2.6% of the vote in Germany's last genuinely democratic election in 1928.[2]

Ireland during the Emergency, however, by definition was not living through normal times. Although, as noted above, the exigencies of wartime led to extensive powers of direction being placed in the hands of the government – powers that could be, and were, used to hold movements like Ailtirí na hAiséirghe in check – that very fact lent

---

1 R. Griffin, *The Nature of Fascism* (London: Routledge, 1991), pp. 44–5.
2 Although the Weimar Republic is conventionally dated as having come to an end with the accession of Hitler to power in January 1933, the last government to derive its authority from a Reichstag majority, rather than emergency decrees, collapsed in March 1930. Thereafter the Weimar regime was in fact, if not in name, a presidential dictatorship.

credence to Aiséirghe's contention that rule by decree was a necessary tool to promote the safety and efficiency of the state. The argument was a difficult one for the government to counter. If such measures proved effective, there was surely a case for retaining them into the postwar era as well. On the other hand, assertions that the purpose of emergency legislation was to preserve intact through this period of temporary crisis the Irish democratic regime as it had been in 1939 ran into the objection that the prewar system, with its appallingly high unemployment and emigration figures, hardly represented a model that could or should be recreated.

Nonetheless, in formally democratic societies a political movement whose programme is predicated entirely upon the electorate having first entrusted it with supreme powers is rarely, if ever, successful. Elections are not merely referenda on the prevailing system of government, although their outcome may be strongly influenced by voters' perception of how well that system is functioning. Constituents also expect their immediate problems to be addressed by their political representatives. The history of abstentionist Sinn Féin in the years immediately following the Civil War made clear that the Irish people were not willing to defer their day-to-day concerns until such time as the republican millennium had been achieved. During the Emergency, Aiséirghe was to demonstrate that it had learned little from the example of the party to which it most frequently compared itself.

The 1943 general election

The announcement that a general election would be held in the summer of 1943 found Ailtirí na hAiséirghe completely unprepared for a contest. There was no reason that it should have been so. Under the Constitution, a dissolution of the Oireachtas was required no later than five years after the date of the previous general election, which had taken place in June 1938. Although the possibility existed of extending the life of the existing parliament by making use of the Emergency Powers Act – an option favoured by several government backbenchers – de Valera was never likely to entertain such an idea. To do so would either have compelled him to invite the opposition parties to join a National Government, a proposal he had strenuously resisted since the beginning of the Emergency, or exposed him to accusations of preferring to undermine the democratic process rather than face the verdict of the people. As early as the previous November, therefore, two senior Fianna Fáil ministers had stated publicly their belief that a general election could not be long delayed; and by late February 1943 unofficial campaigning had already begun on platforms and in parish halls around the country.

From Aiséirghe's point of view, the prudent course appeared to be not to participate in the contest. Nationally, the organisation was still in a rudimentary state. Several counties still lacked a single established branch, while none of those in operation had been in existence for so much as a year. Aiséirghe's unique demographic composition meant that a significant proportion of its membership, being under the age of twenty-one, would not themselves be eligible either to vote or to present themselves as candidates. The movement's finances were in no condition to support the expenses of an election campaign. Lastly, and most critically, Ó Cuinneagáin had still not reached a decision on whether it was permissible for Aiséirghe members to participate in electoral politics.

As noted in Chapter 4, the precise means by which Aiséirghe was expected to come to power was deliberately shrouded in vagueness. Ó Cuinneagáin had always emphasised that his was a national movement [*gluaiseacht*], not a political party.[3] 'A spiritual political party is a contradiction in terms.'[4] Aiséirghe wanted no part of the 'godless liberalistic corrupt governmental system which is ... our inheritance from England'.[5] To take part in that system to the extent of engaging in political campaigning risked obscuring the distinction Ó Cuinneagáin wished to preserve between Aiséirghe and the 'old gang' of discredited party politicians. An even thornier question was what Aiséirghe representatives should do in the event of their being elected. To take their seats in the Dáil would imply recognition of the legitimacy of the state, a position that was unacceptable to many of the republican activists whose support Ó Cuinneagáin had assiduously courted. An abstentionist stance, on the other hand, would condemn the movement to political impotence, as the record of Sinn Féin over the previous two decades had sufficiently demonstrated.

The solution devised by Ó Cuinneagáin in the spring of 1943 was an uneasy compromise between the two alternatives. Successful Aiséirghe candidates would take their seats and use the facilities of Leinster House 'as efficiently and energetically as possible in the service of the people of Ireland'. Ó Cuinneagáin himself, however, if elected,

---

3　*The Leader*, 29 July 1944. The same rhetorical strategy had been pioneered by National Socialism in the late 1920s and early 1930s, for identical reasons. See R. Evans, *The Coming of the Third Reich* (London: Allen Lane, 2003), p. 265.
4　'The People and Partition', 18 December 1944, 8/5/7, GÓCP.
5　Ailtirí na hAiséirghe. *Aiséirghe Says ... The New Order in the New Ireland* (Dublin: Ailtirí na hAiséirghe, 1943).

would abstain from attendance so as to 'protect the party [*sic*] against the corruptive influence of that house'.[6] To guard further against the same tendency, Ó Cuinneagáin required each Aiséirghe candidate to sign a covenant signifying his or her acceptance of a stringent set of conditions. Elected representatives undertook to speak and vote in the manner prescribed by the *Ceannaire*; either to retain only a quarter of their Dáil salary or to give up any outside employment and become a full-time Aiséirghe worker at five-eighths of their parliamentary pay, the balance in each case to be turned over to the movement; to resign their seats when instructed by Ó Cuinneagáin to do so; and not to 'waste time engaging in lengthy foolish unprofitable debates'.[7] The movement's aim was 'to increase the importance of the Aiséirghe congress such that it will be respected by the people of Ireland to a greater degree than Dáil Éireann'.[8]

Aiséirghe's ambivalence over the notion of participation in the democratic process was further reflected in its lackadaisical and unsystematic attitude to political campaigning. As late as three weeks before polling day, Ó Cuinneagáin still had not decided how many candidates would be fielded, nor in what constituencies. Initial plans to put forward ten or twelve representatives were rapidly scaled down to four: Ó Cuinneagáin himself, standing in Dublin North-West; Tomás Ó Dochartaigh in Waterford; Seán Ó Dúbhghaill in Cork Borough; and Eoin Ó Coigligh in Louth, who after initially deciding not to stand changed his mind on the last possible day, forcing his constituency organisation to engage in a frantic scramble in the few hours before nominations closed to raise his deposit and complete his papers.[9] Although it is probable that an informal agreement had been concluded with Córas na Poblachta to avoid contesting the same areas, the choice of Aiséirghe candidates and constituencies seems to have been dictated largely by the willingness of the local organisation to finance a campaign. Thus the candidature of Ó Dochartaigh, another eleventh-hour selection for a district in which he was completely unknown, was made possible by a contribution of £100 from a donor of ardent anti-Semitic views from Waterford city, whereas a plan to put forward Feardorcha Ó Carra [Fred Carr] in the Dublin County constituency had to be abandoned before the close of nominations after funds for his campaign ran out. The latter, a police informant and former Córas na Poblachta official who had left that movement

---

6 Ó Cuinneagáin to editor, *Dublin Evening Mail*, 1 June 1943, 4/1/12, GÓCP.
7 'Iarrthóirí Tóghacháin – Coinghiollacha', *ibid*.
8 Minutes of a meeting of Comhairle Laighean, 11 March 1943, 5/14/1, *ibid*.
9 M. Ó Flannagáin to Ó Cuinneagáin, 17 May 1944, 4/2/6, *ibid*.

under a cloud, served instead as Ó Cuinneagáin's election agent.[10]

Aiséirghe's election campaign gave little basis for concluding that much thought or preparation had been invested in the problem of making an effective appeal to voters. A series of posters, probably designed by Ó Carra, harped on the themes of 'Alien Infiltration' and 'Masonic Domination'; by the time these had been prepared, however, nearly all the commercial poster sites in Aiséirghe's selected constituencies had already been reserved by the mainstream parties.[11] Only three small and inconspicuous advertisements were placed in the national press, the cost of which nonetheless absorbed two-thirds of the movement's modest publicity budget. Although some 95,000 election handbills were printed, it was only with considerable difficulty that Dónall Ó Maolalaí and other members of the Ard-Chomhairle prevailed upon the *Ceannaire* not to repeat in them his earlier public boast that he himself had 'never voted in any election'.[12]

Attacks against the political system and the Judaeo-Masonic conspiracy formed the principal elements of Aiséirghe's electoral campaign. As an official from the American Legation recorded, 'The Ailtirí na hAiséirghe meetings were a common sight in downtown Dublin during the election campaign, and the speakers varied their denunciation of democracy with arguments of a pronounced anti-Semitic bias'.[13] In the countryside also, Aiséirghe speakers played on similar themes. Éamonn Ó Riain, for example, assured Water-ford voters that 'in the Aiseirghe Ireland there would be no place for Masonic, Jewish, or Communistic cliques'.[14] Sentiments of this kind may have impelled the Germans, through their mouthpiece Francis Stuart, obliquely to urge Irish voters to support Aiséirghe and Córas na Poblachta in an *Irland-Redaktion* broadcast of 10 April 1943, though the appeal was issued in sufficiently vague terms as to pass over the

10 Ó Carra had been accused of misappropriating the organisation's funds; a similar charge would later be levelled against him by Ó Cuinneagáin. Judgment in a 1945 slander action brought by Ó Carra against a fellow Córas na Poblachta official, Kevin Cahill, who repeated the allegations against him to third parties, was given, with costs, in favour of the defendant. Unsigned 'Extract from Minute from Eastern Command Dated 15th November, 1943', G2/X/1231, DDMA; Tóghacán [*sic*] na Dála 1943: Cúnntas ar Cheanntar Conndae Portlairge', n.d.; nomination paper of Ó Carra, 4/1/12, GÓCP; *Irish Times*, 22 and 23 February 1945.
11 M. J. Mullen, David Allen & Sons Billposting Ltd., to Ó Cuinneagáin, 12 June 1943, 4/1/12, GÓCP.
12 Dónall Ó Maolalaí, author interview, 15 July 1999.
13 T. A. Hickok, chargé d'affaires *ad interim*, to Cordell Hull, telegram no. 674, 'Irish Totali-tarian Party', 9 July 1943, Record Group 84, 'Ireland: Dublin Legation: General Records, 1936–1948', 350/61/29/4, Box 13, NARA.
14 *Waterford Standard*, 19 June 1943.

heads of most listeners.[15] Aiséirghe's own proposal to take up where Sinn Féin had left off at the end of the War of Independence similarly confused rather than clarified its political stance. Liam de Róiste, for example, was unsure whether 'the young men [of Aiséirghe] visualise another "Black-and-Tan" fight? If so, they fail to realize that the science and art of war has changed, even since the present world war began'.[16]

Ó Cuinneagáin, for his part, appears to have invested his hopes for Aiséirghe's electoral fortunes in an old-fashioned political stunt. Two weeks before polling day, he used his privilege as a candidate of sending post-free literature to voters to appeal for contributions to an 'Election War Chest' and to draw attention to an Aiséirghe *céilí*, or traditional Irish dance, scheduled in Belfast for 4 June. Ó Cuinneagáin himself crossed the Border to preside at this event and, during an inter-mission, ascended the platform and began to deliver what one local activist described as a 'fire-breathing speech' to the 400 or so dancers in attendance. A squad of some thirty-five officers of the Royal Ulster Constabulary (RUC), which had been standing by outside the premises since the beginning of the evening and had already interviewed the organisers, immediately broke up the event, took Ó Cuinneagáin into custody, and removed him to gaol.[17]

There can be little doubt that Ó Cuinneagáin travelled to Belfast with the definite intention of being arrested. As a native of Northern Ireland, he could have harboured no illusions as to the response of the Stormont regime to any act of nationalist provocation, far less one offered by so radical an organisation as Ailtirí na hAiséirghe. His advertisement of the Belfast event in his letter to voters had clearly been intended to ensure that the persecuting zeal of the Northern authorities would not go unnoticed. The catch-cry 'Put Him In to Get Him Out' was a time-honoured electoral stratagem in Irish politics, and Aiséirghe activists lost little time in seeking to generate political capital from the incident. A telegram by Prionnsias Mac Fógartaigh [Francis Gogarty Jr], the leading light of the Belfast Ailtirí, to the Dublin headquarters a few hours after the incident consisted of the succinct message: 'Cunningham detained for questioning. Propagandise'.[18] Suiting the action to the word, Aiséirghe promptly called upon the Irish government to demand Ó Cuinneagáin's release and sent protests to

15 D. O'Donoghue, *Hitler's Irish Voices: The Story of German Radio's Wartime Irish Service* (Belfast: Beyond the Pale Publications, 1998), pp. 114–15, 119 n. 1.
16 Liam de Róiste diary, 7 June 1943, U 271/A56, Cork Archive Institute.
17 *Irish News*, 5 June 1943; Tom Mageean, author interview August 8, 1999.
18 Mac Fógartaigh to Ailtirí na hAiséirghe, 5 June 1943, 7/6/4, GÓCP.

the leading media organisations in hope of gaining sympathetic press coverage for Ireland's latest 'political prisoner'.

Unfortunately for Ó Cuinneagáin, the status of nationalist martyr proved more elusive than he had hoped. After fewer than forty-eight hours in detention, he was escorted by detectives to the Belfast railway station and placed aboard a Dublin-bound train. The anticipated publicity dividend never materialised, as the national newspapers, whose editorial line favoured one or other of the mainstream parties, saw no reason to provide free advertising for Ó Cuinneagáin or his movement in the midst of an election campaign.[19] On the other side of the ledger, this coat-trailing exercise resulted in a swift crackdown by the Stormont security apparatus against the vulnerable Aiséirghe organisation in Northern Ireland. In the weeks following the céilí, Aiséirghe members known to the Royal Ulster Constabulary were rounded up or visited by detectives and offered the alternative of severing their links with the movement or being immediately imprisoned as suspected subversives under Northern Ireland's draconian Special Powers Act. In each case those interviewed wrote letters of resignation to Ó Cuinneagáin, using a form of words helpfully dictated to them by one of the RUC detectives, Sergeant Davis:

> I beg to offer my resignation from Ailtirí na hAiséirghe. I cannot approve of any organisation that is prepared to use physical force to attain any of its objects. I must also ask you not to send me any more papers in connection with it.[20]

> I feel I must tend to you my resignation from Altire na H,Aiseirge as its advocasey is ficical forse.
>
> Please do not send me any further publications in connection with it.[21]

> You will probably have recieved or will recieve my resignation. Cannot relate circumstances under which this resignation was made. An Ceannaire himself was a victim of same circumstances on a recent visit to Belfast.[22]

The only other consequence of the incident, apart from providing a pretext for Ó Carra to claim mendaciously that he had been compelled

---

19 The *Irish Press*, the newspaper with the second-highest circulation in the country, was operated by a Delaware corporation headed by Éamon de Valera and was regarded as the house organ of Fianna Fáil. The market-leading *Irish Independent* and its Sunday offshoot strongly favoured Fine Gael, in which the editorial sympathies of the *Irish Times* were likewise invested *faute de mieux*.

20 Raymond J. Moore (Réamonn Ó Mórdha) to Ó Cuinneagáin, 12 July 1943, 7/6/16, GÓCP.

21 Pádraig Ó Lochlainn to Ailtirí na hAiséirghe, 24 June 1943, 7/6/14, *ibid*.

22 Letter by Annraoí Mac Aodha [Harry McKee], 24 June 1943, 10/4/24, *ibid*.

to 'withdraw' his candidature from Dublin South, was the issuance of a banning order under the Special Powers Act forbidding Ó Cuinneagáin to enter Northern Ireland in the future.[23] This was a high price to pay for a publicity stunt, especially one that had failed to yield any significant results.

The outcome of the election thereafter was from Aiséirghe's point of view a foregone conclusion. All four candidates lost their deposits, two of them finishing at the bottom of the poll in their respective constituencies. Ó Cuinneagáin himself barely avoided this ignominious outcome, gaining just 607 first preferences and avoiding the last place by a mere eight votes. The distribution of the eliminated Aiséirghe candidates' ballots also revealed that the movement's campaign against the party system had made little impression even upon its own supporters, with most second-preference votes going to Fianna Fáil or Labour candidates. In the election's aftermath, Feardorcha Ó Carra noisily departed Aiséirghe in favour of a new far-right anti-partitionist movement, the Green Front, which he established in the autumn with the co-operation of the former CCOG official Dermot Brennan.[24] Its membership, according to MI5, consisted largely of 'a hotch potch of personnel from "Ailtirí na hAiséirghe," the "Young Ireland Association" and "Córas na Poblachta"'.[25]

Nonetheless, neither Ó Cuinneagáin nor his officials regarded the episode as a failure: 'We seek not votes', he reminded delegates at the 1943 annual convention, 'but to arouse the spirit of the people'.[26] The mission remained unchanged: 'the conquest of the universe for Christianity'. A member of the Cork City executive drew encouragement from his candidate's performance, reporting that, 'We would have had thousands [of votes] in the second count if the Fianna Fáil candidates had not all been ahead of us'.[27] In the *Leader*, Ernest Blythe also considered

23 The issuance of an order providing in effect for the administrative exile of a person born in Northern Ireland from his homeland was technically illegal under the Government of Ireland Act, 1920. To circumvent this provision, the Stormont authorities routinely issued orders prohibiting the recipient from entering any part of Northern Ireland, with the exception of a single specified locality. Thus Ó Cuinneagáin's banning order applied to the entirety of Northern Ireland with the exception of the district of Crookstown.

24 An assistant editor of *An tIolar*, Brennan had recently been released following an eighteen-month sentence imposed on him for IRA membership and possession of incriminating documents. *Irish Times*, 8 January, 8 February1941. The Green Front proved abortive; for particulars of its activities, see Commandant N. C. Harrington, G2 Eastern Command, to Bryan, 10 November 1943; unsigned minute, 'The Green Front', November 1943, G2/X/1231, DDMA.

25 'Irish Affairs (The General Situation in Éire)', QRS/205, 1 November 1943, TNA DO 121/85.

26 Undated notes of discussion at Comhdháil Náisiúnta, 30 October 1943, 5/1/1, GÓCP.

27 Pádraig Ó Coileáin to Ó Cuinneagáin, 6 July 1943, G2/2988, DDMA. Under Ireland's electoral system of the single transferable vote with multi-member constituencies, a

that in light of how recently it had appeared on the scene, Aiséirghe's election results gave grounds for mild optimism. The same could not be said for Córas na Poblachta, which despite being in existence for three years had fared no better than Ó Cuinneagáin's movement. 'There is no future for Córas na Poblachta', the *Leader* asserted, recommending its active members to throw in their lot with Aiséirghe. But if a second election were to be held in two years and Aiséirghe did not succeed in quadrupling its 1943 vote, it too would be 'finished'.[28]

The 1943 general election did yield one unexpected benefit for the movement. Although Aiséirghe remained without parliamentary representation of its own, one of the newly elected TDs, Oliver J. Flanagan, proved almost as assiduous a champion of the party's interests as an acknowledged Aiséirghe deputy would have been. At the time the youngest person ever to have been elected to the Dáil, the twenty-three-year-old Flanagan was returned for the Laois-Offaly constituency as the single candidate of the 'Monetary Reform Party'. This success owed more to the candidate's extraordinary charisma and the local unpopularity of the government, especially on the issue of old-age pensions, than to his political affiliation: although it professed a variant of Social Credit ideology, the Monetary Reform Party in Laois-Offaly was little more than a vehicle to secure Flanagan's election. After joining Fine Gael in 1953, he went on to become the longest-serving TD in Irish history, eventually securing office as Minister of Defence in 1976–77 and gaining a nationwide reputation as the most outspoken figure on the right wing of parliamentary politics.

The circumstances under which Flanagan became a supporter of Ó Cuinneagáin are unclear. Since August 1942 a close relationship had existed between Maurice O'Connor, Ó Cuinneagáin's erstwhile colleague in the Irish Friends of Germany/Cumann Náisiúnta, and the new TD; according to G2 O'Connor was believed 'to have been in some measure responsible for Flanagan's election manifesto'.[29] It is thus possible that O'Connor acted as the initial conduit between the two men; on the other hand, Flanagan himself may have regarded

---

first-preference ballot that has not been 'used' to elect a candidate – either because he or she has received so few votes as to make victory impossible or so many as to exceed the 'quota' required for election – is ignored, and the vote applied instead to the candidate listed on the paper by the voter as a second preference. The process continues, with later preferences taken into consideration in subsequent counts as each candidate is elected or eliminated until all votes have been distributed and all seats in the constituency have been filled. In the event of the voter not providing a complete list of his or her preferences, the ballot paper is said to be 'non-transferable' and excluded from later counts.

28 *The Leader*, 3 and 10 July 1943.
29 Unsigned and undated memorandum [c. 1943] on Maurice O'Connor's political activities, G2/2571, DDMA.

Aiséirghe as an ideologically congenial movement worth cultivating. In any case, the Laois-Offaly TD, who would himself achieve notoriety for his anti-Semitic diatribes, admired both Ó Cuinneagáin and his movement and was eager to do whatever he could to assist them. In the winter of 1943–44 he offered his congratulations to the *Ceannaire* on the latter's 'great work for Ireland' and promised that if Aiséirghe should desire 'any matter [to be] raise[d] in the Dáil – I'll do so with the greatest of pleasure'.[30] To that end he furnished Ó Cuinneagáin with a regularly replenished supply of blank Parliamentary Question forms, enabling Aiséirghe to submit its own questions to Ministers in Flanagan's name. In addition to serving as the party's parliamentary proxy, Flanagan volunteered to spend a week speaking on behalf of the Aiséirghe candidate in a by-election to be held in Tipperary in spring 1944, subject to the agreement of his own executive council.[31] In the event, the dissolution of the Dáil that May and the consequent holding of a general election in the summer meant that Flanagan was never called upon to make good on this offer.

While Flanagan was cultivating Gearóid Ó Cuinneagáin, Aiséirghe's National Organiser was seeking allies in another quarter. On an organisational tour of the southeast, Tomás Ó Dochartaigh had found that 'all the priests here support Aiséirghe and are afraid of the Communists'.[32] Archdeacon John Kelleher of Waterford, an Irish Christian Front veteran and founder in 1937 of the anti-Communist organisation Catholic Union, had been particularly supportive and volunteered a donation to the party. Ó Dochartaigh considered that this opening should be pursued, and in a lecture at Thurles in March 1944 declared that the Catholic Church 'had a right to interfere in politics. It was appointed by God to teach men what was right and what was wrong, and there was not a thing they did which had not a religious significance'.[33] Though Ó Cuinneagáin did not share his deputy's belief in the likelihood, or desirability, of significant clerical support, he did nothing to restrain him.

Notwithstanding its disappointing poll results, therefore, Aiséirghe could claim some tangible results from its first foray into electoral politics. It had gained a measure of visibility on the national stage, and established relations with well-placed external supporters who might prove helpful in the future. Morale among the rank-and-file remained undimmed. Although the depletion of the party's coffers

30 Flanagan to Ó Cuinneagain, 17 November 1943, 12 February 1944, 9/1/16, GÓCP.
31 Flanagan to Ó Cuinneagáin, 12 February 1944, *ibid*.
32 Ó Dochartaigh to Ó Cuinneagáin, 8 March 1944, 3/3/8, *ibid*.
33 *Tipperary Star*, 4 March 1944; Ó Dochartaigh to Ó Cuinneagáin, 13 March 1944, 3/3/8, GÓCP.

gave grounds for concern, the mere fact that Aiséirghe had taken part in the electoral arena made it far more difficult for ministers to contemplate suppressing it as a subversive movement without being perceived as undemocratic in their turn. Most importantly of all, the national election results confirmed the trend revealed in the previous year's local government poll of growing disaffection with the 'establishment' parties. Fianna Fáil lost ten of its 77 seats, being reduced to a parliamentary minority for the first time since 1932. Fine Gael fared even worse, relinquishing almost 30% of its representation in the Dáil. Though the beneficiaries on this occasion had been Clann na Talmhan, the Labour Party and anti-establishment independents like Flanagan, the prospects for a still more radical 'outsider' movement were clearly still bright. What the general election campaign had proved, though, was that Aiséirghe could expect few favours at the hands of the mainstream media. If its message was to be communicated to the Irish voting public, the task would have to be accomplished almost entirely through its own efforts.

The propaganda problem

Throughout its existence Ailtirí na hAiséirghe complained continuously, and with some justification, of its treatment at the hands of the national media. With the exception of a few very brief items, more often than not in Irish, the mass-circulation Dublin daily papers maintained a de facto embargo on reports relating to its activities while according considerably more space to less newsworthy organisations. There is no record of Aiséirghe ever receiving attention of any kind from Raidió Éireann, the state broadcasting service. It is unnecessary to infer, as Gearóid Ó Cuinneagáin did, the existence of a conspiracy among proprietors and editors to 'black' reporting of his movement. Although each of the Dublin dailies did indeed have strong political biases in favour of one or other of the mainstream parties, rival movements – e.g. Clann na Talmhan – could normally expect to receive adequate if not always sympathetic coverage. Aiséirghe, however, was a highly controversial body, dedicated to the destruction of the state and widely perceived as pro-Axis in its character and sympathies; reports of its doings were certain to receive the closest possible scrutiny by the censorship authorities. Hard-pressed newspaper staff, with dozens of important stories vying for the few column-inches available,[34] could be forgiven for deciding not to go to the trouble of commissioning and writing

---

34 By the time of Aiséirghe's formation in 1942, paper shortages had already reduced the Dublin dailies to a scant four pages.

articles they knew were unlikely ever to appear in print. Moreover, Ó Cuinneagáin's penchant for splenetically demanding corrections, more often than not with regard to fine details of party policy, from those editors who did from time to time accord space to his movement can have encouraged few of them to repeat the experiment.[35]

Ó Cuinneagáin himself had no doubt that Aiséirghe was the victim of a politically motivated, as well as Jewish-inspired, vendetta. The 'tied and bought daily press', he complained in a 'Personal Letter' to Aiséirghe members, had no shortage of space for news about 'the war front in Timbuctoo', but 'not a line about the battles waged and won for a Free Gaelic and Christian Ireland in one day in Sráid Uí Chonaill [O'Connell Street, Dublin]'.[36] Whether as the result of a concerted boycott or of exceptional wartime conditions, however, the consequences from the movement's point of view were the same. By November 1943, Ó Cuinneagáin had concluded that the only way of gaining Aiséirghe the publicity it needed was for the party to launch a newspaper of its own.

The factor leading the *Ceannaire* to this decision appears to have been the imposition of a ban on the publishing of accounts in provincial newspapers – which had always taken a more favourable stance with regard to Aiséirghe activities – of a pair of significant events in October 1943. A speech by Riobárd Breathnach in Cork at the annual commemoration of the death of the War of Independence leader Terence MacSwiney was stricken from the *Cork Examiner* by order of the Office of the Controller of Censorship. The *Tipperary Star*'s coverage of a well-attended meeting addressed by Ó Cuinneagáin a week previously met a similar fate. In both cases the justification given was that the speakers had advocated unconstitutional means to abolish the institutions of state.[37] Indignant, Ó Cuinneagáin promptly submitted an application for a permit to publish his own Irish-language fortnightly newspaper, *Aiséirghe*, to be priced at twopence and with an initial print run of 5,000 copies.[38] At the same time he approached Oliver J. Flanagan for assistance in protesting against the censorship of his speeches. Flanagan promised to 'raise hell' in the Dáil over the suppression of the *Tipperary Star* report and provided Ó Cuinneagáin

35 See, e.g. Ó Cuinneagáin to the editor, *Dublin Evening Mail*, 1 June 1943, 4/1/12, GÓCP.
36 'Litir Pearsanta', 12 April 1943, 6/2/5, GÓCP.
37 Ó Cuinneagáin to the Newspaper Censor, 3 November 1943, 9/1/16, *ibid.*; M. J. Coyne, Office of the Controller of Censorship, to Ó Cuinneagáin, 6 November 1943, *ibid.*; Ó Cuinneagáin to the censor, 13 January 1944, 8/8/5, *ibid.*; T. Ó Muircheartaigh, Office of the Controller of Censorship, to Ó Cuinneagáin, 29 January 1944, *ibid.*
38 Ó Cuinneagáin to the Secretary, Stationery Office, 4 November 1943, 9/1/16, *ibid.*

with another Parliamentary Question form, inviting him to draft his own question on the matter for submission in Flanagan's name.[39] In the event, the strategy of calling one government department's attention to Ó Cuinneagáin's proclivity for rhetorical extremism at the very moment that he was attempting to persuade another that he was a suitable person to be granted a newspaper licence proved unwise. The ministerial response to Aiséirghe's Dáil question was a reiteration of the censor's objections; four days later, Seán Lemass, Minister of Industry and Commerce, turned down Ó Cuinneagáin's application on the ground that supplies of paper were too limited to grant approval to any new publications.[40]

Ó Cuinneagáin, for his part, was determined not to take no for an answer. Correctly identifying the inadequacy of the movement's propaganda as the principal reason for its inability to make any significant breakthrough on a national scale, he declared the launching of a paper to be Aiséirghe's single most important task for the year ahead. A vigorous campaign to exert pressure on the government was immediately set in train. Ó Cuinneagáin sent numerous letters to the press, protesting that the paper requirements of his proposed journal was 'not more than .0001%' of the supply made available to English-language publications in Ireland and drawing attention to the 'hypocrisy' of the government in calling for the wider use of Irish in daily life but denying facilities to an organisation seeking to do just that in the field of journalism. Aiséirghe members wheeled a 'trolley-poster' bearing a caricature of de Valera and the legend 'The Old Man Says NO! to a Gaelic Paper for Aiséirghe' through the streets of Dublin during the week of the 1944 St Patrick's Day celebrations.[41] The assistance of sympathetic figures in Comhdháil Náisiúnta na Gaeilge and other Irish-language revival bodies was enlisted, and a programme of public protest meetings launched. An Aiséirghe petition-drive was inaugurated, although the number of signatures received fell far short of the 20,000 sought.[42] As a final expedient, Ó Cuinneagáin attempted to purchase an existing title, the Skibbereen, Co. Cork-based *Southern Star*.[43] The approach was made anonymously through a firm of solici-

39 Flanagan to Ó Cuinneagáin, 17 November 1943, *ibid*.

40 C. Ua Dubhgáin, Department of Industry and Commerce, to Ó Cuinneagáin, 27 November 1943, 9/1/16, *ibid*.

41 'Litir Pearsanta', 29 March 1944, 6/2/21, GÓCP.

42 Only 916 signatures were gathered, the result of the apathy of Aiséirghe *cumainn* – the majority of which failed to return a single completed form – and Ó Cuinneagáin's insistence that signatures be accepted only from those using the Irish form of their names.

43 This may have been a suggestion from Ernest Blythe, who had edited the *Southern Star* in the early 1930s.

tors – 'the proprietors are *at best* Fine Gael and it is only too likely they would not consider a direct application from us' – but the journal turned out not to be for sale except at prohibitive cost.[44]

The government was unmoved by Aiséirghe's protest campaign, which, in view of the public's long record of indifference to controversies involving the Irish language, was never likely to cause it serious embarrassment. But it found the campaign waged on Ó Cuinneagáin's behalf by Aiséirghe's patron in the Dáil, Oliver J. Flanagan, harder to ignore. In February 1944, Flanagan laid down an Ó Cuinneagáin-drafted question in the asking the Minister for Supplies, Seán Lemass, to justify his refusal of a newspaper licence to Aiséirghe. Simultaneously, the deputy for Laois-Offaly drew Ó Cuinneagáin's attention to the recent appearance of a periodical entitled *Dublin Jewish Youth Monthly*, and declared his intention of submitting a second question of his own to find out 'when did the Jews get the permit?'[45] Ó Cuinneagáin was highly gratified by the coupling of the two questions, and still more pleased by the opportunity for propaganda provided by the Minister's admission that the youth monthly had failed to submit an application for approval.[46] From Aiséirghe's point of view, however, the salient part of Lemass' answer was that a licence had been denied Ó Cuinneagáin 'in accordance with the general policy of restricting the publication of periodicals which were not in existence when the [Emergency Powers] Order relating to periodicals was made'.[47] If it could be shown that other journals had in fact been launched with the government's approval since the beginning of the Emergency, the rationale for continuing to withhold sanction for an Aiséirghe newspaper would be seriously undermined. Six months later, Ó Cuinneagáin wrote to the Department of Industry and Commerce to point out that Muintír na Tíre had just been granted permission to begin a monthly publication of its own, and that the restrictive policy referred to in the Minister's reply in February no longer appeared to be operative. The grant of a publication licence for a party fortnightly followed two weeks later.[48] The first issue of *Aiséirghe*, a four-page tabloid-style paper with a maximum authorised print run of 5,000 copies, appeared in November.

44 Ó Cuinneagáin to James Charleton, J. J. Bastow & Co., chartered accountants, 5 July 1944; Crowley, Bolger & Cusack, solicitors, to Bastow's, 29 July 1944, 9/1/16, GÓCP. Emphasis in original.
45 Flanagan to Ó Cuinneagáin, 12 February 1944, *ibid*.
46 Ó Cuinneagáin to Flanagan, 1 March 1944, *ibid*.
47 92 *DP–Dáil*, cols 1512–13 (23 February 1944).
48 Ó Cuinneagáin to the Secretary, Department of Industry and Commerce, 30 August 1944; Conchubhar Ó Síothcháin, Department of Industry and Commerce, to Ó Cuinneagáin, 15 September 1944, 9/1/16, GÓCP. Due to paper shortages, *Aiséirghe* was initially published as a monthly.

Lemass could console himself that he had succeeded in delaying the appearance of Aiséirghe's paper for almost a year. But in being forced to give ground in this fashion, the government had by no means exhausted the tools at its disposal for holding the movement's propaganda effort in check. Few organisations in Ireland during the Emergency can have suffered more severely at the hands of the censor than Ailtirí na hAiséirghe. The rigidity and, in the view of many commentators, irrationality of wartime censorship policy – of which an oft-cited example was the banning of a photograph of a government minister ice-skating on a frozen pond for fear that the image might provide meteorological information of use to a belligerent power – has been the subject of much recent scholarship.[49] Aiséirghe, however, had more reason for complaint than most. To be sure, much of the material it submitted for approval was objectionable by any reasonable standard. An article in *Aiséirghe* inviting readers to forward denunciations of 'alien scoundrels' [*boicíní gallta*] who had been observed flying the Union Jack on 11 November was clearly intimidatory in intent and duly blue-pencilled by the censor.[50] Other acts of suppression were much more questionable. Feargus Ó Mordha's pro-Salazar pamphlet 'The Resurrection of Portugal', and a lengthier Irish-language treatment of the same theme, 'Éire ag Féachaint ar an Phortingéil', by Riobárd Breathnach, were banned on the highly dubious grounds that if the government permitted publications inviting the public to regard foreign heads of state admiringly, it would have no basis for prohibiting countervailing publications holding them up to public contumely.[51] (Ó Cuinneagáin's protest in *Aiséirghe* that books with titles like *King George VI and His People: A Tribute to Britain* were freely available in Dublin bookshops was itself made the subject of a banning order.) Unquestionably a great deal of the censorship to which Aiséirghe publications were subjected – when it was not so arbitrary as entirely to defy explanation[52] – was

49 See especially D. Ó Drisceoil, *Censorship in Ireland 1939–45: Neutrality, Politics and Society* (Cork: Cork University Press, 1996) and R. Cole, *Propaganda, Censorship and Irish Neutrality in the Second World War* (Edinburgh: Edinburgh University Press, 2006). It should be noted, though, that many supposedly irrational decisions by the Office of the Controller of Censorship came about as a direct response to demands by the British Ministry of Information for matter of this kind to be suppressed. The fact that, following Irish acquiescence, the censored material would often appear in British publications was the occasion of much ill-feeling on the part of the Irish authorities.

50 Censored draft, April 1945, 9/1/18, GÓCP.

51 Minute by Frank Aiken, 3 December 1943, Department of Justice: Office of Controller of Censorship 4/45, file 135, NAI.

52 An example was the censor's veto of the original title of *Ireland's Twentieth Century Destiny*: 'Ireland Will Rise Again'.

politically motivated. Frank Aiken, the Minister for Co-Ordination of Defensive Measures, took a keen personal interest in Aiséirghe's propaganda output, and did not hesitate to prohibit or edit material that had no conceivable security implications, but that he regarded as unfair, unbalanced or excessively critical of the government. In view of the exceptionally broad and vaguely-defined character of the legislation governing censorship, it is difficult to say that Aiken exceeded his powers by doing so.[53] That he was flouting the spirit of the law and the Oireachtas' intent in granting such extraordinary powers to the executive, on the other hand, cannot be disputed. For his part, Aiken was wholly unapologetic about his actions. A hard-bitten veteran of the War of Independence and Civil War, he was especially contemptuous of Aiséirghe's martial rhetoric: 'We must spout our heads off at all times & the less guts we have for fighting the more we must talk about it'.[54]

It is difficult, however, to avoid the conclusion that the government's best efforts to undermine Aiséirghe's propaganda campaign were less successful than the actions of Ailtirí na hAiséirghe itself. The party's uncompromising adhesion to the Irish language in its publications meant that the paid circulation of *Aiséirghe* was significantly higher than its actual readership. Not until April 1945 did Ó Cuinneagáin unbend so far as to permit the lead headline of the newspaper to appear in English, though the remaining content continued to use Irish exclusively. Even for the minority capable of comprehending the articles, *Aiséirghe* made few concessions to the uncommitted reader, consisting largely of recapitulations of party statements interspersed with caustic commentary on the manifold deficiencies of the Fianna Fáil government. Far too great a proportion was written by the *Ceannaire* himself, less a reflection of any desire on his part to monopolise the paper's columns than of the paucity of Aiséirghe members capable of producing informed political commentary in the first official language. The consequences of this communications strategy, then, were doubly unfortunate. A disproportionate amount of the leader's time and

53 In addition to fifty-four itemised subjects, mention of which was prohibited unless specifically cleared by the state censor (ranging from details of defensive measures to 'matter in which use is made of the expression "black bread" or of the word "black" in relation to bread'), a catch-all article 55 of the Emergency Powers (No. 5) Order, 1939 – the contents of which itself could not legally be published – banned 'matter not included in any of the foregoing classes the publication of which would be likely to be prejudicial to the public safety or the preservation of the State, or to the maintenance of public order, or to the provision and control of supplies and services essential to the life of the community'.
54 Marginal comment by Aiken on Aiséirghe draft article, 'An Teorann', n.d. [c. December 1944], Department of Justice: Office of Controller of Censorship 4/45, file R. 42, NAI.

energy had been dissipated in a publicity effort that largely failed to achieve results, leaving the party little better prepared to fight a new general election than it had been in 1943. In the event, the necessity of doing so loomed closer than any of Aiséirghe's leaders realised.

Confusion worse confounded

Aiséirghe's general election campaign in 1944 was in many respects a repeat of the debacle of the previous year, on a larger scale. Once again the movement was taken unawares by the government's announcement that it intended going to the country, although on this occasion with more excuse. The event that precipitated the election was the crisis over the so-called 'American Note'. The US envoy in Dublin, David Gray, who owed his appointment in 1940 to the fortunate circumstance of being Eleanor Roosevelt's uncle, had developed during his stay in the Phoenix Park a moderate distaste for the Irish people;[55] a melodramatic overestimation of the capacity for evil of the Fianna Fáil government ('believe me we are dealing with a very charming, astute, unscrupulous and dangerous outfit');[56] and a virtual monomania with the personality of Éamon de Valera, who he viewed as the 'malign genius' standing in the way of Ireland's entry into the war on the side of the Allies.[57] In February 1944 Gray, supported by his British counterpart Sir John Maffey,[58] prevailed upon the governments of the United States and the United Kingdom to despatch a communiqué to the Taoiseach demanding in peremptory terms the closure of the Axis legations in Dublin and the expulsion of the German and Japanese representatives. Gray was under no illusions that the Irish government would acquiesce in such an unneutral action. His true purpose, as he made clear to Maffey, was to use de Valera's expected refusal as the basis for a press campaign in the US and Britain denouncing Ireland's supposed partiality in favour of the Axis powers, thereby

55 'I suppose the truth is that they are like all other people … the worst of them perhaps a little more despicable.' Gray to W. Cameron Forbes, 12 December 1940, RG 84, 'Ireland: Dublin Legation: General Records, 1936–1948', 350/61/29/4, Box 7, NARA.

56 Gray to Col. David Bruce, Director, European Theater of Operations, Office of Strategic Services, 17 June 1944, OSS files, RG 226, Entry 210, Box 299, 'Éire' file, NARA.

57 Gray to Winston Churchill, 11 May 1942, TNA DO 35/1109/8, WX 11/116.

58 Maffey can in a sense be considered the originator of the 'American Note', having suggested in February 1943 that a joint US–British demand be made for naval and air facilities in Ireland. Four months later, he proposed to Gray that the latter should advocate to Washington a '*joint exploratory approach without specific demands or specific reference to Partition*, followed possibly by curtailment of supplies if response were not satisfactory'. The British government rejected both of Maffey's suggestions. J. L. Maffey, 'Memorandum covering talk with Mr. Archer on points arising from my telegram No. 79 of 24th August, 1943', TNA DO 130/32. Emphasis in original.

ensuring its marginalisation at the end of the war – an unusual instance of an diplomat conceiving his ministerial duty to be the worsening of relations between his own government and the country to which he was accredited.[59] In the event, however, Gray's démarche badly backfired. The Irish government, fearing the Note to be the diplomatic prelude to the incursion from the North that they had apprehended since the beginning of the Emergency, placed the armed forces on full invasion alert and rushed troops to the Border. De Valera took pre-emptive action in the ensuing propaganda exchange, leaking the terms of the Anglo-American demand to the press and describing in considerable detail in a Dáil speech the measures the government had taken since the beginning of the war to ensure that the presence of the Axis legations would not compromise the security of the Allies. As a result, the two Allied governments were placed in the embarrassing position of being obliged to explain that the Note had merely been a request rather than an ultimatum, and that they had no intention of violating Irish neutrality to secure compliance. De Valera's prestige soared as a result of his refusal to be bullied by the Anglo-Americans and his success in surmounting what appeared to be the most serious threat to Ireland's neutral status since the summer of 1940. Quick to perceive his advantage, the Taoiseach found a suitable pretext for calling a snap general election to be held at the end of May.

In the twelve months since the previous campaign, the arguments in favour of Aiséirghe refraining from contesting the election had only grown stronger. From the outset it was plain that Fianna Fáil was heading for a sweeping victory, and that an appeal based on discontent with the government's performance was unlikely to resonate with the electorate as it had done in 1943. Aiséirghe's meagre results on the previous occasion had confirmed how much organisational work remained to be done before the movement could take on the establishment parties on anything like equal terms. The constituency organisations that had put forward candidates in 1943 were still burdened with heavy debts, while the finances of Aiséirghe as a whole remained in a fragile state.

Ó Cuinneagáin, however, was determined that Aiséirghe should not only put forward its own slate of candidates, but do so on an even wider scale than the previous year. It is tempting to conclude that in making this decision he had fallen victim to his own propaganda: and

59 Gray's initiative was also intended to neutralise the Irish-American lobby within the Democratic Party in advance of the 1944 presidential election. It should be remembered that in his approach to Irish affairs the US envoy was carrying out the policy of his president, who held him in high regard.

certainly the relentlessly upbeat tone of the *Ceannaire*'s monthly letters to members and the fury with which he reacted to any suggestion that the movement was on the wrong track would lend colour to such an interpretation. But according to Aindreas Ó Scolaidhe, Ó Cuinneagáin did not regard the winning of seats as the only, or even necessarily the primary, advantage to be gained from nominating candidates. During the Emergency, censorship rules were relaxed to a considerable extent for the duration of election campaigns. For Aiséirghe, they thus represented brief windows of opportunity in which the movement's message could be communicated to voters, and published by the newspapers, without attracting government interference. Hence Ó Cuinneagáin was keen that as many Aiséirghe candidates as possible should go forward, even – or especially – in those areas in which the movement was not yet well established.

Not all Aiséirghe constituency organisations were of a like mind. The Waterford branch was aghast to learn that Tomás Ó Dochartaigh, its candidate in 1943, had decided to stand on this occasion in his home constituency of Tipperary and now required it to find an entirely new local candidate two weeks before polling day. Three potential nominees declined to put their names forward, and the meeting to select a candidate broke up without any decision having been reached. In Limerick, a similar meeting failed to attract a quorum.[60] The Dundalk branch openly mutinied against Eoin Ó Coigligh's reselection, declaring that it was 'unwise & immoral to contract debt on top of debt, with no prospect of paying same', and declined to assist its own candidate in the election.[61] In the event, only seven candidates were put forward: Ó Cuinneagáin, Seán Ó Dúbhghaill and Eoin Ó Coigligh in the constituencies they had contested the previous year, and Oisín Ó Droighneáin, Seosamh Ó Ceallaigh and Tomás Ó Dochartaigh in Dublin County, Roscommon and Tipperary respectively. After immense difficulty, a last-minute nominee, Liam Breathnach [Willie Walsh], was persuaded to stand in the Aiséirghe interest for the constituency abandoned by Ó Dochartaigh in Waterford. Hostile commentators, however, did not fail to draw attention to the ironic contrast between Aiséirghe's claim to represent Irish youth and its choice of a champion in Breathnach, a sextuagenarian store manager and veteran of the War of Independence.[62] The pro forma nature of Breathnach's nomination

60 Ristéard Mac Siacuis to Ó Cuinneagáin, 15 May 1944, 4/2/6, GÓCP.
61 M. Ó Flannagáin to Ó Cuinneagáin, 17 May 1944, *ibid.*
62 This individual is confused with Capt. Liam Walsh of the Blueshirts and IFG/CN in Martin White's 'The Greenshirts'; other than the coincidence of names, there was no connection between the two.

was conceded by his own election manager, who admitted that it would be impossible for the candidate to make many appearances in his home constituency before the election.[63] Nonetheless, Breathnach did satisfy the essential requirement of Aiséirghe's principal financial backer in the district, having given speeches from party platforms in the previous year descanting upon the threat of 'International Jewry and Freemasonry'.[64]

Though once again the product of frenetic improvisation, in one respect at least Aiséirghe's performance showed improvement over 1943. The party's campaign rallies and meetings drew large crowds, and earned praise for their energy even from neutral or unsympathetic commentators. The only significant exceptions were those headed by the *Ceannaire* himself. Ernest Blythe's *Leader*, which was coming to adopt a steadily more critical stance vis-à-vis Ó Cuinneagáin's direction of the organisation, did not fail to notice the contrast. In a lengthy editorial provoked by Ó Cuinneagain's address at the 1944 St Patrick's Day rally in Dublin, the weekly wondered whether the *Ceannaire* might not be more valuable to his party in another capacity:

> As we listened to the opening remarks of the speaker who followed him, certain ideas that have been gathering in our mind in recent months crystalised into a definite opinion. Gearoid Ó Cuinneagáin, though he had the advantage of a microphone, was shouting himself hoarse making much more noise than was necessary but articulating so badly that, with the distraction inseparable from an outdoor meeting in a busy street, it was next to impossible to follow the trend of his remarks. Two friends of ours to whom we talked about the speech afterwards told us that they had not been able to catch half of it.
>
> [W]e came to the conclusion that the Ailtirí will get nowhere unless Gearoid Ó Cuinneagáin either manages to improve himself almost out of recognition as a public speaker or leaves the platform work of the organisation practically entirely to others ... We are aware that Mr. de Valera is regarded by many people as a very poor public speaker; but it cannot be suggested that he is anywhere near as bad as Gearoid Ó Cuinneagáin. Mr. de Valera never makes himself unintelligible by speaking through clenched teeth, he offers some variety in tone and expression, he is occasionally mildly humorous; and now and again, when roused, he rises to a kind of eloquence.
>
> ... A good plan might be for Gearóid to surrender the position of Ceannaire, altering the Constitution so as to enable him to remain as Secretary or Director of Organisation with sufficient authority to give scope to his invaluable driving power. We have become convinced that if he

63 *Waterford Standard*, 27 May 1944.
64 *Ibid.*, 5 June 1943.

continues as Ceannaire on the present basis the Ailtirí will undoubtedly miss the tide; and that would be a thousand pities when the country so badly needs such a movement.[65]

Though Ó Cuinneagáin wisely chose not to respond publicly to this suggestion, the outcome of the election bore out Blythe's contention that structural changes were vitally necessary. Though they should have been assisted by Córas na Poblachta's decision not to participate in the contest, all seven of Aiséirghe's candidates finished at the bottom of their respective polls and lost their deposits. Only in Roscommon and Tipperary, where Seosamh Ó Coigligh and Tomás Ó Dochartaigh secured 16% and 14% respectively of the votes necessary to meet the electoral 'quota', could the movement claim to have performed creditably. Given the circumstances of the election and the inadequacy of the canvassing effort – the *Leader* noted that in Ó Droighneáin's north Dublin constituency, the only indication voters appeared to have been given that an Aiséirghe candidate was standing in their district was when they read his name on their ballot papers on polling day – such a result was perhaps inevitable.[66] But while it probably said less about the true extent of Aiséirghe's following than at first sight it appears to do, it was nonetheless a meagre reward for almost two years of sustained effort.

Ó Cuinneagáin did not attempt to conceal his disappointment with the result. In his post-election 'Personal Letter', he acknowledged frankly that little headway had been made since 1943. The contest, he noted, had been conducted on the basis of the old electoral register, thereby making it impossible for those who had recently attained the voting age to participate. This did undoubtedly cost Aiséirghe some support, if not the 'thousand and more votes in each area' that the *Ceannaire* optimistically claimed. Still more hopefully, he announced that the movement must be ready to field at least 107 candidates at the next general election.[67]

Ó Dochartaigh too put a brave face on the defeat. In a letter of appalling frankness published in the Waterford newspapers, he attributed his own and Aiséirghe's failure to increase their vote to a variety of factors, the most important of which was that 'most of our time is not given to preparations for elections, but rather to expounding a new order of society and forwarding a culture which others have forsaken. That we lost a few hundred votes signifies nothing to us or those who grasp the true meaning of this national resurgence ... For us those

65 *The Leader*, 25 March 1944.
66 *Ibid.*, 17 June 1944.
67 'Litir Pearsanta', August 1944, 6/2/26, GÓCP.

elections are only side-shows'. Ó Dochartaigh went on to promise a settling of accounts, once Aiséirghe ultimately achieved power, with 'those who are celebrating their victory all over Éire not with Céilid-ithe, but with the dances from Paris, London and with Nigger music. As for the actions of enmity against us by the so-called national Press. Those go into the book of reckoning'.[68]

More significant than this, though, was Ó Dochartaigh's reaction to the outcome of the contest in his own Tipperary constituency. Throughout the election, Aiséirghe had ceaselessly reiterated its aversion to the party-political system and all those associated with it. Ó Dochartaigh himself on the hustings had characterised the existing Irish parties as mere tools of the true rulers of Ireland: the powerful vested interests of industry, finance and exchange. While campaigning, however, he had discovered much common ground between himself and two of his fellow candidates, the pro-Hitler Fianna Fáil TD Dan Breen and the Clann na Talmhan representative Jack (John P.) Stakelum, a member of a well-connected North Tipperary political family.[69] During his concession speech Ó Dochartaigh paid public tribute to both men, amplifying his warm comments a week later in a letter to the *Tipperary Star*:

> I must mention Mr. Stakelum and Mr. Dan Breen. There is so very little between these men and Aiséirghe and they are so obviously sincere that I feel justified in hoping that they will be with us next time. Meanwhile, if they follow their consciences (and I am sure they will) Breen in the Dáil and Stakelum in the Co. Council, will prepare the road for the Aiséirghe Ireland.[70]

Breen reciprocated Ó Dochartaigh's overtures in equally generous terms, saying that 'he was sorry Ailtirí na h-Aiseirighe had not done better, that he had studied their programme and that there was a lot in it to commend'.[71]

As some officials were quick to perceive, this initiative by Aiséirghe's second-in-command implied a marked tactical departure from the traditional approach, and possibly an entirely new strategy for the movement. Ever since Aiséirghe's launch, Ó Cuinneagáin had taken every opportunity to sharpen the distinction between his own

68 Letter by 'An Fíolar' [T. Ó Dochartaigh], 3/3/1, GÓCP.
69 Visitors to Breen's home noted the presence of a portrait photograph of Hitler on the Deputy's living-room wall. In 1943 Breen had sent to the German Legation, on Dáil notepaper, his 'congratulations to the Fuehrer on his birthday. May he live long to lead Europe on the road to peace, security and happiness'. Breen to Hempel, 20 April 1943, Office of Strategic Services, RG 226, Entry 210, Box 299, 'Éire' file, NARA.
70 *Tipperary Star*, 1 July 1944.
71 Memorandum by G. C. Ryan, G2, 8 June 1944, G2/X/1320, SI/256. DDMA.

organisation and conventional political parties. Coexistence, far less co-operation, was contrary to everything for which the one-party 'national movement' stood. But whereas Ó Dochartaigh's expressions of admiration for Breen and Stakelum might be seen as nothing more than an attempt to separate them from their existing allegiances and draw them into the Aiséirghe camp – and were so interpreted by the *Ceannaire* – they could also suggest a tactical alliance between Aiséirghe and radical-right elements in other parties, in a kind of 'pan-extremist front'. Over the next year, it would become clear that this was in fact the direction towards which Ó Dochartaigh wished to draw the movement. Nor was he alone in attempting to do so. These conflicting visions – of a vanguard all-Ireland party that stood beyond and against the existing order, versus a body that would seek collaborators and alliances from within the twenty-six-county political structure – would become the principal, though by no means the only, bone of contention between Ó Cuinneagáin and his lieutenants in the following year.

Internal divisions

By the spring of 1944 a distinct chill had begun to emerge in relations between Harcourt Street and some branches in the provinces. In the case of the Cork city and county organisation, exchanges of mutual recriminations became the principal form of communication with national headquarters. The grievances of the *Ceannaire* centred mainly upon the Cork organisation's failure during much of 1943 to provide regular monthly reports and remit head office's share of receipts from sales of literature and collections in a timely fashion. Ó Cuinneagáin further alleged that this indiscipline had communicated itself to many of the smaller branches in the country, and that Riobárd Breathnach's inability to keep local officials up to the mark – if necessary by summarily dismissing the less competent or committed among them – was causing administrative chaos.[72] There was some basis for these complaints. Due to a number of personal problems, most notably the death of his infant son, Breathnach was unable during 1943 and much of 1944 to devote sufficient attention to his duties as *Ard-Cheannasaidhe*. In March 1944 Ó Cuinneagáin went so far as to suggest that Breathnach might like to step down from the position, while retaining his seat on the Ard-Chomhairle. A temporary solution was found by bisecting the Cork organisation into city and county divisions and appointing Seosamh Ó Coigligh [Joseph Quigley] as acting *Ard-Ceannasaidhe* to

---

72 Ó Cuinneagáin to Riobárd Breathnach, 13 March 1944, 7/1/74, GÓCP.

assist Breathnach, a step which restored order and direction to the local organisation's affairs.

Ó Coigligh's promotion, however, provided an object-lesson to Ó Cuinneagáin in the danger of getting what one wishes for. Employed at the time as a local government official, Ó Coigligh was one of the most capable individuals ever to hold office in Ailtirí na hAiséirghe. A self-taught linguist who spoke several modern languages fluently and read widely in all of them, he possessed an international perspective and a breadth of vision that the *Ceannaire*, for all his many gifts, conspicuously lacked. Unlike Ó Cuinneagáin, moreover, Ó Coigligh was not merely respected but regarded with genuine affection by many of his colleagues in the movement. Lacking in personal or political ambition, he had no desire to rise higher in Aiséirghe's ranks than the position he held, and on more than one occasion asked to be relieved of the *ceannasaidheacht*. But this quality was not accompanied by any tendency towards reticence: and almost from the moment of his assuming office Ó Coigligh had begun to respond to Ó Cuinneagáin's criticisms with suggestions of his own for improving the higher direction of the movement, expressed in terms almost as pungent as those of the *Ceannaire* himself.

Ó Coigligh's unhappiness, shared by most other officers in the Cork organisation, was fuelled above all by the negativity, captiousness and injudiciousness of Aiséirghe's public propaganda. The aura of extremism that had alienated many potential supporters from the movement, they believed, was almost entirely due to the rhetorical excesses of leading members of the Dublin city and county branches – not least among them the *Ceannaire* himself. The ideological bankruptcy of Fianna Fáil was so great, and the failure of Fine Gael and Labour to offer any credible alternative so transparent, that Aiséirghe was almost certain to become a significant political force if only it could refrain from driving away uncommitted voters. Destructive criticism and *ad hominem* attacks on mainstream party leaders – many of whom, regardless of their political affiliations, enjoyed considerable public respect for having put their own lives at hazard in the struggle for Irish independence – undermined the national unity Aiséirghe professed to value and projected a deeply unattractive image of the party as a whole. In the same fashion, constantly reiterated demands that the six counties be 're-taken' by force of arms served only to confuse ordinary people as to the distinction between Aiséirghe and republican parties like Sinn Féin, and to throw a lifeline to the government by providing it with a pretext to ban the movement as a subversive organisation.

A visit by Ó Cuinneagáin to Cork in January 1944 provided county officials with an opportunity to make these points to him personally. To their dismay, they found him eager to discuss what they considered to be still more wrong-headed and impractical ideas, such as the organisation of hunger-strikes in Northern Ireland as a means of protesting against partition. By the end of the visit, however, they believed that the air had been cleared to some extent and that Ó Cuinneagáin would henceforth take note of their concerns. The *Ceannaire's* actions two months later, in response to the 'American Note' crisis, revealed how wrong they had been in this assumption. It also led to an open confrontation between the two most important regional components of the Aiséirghe organisation.

The turmoil over the American Note, coinciding as it did with the previously-planned St Patrick's Day activities, provided Aiséirghe with an ideal opportunity to take advantage of the prevailing atmosphere of patriotic fervour. In a hastily drafted address delivered by Riobárd Breathnach before the annual 17 March rally, the Cork organisation characterised the national unity and setting-aside of party differences that David Gray had inadvertently produced in Ireland as a practical manifestation of the Aiséirghe ideal, one that could and should be extended to other aspects of life.

> Our whole effort in Aiséirghe has been to secure that in national questions we should act as a united people and we therefore welcome the unanimity with which this latest demand has been rejected. We believe, moreover, that this same unity of mind and purpose can be brought into being on other national issues also and that it can and must ultimately defeat the attempt of any outside power to dominate us, whether that attempt is [sic] at physical domination, as in the Six Counties, or domination through the enslavement of the mind of our people which the loss of the Irish Language would ultimately entail.[73]

In Dungarvan, too, Tomás Ó Dochartaigh pledged Aiséirghe's support for the Taoiseach 'in the stand he had taken against Anglo-American pressure', and called for the young men and women of the area to enlist in the state Emergency Services.[74] A very different note, however, was struck at the mass meeting held by the Dublin city branch in O'Connell Street the same day, at which Ó Cuinneagáin spoke – the same address that had led Ernest Blythe to recommend that he consider giving up the *ceannaireacht*. Not only did much of Ó Cuinneagáin's speech consist of an unmodulated attack upon the Fianna Fáil government,

---

73 Text of Cork address, covered by letter from Séamus Ó Coigligh to Ó Cuinneagáin, 17 March 1944, 7/1/72, GÓCP.
74 *Dungarvan Observer*, 25 March 1944.

but it went on to intimate that should the Anglo-Americans persist in their demands, Aiséirghe's response would not be confined to words alone.

The heads of the Cork branches greeted the news of the actions of their counterparts in Dublin with undisguised exasperation. Regarding the O'Connell Street address as a sign that Ó Cuinneagáin had either misunderstood or ignored their representations of the previous January, officers of the city organisation resolved in April to restate their views in terms that would not be open to misinterpretation. The resulting letter, drafted by Ó Coigligh on behalf of the local executive, was one of the most uncompromising documents ever addressed to Ó Cuinneagáin by any of his subordinates and represented, in fact if not in so many words, a direct challenge to his authority as leader.

[T]he name of the Dublin Ailtirí is now associated with oratorical extremism and thoughtlessness – something, in our view, that will arrest the forward progress of the movement not only in Dublin but throughout the country as well …

If the movement is conducted correctly at this time, in our view it will not be able to be stopped … but if [the people] should come to believe that we are merely a kind of appendage of the I.R.A. or of latter-day Sinn Féin, we are convinced that they will give their support to some organisation other than Ailtirí na hAiséirghe.

We have not yet received an account of your meeting on St Patrick's Day but we have heard that the greater part of it consisted of an attack upon the Government – this when the Government's reputation is riding high on account of the threats from the Yanks [*bagartha na puncánach*]! We cannot imagine that this helps the movement; rather the reverse.

… [We recommend]: That you rigorously prohibit very young Ailtirí from speaking in public;

That you, in your capacity as *Ceannaire*, speak [publicly] as infrequently and with as much restraint as lies within your capability; [and] …

That you make clear to the people as often as may be required that not only our aims but our methods are transparent and in conformity with the law.[75]

Ó Cuinneagáin's response to this lengthy and peremptory missive gave no indication that he appreciated the extent to which his leadership had been called into question. Faced with a challenge that on its face called either for earnest conciliation or open confrontation with his critics, he sought instead to brush aside their concerns as trivial misunderstandings, born of lack of self-confidence. It was true, he acknowledged in a letter of response two weeks later, that some of Aiséirghe's

75 S. Ó Coigligh to Ó Cuinneagáin, 2 April 1944, G2/2988, DDMA.

speakers in Dublin were very young and that from time to time they forgot themselves on the public platform, notwithstanding the best efforts of their elders to hold them in check. But trained speakers were in exceedingly short supply and in a city as large as the capital, with meetings being held on a daily basis, occasional intemperate remarks were quickly forgotton by their hearers. In fact, Ó Cuinneagáin was not sure that in the long run, appeals to the emotions of the public, however unrestrained their phraseology, were not likely to do as much good as harm:

> I myself believe most firmly that the awakening of a *spirit of courage* in the people is the most important thing and that the best way of accomplishing this is not through their *intellect*. The people who have courage are the people who will do most to help the national movements in Ireland and it is not usual for *those* to be advanced in years.

As for his own address on St Patrick's Day, he had done his best 'to be as gentle with the Government as I could, but without denying the right of Ireland to freedom as Pearse and [Terence] MacSwiney understood it'. If the speech had not been well received by Ernest Blythe, doubtless that was not unrelated to the fact that Blythe himself was notorious for his irritation with any public stance supportive of republicanism. Ó Cuinneagáin conceded that 'it is bruited about both here and in other towns that Aiséirghe is nothing more than the above-ground wing of the [Irish] Republican Army', rumours that he claimed were being actively disseminated by 'politicians evilly disposed to us' as well as government officials. These insinuations were no more to be taken seriously than their predecessors of two years previously – that Aiséirghe was in receipt of 'German gold' or 'Russian gold'. The *Ceannaire* made no apology, however, for the martial tone of his statements regarding the American Note, even though these had been misreported in the press. It was appropriate not only that the 'dedicated people [*críonna*] in the movement understand that we, the members of Aiséirghe, will stand shoulder to shoulder with other Irishmen against any occupying force whatsoever, but that *we are resolved to fight for the freedom of the entire country should war be waged against us*'. The *Ceannaire* concluded by exhorting his followers in Cork to draw inspiration from the life of Fr Theobald Matthew, the nineteenth-century Cork-born apostle of temperance, and not 'to assume that ours is a movement without obstacles, rumours, misunderstandings etc ... Life has been thus since the beginning of time. *Nulla crux, nulla corona!*'[76]

---

76 Ó Cuinneagáin to Riobárd Breathnach, 18 April 1944, 7/2/13, GÓCP. Emphases in original.

The result of this unsatisfactory exchange was to aggravate greatly the divisions within the movement. Concluding that there was little point in attempting to reason further with Ó Cuinneagáin, the Cork organisation increasingly went its own way. Several influential members decided that the only way forward for Aiséirghe would be with a new face in the *ceannaireacht*. For his part, Ó Cuinneagáin's failure to recognise the disaffection of his most important regional organisation as representing more than a little local difficulty not only left a potential internal rebellion simmering, but allowed the growing tendency of the movement to engage in the kind of immoderate and provocative behaviour of which the Cork representatives had complained to go unchecked.

The intensification of militancy

As if positively to defy his Cork-based lieutenants, Ó Cuinneagáin presided over a series of actions in later 1944 and the first half of 1945 that seemed to have no other purpose than to cement Aiséirghe's reputation for extremism and irresponsibility.

At the end of 1944, the *Ceannaire* appears to have hoped that tarring Fianna Fáil with the anti-Semitic brush might yield political dividends. To assist him in this endeavour, he approached the head of the Imperial Fascist League in Britain, Arnold S. Leese. His choice of correspondent was a curious one. The most monomaniacal British representative of what Richard Thurlow has aptly styled 'the Hitler fan club', Leese had spent much of the 1930s attempting to persuade his compatriots of the racial inferiority of the Irish and other biologically 'Mediterranean' peoples, who in his view were 'frequently misleadingly called "Celts"'.[77] In his newspaper, *The Fascist*, he had persistently urged the military reconquest of Ireland as a strategic and racial imperative.[78] Notwithstanding this unpromising pedigree Ó Cuinneagáin turned to Leese, the author of a widely distributed series of foaming-at-the-mouth exposés of the worldwide Judaeo-Masonic conspiracy and proprietor, following his release in 1944 from internment as an enemy sympathiser, of a one-man 'Anti-Jewish Information Bureau', as an authority who could provide a definitive ruling on Éamon de Valera's

---

77 Imperial Fascist League, *Race and Politics: A Counter-Blast to the Masonic Teaching of Universal Brotherhood* (London: Imperial Fascist League, n.d. [c. 1934]), p. 5.

78 See, e.g., 'The Division of Ireland: The Part of the Jews', *The Fascist*, October 1937; 'Our Policy in Ireland – Realism', *ibid.*, December 1938; 'The Necessity for Re-Occupying Ireland', *ibid.*, June 1939. For a more detailed discussion of Leese's Hibernophobic ideology, see R. M. Douglas, 'The Swastika and the Shamrock: British Fascism and the Irish Question, 1918–1940', *Albion* 29:1 (Spring 1997): 57–75.

supposed Semitic antecedents. While the *Ceannaire*'s initial communication has not been traced, Leese's reply to Ó Cuinneagáin sufficiently reveals the character of their exchange:

> In answer to your letter undated about Mr. De Valera, I have not been able to identify the booklet in which you say that De Valera is said to be a Jew. Therefore, I am unable to trace the authority for the other reference you mention. If you will name the pamphlet, I should be glad to look into it. Mr. De Valera I believe to be Jewish, but not 'a Jew' on the following grounds. His mother is accepted by me as Irish.
>
> 1. His father is stated to have been a Spaniard from New York. A very high proportion of Spaniards have Jewish blood, and one third or more of the inhabitants of New York are Jews.
>
> 2. His personal appearance is decidedly of Hither Asiatic race, and more like a caricature of a Jew than a Jew.
>
> 3. *Doar Hayom*, Hebrew paper of Jerusalem, 9.5.1932, says he is descended from Spanish Jews.
>
> 4. A.F. Tschiffely in *Don Roberto* (Heinemann 1937) page 381 refers to 'criminal Bolshevik Jews who run "De" Valera in New York'. You are aware of course that his father is supposed to be a Bowery Jew.
>
> 5. Pre-War activities of Mr. De Valera show that he accepted assistance from Jews to enforce the separation of the country of Ireland from Britain at a time when it was the Jewish plan to weaken us.
>
> His conduct during the [present] war, as you say, has not been Jewish.
>
> But part-Jews are strange creatures, with sometimes one side, sometimes the other, uppermost, and I know many cases where the Aryan psychology predominates when the facial race-marks make the individual miserable.
>
> Valerio and Valery are common Jew names.[79]

In addition to the more traditional forms of political expression, Aiséirghe at this time embarked upon several extra-legal manifestations of 'propaganda of the deed'. The targets were selected not merely for the purpose of advertising the movement's commitment to action in contradistinction to the national and local governments' preference for talk, but to draw attention to the state's tolerance of 'antinational' symbols and mentalities. A typical example was Aiséirghe's long-running campaign to compel Dublin Corporation to change the name of Talbot Street, one of the city's main thoroughfares which commemorated an eighteenth-century Anglican archbishop, to 'Seán Treacy Street', in memory of a War of Independence leader who had died there during a famous gun-battle in 1920. When the Corporation proved unaccommodating, Aiséirghe took matters into its own

---

79 Transcript of intercepted letter from Leese to Ó Cuinneagáin, n.d. [postmarked 3 December 1944], G2/5235, DDMA.

hands, defacing the official street-signs and attaching replacements of its own to the exterior of prominent buildings. Photographs of the operation, carried out in broad daylight, were published in the party newspaper.

Emboldened by the lack of response from the authorities to these provocations, Aiséirghe turned its attention to a more visible symbol of the imperialist legacy, the Gough Monument in the Phoenix Park. One of the finest equestrian statues in Europe, the monument depicted an Irish-born field-marshal who had commanded British forces in India during the First and Second Sikh Wars. On Christmas morning 1944 a party of four Aiséirghe activists, led by Gearóid Ó Broin and including another member of the Ard-Chomhairle who stood as look-out, used hacksaws to cut away the head of the bronze figure of Gough and a three-foot length of the sword. The raiders carried both pieces away as trophies.[80] The identity of the miscreants was an open secret in Dublin, and nine days later the Aiséirghe offices in Harcourt Street were raided by the police. Ó Cuinneagáin himself was not present; according to his wife, Síle, the head was successfully concealed from detectives by being wrapped in old clothes and secreted in a suitcase underneath his bed.[81] Having successfully tweaked the government's tail, however, there was little point in Aiséirghe retaining such an incriminating piece of evidence. Gough's head was dumped at dark of night into the river Liffey near Islandbridge, from which it was subsequently fished out at low tide by the Office of Public Works.[82]

More significant still was the part played by Aiséirghe in the VE Day riots in Dublin. These disturbances, which commenced when exuberant pro-British students of Trinity College, Dublin, held a celebratory demonstration involving a perceived insult to the Irish flag, have entered into political mythology on account of the retaliatory action supposedly taken by the future Taoiseach of Ireland, Charles Haughey. Then an undergraduate at the National University of Ireland, Haughey is alleged to have burnt a Union Jack in College

80 Private information in the possession of the author.
81 Síle Bean Uí Chuinneagáin, author interview, 24 July 1999.
82 Aiséirghe's action started a vogue for vandalising the Gough monument, which was subjected to a catalogue of indignities in later years. After the head was re-attached (at a cost of £18.10.0), the statue was defaced with paint by an unknown hand. In November 1956 the monument was the target of an IRA bomb attack, causing damage estimated at £700. Repairs had not been completed when a second explosion in July 1957 again decapitated the figure of Gough; blew the horse off its pedestal; severed two of the legs; and opened up a gaping hole in the belly. The monument was never restored. Department of Finance, 'The Gough Statue in Phoenix Park', 3 September 1957, Department of the Taoiseach file S 16037A, NAI.

Green, thereby precipitating the riots that followed.[83] Evidence from a variety of sources, however, shows that whatever part, if any, Haughey played on VE Day was insignificant in comparison to the day-long disorders on the south side of Dublin orchestrated by Aiséirghe members. The trouble began when two undergraduates at Trinity College, later identified by a fellow student as 'Orangemen',[84] hoisted a Union Jack above the Irish tricolour upon the main flag-pole above College Green. The two provocateurs were joined on the roof of the College by up to a hundred other students of both sexes, one of whom brandished a Soviet banner. An indignant crowd gathered below and was joined by 'a procession of members of Ailtirí na hAiséirghe', whose members 'staged an anti-Trinity demonstration in the street, in the course of which a Union Jack was burnt'.[85] The students responded by setting the tricolour on the flag-pole alight, precipitating a general mêlée involving Aiséirghe members, joined by outraged passers-by, on the one hand, and Trinity undergraduates on the other. Following this initial confrontation, Aiséirghe returned in greater numbers to the fray. After an evening meeting in Middle Abbey Street, 'demonstrators marched to the front of the college and, headed by a young man waving a large tricolour hoisted on the shoulders of comrades, attempted to force their way through the gates'.[86] The Gardaí thereupon baton-charged the attackers, causing a stampede in which several people were injured and removed to Mercer's Hospital. Shortly thereafter, an Aiséirghe representative climbed a lamp-post and appealed to the demonstrators through a megaphone to return to the Harcourt Street headquarters: 'There is no sense', he said, 'of getting yourself and the Guards beaten up just to entertain the brats in Trinity College'. Aiséirghe found, however, that the disturbances were easier to unleash than to control. The speaker's words were applauded but his request ignored. A member of staff of the British diplomatic representative in Ireland[87] – probably Norman Archer, a high-ranking Dominions Office official on secondment in Dublin – arrived in time to observe a 'fairly large baton charge' of Gardaí breaking up 'an organised body of

83 The tale is related in many historical accounts; none, however, offers corroborating evidence of Haughey's involvement. See, e.g., B. Arnold, *Haughey: His Life and Unlucky Deeds* (London: HarperCollins, 1993), p. 14; T. Gray, *The Lost Years: The Emergency in Ireland, 1939–45* (London: Little, Brown, 1997), p. 234; I. S. Wood, *Ireland During the Second World War* (London: Caxton, 2002), p. 100.
84 *Irish Times*, 10 May 1945.
85 R. B. McDowell & D. A. Webb, *Trinity College Dublin 1592–1952: An Academic History* (Cambridge: Cambridge University Press, 1982), pp. 464–5.
86 *Irish Times*, 8 May 1945.
87 Because the British government did not recognise Ireland's formal independence, its envoy in Dublin bore the formal title of 'United Kingdom Representative in Ireland'.

Altire na hAiseirge [*sic*]' advancing on the college from Dame Street.[88] Meanwhile, a detachment of 'about fifty young men attacked the doors of the Wicklow Hotel to cries of "Give us the West Britons," "Put out the traitors." The hotel was rushed, and three men broke into the hallway, but were forced to retire under the blows of defending bellboys'.[89] Several more baton-charges ensued before the Gardaí succeeded in regaining control of College Green.

Later in the evening, the same British witness saw a fresh procession of young men from Aiséirghe, 'many holding up their hands in the Fascist salute', marching past Jammet's restaurant in Nassau Street, a fashionable establishment widely known as a meeting-place for those of pro-British sympathies. Joined, according to the *Irish Times*, by 'hundreds' of reinforcements from surrounding streets, including a strong contingent from University College Dublin, the demonstrators sang *Amhrán na bhFiann*, the Irish national anthem, in front of the restaurant before unleashing a volley of stones at its windows. The British diplomat went home, but was recalled to the Representative's offices in Upper Mount Street shortly before midnight.

> We there heard from one of our R.A.F. staff and the duty messenger and policeman what had occurred. They said that an organised crowd of about 150 carrying a Tricolour and a Swastika paper flag and accompanied by 200 or 300 others, mostly spectators apparently, had filled Upper Mount Street, thrown three missiles at the windows and demonstrated with speeches, etc., outside the Office for about five minutes until some ten policemen, summoned by telephone from a Garda Station nearby, had, without difficulty, chased the entire crowd away with batons. It seems clear, from the time involved, that these demonstrators were the Altire na hAiseirge procession which we had seen marching past Jammet's.
>
> We drove home round Merrion Square to see whether the US Consulate-General had suffered any damage but at that time (11.45 p.m.) it appeared untouched. Apparently, however, about half an hour later a demonstration and stone throwing, similar to that which occurred at our Office, took place outside the US Consulate-General.

Another eyewitness, the newly appointed minister of the Italian Republic, noted evidence of the demonstrators' pro-Axis sympathies: 'many of the participants wore swastika badges in their button-holes and a few Nazi flags were waved around'.[90] A swastika flag was also

---

88 Unsigned and undated memorandum, covered by letter from N. E. Archer, United Kingdom Representative's Office in Ireland, to Sir John Stephenson, Dominions Office, 25 May 1945, TNA DO 130/57.
89 *Irish Times*, 8 May 1945.
90 D. Keogh, *Ireland and Europe 1919–48* (Dublin: Gill & Macmillan, 1988), p. 198. Keogh

reported to have been hoisted the same day at University College Galway.[91]

The Aiséirghe mobs' conduct, coming as it did so soon after Éamon de Valera's punctilious and injudicious expression of condolence to the German minister on the death of Hitler, was a grave embarrassment to the government. The following day, the Department of External Affairs offered a formal apology to Sir John Maffey and David Gray for the damage done to their premises.[92] This transpired to be premature. Showing that the riots were more than a spontaneous and momentary eruption of anger, 'thousands' of demonstrators of both sexes returned on the evening of 8 May for a second night of disturbances that proved to be almost as serious as the first. The windows of Trinity College were smashed with volleys of stones, and fireworks and smoke bombs unleashed at the Gardaí, who once again were forced on several occasions to baton-charge the crowds.[93] In Dundalk Eoin Ó Coigligh, who a week previously had anticipated de Valera by demanding of his colleagues on Louth County Council that the national flag over the municipal buildings be flown at half-mast in mourning for the death of Benito Mussolini, generated another small diplomatic incident when he led a crowd of Aiséirghe demonstrators to vandalise the car of Sir John Maffey as the British Representative was alighting at a local function.[94]

The efforts of the government to divert attention from these acts of lawlessness may indicate that ministers feared that Aiséirghe on this occasion was expressing the public mood. Joe Walshe of the Department of External Affairs, seemingly under the misapprehension that the members of the American diplomatic corps were incapable of reading the daily newspapers, called on the US Consul General in the hope of persuading the latter that the attack on his offices had been 'the work of communists and certain Irish extremists whose object was to embarrass the Irish Government'.[95] Addressing the Philosophical Society, a debating club at Trinity College a week later, Erskine

considers that because there was no mention of these emblems in contemporary newspaper accounts, 'it is doubtful if they were very much in evidence'. In view of the fact that the press censorship was not lifted until three days later, however, it is probable that any such references would have been suppressed in the same manner as reports of all other expressions of support for any of the belligerents.

91 B. Girvin, *The Emergency: Neutral Ireland 1939–45* (London: Macmillan, 2006), p. 319.
92 *The Times*, 9 May 1945.
93 *Irish Independent*, 9 May 1945.
94 *Daily Express* (London), 2 May 1945.
95 Thomas McEnelly, Consul General, Dublin, to Cordell Hull, 9 May 1945, Department of State, Dublin Legation General Records 1936–48, RG 84 350/61/29/07, Box 15, File 700–7113, NARA.

Childers, Parliamentary Secretary to the Minister for Local Government, similarly attempted to smooth over the affair, claiming that 'the young men who brandished the Swastika in Dublin streets the other day were no more representative of the people as a whole than the young men who caused the provocation'.[96] Few were taken in by such obvious red herrings. P. S. O'Hegarty defended the rioters' actions in the *Sunday Independent*, asserting that it had not merely been 'the young men of the *Ailtirí*' who resented the insult offered to the Irish flag, but 'all sorts and conditions of people'.[97] David Gray, too, was equally unpersuaded, informing de Valera that 'The mentality of such people is favourable soil for the seed of National Socialist resurgence'.[98]

Aiséirghe's record of subversive associations and actions during the last year of the Emergency begs the question of how it was able to remain immune from governmental counter-measures when seemingly less dangerous bodies had already been suppressed. According to an MI5 report of December 1944, 'the man in the street wonders why, since it is avowedly Fascist, the organisation has not been prohibited as an illegal body'.[99] While part of the answer no doubt lies in the support Aiséirghe enjoyed from influential patrons like Blythe and Walsh, that would not have been sufficient to shield it completely. Paradoxically, Aiséirghe probably owed its continued survival to the fact that Allied intelligence agencies by now were taking so close an interest in it. David Gray had warned Colonel David Bruce, the OSS' Director in the European Theater of Operations, in March 1943 of the existence in Ireland of 'a secret political organization supported by the Nazis who would attempt a coup d'état'.[100] Six months later, in one of the Emergency's more bizarre episodes, Gray wrote to Franklin D. Roosevelt to inform the President of the results of a seance in which the ghost of a deceased British Prime Minister, Arthur J. Balfour, had addressed a message to him. Confirming that Britons' notorious ignorance of languages other than English extends into the afterlife, the Premier's shade told Gray that 'the Fifth Column here have established a new political organisation called "Society of the Rising," or some strange name that sounds like "Ashereee"'.[101] Thus alerted, the

96 *Irish Times*, 16 May 1945.
97 *Sunday Independent*, 20 May 1945.
98 Gray to de Valera, 5 December 1945, quoted in T. Ryle Dwyer, *Irish Neutrality and the U.S.A. 1939–47* (Dublin: Gill & Macmillan, 1977), p. 206.
99 'Irish Affairs (The General Situation in Éire)', QRS/202, 1 May 1943; QRS/212, 31 December 1944, TNA DO 121/85.
100 Unsigned 'Memorandum on Visit to US Minister in Dublin March 13–15 1943', Office of Strategic Services, RG 226, Entry 210, Box 480, Folder 4, NARA.
101 T. Ryle Dwyer, *Strained Relations: Ireland at Peace and the U.S.A. at War 1941–45* (Dublin: Gill & Macmillan, 1988), p. 40. Alarmingly, the President encouraged Gray in his psychic

American Minister had insisted that the OSS maintain the closest possible scrutiny over Ó Cuinneagáin's movement. This in turn placed G2 in a highly awkward position. Any independent investigations by OSS could only strengthen American suspicions of pro-Nazi activity in Ireland. On the other hand, to pre-empt such enquiries by moving to suppress Aiséirghe, in the wake of the American Note controversy, would be to concede the original allegation that Ireland represented a security risk to the Allied forces.

Colonel Bryan's solution to this dilemma, when OSS officers arrived from London in June 1944 to discuss the Aiséirghe problem with him, was to lie unblushingly to his American counterparts. The movement, he told the OSS visitors, was made up of young people 'primarily interested in Gaelic culture' and had little in the way of funds. There was 'no evidence of pro-Axis sentiment on the part of the organization'. Its interests were 'solely Irish and Gaelic'. Understandably, Gray remained sceptical in the face of these improbable assurances and demanded that further information be obtained. The OSS officers accordingly returned to spend much of a week 'in conferences with Col. Bryan and studying his files. The various rumors which Mr. Gray requested be checked were discussed with Bryan'.[102] Even this did not dispel the Americans' anxieties about Aiséirghe, however, as evidenced by Bryan's dispatch of further G2 reports about the party – no doubt equally misleading in content – in July and August.[103]

The end of the European war in May 1945 relieved both Bryan and Ó Cuinneagáin of the need for further anxiety about each other's activities. It was true that not all the emergency laws were immediately repealed. Joe Walshe, clearly with Aiséirghe in mind, advised that even in time of peace the government could not 'safely divest itself of the powers necessary to enable it to deal with … Fascist or other subversive organisations etc'..[104] De Valera and his ministers, though, were keen to revert to normal conditions as quickly as possible, and

---

enthusiasms. 'These are real contributions and I hope you will continue', he wrote to the Minister in April 1942.

102 Lieut. Edward J. Lawler Jr, OSS, to Norman H. Pearson, Chief, X-2 Branch, London, 26 September 1944, OSS papers, RG 226, Entry 210, Box 299, 'Éire' file, NARA.

103 Bryan to Lawler, 22 July and 4 August 1944, *ibid.* Cecil Liddell, head of MI5's Irish section during the Emergency, also suspected the Irish authorities of similar concealment: 'Information is probably being withheld [by the Irish defence authorities], which would provide us with a handle for saying that the Germans in Éire must be all interned or kicked out, or which would strengthen our hand in asking for the use of the Éire ports as bases'. Liddell to John Stephenson, Dominions Office, 29 January 1942, TNA KV 4/280.

104 Quoted in S. Ó Longaigh, *Emergency Law in Independent Ireland 1922–1948* (Dublin: Four Courts Press, 2006), p. 274.

the most onerous wartime measures were speedily repealed. Censorship and other restrictions on publication came to an end on May 11, and all internees were released by the close of July.

In spite of its various tactical missteps, Aiséirghe could congratulate itself upon surviving the war years relatively unscathed. If the defeat of the Axis powers had deprived right-wing totalitarianism of much of its credibility, it also relieved Aiséirghe of opponents' taunts that it was no more than an Irish stalking-horse for some Continental fascist party. The Emergency, moreover, while providing Aiséirghe with its greatest opportunities, had also confronted it with its most immediate dangers. Merely to preserve the organisation from the menace of governmental counter-measures had been an achievement in itself. Now, with the lifting of emergency laws, Aiséirghe would for the first time be in a position to place its undiluted message before the Irish people. It could draw upon the resources of a national organisation that was daily growing in political experience. In its own newspaper it possessed the means of appealing directly to the electorate. Nor was there any reason to suppose that the democratic regime in Ireland would prove more effective in dealing with the country's fundamental problems in the difficult postwar transition period than during the more tranquil years before the Emergency. From Gearóid Ó Cuinneagáin's perspective in the summer of 1945, there was still everything to play for.

6

Autumn of discontent

It is frequently asserted that the lifting of censorship at the close of the European war, and the ensuing revelation of German atrocities, brought about a sea-change in the attitude of Irish people to the conflict. Newsreel footage of the liberated concentration camps, according to various historical accounts, made a deep and shocking impression on Irish minds. Tim Pat Coogan, for example, records Sir John Maffey's perception that 'a sense of disgust slowly manifested itself' throughout the country as Nazi barbarities were revealed.[1] The censorship regime has thus conventionally been appealed to as a complete explanation for Irish wartime attitudes which, it is implied, would have been very different had more light been allowed to penetrate to the deeper recesses of Plato's cave. As the Minister for Defence, Paddy Cooney, rhetorically asked in 1979, 'What would our attitude to neutrality have been in the last war if we had been aware of the existence of Belsen?'[2]

Contemporary evidence, however, makes clear that photographs, films and even first-person testimonies from Irish aid workers in Belsen itself as well as other German concentration camps changed few minds in the summer of 1945 about the issues involved in the war. In the immediate postwar period, Irish sympathies remained, to all appearances, largely unaltered from what they had been during the Emergency. That Hitlerite Germany's treatment of the Jews had been, in the *Leader*'s words, 'deliberately and ferociously unjust' came as a surprise to few Irish citizens in 1945.[3] Even while the war was under way, the possibility that Nazi intentions for the Jews might extend to physical annihilation rather than mere persecution was being discussed in Ireland as in other European countries. In October 1944,

---

1 T. P. Coogan, *Ireland in the Twentieth Century* (London: Hutchinson, 2003), p. 277.
2 Cooney interview in *Irish Times*, 5 April 1979, quoted in R. Kee, *In Time of War: Éire, Ulster and the Price of Neutrality 1939–1945* (London: André Deutsch, 1983), p. 475.
3 As Mary Kenny notes, well before the war began 'Catholic Ireland … had few illusions about the Nazis'. M. Kenny, *Goodbye to Catholic Ireland* (London: Sinclair-Stevenson, 1997), p. 202.

for example, the Department of External Affairs requested Con Cremin, chargé d'affaires at the Irish legation in Berlin, to investigate rumours current in Dublin that 'the Germans plan to exterminate all Jews'.[4] The seventeen-year-old Belvedere College student who expressed during the war, in an essay for his German language class, the conviction that 'The Jews are vermin, and Hitler is right to exterminate them' also appeared to labour under few illusions about the true purpose of Nazi racial policy.[5] Newspaper coverage of the liberated concentration camps, consequently, was perfunctory and little commented-upon. The three main Dublin dailies, while acknowledging that conditions in the camps could scarcely be exaggerated, quickly lost interest in the story. The most pro-British among them, the *Irish Times*, devoted far more column inches to the VE Day disturbances than to the Holocaust, while the *Irish Press* confined its news coverage of the camps to a single inside-page article. Most provincial papers ignored the subject entirely. The sum total of the *Cork Examiner*'s reportage of Nazi atrocities throughout the summer of 1945 consisted of a 180-word Reuters' item on 14 May bearing the less-than-enlightening headline, 'Clothes Levy for Camp Victims'.[6] Nor did Pathé newsreel footage of Belsen and Buchenwald, first shown at the Carlton cinema in Dublin at the beginning of June and in Cork later in the month (where it was twinned on the bill with a Lon Chaney horror film), make any greater impact.[7] To many Irishmen and women, including Éamon de Valera, such images merely provided retrospective justification for the thoroughness of wartime censorship. As the Taoiseach asked his audience in an address at Galway in June, 'You see more atrocity pictures and so on [since the lifting of restrictions], and are you any the better for seeing them?'[8] Others protested in letters to the newspapers that the films of the camps were obvious fabrications.[9] On the whole, therefore, Irish newspapers' treatment of the Holocaust after the ending of censorship provides little evidence to support their editors' complaints that governmental restructions alone prevented them from providing adequate coverage of the most controversial aspects of the war.

4 N. Keogh, *Con Cremin: Ireland's Wartime Diplomat* (Cork: Mercier, 2006), p. 76.
5 G. Holfter, 'Ernst Scheyer', in G. Holfter, ed., *German-Speaking Exiles in Ireland 1933–1945* (Amsterdam: Rodopi, 2006), p. 153.
6 *Cork Examiner*, 14 May 1945.
7 For a discussion of the ways in which the atrocity newsreels paralleled the structure of the horror genre, see J. Shandler, 'The Testimony of Images: The Allied Liberation of Nazi Concentration Camps in American Newsreels', in R. M. Shapiro, ed., *Why Didn't the Press Shout? American and International Journalism During the Holocaust* (Jersey City, NJ: Yeshiva University Press, 2003), esp. p. 116.
8 *Sunday Independent*, 3 June 1945.
9 *Ibid.*, 10 June 1945.

In part, such reactions were responses to what many people saw as an unattractive display of Allied triumphalism. The revocation of censorship in early May was quickly followed by the release in Irish cinemas of a tidal wave of previously banned war films. Many of these, often dating from a much earlier period in the conflict, were strongly propagandistic, if not belligerent, in tone. Their screening at a time when a defeated Germany lay in ruins at the feet of the victorious Allies was widely perceived as the cinematic equivalent of kicking an opponent when he is down, and is likely to have coloured the response of audiences to the newsreel footage a month later. Elizabeth (Bowen) Cameron, for example, reported in June that at screenings of some of the more strident war films in Dublin, '*e.g.* during *Tunisian Victory*, there was cheering of Rommel'. In consequence, '"Sales Resistance" to Nazi atrocity stories is ... I am told, very strong'.[10] It may also safely be assumed that Winston Churchill's inflammatory assertion in his victory broadcast that the de Valera administration had 'frolic[ked] with the Germans and later with the Japanese representatives' during the war – a claim its author knew to be unfounded – did little to encourage retrospective Irish identification with the Allied cause.

It is no less true, however, that many Irishmen and women to a greater or lesser degree openly regretted the defeat of the Axis powers. In its immediate aftermath, Dublin's Jewish community became the targets of 'threatening letters, purporting to be signed by an organised body', a campaign of intimidation that the Minister for Justice declined to investigate in spite of strong pressure to do so from James Dillon.[11] The VE Day disturbances had likewise been in part an expression of chagrin over the outcome of the war, as the presence of swastika banners among the rioters and the disproportion of their reaction to the original provocation served to indicate. Even relative moderates like Liam de Róiste observed during the last year of the conflict that 'of the two combinations in the war ... I regard the Allied Powers as the greater danger to religion, to Catholicism, to the Church'.[12] With the return of peace in Europe, expressions of sympathy for the defeated were much more common than condemnation of their crimes. A requiem mass was offered in the Pro-Cathedral in Dublin after VE Day

10 E. (Bowen) Cameron, 'Notes on Éire', 10 June 1945, TNA DO 130/68. Based on his own cinemagoing experiences, R. M. Fox maintained that to the contrary, 'Now that the military battle has been fought out in Europe the cinema is recruiting Éire for the ideological battle on the side of the democracies'. Others, like William Humphreys of the *New York Herald Tribune*, disagreed. *Manchester Guardian*, 2 July 1945; *New York Herald Tribune*, 15 July 1945.

11 97 *DP–Dáil*, cols 341–3 (15 May 1945).

12 Liam de Róiste diary, 20 June 1944, U 217/A56, Cork Archive Institute.

for the repose of the soul of Benito Mussolini; only the intervention of Archbishop McQuaid prevented another from being offered for Hitler.[13] For many Irish citizens, succouring the defeated German nation in the war's chaotic aftermath had a higher claim to their attention than did binding up the wounds of Nazism's victims. At the launch of the well-supported Save the German Children Society in October 1945, J. J. O'Byrne, a Fianna Fáil councillor from Dublin, declared publicly that 'he supported the formation of the Society on the grounds of his pro-German feelings and his hatred of Britain'. Another founder-member, Kevin Cahill, formerly of Córas na Poblachta, concurred, pointing out that Ireland 'had a debt to pay to Germany' and crying *'Heil dem Führer!'* as he departed the meeting.[14] Other longstanding pro-Axis activists and sympathisers, including Maurice O'Connor, Dan Breen, Liam Gogán and P. S. O'Sullivan, occupied prominent positions in the Society, which was later to take on as its secretary Hermann Goertz, the *Abwehr*'s leading wartime operative in Ireland. There is every reason, therefore, to accept as accurate the *Irish People*'s rueful conclusion at the end of October 1945 that 'there are still a great many people in this country who, because of their perfectly understandable hatred of everything British, still have strong Nazi sympathies'.[15]

To those Irishmen and women to whom Soviet *gulags* already seemed little different in kind, and Stalin's numerous aggressions against his neighbours no less flagrant contraventions of international law, than their Hitlerite counterparts, the sudden and shocking conclusion of the war in the Pacific served to dispose of any pretensions of moral superiority on the part of the Western Allies as well. The use of atomic weapons against Hiroshima and Nagasaki, at a moment when Japan seemed to be on the brink of defeat, was greeted with almost unanimous disapproval in Ireland. Even the normally pro-Allied *Irish Times* was moved to declare in an editorial a year later: 'All the crimes of the Goerings and the Himmlers, the horrors of the concentration camps and lethal chambers, all the brutalities of the Japanese sadists in Malaya and Burma seem to us to be peccadilloes in comparison with the supreme crime of the atomic bomb'.[16] The authors of the attacks against the Japanese cities, its editor opined, were no less guilty of 'crimes against humanity' than any of the Nazi leaders hanged at

13 D. Keogh, *Twentieth Century Ireland: Nation and State* (Dublin: Gill & Macmillan, 1994), pp. 158–9.
14 *Irish Times*, 17 October 1945; DFA 419/6. Dr Kathleen Lynn, another ex-Córas office-holder, became the Society's vice-president.
15 *Irish People*, 27 October 1945.
16 *Irish Times*, 31 October 1946.

Nuremberg.[17] So far from retrospectively repenting their stance during the Emergency, then, many if not most Irish citizens would have seen no reason to dispute the *Leader's* assessment in September 1945 that 'the war was fundamentally a selfish struggle between groups of rival Imperialisms from which considerations of self-respect as well as physical safety suggested that we should stand apart'.[18]

For Aiséirghe, then, fascism's collapse on the Continent was of far less consequence than might have been predicted even a few months previously. There was no cause for apprehension that the Irish electorate in the summer of 1945 was in a mood to punish any political party for its excessively close association with far-right totalitarianism. Indeed, some voters might be all the more ready to give such a movement their support as a gesture of defiance. Paradoxically, as Aiséirghe prepared for its third campaign in two years, the political climate was more favourable for Irish fascism than ever before.

The 1945 local government election

The local government contest of June 1945 constituted the most important electoral advance made by Ailtirí na hAiséirghe, and provided an indication of the potential level of support that a right-wing extremist movement, if competently directed, could mobilise. That is not to say that Aiséirghe on this occasion did in fact show that it had fully absorbed the lessons of its previous shambolic forays into electoral politics. As in the past, the party's campaign was marked by high levels of amateurism, administrative incoherence and last-minute improvisation. Once again, candidates were selected and constituencies contested without any attempt being made to assess their viability or balance available resources against prospects of success. But uniquely in Aiséirghe's history, some effort was invested in preparing in advance for the poll and tailoring the movement's agenda to local concerns. The 1945 election was also the first in which, following the end of the war and the consequent lifting of emergency regulations, Aiséirghe was free to place its entire programme before the electors without having to run the gauntlet of state interference. The successes it achieved, at a time when fascism was being comprehensively and conclusively discredited everywhere else in Europe, offers disturbing

17 *Ibid.*, 19 October 1946. In a dispatch to Washington at the same time, David Gray reported the existence of 'a considerable section of Irish opinion which is highly critical of the Nuremberg trials. In most of the comment the United States is singled out as being in the wrong'. Gray to James F. Byrnes, 24 October 1946, Dublin Legation General Records 1936–48, file 711.3, RG 84 350/61/29/07, NARA.
18 *The Leader*, 15 September 1945.

evidence of the appeal to many Irish voters of political extremism, ultranationalism and xenophobia more than two decades after the establishment of the state.

The idea of seeking to establish a foothold in local politics was first mooted by Aindrias Ó Riain, a leading activist in the Cork branch and one of the few Aiséirghe members to hold an advanced degree. In the aftermath of the 1944 general election, Ó Riain composed a memorandum assessing the costs and benefits of pursuing seats on municipal and county councils. While the party constitution had left open the possibility of participating in local government, the sugges-tion was a controversial one inasmuch as Aiséirghe had frequently poured scorn upon these bodies as 'effete', 'corrupt' and 'of genuine English manufacture'. To reverse this stance and contest local elections, Ó Riain acknowledged, was by no means a risk-free strategy. At the very least it would distract the movement from national questions and divert some of the attention of Aiséirghe's most dedicated activists to matters of purely local concern. There was also a danger of tactical or ideological gaps appearing between individual Aiséirghe councillors and the agenda of the party as a whole, the prevention of which would require close monitoring by the national leadership. On the other hand, success in local government would boost Aiséirghe's public standing after two disappointing general election campaigns; counteract the widespread perceptions that it was either 'merely a Left-Wing F[ianna] F[áil] reaction' or a 'purely cultural Gaelic Movement that happened to Stumble into Politics'; and above all 'would be acknowledged by the Public, as a gesture of good faith, so to speak. We should have staked a claim for their consideration, when a general election next takes place'. Lastly, an effective campaign was within Aiséirghe's means inasmuch as no deposit was required of candidates, whereas the small size of each constituency meant that a sufficient quantity of election material could be produced at moderate cost.[19]

Gearóid Ó Cuinneagáin was quickly persuaded of the merits of Ó Riain's proposal, an additional benefit of which was that participa-tion in local government did not signify any recognition of the legiti-macy of the state.[20] The fact that Eoin Ó Coigligh, who had been elected as a Labour representative to Louth County Council, had served Ailtirí na hAiséirghe faithfully since his defection to Ó Cuinneagáin's banner in 1942, served as additional reassurance of the compatibility of party ideology and local politics. Accordingly, the *Ceannaire*'s 'Personal Letter' of August 1944 exhorted members to prepare for the poll the

19 Untitled and undated memorandum by Aindrias Ó Riain, c. July 1944, 4/3/48, GÓCP.
20 Domhnall Ó Maolalaí, author interview, 22 July 1999.

following year, anticipating the Ard-Chomhairle's eventual decision in January 1945 to contest the elections 'in each area that suitable candidates would be available'.[21] In the Cork branch's newsletter *Aisling*, Ó Cuinneagáin emphasised the importance of mounting a sustained nationwide challenge and urged supporters not to be daunted by the magnitude of the task.[22] Notwithstanding this promising beginning, head office's own preparations for the campaign, under the supervision of Tomás Ó Dochartaigh, were conducted with little more urgency than had been evident in previous contests. As late as three months before the date fixed for the election, the National Organiser had failed to inform himself of such basic matters as the legally prescribed nomination procedure. Not until six weeks before polling day were branch leaders instructed to convoke meetings to select a candidate for their area.[23]

The task of recruiting suitable representatives to carry the Aiséirghe banner was once again to prove the movement's most intractable problem throughout the campaign. Máire Uí Nuanáin, one of Aiséirghe's most dedicated workers, was obliged to decline Ó Cuinneagáin's invitation to stand for Limerick when her husband withheld his permission for fear that she would neglect her household duties and contravene St Paul's instructions to wives (the *Ceannaire* consoled her by declaring that in his view too it was 'highly preferable that married women take no part in public affairs').[24] Éamonn Ó Riain, head of the Waterford city branch, was one of several prospective candidates from that district to withdraw his name from consideration, causing a dismayed Ó Cuinneagáin's to protest that the prospects there were no worse than in Sligo, a town 'equally alien- and even more Freemason-ridden [*saor-mhasúnaighe*]' in which two Aiséirghe candidates were already standing.[25] Another nominee from Thurles, one of three put forward by the local *cumann*, was vetoed by Ó Cuinneagáin, who considered the prospective candidate's leisure-time activities to be insufficiently in keeping with the movement's austere public image. In consequence, the final weeks of the campaign witnessed a repetition of the familiar pattern of last-second nominations, an example of which was Ó Cuinneagáin's endorsement of Stiofáin Ó Fearghail [Stephen J.

21 *Kerryman*, 13 January 1945.
22 Ó Cuinneagáin, 'Aiséirghe and the Local Elections', *Aisling* no. 5 (February 1945).
23 Ó Dochartaigh to the Secretary, Department of Local Government, 12 March 1945, 5/3/20, GÓCP; circular letter from Ó Dochartaigh to *ceannasaidheanna cumainn*, 23 April 1945, 5/3/41, *ibid*.
24 Máire Uí Núanáin to Ó Cuinneagáin, 5 May 1945; Ó Cuinneagáin to Ó Nuanáin, 10 May 1945, 5/3/35, *ibid*.
25 Ó Cuinneagáin to Éamonn Ó Riain, 9 May 1945, 4/3/38, *ibid*.

Farrell] a radio engineer from Athy, as an Aiséirghe candidate before the latter had enrolled as an ordinary member of the movement and before he had specified whether it was his intention to stand for the Athy municipal board or for Kildare County Council.[26]

In certain respects, nonetheless, the lack of national co-ordination had positive benefits, enabling individual branches to exercise their own initiative in selecting locally known candidates and stressing grass-roots concerns likely to resonate with voters. If over-enthusiastic office-seekers were sometimes prone to make injudicious policy commitments – for example, the assurance by the two remaining Aiséirghe contestants for seats on the Thurles Urban District Council, Seán Breathnach and Éamonn de Róiste, that in the event of their election they would seek to have 'the main Dublin to Cork road pass through Thurles' – the overall calibre of Aiséirghe's campaign was noticeably higher than in previous elections. Leaflets and other forms of propaganda, produced by and in many cases paid for by the candidates themselves, were in general more professional in appearance than the verbose and visually unappealing productions emanating from Harcourt Street. North of the Border, the Prime Minister at Stormont, Sir Basil Brooke, offered Aiséirghe a valuable negative endorsement during the campaign when he condemned one of the party's anti-partition posters for having 'outraged the sentiments of every true Ulsterman' and constituting an 'insult to the British people and the British Empire'.[27] Aiséirghe's public meetings also received unprecedented levels of coverage in the provincial press, thanks to the ending of wartime censorship and the fact that in several constituencies the movement for the first time was perceived as having a genuine chance of success.

The results of the poll, indeed, exceeded the expectations of most independent observers. Of the thirty-one seats contested, involving sixteen local authorities, Aiséirghe candidates won nine, gaining a total of more than 11,000 first-preference votes. Eoin Ó Coigligh was returned for both Louth County Council and Drogheda Corporation, topping the poll in both counts. He was joined on the latter body by Tomás Ó Muireagáin [Tom Morgan]. Seán Ó Dubhghaill [Seán Doyle] was successful in the Cork Corporation race; his Wexford namesake was elected to New Ross Urban District Council. Tomás de Stocdáil [Thomas Stockdale] gained a seat on the Cobh Town Council. A further three Aiséirghe candidates, Caoimhín Mac Cárthaigh [Kevin McCarthy], Tadhg Ó Condúin [Timothy Condon] and Concubhar

26 Ó Cuinneagáin to Ó Fearghail, 18 May 1945, 4/3/37, *ibid*.
27 *Daily Express* (London), 14 June 1945.

Ó Maothagháin [Cornelius Mehigan], were returned unopposed to Bandon Town Council. The party had at least two more successes within its grasp. In Limerick, where the local organisation had put forward a pair of energetic and articulate candidates, Micheál Brianach Ó Ceallaigh [Michael O'Brien Kelly], a well-known local solicitor, obtained a higher number of first preferences than two former mayors of the city and failed by just thirty-five votes to take the last seat from his Fianna Fáil opponent. In Thurles, the prospective candidate vetoed by Ó Cuinneagáin had responded to the slight by severing his links with the movement and standing as an independent; he went on to obtain the highest number of first-preference votes in the constituency and was duly elected.

Elsewhere around the country, Aiséirghe's record was less impressive. Dublin continued to be a weak link: none of the party's seven representatives in the capital, all of them drawn from the Ard-Chomhairle, came close to election – the result in part of the tactical error of nominating a single candidate for each constituency rather than seeking to maximise transfers from one candidate to another. In Passage West, Dungarvan and Midleton, Aiséirghe candidates performed especially poorly; the picture was little better in Waterford and Roscommon. Nor had the promise to re-orient the country's road network for the benefit of the citizens of Thurles proven a winning formula for the pair of Aiséirghe aspirants there.

Many obstacles undoubtedly stood in the way of the replication of Aiséirghe's achievement on a larger scale. Only in Louth did the party gain any seats outside the province of Munster, showing how serious were the gaps that remained in its national organisation. Aiséirghe's Irish-only policy was also identified as a major stumbling block by several candidates.[28] In a post-mortem on Aiséirghe's near-miss in Limerick, Pádraig Mac Giobúin [P. J. Fitzgibbon] underlined some of the long-standing difficulties the movement continued to face. As a result of the perception that 'Aiseirghe is out to establish a dictatorship in this country', many would-be members and backers were fearful of associating themselves with it publicly. Aiséirghe's social programme, furthermore, was widely considered 'fantastic' and '[w]e have been told that … it antagonises Civil servants, industrialists, and workers alike'.[29]

Nonetheless, the significance of Aiséirghe's electoral performance in 1945 should not be understated. The *Drogheda Independent* described the result as a 'remarkable advance' that had 'come as a big surprise

---

28 See, e.g., Seosamh Ó Ceallaigh [Joseph O'Kelly], Ballaghaderreen, to Ó Cuinneagáin, 1 June 1945, 4/3/34, GÓCP.
29 Pádraig Mac Giobúin to Ó Cuinneagáin, n.d. [*c.* 18 June 1945], 4/3/31, *ibid.*

to the majority of the citizens'.[30] Although Aiséirghe's success is best regarded as indicative of the continuing potential for right-wing extremist movements rather than the sudden discovery of a vote-winning formula, it is clear that the party's message was starting to evoke a positive response from elements of the Irish electorate. While Ó Cuinneagáin compared Aiséirghe's achievements to those made by Sinn Féin during the early years of the century, a more appropriate frame of reference may be the far less impressive record of compa-rable movements overseas like the British Union of Fascists, which, in spite of the advantages conferred by a much more favourable political environment in which to operate and enormous subsidies from Musso-lini's government, succeeded in winning only a single local govern-ment seat during its eight-year history.[31] Aiséirghe, by contrast, had gained its electoral successes virtually without financial resources; in the immediate aftermath of three years' determined effort by the state to strangle the movement in its cradle; and without repudiating or attempting to conceal the totalitarian, anti-democratic and intolerant character of its ideology. That so many Irish voters should have given it their support at the precise moment when the barbarities for which European fascism was responsible were being displayed in horrific detail in newspapers and on cinema screens throughout the world, and that so many more would undoubtedly have done so if given the opportuntity to vote for an Aiséirghe candidate, raises disquieting questions about the well-being of Irish democracy at mid-century.

'Briathar Ghearóid, briathar Dé!'[32]

To participate in local elections was one thing; to have a coherent programme for local government entirely another. It quickly became apparent that Aiséirghe had given no thought to what its elected repre-sentatives were to do while in office. Arguably, the pledge required of candidates to speak and vote only in the manner prescribed for them by Ó Cuinneagáin implied that in the leadership's view no such consideration was necessary. However impractical the idea of trying to turn all Aiséirghe's councillors into the *Ceannaire*'s mouthpieces may have been, such a policy, if implemented, would at least have

---

30 *Drogheda Independent*, 23 June 1945.
31 In 'The Pro-Axis Underground in Ireland, 1939–42', I incorrectly stated that no BUF candidate had ever been voted into office (p. 1179). In fact, Ronald Creasy was elected for Eye (Suffolk) in 1938. (His BUF colleague 'Captain' Charles Bentinck Budd, briefly a West Sussex councillor, was not a party member when he gained his seat in 1932.) I am grateful to Dr Martin Durham of the University of Wolverhampton for this information.
32 'The Word of Gearóid is the Word of God!'

ensured that the party spoke locally as well as nationally with a single voice. In the event, no guidance, far less direction, was ever issued by Harcourt Street, leaving it to individual councillors themselves to attempt to reconcile their official activities with what they believed to be Aiséirghe policy.

The results were on the whole unimpressive. An early presentiment of the kind of compromises to which electoral politics were likely to drive Aiséirghe came at the first meeting of the new Drogheda Corporation. After Eoin Ó Coigligh's bid to become mayor failed at the first hurdle when no other councillor – not even his party colleague – seconded his nomination, both Aiséirghe representatives joined an impromptu coalition to secure the post for a septuagenarian non-party member so as to block the election of the Fianna Fáil nominee. The irony of Aiséirghe, a party that, as a commentator noted, had so recently bedaubed 'every dead wall in Drogheda' with the slogan 'Give Youth Its Just Opportunity!' backing so venerable a candidate was not lost on local voters.[33]

Unwilling to sacrifice their independence by collaborating with other parties and lacking any distinctive ideas of their own, Aiséirghe councillors had little alternative but to fall back upon populist gestures. In July 1945, Ó Coigligh proposed that 'the mace and sword and all other imperial decorations, which are the property of Drogheda Corporation, be sold…and the entire proceeds devoted to a boot fund for the poor children of the town'.[34] Seán Ó Dubhghaill, Aiséirghe's lone representative on Cork Corporation, announced his refusal to participate in the vote for a Lord Mayor for the city because he could support no candidate who lacked fluency in the Irish language.[35] The question that monopolised the attention of his Bandon colleague, Caoimnín Mac Cartaigh, during the latter's first months in office was the alleged failure of the manager of the local cinema to play the National Anthem at the conclusion of each evening's performance.[36]

Despite its failure to make the most of its opportunities, Aiséirghe's presence on local bodies was beneficial to the movement. Eoin Ó Coigligh showed what could be achieved by an energetic councillor even in the absence of any coherent local programme. In a two-month span he used his position in Drogheda Corporation as a platform to advertise Aiséirghe's demands for representatives from Northern Ireland to be included in the Dáil, the abolition of the means test for

33 *Drogheda Argus*, 30 June 1945.
34 *Ibid.*, 7 July 1945.
35 *Irish Times*, 3 July 1945.
36 *Southern Star*, 27 September 1945.

unemployment benefits, the augmentation of old-age pensions, and the payment of a gratuity to members of the part-time Local Defence Force, which had been disbanded at the end of the Emergency. Although many of his resolutions and orations were ruled out of order or *ultra vires*, occasional victories were achieved, as when Ó Coigligh persuaded the Corporation to call for the immediate and uncondi- tional release of all political prisoners in Britain and Ireland. Tomás de Stocdáil's election as vice-chairman of Cobh Urban District Council, moreover, was an indication that Aiséirghe's isolationist stance was not always incompatible with the attainment of leadership positions.

Throughout the second half of 1945, Gearóid Ó Cuinneagáin continued to depict the local government election as a triumph for Aiséirghe: the party remained on course, he asserted, to mount a nationwide challenge in every Dáil constituency before 1949, when the next general election would have to be held. Some of those associ- ated with the movement took a similarly optimistic view. The *Aiséirghe* film-critic Deasún Breathnach ['Rex Mac Gall'] congratulated the *Ceannaire* on the Drogheda victory – 'your Munich' – and lamented the publicity opportunity that had been lost by the failure to put forward a candidate in the 1945 presidential election.[37] For a very large propor- tion of Aiséirghe activists, however – including virtually the whole of the Cork city and county organisations, probably a narrow majority of their counterparts in Dublin, and the National Organiser and de facto second-in-command, Tómas Ó Dochartaigh – the June 1945 poll constituted the final straw so far as the *ceannaireacht* was concerned. The election had indeed proved that Irish voters were responsive to the Aiséirghe message and that a significant measure of electoral success was within reach; it had also, in the view of an increasing number of the movement's most important figures, demonstrated beyond dispute that that potential could never be realised so long as Gearóid Ó Cuinneagáin remained as leader.

If one of the principal motive forces propelling Ailtirí na hAiséirghe forward had been disappointment over the inability of the Irish state to fulfil the promise of national independence, then the chief griev- ance of the dissident elements within the party was Ó Cuinneagáin's similar failure to make good upon his own promises. The abandon- ment of Craobh na hAiséirghe in 1942 and the creation of a political movement had been predicated on the belief that, as a result of the world war and the simultaneous rising to political maturity of the first post-independence generation, a uniquely favourable set of circumstances existed for the revolutionary transformation of Irish

37 'Rex Mac Gall' [Breathnach] to Ó Cuinneagáin, 21 June 1945, 3/7/1, GÓCP.

political, economic and cultural life. That the outcome of the war was very different from what had been foreseen in 1942 was not something for which Ó Cuinneagáin could be blamed. His culpability, the dissidents claimed, lay rather in his inability to adjust to what clearly had become a radically different political environment. Eighteen months earlier, they recalled, Ó Cuinneagáin had proclaimed 1944 'the year of victory' [*bliain na buaidhe*] for Aiséirghe.[38] The results of that prediction had been an electoral triumph for de Valera and Fianna Fáil; an Aiséirghe general election campaign that had learned none of the lessons of 1943; a string of lost deposits; the lowering of party morale; and the saddling of the organisation with an unsustainable level of debt. Yet, far from causing him to re-evaluate his approach, Ó Cuinneagáin had proclaimed the election debacle a vindication of his methods.

Compounding their discontent was an acute sense of frustration over the manner in which the party's organisation was being conducted. The shortcomings, as they saw it, were both structural and personal. In the former category was what they perceived as an absurd degree of over-centralisation. Although Ó Cuinneagáin had castigated the local organisations in the 1944 Annual Report 'for doing nothing, by all appearances, unless an officer from Dublin is on his way or on the scene',[39] his critics viewed this passivity as the inevitable consequence of headquarters' refusal to loosen the reins. The lack of any coherent structures at provincial or county level and the constant attempts at micro-management by head office deprived local leaders of scope for initiative. That they should have the ability to make use of their knowledge of local conditions to maximise Aiséirghe's appeal in their own areas was all the more necessary in light of the fact that the Ard-Chomhairle, partly as a result of wartime transport difficulties, rarely met and had degenerated in practice, if not in intent, into a rubber-stamp for the *Ceannaire*'s ideas.[40] The insistence that all pamphlets and other forms of propaganda material be obtained exclusively from head office, and that no publications or statements be disseminated in Aiséirghe's name without Harcourt Street's prior approval, meant that ideas flowed in one direction only – from Dublin to the provinces – contributing to the increasingly evident ideological sclerosis of the movement. It also had accentuated the demoralisation of the branches, which tended to perceive themselves as little more than fund-raising adjuncts of the national headquarters.

38 'Litir Pearsanta', 1 February 1944, 6/2/19, *ibid.*
39 Ailtirí na hAiséirghe, *Tuarascbháil Bhliantúil go 30ú Meán Fómhair 1944*, 6/1/2, *ibid.*
40 This tendency was reinforced, some members complained, by Ó Cuinneagáin's record of ignoring those Ard-Chomhairle decisions with which he did not agree.

Ó Cuinneagáin's style of interaction with his subordinates was the source of still greater dissatisfaction. The endless stream of circulars, monthly 'Personal Letters' and other communications from Dublin reminding officers in peremptory terms of their duties and accusing them *inter alia* of 'neglect', 'carelessness', 'laziness' and even 'murder' when these were not carried out to the *Ceannaire*'s satisfaction aroused bitter resentment in many recipients; few officials at the level of *ceanna-saidhe cumainn* or higher failed to receive several such missives within the first twelve months of their assumption of office.[41] The sense of vexation was most keenly felt by members of the Cork city and county organisation, who contrasted the scale of their activities and the extent of their financial contribution to what they regarded as the meagre accomplishments, in terms of membership, fundraising and electoral success, of the Dublin branches. Added to this was Ó Cuinneagáin's notorious resistance to suggestions or counsel, even from members of his own *Ard-Fhuireann* or advisory team, a trait that in the opinion of some Aiséirghe officials was progressing from 'dictatorship' to full-blown 'messianism'. The growing tendency of Ó Cuinneagáin's Dublin-based acolytes to treat him as a leader carrying the mandate of Heaven and his lightest words as unchallengeable truths (as one of them, Caoimhín de Eiteagáin, was later to recall, 'You accepted Gearóid as a sort of prophet – with all due respect, you'd look on him as a sort of Son of God'[42]) was, it was feared, going to his head. Riobárd Breathnach noted the *Ceannaire*'s reliance upon the formula '*Do chuir Dia annso mé ...*' ['God put me here ...'] when dismissing counsel or complaint as symbolising a growing sense of infallibility, as well as indispensability, on Ó Cuinneagáin's part; the future of the movement would be in grave peril, he observed, if the sole criterion for assessing the correctness of policy was to be Divine Right.[43]

Lastly, Ó Cuinneagáin's conduct during the 1945 election campaign itself served as final confirmation to the dissidents that he had become a liability to the movement. In the view of Ó Dochartaigh and a growing number of like-minded activists, Aiséirghe could make real progress only if it built bridges to powerful individuals and institutions. Alone, it was too small, under-resourced and tainted by what by 1945 had become a damaging reputation for irresponsibility and immaturity, to have a prospect of gaining power. Ó Dochartaigh and others were convinced, however, that there were a large number of 'respectable

41 See, e.g., letters from Ó Cuinneagáin to *ceannasaidheanna cumainn* whose branches were in arrears, dated 'February 1945' and 18 June 1945, 6/2/31, 6/2/36, GÓCP.
42 Caoimhín de Eiteagáin, author interview, 25 July 1999.
43 Breathnach to Eoin Ó Coigligh, 7 November 1945, 5/3/5, GÓCP.

citizens' of all parties who, while not subscribing to the entirety of the Aiséirghe philosophy, were sympathetic to its broader aims and anxious to break the log-jam obstructing the progress of Irish nationalism. These individuals – in whose ranks such noteworthy figures as Ernest Blythe, Dan Breen and Oliver J. Flanagan could already be numbered – were willing to co-operate with Aiséirghe, to provide it with material and political support, and to obtain for it *entrées* into areas of influence, like the national media and the business world, from which it continued to be excluded. But they were unlikely to do so as long as Aiséirghe retained its reputation for fanaticism and unreliability. Nor could they be expected to put themselves out on the movement's behalf while it continued to denounce those active in mainstream political parties as *ipso facto* corrupt, complacent and indifferent to the welfare of the Irish people.

For Aiséirghe members eager to take advantage of such alliances, Ó Cuinneagáin's actions during the summer campaign gave grounds for despair. Not only were his rhetorical broadsides against the existing parties sustained if not intensified ('An Aiséirghe Minority is Better than a Political-Party Majority' was the uncompromising, if pessimistic, campaign slogan adopted by Harcourt Street in 1945), but his address at the movement's final pre-election rally in Dublin aroused once again all the apprehensions that had been expressed by the Cork organisation at the time of the 'American Note'. In the course of this speech, the *Ceannaire* referred to the order prohibiting him from entering Northern Ireland, and announced that on the next occasion that he crossed the Border he would do so with 100,000 green-clad men at his back. Tomás Óg Ó Murchadha's lament that '[i]nstead of winning us votes that Final Rally cost us thousands' was almost certainly an exaggeration – if only because the Dublin newspapers' practice of withholding coverage of Aiséirghe events limited any damage done to those who heard the speech in person – but it undoubtedly did little to persuade uncommitted observers of the party's maturity and sense of reality. Although a secondary concern for his Aiséirghe critics, Ó Cuinneagáin's invocation of physical force as a solution to the Northern question once again raised questions about the influence of IRA members within the movement, and the extent to which the *Ceannaire* was privately beholden to these elements.

In the late summer of 1945, consequently, moves began to force a showdown with Ó Cuinneagáin over these grievances and, if he proved intractable, to remove him. The leading figure among the rebels was Tomás Ó Dochartaigh. Although he had once been closer to Ó Cuinneagáin than any other Ard-Chomhairle member with the possible exception of Gearóid Ó Broin, relations between the two had cooled perceptibly over the previous twelve months. On social and economic questions Ó Dochartaigh stood well to the left of the Aiséirghe spectrum, becoming increasingly critical of what he regarded as Ó Cuinneagáin's indifference to issues of class and unwillingness to develop policies to appeal to the immediate concerns of the working voter.[44] Ó Dochartaigh was also resentful over the rejection of his plan for the local government election campaign, the correctness of which he considered to have been proved by events, and attributed his own defeat in the Dublin Corporation race largely to the *Ceannaire's* ill-timed interventions.[45] Lastly, the two had clashed when Ó Dochartaigh pressed for the full-time secretary at Harcourt Street, Síle Ní Chochláin, to be made to give up her job following her marriage to Ó Cuinneagáin in 1945.[46]

In view of their temperamental similarities, it was all but inevitable that Aiséirghe's two most senior figures would come into conflict sooner or later. Both were highly ambitious; energetic; strong-willed; intolerant of dissent; former Anglophone monoglots who as adults had dedicated themselves to Irish-Ireland and Christian ideals – as they themselves interpreted those philosophies – and autocratic in manner (many within the movement considered Ó Dochartaigh to be more than his leader's equal in this respect). Though possessing a 'loud, harsh voice', however, Ó Dochartaigh was far superior to Ó Cuinneagáin as a platform speaker. Notwithstanding his frequently ventilated anti-Semitic and anti-democratic views, his speeches were usually well crafted and calculated to gain support by means of persuasion rather than mere denunciation or repetition. In contrast, as the *Leader* noted, whenever the *Ceannaire* spoke before a group of uncommitted hearers 'he is just as likely to lose support as to gain it'.[47]

Ó Dochartaigh made full use of these rhetorical talents during a major speaking tour of Munster in the weeks after the local govern-

---

44 In a March 1945 lecture, Ó Dochartaigh had gone so far as to declare that 'it was the duty of everyone to be a member of some [trade] union'. *Clonmel Nationalist*, 21 March 1945.

45 According to Tomás Óg Ó Murchadha, 'Our recent defeat has awakened Tomás [Ó Dochartaigh] to the realities of life & has made him a sadder & a wiser man'. Ó Murchadha to Ó Coigligh, 19 June 1945, 5/3/11, GÓCP.

46 Ard-Chomhairle minutes, 17 March 1945, 5/12/1, *ibid*. Ní Chochláin came to the attention of MI5 as early as February 1942, when she wrote to the British Representative's office requesting to be supplied regularly with 'British War News'. Rightly suspecting this to be 'an attempt to expose our propaganda methods', the office requested MI5 to provide all available information concerning her. Unsigned minute no. 1216, 18 February 1942, 'Miscellaneous Enquiries' file, part II, 284, G2/X.1091, DDMA.

47 *The Leader*, 23 June 1945.

ment election, in what appears to have been a bid to establish his
credentials as a plausible candidate for the *ceannaireacht*. Taking the
neglected ninth point of the Aiséirghe programme as his theme, he
declared that the party was committed to the fight against 'what we
call the vested interests – financiers; industrial magnates, rulers of
commerce, etc.'.[48] In an even more outspokenly anti-capitalist address
a week later, Ó Dochartaigh asserted that the claims of labour for
'higher wages, shorter hours and better working conditions [were]
… for the most part just demands'. Aiséirghe, he said, stood with the
working class against exploitative employers, whom he described as
'hypocrites or fools'; 'modern Pharisees'; and 'the greatest enemies of
Christianity'. Either social justice would be done, he warned, or 'their
heads will be the first to fall'.[49] Ó Dochartaigh was at pains to reassure
his audiences, however, that despite the downfall of the Axis powers
Aiséirghe did not intend to compromise its core principle of creating
a one-party state:

> [N]ote the fact that party-politics has so far failed to solve unemployment
> while in every instance where there was a one-party system of Govern-
> ment, this problem has been solved … To state that the one-party system
> of government is Fascist is to confuse the means with the end … In truth,
> the system of government is merely the machine. We, of Aiséirghe, shall
> use the machine to establish a Christian, social and economic order; let
> Stalin or Hitler or anyone use it for what they may.[50]

If Ó Dochartaigh's aim in mid-1945 was to position himself as an
Irish analogue of Gregor Strasser and to succeed where the latter
had failed, the parallel broke down over the fact that to most of the
dissenting elements within the party he was even less acceptable as
a leader than Ó Cuinneagáin himself. Sometime in August, he and
Seán Ó hUrmoltaigh, after discussions with the Cork party officials,
obtained an interview with the *Ceannaire* to lay their combined grievances before him. According to Ó Dochartaigh's account of events, the
deputation carried out this task 'as tactfully as we could; but perhaps
we were too tactful inasmuch as the final response he gave us was
that these were "small trivial matters" and that we were "ignoring
many other things" [to the contrary]'. In the wake of this meeting,
and Ó Cuinneagáin's unsatisfactory response to similar representations from the Cork officials, Ó Dochartaigh and Ó hUrmoltaigh
sought out Ó Cuinneagáin once again on 27 August to demand that he
convene a meeting of the Ard-Chomhairle. The *Ceannaire* denied that

48 *Tipperary Star*, 28 July 1945.
49 *Ibid.*, 4 August 1945.
50 *Ibid.*, 28 July 1945.

there was any necessity for such a meeting, but promised to give the matter his consideration. When Ó Dochartaigh refused to accept such a temporising reply and threatened to convoke the Ard-Chomhairle on his own authority, Ó Cuinneagáin's response was swift, decisive and unexpected. On 1 September he called a meeting of those Ard-Chomhairle members resident in Dublin and the surrounding districts to discuss 'the question of insubordination and the demand in the form of an ultimatum that he had received'. Although the *Ceannaire* was unable to dissuade the group from agreeing to the request for a further meeting of the full Ard-Chomhairle three weeks later, he concluded the gathering by suspending Ó Dochartaigh and Ó hUrmoltaigh from their offices and declaring that the only issue on the agenda would be the 'insubordination' of the two men.[51]

The boldness and aggression of Ó Cuinneagáin's pre-emptive action took Ó Dochartaigh and Ó hUrmoltaigh by surprise. From such evidence as is available, it appears that they had counted upon a lengthy period of confrontation, with the *Ceannaire* displaying his customary defensiveness and indecisiveness in the face of thorny problems, as a way of demonstrating to the movement as a whole that no change could be expected so long as he remained in power. An additional complication was that even his severest critics, with the exceptions of Ó Dochartaigh and Tomás Óg Ó Murchadha, were anxious not to drive Ó Cuinneagáin out of the movement but rather, in the manner advocated by Ernest Blythe a year earlier, to redeploy him to a position in which his unquestioned talents and energies could be harnessed to the benefit of the movement. It quickly became clear, however, that Ó Cuinneagáin himself harboured no such inhibitions, and that he was determined to crush all opposition to his leadership regardless of the damage the organisation might sustain as a result.

Although Ó Cuinneagáin was subsequently to accuse Ó Dochartaigh and a 'Cork clique' of secretly plotting for his removal since the summer of 1945, no such scheme appears ever to have existed. On the contrary, the events that followed the suspension of the two officers lead strongly to the conclusion that Ó Dochartaigh and Ó hUrmoltaigh acted without the knowledge or approval of other dissidents either on the Ard-Chomhairle or throughout the country. The Cork organisation was so unprepared for a confrontation that the list of proposals it presented to the full Ard-Chomhairle on 22 September was finalised only on the morning of the meeting itself. The fact that the first item of business dealt with was the passage of

---

51 Ó Cuinneagáin to Ó Dochartaigh and Ó hUrmoltaigh, 3 September 1945, 3/4/4, GÓCP; Ó Dochartaigh to Conall Ó Domhnaill, 12 September 1945, 3/3/7, *ibid*.

a unanimous resolution censuring Ó Dochartaigh for the manner in which he had attempted to dictate to the *Ceannaire* likewise indicates that the National Organiser had not taken the Cork dissidents into his confidence before doing so.

This resolution, however, represented the sum of the unanimity to be found at the Ard-Chomhairle meeting. Three hours before it convened, Seosamh Ó Coigligh and the other Cork delegates met privately with Ó Cuinneagáin to present him with the list of organisational changes they intended to submit to the council that afternoon. Of the eight recommendations, the most unwelcome from Ó Cuinneagáin's point of view were proposals to reduce the *Ceannaire*'s term of office from three years to one; to disqualify the leader from serving simultaneously as *Ard-Cheannasaidhe* of the Dublin district; to reorganise the party organisation so as to provide each province with 'the largest measure of autonomy consistent with the strength and welfare of the movement'; and to ensure that 'all communications, reports, subscriptions, monies etc. from each province go in the first instance to the *Ard-Ceannasaidhe* of that province'.[52]

These suggestions were poorly received by Ó Cuinneagáin, who viewed them as a second ultimatum and regarded the lack of notice given as a deliberate tactic to prevent him from preparing counter-arguments of his own. His temper was not improved by proceedings at the Ard-Chomhairle meeting itself later that afternoon. As the Cork delegation recorded, 'over 2 hours of the members' time was taken up in listening to a bitter and acrimonious discussion between *An Ceannaire* and *An Timthire Náisiúnta* [the National Organiser] which made it clear that the position of affairs at H.Q. was even worse than we had been led to believe'.[53] After its reproof of Ó Dochartaigh, moreover, the Ard-Chomhairle proceeded to censure the *Ceannaire* for exceeding his authority by suspending Ó Dochartaigh and Ó hUrmoltaigh, and, ruling that no blame attached to the latter, reinstated him in his office.[54] Lastly, a resolution was adopted amending Article 2 of the constitution to provide that officers, including the *Ceannaire* himself, should serve for one year rather than three, over Ó Cuinneagáin's strenuous objection that the Ard-Chomhairle possessed no power to do so.[55] The

---

52 'Proposals of *Ard-Ceannasaidhe*, Corcaigh, and his Advisory Council', n.d. [c. 22 September 1945], 7/2/9, *ibid.*
53 'Ráiteas Ó Cumann Corcaighe d'Aiséirghe', September 1945, 7/2/8, *ibid.*
54 A subsequent resolution, seconded by Ó Dochartaigh himself, granted the *Ceannaire* power to suspend a member of the Executive subject to the confirmation or counter-manding of his decision by an extraordinary meeting of the Ard-Chomhairle to be held within fourteen days of the action.
55 Ard-Chomhairle minutes, meeting of 22 September 1945, 5/11/1, GÓCP. The constitution as adopted in 1943 did not contain any mechanism providing for its amendment.

meeting concluded with Ó hUrmoltaigh requesting to be relieved of his office as Deputy Treasurer on the grounds of his personal 'unsuitability' for the position, and Ó Dochartaigh submitting his resignation as National Organiser.

Smarting from his treatment at the hands of the Ard-Chomhairle, convinced that events at the meeting had been meticulously co-ordinated by his opponents and confronted with the necessity of submitting himself at the annual convention a month hence to a leadership election, the first in Aiséirghe's history, Ó Cuinneagáin once again went over to the offensive. A week after the Ard-Chomhairle meeting, he dismissed Seosamh Ó Coigligh from his position as *Ard-Cheannasaidhe* for Cork, and Muiris Mac Gearailt as head of the Tipperary organisation. In both cases the reason stated was that the *Ceannaire* 'no longer had any confidence in them'. As he revealed in a letter to the head of the Glasgow branch, his intention by now was no longer to force the dissidents to back down, but rather 'to run people like that out' of the movement [*an ruaig a cur ar dhaoine mar sin*].[56] By thus removing the most popular figure in Munster (Mac Gearailt, on the other hand, appears to have been targeted as a near neighbour, and presumed supporter, of Ó Dochartaigh), Ó Cuinneagáin ruled out any possibility of a negotiated settlement and ensured that the forthcoming convention would constitute a fight to the finish.

A coup from above?

Only at this inconvenient juncture did Ó Dochartaigh discover the full extent of his personal unpopularity and the seriousness of his miscalculation in provoking a premature showdown with the leader. Although the heads of the Dublin Aiséirghe branches unanimously agreed that a change of leader was necessary, they were prepared to accept Ó Dochartaigh only in the capacity of interim *ceannaire* until the October convention took place.[57] Soundings taken on his behalf by Tomás Óg Ó Murchadha at the end of September revealed that key members of the Ard-Chomhairle were no less determined to prevent him from ascending to the *ceannaireacht* than to secure Ó Cuinneagáin's removal from it. Women members recalled bitterly that Ó Dochartaigh had summarily dismissed the popular secretary of the Waterford City branch, Barbara Nic Giolla Choilín, for no more substantial reason than his belief that 'the girls should be segregated

---

56 Ó Cuinneagáin to Séamus C. Mac Fhinn, 27 September 1945, 9/2/33, GÓCP.
57 Telegram from Dublin *ceannasaidheanna* to Eoin Ó Coigligh, 5 October 1945, 5/3/4, *ibid.*

240Architects of the Resurrection

from the boys'.[58] Seán Glanbhille and Risteárd Ó Murchadha had not forgiven him for his Waterford speech in 1943: 'nothing you might do now could make up for what you said at that meeting'. Gearóid Ó hAodha and Piaras Mac Maghnúsa might 'thoroughly detest the name of Géaroid Ó Cuinneagáin', Ó Murchadha reported, 'but that doesn't bear comparison with their detestation of you. You are too "taken up with your own infallibility." "Ó Cuinneagáin is a dictator but Ó Dochartaigh is twenty times worse." "We will accept anybody except Ó Dochartaigh!"' Eoin Ó Coigligh, his dissatisfaction with Ó Cuinneagáin notwithstanding, was another who saw no point in ousting the *Ceannaire* if the consequence was to enable Ó Dochartaigh to take over: '"Out of the frying pan into the fire," he says'.[59]

The result was that as the date for the convention approached, those seeking Ó Cuinneagáin's removal had no substitute of their own to offer. Seosamh Ó Coigligh, perhaps the best-qualified candidate on the Ard-Chomhairle, chose not to put himself forward. Risteárd Mac Siacuis, though regarding Ó Cuinneagáin's continuance in the *ceannaireacht* as disastrous, was so determined not to contribute in any way to a split that he resigned from the Ard-Chomhairle in advance of the convention and reverted to associate membership of the movement rather than cast a negative vote against the leader.[60] Eoin Ó Coigligh, Aiséirghe's leading vote-winner and an important swing vote courted by both factions, was disqualified from candidacy on the grounds of knowing no Irish. Lacking any better alternative, the officers of the Cork City branch nominated Riobárd Breathnach for the *ceannaireacht* a week before the convention. In light of his inability to devote more than a fraction of his time to the movement during the previous two years, there is no reason to doubt Breathnach's assertion that he had no personal designs upon the leadership and was standing merely to ensure that a contest took place. To the degree that it persuaded others of his sincerity, however, such a stance served only to raise further questions as to the level of commitment that could be expected from him should he succeed in replacing Ó Cuinneagáin as Aiséirghe's head.

So lacking in forethought and haphazard in execution were the preparations of the dissidents in the days before the convention that it is hard not to conclude that even at this late stage several had not given up hope that Ó Cuinneagáin might save the movement from a damaging confrontation by stepping down of his own volition. Any

58 Ó Dochartaigh, '*Memo* ar Litir Éamonn Uí Riain (Ard Ceannasaidhe Co. Phortlairge), de'n 29adh Márta 1944', n.d. [c. April 1944], 3/4/11, *ibid*.
59 Tomás Óg Ó Murchadha to Ó Dochartaigh, 28 September 1945, 3/3/2, *ibid*.
60 Mac Siacuis to Ó Cuinneagáin, 25 October 1945, 5/3/10, *ibid*.

illusions of the kind were rudely dispelled by the *Ceannaire*'s Annual Report on Aiséirghe's activities, issued to all members in mid-October. Published for the first time in an English- as well as an Irish-language edition to ensure maximum readership, the greater part of the report consisted of a polemical attack on the dissident elements. Omitting any mention of the complaints made against his own leadership style and characterising the issue in dispute as an attempt 'by a small number of our own officers ... to weaken if not wholly alter the extremely important portion of Aiséirghe policy which deals with the Border problem and the independence of our country', Ó Cuinneagáin accused Ó Dochartaigh and the Cork City officials of seeking to abandon the ideal of a united republican Ireland in favour of 'a new policy designed to attract the people (as they imagine) in the 26 Counties very rapidly in favour of Aiséirghe'. He attributed this stance to 'the disappointment they felt at the results of the Local Government Elections and the unsatisfactory progress in the area under their own control during the past twelve months'. After ventilating a number of extraneous complaints about Ó Dochartaigh's and the Cork officers' alleged organisational shortcomings, Ó Cuinneagáin warned against the rise of 'a dangerous tendency in the organisation' and declared his conviction that the people of Ireland would not permit themselves to be 'deceived and misled by a new troupe of party politicians!'. He also issued a veiled but unmistakable threat that if defeated in the leadership election he would not hesitate to split the organisation, as he had done twice previously in 1940 and 1942 when thwarted in his leadership ambitions:

> I am of course fully prepared to retire from An Ceannaireacht *if that is the best thing to do in the Movement's and the country's interest.*
>
> I am also fully prepared to use every ounce of my energy to prevent the formation of a new 26 County Political Party on nobly Republican and National Organisation [sic] that is to-day Aiséirghe.[61]

The issuance of this report provided the first indication to those within Aiséirghe, other than the principals immediately concerned, that anything was amiss, and gave rise to much bewilderment and confusion among ordinary members throughout the country as to the precise nature of the dispute. For their part, the dissidents had little opportunity to put their side of the case in advance of the convention, which was scheduled for 22 October. Not until ten days before this date were official invitations to the convention extended to the branches,

---

61 Ailtirí na hAiséirghe. *Annual Report 1944–45*, 12 October 1945, 6/1/3, *ibid*. Emphasis in original.

which were requested to submit nominations for the *ceannaireacht* and Ard-Chomhairle elections within the week. To Ó Cuinneagáin's opponents, already infuriated by the contents of the Annual Report, the criteria laid down by the *Ceannaire* for participation constituted an additional source of grievance. No mention was made of the provision laid down in Article 8 of the Aiséirghe constitution withholding nominating and voting rights from branches formed less than three months previously; nor would the requirement that a branch have a minimum of ten active members to be represented be adhered to on this occasion. Instead, Ó Cuinneagáin authorised the respective *Ard-Cheannasaidheanna* to waive this rule in the case of branches which had done 'especially good work' on behalf of the movement, a formula that was interpreted by his opponents to mean those branches that had demonstrated their personal loyalty to the leader.

The rebels' conviction that Ó Cuinneagáin and his supporters were attempting to gerrymander the convention was strengthened by two controversial episodes in mid-October in which the *Ceannaire* was directly involved. After offering several conflicting explanations as to the whereabouts of party funds for which he was responsible, Tomás Óg Ó Murchadha signed a statement on 11 October acknowledging having diverted the money to his own use; resigning from his salaried position as organiser for Co. Dublin and from the Ard-Chomhairle; and agreeing not to communicate with any other member of the Ard-Chomhairle before the convention. News of the affair inevitably leaked, and, in light of Ó Murchadha's personal antipathy to Ó Cuinneagáin, the *Ceannaire*'s gagging order was taken by his opponents as evidence of an attempt on his part to neutralise a known opponent by holding the threat of a criminal prosecution over his head and derive political advantage from the scandal. Suspicions were intensified further by the unusual method by which the leadership of Cumann na gCailíní, a position which carried with it the right to attend and vote at the convention, was determined ten days before the assembly took place. At a weekly meeting of the women's group, Denise Nic Réamoinn, a staunch Ó Cuinneagáin loyalist, moved that she be elected by acclamation for the following year. This unorthodox procedure was challenged by five of her subordinates, who in a written complaint to Ó Cuinneagáin in his capacity as Dublin city *Ard-Cheannasaidhe* pointed out that a proper election had not been held; that no notice of Nic Réamoinn's intentions had been given to members; and that nominations for the appointment of group officers were not in order. In a hastily convened hearing thirty-six hours before the convention, Nic Réamoinn admitted that no advance notice of election had been distributed but claimed in her defence that eight members of the body had been present on the evening in question, which constituted a good average attendance. She had, she said, stated her lack of desire for the *Ceannasaidheacht* and her willingness to stand down in favour of any other nominee, but nonetheless had been elected unopposed. Ó Cuinneagáin dismissed the complaint; confirmed Nic Réamoinn in her post; and sternly admonished members of the organisation to pay more attention to their duties.[62]

In the final days before the convention, much jockeying for position took place between the respective camps. The Cork officials struck back at Ó Cuinneagáin's Annual Report with an eight-page statement of their own, disputing his version of events and maintaining that 'if the movement [is] to make progress, it [is] essential that it should have as leader someone who, as a minimum qualification, would at least not antagonise his most active workers'.[63] As well as submitting nominations for the elected offices, several branches took the opportunity to append unsolicited resolutions of their own for discussion at the convention. Cumann Cathal Brugha, the branch to which Tomás Ó Dochartaigh belonged, indicated its support for the suspended National Organiser by demanding 'that our propaganda be aimed more directly at the working class than it is at present'. The Dublin South branch requested the convention to reject the 1945 Annual Report on the ground that of its seven pages, four contained 'nothing but attacks upon the officers of the movement, attacks based on the personal opinions of Gearóid Ó Cuinneagáin'. Cumann Mac Piarais, another rebellious Dublin branch, proposed that no officer be permitted to hold more than one position – a criticism of Ó Cuinneagáin, who combined in his own person the offices of *Ceannaire*, National Secretary and National Treasurer, as well as head of the Dublin County and Leinster provincial councils – and desired that a balance sheet showing the movement's finances be presented to the Ard-Chomhairle. But Ó Cuinneagáin too received numerous pledges of support from his admirers. Seán Ó hUrmoltaigh, displaying a previously unrevealed appetite for humble pie, put his name to a circular letter to all members extolling Ó Cuinneagáin and calling for the movement to unite behind the *Ceannaire*.[64] Another prominent loyalist was Liam Ó hArgadáin [William Hargadon], onetime head of the Aiséirghe branch in Sligo,

---

62 Róisin Nic Piarias, Máirín Nic Aodagháin, Máire de h-Altúin, Monica Halton and Máirín de Ghrás to Ó Cuinneagáin, 21 October 1945; minutes of a meeting between Ó Cuinneagáin and members of Cumann na gCailíní, 25 October 1945, 7/11/1, GÓCP.
63 'Ráiteas Ó Cumann Corcaighe d'Aiséirghe', 7/2/8, *ibid*.
64 Circular letter by Ó hUrmoltaigh, 12 October 1945, 6/2/9, *ibid*.

who hoped he would 'see the day when the Seóiníns [*recte: seóiníní*] will be suitably dealt with', and went on to express confidence that 'What Franco did for Spain, what Hitler did for Germany, surely we of Aiséirghe can do for Ireland from top to bottom'.[65]

If it achieved nothing else, the outcome of the convention went far to satisfy Ó hArgadáin's unintentionally risible expectations. The meeting was a bad-tempered one, with the *Ceannaire*, who commenced by announcing that he would not go through the Annual Report point by point, spending much of the day doing precisely that. Accusing his critics of having held a secret gathering at Limerick Junction to intrigue against him, he reminded the convention of the fragility of the movement. Lack of money and of full-time organisers had limited the progress he had been able to achieve, as had the difficulty of establishing the newspaper: 'One might say that it's a *paper* [rather than a party] that we have at present'.[66] Ó Cuinneagáin pointed out, though, that *Aiséirghe* was growing into a considerable asset, and promised brighter days ahead so long as it was borne in mind that the task of freeing Ireland would be accomplished through patriotism and divine assistance, 'not lectures & talk'. For the Cork delegation, Séamus Ó Coigligh made the most effective rebuttal. He was tired, he said, of the *Ceannaire*'s repeated demand for greater 'confidence in God'. Christianity had become the movement's 'catch cry', amounting in practice to the presentation of an 'ultimatum to God'. The essential problem was that Ó Cuinneagáin was 'not satisfied to have [any] strong man about him', but would get rid of any excessively outspoken subordinate. Ó Coigligh declared that he and the other dissidents had 'no further faith' in Ó Cuinneagáin, though they acknowledged his 'great work in the past'. Ó Dochartaigh defended his association with Jack Stakelum and Dan Breen, pointing out that the former had championed Aiséirghe's abortive 1944 'partition plebiscite' and the latter had been instrumental in helping to obtain the permit to publish *Aiséirghe* as well as supplies of petrol for the movement. Fionntáin Mac Guill reminded delegates that Aiséirghe was 'the only body capable of saving Ireland [and] possibly the world'; the best solution, he declared, was for one of the candidates to sacrifice his 'petty ambitions' and withdraw in the interest of unity. After others had spoken, a secret vote was held at the conclusion of the day-long meeting, with 22 officials backing Ó Cuinneagáin's continued leadership, and 13 supporting

---

65 Liam Ó hArgadáin to Ó Cuinneagáin, 21 October 1945, 5/3/10, *ibid.*
66 Manuscript minutes by Aindrias Ó Scolaidhe, 28 October 1945, 5/3/2, *ibid.* Emphasis in original.

Riobárd Breathnach. One delegate recorded a spoiled ballot; another abstained.[67]

With the exception of Ó hUrmoltaigh, the *Ceannaire*'s challengers had made clear that they would take no further part in a movement under Ó Cuinneagáin's leadership. The convention was thus followed by the immediate resignation of Ó Dochartaigh and of the entire Cork delegation from Ailtirí na hAiséirghe. A remarkable feature of the split was the acquiescence of the defeated minority in the verdict. Though Riobárd Breathnach, on behalf of his colleagues, briefly held out the possibility of a reunification on condition of the removal of Ó Cuinneagáin from the *ceannaireacht*, it soon became apparent that no further challengers would come forward.[68] With the exception of a small and short-lived body, Comhdháil Laochra Poblacht na hÉireann ['Republic of Ireland Heroes' Congress'], in which some former members of Aiséirghe participated, no attempts were made to form splinter organisations or to obtain a new hearing in the court of public opinion. Instead, the leaders of the Cork organisation chose to withdraw not only from Aiséirghe but the political scene altogether. While exhaustion and demoralisation no doubt provide part of the explanation, it is also likely that the dissidents tacitly acknowledged the force of one of Seán Ó hUrmoltaigh's arguments in defence of the *Ceannaire*. Each member, Ó hUrmoltaigh reminded recipients of his circular letter, had to acknowledge that regardless of their personal opinion of him 'it was Gearóid Ó Cuinneagáin who conceived the programme. It was he who laid it out for us in *Aiséirghe Says* ..., etc. He instructed us in his vision. He demanded self-sacrifice of us. He instilled courage in us'.[69]

Ó Cuinneagáin's critics were capable and dedicated party activists. Many of them had given years of devoted work to the movement, in whose service they had spared themselves no more than had the *Ceannaire* himself. In many respects their view of the realities of Irish politics, and of Aiséirghe's potential place within it, was clearer than his. They were not, however, visionaries. The most capable of them, Seosamh Ó Coigligh, was prepared to challenge Ó Cuinneagáin, but not to supplant him. Tomás Ó Dochartaigh, who was more than willing to assume leadership of the movement, lacked the ability to inspire it. Nor was it imaginable that a party headed by him would have remained true to its original ethos and objectives. Had he succeeded in replacing Ó Cuinneagáin as *Ceannaire*, its character would surely have

67 *Ibid.*
68 Breathnach to Eoin Ó Coigligh, 7 November 1945, 5/3/5, *ibid.*
69 Circular letter by Ó hUrmoltaigh, 12 October 1945, 7/2/9, *ibid.*

fundamentally changed. For better or worse, Ailtirí na hAiséirghe was inseparable from its creator. Without him it could never have progressed as far as it had done. The outstanding question at the end of 1945 was whether it was fated to reflect his weaknesses as faithfully as his strengths.

7

The 'Cunningham circus'

The October 1945 split was the most grievous blow Ailtirí na hAiséirghe ever sustained. At the very moment when the party had scored a modest but definite electoral victory and seemed poised to make further advances, its momentum was abruptly halted by a bitter inter-necine dispute. The rupture cost Aiséirghe an extremely high propor-tion of its most able and active members, a considerable proportion of whom, disillusioned, withdrew altogether from politics. With the remainder abandoning their normal activities the more completely to give themselves over to mutual recrimination, the prospect of Aiséirghe being able to forge alliances with well-connected figures who had viewed it as a coming force permanently receded into the background. Once again the party's striking inability to take advantage of golden opportunities exhibited itself, for the split could hardly have come at a worse time. Demoralising though the scale of Fianna Fáil's 1944 general election success had been to its opponents, its temporary spike in popularity as a result of the American Note quickly evaporated as the war came to an end. Éamon de Valera and his ministers had been continuously in office since 1932, and were displaying all the signs of physical and mental exhaustion. De Valera's fifth administration was one of the most undistinguished in the country's history, seemingly bereft of fresh ideas. While the Taoiseach's personal standing remained high as a result of his having successfully steered Ireland through the Emergency, like his wartime counterpart Winston Churchill he was widely perceived as having remained in office beyond his time. The 1945 Presidential election, in which the popular and affable Seán T. O'Kelly scrambled to a narrow victory only on the second count, provided an early portent of what the Fianna Fáil parliamentary party could expect when it next sought a mandate from the people.

Immensely debilitating as the setback Aiséirghe had experienced was, the wound need not have been mortal. The party remained a viable concern, with a national newspaper to disseminate its message and a public avid for new approaches to the country's ongoing problems. Gearóid Ó Cuinneagáin could legitimately argue that, whatever his flaws as a leader, such figures as Tomás Ó Dochartaigh or Riobárd Breathnach represented little improvement. The purging of dissentients, if it achieved nothing else, at all events ensured that no future internal divisions need be apprehended: henceforward Aiséirghe would speak with a single voice.

This was, however, the only question resolved by the split. All the party's fundamental problems – ideological inflexibility, organisational dysfunction, chaotic finances and inadequate leadership at all levels – either remained unaddressed or had been deeply aggravated by the loss of key members and in many cases whole branches. As a result, whatever margin for error Aiséirghe may once have possessed no longer existed at the end of 1945. Unless Gearóid Ó Cuinneagáin showed himself capable of learning the lessons of his Pyrrhic victory, the future of the party he led was bleak. Nothing in his record to date provided any basis for believing that he could do so.

Consequences of the split

The resignation of Séamus Ó Coigligh, Riobárd Breathnach and Seán Ó Dúbhghaill, among others, had a devastating impact on Aiséirghe especially in its Munster heartland. These men had been responsible for recruiting a large proportion of the movement's leadership cadre in the south of Ireland, and many of these in turn departed either in solidarity or in despair. The Cork City branch elected to remain in being as a non-political Irish language society, separating itself from Aiséirghe but retaining the party headquarters in Patrick Street for its own meetings.[1] In Aherlow, Co. Tipperary, where as recently as the previous July interest in Aiséirghe was reported to be increasing, along with a keen local demand for party emblems, 'every single one [of the members]…resigned in disgust from the movement when they heard that a split had occurred'.[2] Caoimhighin Mac Cartaigh, one of Aiséirghe's councillors in Bandon, informed Ó Cuinneagáin in February 1946 that there too the membership had resolved to disband the *cumann* and sever their connections with the party.

> Cork has unfortunately finished completely with Aiséirghe now, and I can assure you that it would be quite useless for you to attempt to start the movement there again…We have been informed that Cobh is

1 Eoghan de Leastar to Ó Cuinneagáin, 4 March 1946, 7/3/6, GÓCP.
2 M. Ó Murchadha to Ó Cuinneagáin, n.d. [c. 29 July 1945]; same to same, n.d. [c. December, 1945], 7/3/5, *ibid.*

finished also, and T. Stockdale has left for Canada working as a ship's carpenter on a boat...

Personally I think that you yourself are a fine sincere Irishman with the cause of Ireland at Heart, but I think you adopted a rather dictatorial attitude at times. The Programme and policy of Aiséirghe was the finest that could be put before the Irish people, and perhaps the 'Leader' was Correct when they stated that you had not the qualities of leadership...

[I]f we failed [in Bandon] it was not our fault as we spent hundreds of pounds for the Aiséirghe cause in propaganda etc., through press and posters, and were recognised by the general public as a fine outstanding body. We worked hard for four years and what have we achieved – nothing, and leave behind the remnants of a dead movement.[3]

A more bitter note was struck in Dublin, whose branches were even more sharply divided than the Ard-Chomhairle had been and whose leaders were far less willing to go quietly. A week after the convention, the *ceannasaidhe* of the Cathal Brugha branch, Pádraig Ó Gríobhtha na Coille, invited one of Ó Dochartaigh's partisans, Tomás Ó Muire-adaidh, to speak. The latter described the convention as 'packed and a farce', and accused the *Ceannaire* of using the Annual Report to smear those who questioned his leadership. Ó Gríobhtha na Coille announced to the members that a new organisation was being formed. To this Aindrias Ó Scolaidhe, an Ó Cuinneagáin loyalist, responded by suspending Ó Gríobhtha na Coille on his own authority; 'He then declared the Cumann meeting at an end and took all the files away'.[4] To protest against this action the officers of two other Dublin branches, Cumann Mac Piarais and Cumann Ó Conghaile, resigned en masse from the movement. Their letter of resignation, disdain-fully composed in 'the language of the oppressor', contended that the convention had been illegal and that numerous other provisions of the Aiséirghe constitution had been repeatedly ignored or violated by 'Jerry Cunningham' over the previous three years: 'Having heard so much about compromising, we are convinced it is going a bit too far to countenance the breaking of six Articles in a Constitution of 12 Articles ... We are convinced that any *Ceannaire* who countenanced such breaches of the Constitution *is unfit to lead us'*. In an unconscious note of irony, the defecting officers declared that they had 'no intention of becoming willing tools of a Dictatorship'.[5]

Ó Cuinneagáin's response to this cascade of resignations was to dismiss them as little local difficulties. The 'discord' that had arisen, he

3 Mac Cartaigh to Ó Cuinneagáin, 7 February 1946, 7/4/2, *ibid.*
4 Minute by Dómhnall Ó Maolalaí, 30 October 1945, 6/3/7, *ibid.*
5 Officers of Cumainn Mac Piarais and Ó Conghaile to Eoin Ó Coigligh, 2 December 1945, 3/1/16, *ibid.* Emphasis in original.

told one of the remaining members in Cork, was regrettable. Neverthe-less, 'We in Dublin do not intend to make any changes. The movement is proceeding as usual here and throughout the country. We welcome the people who are willing to help us. Those who aren't, well, they don't matter'.[6]

As far as possible changes were concerned, the *Ceannaire* was practi-cally as good as his word. At organisational level, the only response to the split was the convening of a meeting of the rump Ard-Chomhairle to reverse the decision of September 1945 limiting the term in office of the *ceannaireacht*, and to modify the constitution to enable recalci-trant members or branches to be more easily disciplined or expelled.[7] Ó Cuinneagáin's claim that those who had quit Aiséirghe were people of no importance, however, was not supported by the course of events in the south. The handful of remaining loyalists in Cork City, who had been left without instructions or communications of any kind from Harcourt Street, eventually gathered together on their own initiative and resolved to relaunch the branch. Welcoming this move, Ó Cuinneagáin advised them to avoid any bitterness or vindictiveness with respect to the defectors. 'The best of them will yet come to their senses!'[8] Six months later, though, none had done so, and the Cork City branch could not boast a single new member. In the adjoining county of Tipperary, the situation was no less bleak. Micheál Ó Murchadha, to whom Ó Cuinneagáin eventually turned to rebuild the organisation in the rural areas, made no attempt to sugar-coat the scale of the task: 'You and Aindrias [Ó Scolaidhe] had better understand that I don't deserve to be *Ard-Cheannasaidhe* because there's nobody to lead….Let me tell you that the split played merry hell with us'.[9]

In a few areas a more positive situation prevailed. The South Tipperary electoral area, which had long underperformed, was reorgan-ised by an energetic new *Ard-Cheannasaidhe*, Eoin Ó Dabharáin [Owen Davern], assisted by Seán Treacy, formerly of Cumann Cultúrdha na hAiséirghe.[10] The Cashel branch alone, headed by Ó Dabharáin,

6 Ó Cuinneagáin to Seán Ó Doirinne, 7 February 1946, 7/5/3, *ibid*.
7 Circular letter by Ó Cuinneagáin, 17 January 1946, 8/1/1, *ibid*.
8 Ó Cuinneagáin to Tomás Ó Gríobhtha, 7 January 1946, 7/3/6, *ibid*.
9 M. Ó Murchadha to Ó Cuinneagáin, 12 March 1946, 7/3/5, *ibid*.
10 Treacy was elected Secretary of the Clonmel branch of Ailtirí na hAiséirghe in October 1945 and submitted reports to Harcourt Street in that capacity. His activities on behalf of the party over the following four years included organising and speaking at public meetings; arranging publicity for the movement; raising funds; selling publications; and directing the work of other members. He is listed in Ailtirí na hAiséirghe membership records as having paid his annual subscription fee, and, in letters to Ó Cuinneagáin, signed himself as 'your fellow-Architect' [*do comh-Ailtire*]. See letter reporting results of election by S. Ó Crotaigh, Clonmel branch *ceannasaidhe*, 10 October 1945; letter by Treacy, 1 September 1947; same to Ó Cuinneagáin, 9 April 1949; same to same, 20 June 1949,

reported a membership of nearly 50 in January 1946.[11] His counterpart in Co. Louth, Fionntán Mac Guill, could report in May 1946 that the level of Aiséirghe activity in that area remained undiminished; and Roscommon continued to make progress under Seosamh Ó Ceallaigh. Such isolated successes, however, could not offset the general picture of rapid decline. A pair of reports by Éamonn Ó Ceallacháin, who temporarily assumed Tomás Ó Dochartaigh's functions as National Organiser, in January and May 1946 made for gloomy reading. No activity was occurring in Youghal, whose branch leader 'was interested only in his lunch all the time I was speaking with him'. Only two self-confessed Aiséirghe members could be found remaining in Athy. Though there were some fifty members in Tallow, Co. Waterford, their activities were curtailed by the county organisation's heavy debts incurred by the previous administration.[12] On all sides the branches' appeal was the same: for full-time paid organisers; more funding; and fewer financial exactions from head office.[13]

The *Ceannaire*'s reaction to these unwelcome tidings was to whistle loudly past the graveyard. Aiséirghe, he declared unblushingly in the 1946 Annual Report, had not only stood its ground in the previous year, but was stronger than ever: 'If there were a general election in the morning, we might nominate 15 Aiséirghe candidates'. The movement's debts had largely been cleared; public meetings were continuing in all twenty-six counties; and the sale of *Aiséirghe* had more than doubled.[14] While formidable obstacles remained, 'Another hard strenuous year of enthusiastic work from all, and with God's help the Aiséirghe Movement will definitely be in a position to determine Ireland's twentieth century destiny'.[15] The *Ceannaire* had predicted the advent of the Aiséirghe millennium too often, however, for assurances like these to have any credibility even among his most loyal followers. As many of them realised, Aiséirghe's window of opportunity in Irish politics might already have slammed shut. For four years, the party had been able to present itself as the only source of fresh ideas in political life, the sole alternative to a discredited status quo. That distinction too was now to disappear.

7/8/1–2, GÓCP; *Tipperary Star*, 28 April 1945; *Munster Express*, 3 June 1949; *Aiséirghe*, 24 October 1948.

11 *Tipperary Star*, 19 January 1946.

12 Ó Ceallacháin, 'Tréimhse Nollaig 22ú-Eanair 15ú [1946]', n.d.; 'Turas ó Áth Cliath go Portláirge agus Thar n-Ais Márta 1ú-8ú 1946', n.d.; S. Glanbhille, 'Fiacha Conndae Phortláirge ag 20/5/1946', 3/2/3, GÓCP.

13 *Ibid.*

14 Tuarascbhail Bliantuil go 30ú Mean Fómhair, 1946', 15 November 1946, 5/4/1, *ibid.*

15 'Prophets Confounded: Extract from Report of Ceannaire for Year to 30th Mean Fómhair, 1946', 5/4/2, *ibid.*

Clann na Poblachta – 'Aiséirghe light?'

Ó Cuinneagáin's final – and ultimately fatal – mistake as Aiséirghe's leader was his refusal to take seriously the advent on the Irish political scene of a rival party, Clann na Poblachta ['Tribe of the Republic']. By the summer of 1946 the Fianna Fáil government was visibly running out of steam. Most ministers had been continuously in office for more than fourteen years; only three had not been members of the first de Valera administration in 1932. De Valera himself, by now almost blind, appeared to have no new ideas with which to meet the challenge of the postwar world. His appointment of the loyal but unimaginative Frank Aiken as Minister for Finance in June 1945 was widely perceived as a manoeuvre to prevent Seán Lemass, who was exhibiting alarming signs of independence of mind in economic matters, from publicly upstaging his Taoiseach. Unemployment took a sharp upward leap to 14% as servicemen in the Defence Forces were demobilised, and it seemed to many contemporary observers that only the unexpectedly buoyant labour market in Britain was preventing a social explosion at home. Signs of public discontent were not lacking. Fianna Fáil lost its first by-election since 1932 in December 1945 to the Labour candidate Brendan Corish. Three months later, the national teachers' union, traditionally sympathetic to the ruling party, began a long and bitter strike for better pay and conditions. The final straw came in May 1946 when the former IRA adjutant-general, Seán McCaughey, died in Portlaoise Prison after a twenty-three-day hunger strike. McCaughey's protest, in support of his demand to wear his own clothing rather than a convict's uniform, had been followed closely throughout the country. Resolutions and petitions from public bodies and individuals calling upon the government to yield poured in from all sides. Shops and businesses across Ireland closed as a mark of respect on the day of McCaughey's funeral. Although in a number of areas the IRA took it upon itself to enforce the observance, genuine outrage rather than intimidation lay behind the popular response. That de Valera would allow a fellow veteran of the War of Independence to die over a matter of symbolism appeared to large numbers of erstwhile supporters to demonstrate the bankruptcy of the Taoiseach's pretensions to the republican ideal. At McCaughey's inquest, counsel for the next of kin, Seán MacBride – himself a former IRA chief of staff – forced Dr T. J. Duane, the Portlaoise prison doctor, into the embarrassing admission that the latter would not 'treat a dog in [the] fashion' in which the dead man had been confined during his four-and-a-half-year imprisonment, a revelation that added fuel to the fire.[16]

Had Aiséirghe not divided eight months previously – and had someone other than Gearóid Ó Cuinneagáin been leading it – the party would have been well positioned to capitalise upon this groundswell of political and economic disaffection. Whether in such circumstances the need for a completely new republican movement would have been perceived is at least open to question, and it may not be wholly fanciful to suggest that one of the remote consequences of the Aiséirghe split in October 1945 was the emergence of Clann na Poblachta in July 1946, with Seán MacBride at its head. As matters stood there was little in the prospect of a fragmented movement headed by Ó Cuinneagáin to attract the men who were to found the new party, so they contented themselves with stealing his political clothing. So many elements of the Clann na Poblachta manifesto – a state-sponsored economic and industrial development programme; rural afforestation; the revival of the Irish language using modern media; the admission of Northern Irish representatives to the Oireachtas; the placing of national reunification at the top of the political agenda – had previously appeared in *Aiséirghe Says ...* that several of Ó Cuinneagáin's lieutenants regarded the party as merely a derivative 'copycat' body. This is probably inaccurate. The ideological heterogeneity of Clann na Poblachta's programme was as much a reflection of the need to maintain its disparate elements under a single banner as of any prior inspiration from Aiséirghe. A party that combined social conservatives like Michael Kelly and Con Lehane, democratic socialists like Jack McQuillan and Noël Browne, and disillusioned former Fianna Fáilers like Noel Hartnett and Aodh de Blacam, had little alternative but to draw its policies from across the political spectrum. Nevertheless, Clann na Poblachta's invocation of the need for a 'Christian State'; its denunciation of 'alien, artificial and unchristian concepts of life'; and its proposal to impose legal controls upon emigration echoed well-worn Aiséirghe themes so faithfully that the similarity can hardly have been coincidental. Certainly the new party's programme was sufficiently congenial to radical rightists as to draw support from such figures as Dr Patrick McCartan, who had attended the formative meeting of the Irish Friends of Germany in February 1940, and Dr Joseph P. Brennan, late of Córas na Poblachta and several other pro-Axis organisations.[17] But MacBride's declaration

16 *Irish Press*, 13 May 1946. Overshadowed in the furore over McCaughey's treatment was the fact that, as Niamh Puirséil notes, he was serving his sentence 'for his part in the sadistic torture of former IRA chief of staff, Stephen Hayes'. N. Puirséil, *The Irish Labour Party 1922–73* (Dublin: University College Dublin Press, 2007), p. 125.
17 Dr Brennan, the south Dublin city coroner and onetime national treasurer of Córas na Poblachta, has been confused in some accounts with his namesake Joseph Brennan,

that his movement would serve 'no duce, no marshal, no fuehrer, no dictator, no taoiseach' served notice that Clann na Poblachta had no aspirations to proceed down the same anti-democratic path as Ailtirí na hAiséirghe. From the outset, moreover, Clann na Poblachta was able to attract to its banner figures of far greater political experience and possessing a much higher national profile than anyone who had ever been associated with Gearóid Ó Cuinneagáin. To many Aiséirghe activists, then, the advent of a broadly-based party that professed many of the same ideals as their own while remaining free of the taint of totalitarianism represented an obvious and urgent threat.

The seriousness of the challenge was underlined by the rapidity with which Aiséirghe supporters began to drift into the ranks of Clann na Poblachta.[18] Kathleen Clarke, widow of the 1916 leader, had previously been one of Aiséirghe's financial contributors, but joined MacBride's party in the summer of 1946.[19] So too did Liam Ó Laoghaire, who had directed the motion picture *Aiséirghe* in 1942 and whose talents were now applied to producing *Our Country* on behalf of Clann na Poblachta – the first and most successful party political campaign film ever made in Ireland. Besides those who formally transferred their allegiance to MacBride, many impatient Aiséirghe members volunteered to work for Clann na Poblachta after deciding pragmatically that a party sharing so many ideals with their own was worthy of support. So numerous were these fellow travellers that the alarmed *Ard-Cheannasaidhe* of Waterford issued a public warning in October 1947 that 'any member of Aiséirghe who affiliates with, speaks or works on behalf of any political party, *de facto* ceases to be a member of Aiséirghe'.[20]

As support for their own movement ebbed away, Aiséirghe activists grew steadily more uneasy over their increasing political isolation. A resolution from Cumann Carnán Cloch (Dolphin's Barn, Dublin) at the 1946 convention called upon Aiséirghe to associate co-operatively with 'ultra-nationalist organisations' like Sinn Féin, as well as with Clann na Poblachta.[21] Ó Cuinneagáin pointed out in reply that certain

---

Secretary of the Department of Finance (1922–27) and Governor of the Central Bank (1943–53). The latter was never a member of any political party. See, e.g., E. Keane, *An Irish Statesman and Revolutionary: The Nationalist and Internationalist Politics of Seán MacBride* (London: I. B. Tauris, 2006), p. 27. Other Córas na Poblachta officials who were prominent in MacBride's new party were Roger McHugh, Seán Mac Giobúin and Helena Moloney.

18 D. Ó Maolalaí, author interview, 15 July 1999; K. Rafter, *The Clann: The Story of Clann na Poblachta* (Cork: Mercier, 1996), p. 29.
19 Ó Cuinneagáin to Caitlín Uí Chléirigh [Kathleen Clarke], 5 September 1944, 9/2/23, GÓCP.
20 *Waterford News*, 25 October 1947.
21 Undated resolution from Cumann Carnán Cloch, 5/4/6, GÓCP; minutes of convention by Ó Scolaidhe, 5/4/3, *ibid.*

difficulties might arise in light of Sinn Féin's continuing adhesion to parliamentary abstentionism, while Dónall Ó Maolalaí maintained that Aiséirghe's attachment to Christianity as a bedrock principle ruled out co-operation of any description with other parties.

By the following year, however, the haemorrhage of members to Clann na Poblachta had become so acute that representatives of the Ard-Chomhairle openly challenged Ó Cuinneagáin over the differing trajectories of the two movements. Liam Ó hArgadáin of Sligo and Seosamh Ó Ceallaigh of Roscommon pointed out to him in April 1947 that 'whereas Aiséirghe is in existence for 5 years, practically as much has been done by Clann na Pob[lachta] in as many months'. MacBride's party seemed to have no difficulty in gaining publicity in the national media, while 'Aiséirghe has received nothing but what it paid for'. MacBride had also forged alliances with movements like the Anti-Partition League, but 'nothing has been done by yourself in this respect'.[22]

Ó Cuinneagáin dismissed these concerns as so much needless 'panic'. Since 1943, when the *Ceannaire* accused MacBride of hijacking the annual Wolfe Tone commemoration at Bodenstown so as to depict Tone as sympathetic to Communism, relations between the two men had been poisonous.[23] Because of this personal disdain, Ó Cuinneagáin seemed to find it impossible to believe that others would not come to regard MacBride in the same dismissive light. Other than in Dublin and Galway, the *Ceannaire* brusquely informed Ó hArgadáin, Clann na Poblachta had not succeeded in establishing itself properly anywhere. The rumoured influx of Clann na Talmhan and Labour TDs into the new party had not taken place. On the contrary, 'at least one person resigned from its Ard-Chomhairle, and looked into joining Aiséirghe'. In view of the fact that Clann na Poblachta were headed by 'a pack of politicians', moreover, '[w]ould we welcome the kind of member they customarily get?'[24]

Even after MacBride and two of his lieutenants won Dáil seats in by-elections in the autumn of 1947, Ó Cuinneagáin continued with ostrich optimism to insist that the advance of Clann na Poblachta was no more than a passing phase. To a Bantry member who warned him in January 1948 that 'Clann na Poblachta is telling us that Ailtirí na hAiséirghe is a washout', the *Ceannaire* counselled a policy of studied aloofness: 'Do not allow yourself to be very much perturbed by the mouthings of the new group of professional political opportunists

22 Ó hArgadáin to Ó Cuinneagáin, 14 April 1947, 3/1/3, *ibid.*
23 Ó Cuinneagáin to MacBride, 20 May 1943, 9/2/24, *ibid.*
24 Ó Cuinneagáin to Ó hArgadáin, 2 May 1947, 3/1/3, *ibid.*

prostituting republicanism for party ends ... There was an average attendance of half-a-dozen at each of a series of public after-Mass meetings they held here last Sunday morning'.[25] Another member, who inquired whether it was permissible for an Aiséirghe supporter to vote for Clann na Poblachta in a constituency in which no Aiséirghe candidate was standing, was advised that MacBride and his party could not be considered 'even half as nationalist as Fianna Fáil, bad as those are'.[26]

In the general election two weeks later, Clann na Poblachta gained 13% of the national vote and took office in an Inter-Party Government with Fine Gael, Labour, Clann na Talmhan and several independent TDs. MacBride became Minister for External Affairs, with Noël Browne joining him at the Cabinet table in the Health portfolio. Aiséirghe had oscillated for several months over whether to participate in the contest. At the December 1947 convention, Dómhnall Ó Maolalai, Seosamh de Léigh and Gearóid Ó Broin argued strongly against taking part, the latter expressing the view that 'it might have gone better with us if we had never fought in elections since the day the movement was founded'. The *Ceannaire*, however, was swayed by the counter-arguments of Ó Scolaidhe and Ó hUrmoltaigh that it was essential to do something to keep Aiséirghe in the public eye.[27] Early in the New Year he abruptly reversed tack. 'We are not running candidates in this election', Ó Cuinneagáin informed a Cork supporter, 'because we understand that the majority of people in the 26 counties still lack a sufficiently satisfactory national mentality to subscribe to Aiséirghe policy, let us say as regards freedom or the Irish language; and also because we have insufficient money to contest an election properly.'[28] As polling day approached he retreated again from this realistic stance, and put forward a single candidate, Liam Ó hArgadáin in Sligo-Leitrim. The result was another lost deposit, as Ó hArgadáin obtained the lowest number of votes ever recorded by the party in a general election. This ignominious episode also cost Ó Cuinneagáin what remained of the support of some of his most loyal lieutenants, who had spent the previous eighteen months in a futile attempt to arrest the movement's continuing decline in the face of its leader's entrenched opposition to change.

Since the 1945 split, branch leaders and *Ard-Cheannasaidheanna* throughout the country had recognised that a new departure in

---

25 Dómhnall Ó Dálaigh to Aindrias Ó Scolaidhe, 13 January 1948; Ó Cuinneagáin to Ó Dálaigh, 20 January 1948, 7/3/23, *ibid*.
26 Ó Cuinneagáin to Éarnán Maghuidhir, 6 January 1948, 7/3/41, *ibid*.
27 Minutes of fifth Comhdháil, 13 December 1947, 5/5/5, *ibid*.
28 Ó Cuinneagáin to Carl Ó Néill, 12 January 1948, 7/3/40, *ibid*.

both policy and practice was essential. Aiséirghe was in danger of becoming a youth movement with little or no appeal to the young. As a result of its loss of membership and subscriptions, the organisation became steadily more dependent on the income from its newspaper to finance its operations. In consequence, generating sales became its most important activity. At a meeting of the Dublin City organisation in February 1947, for example, Ó Cuinneagáin decreed that each branch would henceforth be responsible for selling 500 copies of the journal.[29] However necessary this may have been from a financial standpoint, the number of young people who regarded the prospect of becoming unpaid paper boys and girls as a rewarding and fulfilling form of political activism proved to be exceedingly small.

To appeal to recruits and distinguish itself from other parties, some of the leaders of the movement revived the idea of converting Aiséirghe, or some part of it, into a 'shirted' body. As a military intelligence report of December 1945 recorded, some had already taken matters into their own hands: 'A good deal of younger members of Asheiri [sic] are now in possesssion of shirts of a grey pattern with markings showing rank, etc'.[30] The Sligo branch, considering that something had to be done to make the organisation 'more attractive especially for the youth', offered a resolution in 1946 to adopt a uniform consisting of a green shirt, black tie and black trousers.[31] At that year's convention, Liam Ó hArgadáin went further still, proposing that such a distinctive uniform be provided to an armed wing of the movement. He was supported by Seán Ó hUrmoltaigh and Daithí Mac Réamoinn [David Redmond], who called for an Aiséirghe equivalent of Fianna Eireann, the IRA's youth auxiliary.[32] As he had consistently done since 1942, the Ceannaire vetoed all such proposals.

In despair over the continuing erosion of support and Ó Cuinneagáin's refusal to admit the seriousness of the challenge from Clann na Poblachta, the heads of the two remaining Dublin city branches, Daithí Mac Réamoinn and Tomas Ó Beinéid, confronted the Ceannaire in April 1947. They were supported by such figures as Caoimhín de Eiteagáin, Denise Nic Réamoinn and Seán Mac an Bhaird, all of whom were concerned about 'the grave state of the organisation in the city of Dublin'.

> You will admit, we think, that the position in Dublin has steadily deteriorated over a period of more than six months and now could hardly be

---

29 Minutes of Comhairle Áth Cliath, 26 February 1947, 5/13/1, ibid.
30 Memorandum by Capt. Leonard, G2, 7 December 1945, G2/X/0251, DDMA.
31 Letter by Ó hArgadáin, 24 November 1946, 5/4/9, GÓCP.
32 Comhdháil minutes by Aindrias Ó Scolaidhe, 7 December 1946, 5/4/3, ibid.

worse … With practically no exception, all members of the surviving
Dublin cumainn are very discontented and believe that some new and
drastic action must be taken; that some new working policy must be
evolved before progress can be made, or indeed to prevent the remnant
of the city organisation from falling asunder …

We, therefore, as senior officers of the two surviving cumainn, have
taken upon ourselves the calling of a joint meeting of Cumann Carnán
Cloch and Cumann Seáin Uí Tréasaigh … We realise that in doing this
we are going outside the constitution of the movement and laying
ourselves open to suspension or expulsion. We appeal to you to realise
that anything we may do, we do in the interest of Aiséirghe – that our
desir [*sic*] is to save the situation at this eleventh hour.[33]

Sincere as this appeal unquestionably was, the apparent belief of those
who made it that Ó Cuinneagáin would ever countenance what would
in effect have been a second referendum on his record as leader reveals
a surprising level of naivety on their part. Ó Cuinneagáin's all-too-
predictable response to this *cri de coeur* was to upbraid its authors for
their 'lack of Christianity and sense'; to prohibit the scheduled meeting;
and to remind them that complaints and suggestions would be enter-
tained only in accordance with established procedure.[34] Ten days
later, he reorganised the Dublin branches and decreed that any public
meetings organised by them other than in their own districts must
receive his prior permission in each instance.[35] Though the *Ceannaire*'s
confidence that there would be no repetition on this occasion of the
1945 split was justified, the net effect was similar if less dramatic. The
Dublin leaders accepted their rebuke in silence, and one after another
during the following months voted with their feet. Within a year, none
was any longer active in Ailtiri na hAiséirghe.

In fact, neither Gearóid Ó Cuinneagáin nor the remaining hard core
of officials was by any means oblivious to the state of morale within
their rapidly shrinking party. In a bid to arrest the decline, a group of
six ultra-loyalists led by Aindrias Ó Scolaidhe declared their intention
in June 1947 to create an elite branch of full-time workers as an inspiration to their less-committed peers. It was common knowledge, they
conceded, that 'something is missing from the organisation in Dublin
at present. To revive morale and hope at least among ourselves, and
others if we can', they proposed to launch a branch 'as an example to the
movement as a whole & as a support to every other branch that desires
assistance'.[36] Such an initiative smacked too obviously of desperation

33 Mac Réamoinn and Ó Beinéid to Ó Cuinneagáin, 10 April 1947, 3/1/9, *ibid*.
34 Draft letter by Ó Cuinneagáin to Mac Réamoinn and Ó Beinéid, 12 April 1947, *ibid*.
35 Minutes of Comhairle Átha Cliath, 23 April 1947, 5/13/1, *ibid*.
36 'Míniú Gearr ar an Chumann Nua do Chomhairle Átha Cliath', 1 June 1947, 3/1/7, *ibid*.

to succeed in its objectives, and by the end of the year Ó Cuinneagáin was forced to acknowledge that the movement had not succeeded in 'attracting members or financial aid from the ordinary public to the extent to be expected from all the work done....Even many of the members of Aiséirghe have become worn out and disappointed'.[37] To restore the party's fortunes, however, he could conceive of no more imaginative a plan than once again to seek political martyrdom at the hands of the Stormont government. The banning order preventing him from entering Northern Ireland remained in effect, and the Royal Ulster Constabulary could usually be relied upon to crack down violently upon such manifestations of Irish nationalism as displaying the tricolour in the Six Counties. Accordingly, beginning in December 1946, Aiséirghe carried out a series of cross-border 'raids' intended to provoke a response from the Northern authorities. The usual practice was for a party of activists to assemble on the southern side of the Border; advance several hundred yards into Northern Ireland bearing tricolours and republican banners; and conduct an impromptu public meeting until the police arrived. A film unit often accompanied the 'raiders' to record any clashes that might ensue for subsequent propaganda use. At first the RUC responded in a highly satisfactory manner. At one gathering in Jonesborough, Co. Down in April 1947, held in defiance of a ban on public meetings throughout the North, armed officers broke up the event and attempted to arrest the speakers. Scuffles broke out; Tomas Ó Beinéid and Gearóid Ó Broin, after being taken into custody, escaped from a police car and fled across the Border; a second party of 'raiders' was prevented from entering the North by a massed phalanx of RUC men; and a publicity harvest was reaped when the disturbances were widely reported in Irish, British and American newspapers.[38] The RUC, however, quickly learned from its mistake. Accompanied and advised, Aiséirghe complained, by plain-clothes Garda Síochána officers operating on the 'wrong' side of the border, RUC squads soon adopted a hands-off approach at Aiséirghe meetings.[39] Although these invariably attracted a heavy police presence, as a rule no effort was made to interfere with speakers or confiscate flags or banners. As a result, Aiséirghe events not merely in the areas adjacent to the Border, but throughout the nationalist areas of Northern Ireland, had by 1950 become commonplace, peaceful and largely ignored.

---

37 'Annual Report to 30ú Meán Fomhair 1947 (Translation)', 2 December 1947, 5/5/4, *ibid.*
38 *Aiséirghe*, May 1947.
39 Ó Cuinneagáin to O. J. Flanagan, TD, 14 January 1947, 10/1/6, GÓCP.

'Arm Now to Take the North'

Aiséirghe's series of cross-border forays laid the foundation for the last and most controversial of its political campaigns. Since the late 1930s, Ó Cuinneagáin had believed that a renewal of armed hostilities between Ireland and Britain was both necessary and inevitable. Inasmuch as Britain would never yield the North peacefully, she must be compelled to do so by force. A war from Aiséirghe's point of view would have the further benefit of transforming Ireland into a garrison state. Because even a successful conquest of the Six Counties would require much of the country's manpower to remain mobilised for years if not decades to come so as to guard against a possible reinvasion, the 'just war of aggression' could become a powerful tool of social engineering. The rise of a generation of Irishmen and women formed in an all-pervading atmosphere of military discipline, authoritarian government, ultra-nationalism and international crisis would serve to inculturate the Aiséirghe ethos throughout all social classes, providing a solid foundation for the 'new order'. At first, as noted above, Ó Cuinneagáin considered that the conquest of the North was beyond the twenty-six counties' abilities without military assistance from overseas. In the latter days of the Emergency, however, he came to revise this view. Correctly predicting – as did many of his compatriots – that relations between the USSR and the West would deteriorate as soon as the conflict in Europe came to an end,[40] the *Ceannaire* began to view the coming Cold War as something that might bring about a state of British 'imperial overstretch'. While it is not known whether he truly supposed that a military solution to the Northern problem would be as uncomplicated as he professed to believe – one of Aiséirghe's more popular billboard slogans in the mid-1940s was 'Six Counties, Six Divisions, Six Minutes' – his movement had a long-standing policy of deliberately overstating its case as part of a strategy of instilling 'courage' and ambition in the people. Merely to declare that a seemingly intractable problem was capable of being overcome given sufficient effort and self-sacrifice, Ó Cuinneagáin believed, helped to counter the Irish tendency towards apathy and defeatism and promote a spirit of national enthusiasm.[41]

At all events, from the end of the war Aiséirghe emphasised to a much greater degree than formerly the need for a powerful national

---

40 See, e.g., Elizabeth (Bowen) Cameron, 'Notes from Éire', 10 June 1945, TNA DO 130/65.
41 The *Ceannaire* shared this conviction with Benito Mussolini, who had written in 1912: 'It is faith that moves mountains because it gives the illusion that mountains do move. Illusion is, perhaps, the sole reality in life'. Quoted in E. Gentile, *Il culto del littorio: la sacralizzazione della politica nell'Italia fascista* (Bari: Laterza, 1993), p. 28.

army. A lead article in the June 1946 number of the paper, entitled 'Arms and Irishmen', argued that *'the first and fundamental need in the defence of any country [is] the expulsion of the invading army'*.[42] The need for action, Ó Cuinneagáin declared at a well-attended anti-partition meeting in Dublin three months later, was urgent. At that moment the prestige of 'the oldest dictator in Christendom' had never been lower. If Britain were granted a respite to make good her wartime losses, however, the opportunity would be lost: 'To-day is the hour for Ireland to act to wrest from her that final instalment, the rich jewel of the industrial area of north-east Ulster'.[43]

To assist the campaign the *Ceannaire* turned his attention to strategic as well as political questions, proposing that some of Hitler's former generals be recruited from Germany to help reorganise the Irish army and plan its operations.[44] Thereafter, the pages of *Aiséirghe* offered regular if unsolicited advice to the Defence Forces as to how the country's military capability might best be augmented. The opportunity for a still more provocative policy, however, presented itself in May 1949, when, in response to the Inter-Party Government's declaration that Ireland was a Republic unconnected in any way to the British Commonwealth, the Attlee administration introduced an Ireland Bill in Parliament to provide a statutory basis for the constitutional position of Northern Ireland. Marking an advance from the Government of Ireland Act 1920, Section 1 (2) of the Bill asserted that 'in no event will Northern Ireland or any part thereof cease to be part of His Majesty's Dominions and of the United Kingdom without the consent of the Parliament of Northern Ireland'. The copperfastening in legislation of what has come to be known as the 'Unionist veto' over the ending of partition produced a wave of outrage across the twenty-six counties and in the nationalist areas of the North on a scale unknown since the British attempt to impose conscription on Ireland in April 1918. Protests, resolutions and newspaper articles across the entire spectrum of political opinion denounced the measure in unmodulated language. James Dillon, the resolutely pro-Commonwealth Minister for Agriculture, described the bill as the product of an 'evil genius' and expressed the fear that British 'irresolution and reluctance to face facts' over the indefensibility of partition might 'drench with Irish and English blood the land where herds of sheep and cattle are the only forces massing now'.[45] The Taoiseach, John A. Costello – whose own instincts were

42 *Aiséirghe*, June 1946. Emphasis in original.
43 *Ibid.*, November 1946.
44 *Ibid.*, November 1969.
45 *The Times*, 11 May 1949.

Anglophile and gradualist – spoke of the Ireland Bill in no less apocalyptic terms. Referring to an angry Dáil speech he had made in which he threatened in retaliation to 'hit the British Government in their prestige and in their pride and in their pocket', he told the Seanad on 11 May: 'I failed to express in adequate language the feeling of deep resentment that exists amongst our people, North and South, on this issue … [U]nless the terrible consequences that may ensue from this action are made clear…to people in Great Britain, we may be facing a very serious situation which we cannot control'.[46] Few of his listeners at home failed to understand his reference to the IRA, which enjoyed a recruiting bonanza as a result of the British measure.

The dispute over the Ireland Bill appeared to Ó Cuinneagáin to hold out no less attractive prospects to Aiséirghe. In the first place, it constituted a massive blow to the prestige of Clann na Poblachta, which revealed itself no more effective in bringing nearer the end of partition than Fianna Fáil had been. In the second, it appeared to vindicate Aiséirghe's contention that there was no political solution to the problem of Irish unity, and that military action alone would achieve it.

On the morning of 14 May, citizens in Dublin and other large towns awoke to find large numbers of yellow-and-black Aiséirghe posters bearing the legend 'Arm Now to Take the North' attached to postboxes, walls and advertising hoardings. In terms of the notice it attracted, this poster campaign was the most cost-effective publicity stunt ever launched by the party. The Inter-Party Government's Minister for Justice, General Seán MacEoin of Fine Gael, contributed greatly to its success by ordering the Gardaí to tear down the posters wherever they were to be found. Quite apart from the futility of the task – Aiséirghe graffitists proved more than a match for the state's best efforts – these attempts at suppression had the predictable effect of drawing further attention to the spectacle. Fianna Fáil and independent TDs gleefully rallied to the defence of Aiséirghe's right to freedom of speech, demanding in the Dáil to be told by what authority the Gardaí had been empowered to destroy the posters.[47] Photographs of the offending notices were published on the front pages of Irish and British newspapers, carrying their message to the farthest reaches of the country.

The attention generated by the campaign was a propaganda boon to Ó Cuinneagáin, who quickly moved to stir up further trouble. The following month he approached Major-General Eric Dorman

46 115 *DP–Dáil*, c. 807 (10 May 1949); 36 *DP–Seanad*, c. 1035 (11 May 1949).
47 *Irish Press*, 10 June 1949; *Irish Daily Telegraph*, 24 June 1949.

O'Gowan, MC (né Dorman-Smith), former Deputy Chief of Staff of the British Eighth Army in North Africa, for a 'candid scientific appreciation of the possibilities and difficulties' involved in 'a military plan for the recovery of the Six Counties', which he proposed to publish in *Aiséirghe*.[48] The General, a talented but maverick military leader who was in the midst of a conversion to Irish republicanism that would eventually see him turn his Cootehill, Co. Cavan estate over to the IRA as a training ground,[49] professed himself an admirer of Aiséirghe's policy document on partition ('full of good stuff'). He was in no doubt that the operation suggested by Ó Cuinneagáin could be carried out.[50]

> I am one of the few people on the side of Ireland in this dispute to have given 30 years to the study of war & of organization for war and also to have had war experience ...
>
> I could, given government backing, lots of money, a very great deal, say £10 million, organize & execute such an enterprise as a National undertaking. Three years of planning, organizing & training, at least, would be required. The occasion would need to be ripened by government action etc., and as to that aspect, you must remember that as it is now an offence against International Law to plan a violent offensive against a Neighbouring nation, we would need to have created a political situation, an international political situation, in which our right to strike was universally acknowledged.

For that reason, O'Gowan considered it inadvisable to place such an article in the public domain as Ó Cuinneagáin proposed: 'Can you conceive a Japanese strategist putting over in a National Newspaper a plan for the Pearl Harbour [*sic*] operation?'[51] It would also unnecessarily unnerve the Irish people, despite the fact that they would, in his view, one day have to face the reality of such a conflict. 'Believe me had I the people of Ireland behind me in a constitutional manner, and had I the physical means to do the job properly I'd put an end to this Northern Ireland nonsense tomorrow and talk International Law afterwards.' But it was important that all such preparations be made in secret: 'There is no point in fussing a horse before a big lep,[52]

---

48 Ó Cuinneagáin to O'Gowan, 11 July 1949, 10/3/2, GÓCP.
49 For additional details of O'Gowan's eventful career, see L. Greacen, *Chink: A Biography* (London: Macmillan, 1989).
50 This was not mere braggadocio on O'Gowan's part. So accurately did he predict Rommel's intentions and dispositions – the plans for the victories at the first and second battles of El Alamein were largely his doing – that it proved necessary for the War Office in June 1942 to relieve him of duty, lest his duller-witted superiors appear to disadvantage by comparison.
51 O'Gowan to Ó Cuinneagáin, 14 July 1949, 10/3/2, GÓCP.
52 i.e. jump.

let him take it aisy'. In the General's view, 'Our best hope is in some such party as C[lann] na P[oblachta] securing power constitutionally & bending the will of the people to the final act of national creation, the unifying of Ireland ... But, nevertheless, press on'.[53]

O'Gowan's reluctance to assist Ó Cuinneagáin possibly owed more to the fact that he was himself a keen Clann na Poblachta sympathiser and may have harboured ambitions of being asked to conduct the operation by a future MacBride government, than to any concern over premature publicity. But his belief that Aiséirghe was beginning to occupy too conspicuous a position in the British public eye had some basis in fact. On the other side of the Irish Sea, Ó Cuinneagáin's posters were erroneously taken as evidence of a genuine paramilitary threat to Northern Ireland. Reporting on a debate on the Ireland Bill in the House of Commons, *The Times* reported that 'a hush fell on the Chamber' when one member referred to the appearance of these messages in Dublin.[54] Taking up the point, the Home Secretary, James Chuter Ede, declared that if the controversial section of the Ireland Bill 'had not been justified before, it would have been justified by the posters which had appeared in Dublin during the preceding 48 hours'. The London-based *Catholic Herald* feared that the poster campaign represented 'a movement whose most significant activities...are conducted underground'.[55] The *Sunday Empire News* connected it to a massive protest meeting in Dublin that culminated in a rowdy demonstration outside the British Representative's office. Although the paper reported that Aiséirghe was not believed to have more than 3,000 members, it quoted Ó Cuinneagáin as stating: 'If we were the Government, we would have the North back in five years. We would walk in and take it over with 100,000 men'.[56]

Exaggerated as the apprehensions of the British press and politicians were, they were pardonable when measured against the quality of information available on Aiséirghe from the British intelligence community. Maintaining into the post-1945 era its wartime record of tone-deaf incomprehension with regard to Irish affairs, MI5 was able to offer its political masters only the following appreciation of Ó Cuinneagáin and his movement:

> Several new parties have sprung up in Éire, but the only identifiable Fascist party is the semi Secret KNIGHTS OF THE RESURRECTION, which has the close backing of the Vatican, and which is thought to

53 O'Gowan to Ó Cuinneagáin, 14 July 1949, 10/3/2, GÓCP.
54 *The Times*, 17 May 1949.
55 *Catholic Herald*, 10 June 1949.
56 *Sunday Empire News*, 15 and 29 May 1949.

have made considerable progress in Éire. It's [*sic*] leader is a man aged about 35, a fanatic named O'CONINGHAM. Many people have said that O'CONINGHAM lacks drive and personality, but it is thought that he is formidable, and more so because of the financial backing he enjoys. The KNIGHTS hold meetings, many of them in secret, have an 'Inner Circle', and are allegedly very spy-conscious. They have as their symbol a snake with a sort of arrow through it. The KNIGHTS OF THE RESUR-RECTION are in touch with England through a former Scottish M.P., whose name is not known.[57]

So great was the anxiety on the far side of the Irish Sea about the posters that Freddie Boland of the Department of External Affairs thought it advisable to summon the British Representative's private secretary on 17 May and reassure him that a violent Aiséirghe cross-border incursion was unlikely to occur.[58]

Notwithstanding the notoriety it gained, Aiséirghe's poster campaign left the party no stronger than before. Ó Cuinneagáin boasted that 'by their six-word poster, Aiséirghe had done more … than the thousands of words which had been flowing from Dublin', in the course of an address in which he reiterated that partition would never be ended 'by talk that was not backed up by fixed bayonets and loaded rifles'.[59] Assertions of this kind, however, merely aroused expectations that the party was unable to fulfil. When Ó Cuinneagáin's call to action was followed by nothing more tangible than further effusions of overheated and unspecific rhetoric, his hearers drifted away in disillusionment. On 22 June he was compelled to issue a press release denying that he had ever advocated the formation of a 'private army'.[60] The overall effect was to cause Ó Cuinneagáin himself, in the estimation of many Irish citizens, to be included among the ranks of those who preferred talk to action, and morale within the movement deteriorated further. An Ard-Chomhairle member reported that in Wexford 'those posters have done us more harm than good … I have had to face very unfavourable comment on Aiséirghe & our tactics and even some of our own members (few as they are) are threatening to resign unless a reasonable and sound argument in favour of those posters is immediately forthcoming'.[61]

Consciousness of the party's need to restore its credibility as an activist movement may have impelled Ó Cuinneagáin to launch another round of street disturbances, after the fashion of the VE Day

57 Extract from 'Source Report', 4 June 1946, TNA KV 3/226. Emphases in original.
58 N. Pritchard, 'Note of Talk with Mr Boland on 17 May [1949]', TNA DO 35/3973.
59 *Munster Express*, 3 June 1949.
60 'Anti-Partition Policy', June 22, 1949, 10/3/1, GÓCP.
61 R. de Róiste to Ó Cuinneagáin, 27 May [1949], 7/10/2, GÓCP.

riots. The pretext selected on this occasion was the annual Armistice Day dance of the Royal Artillery Association, held at the Metropole Hotel in Dublin. On the morning of 10 November 1949, Aiséirghe posters announced an indignation meeting to be held that evening at the customary site in Middle Abbey Street. A large crowd gathered at the appointed hour, and heard the *Ceannaire* deliver a fiery speech.[62] When the time of the dance approached, Ó Cuinneagáin unveiled a banner bearing the words 'English Dance at Threshold of G.P.O'. (the headquarters of the 1916 Easter Rising). The crowd then marched upon the Metropole, a few hundred yards away in O'Connell Street. A cordon of Gardaí intercepted the marchers as they passed Prince's Street, wrested the banner from Ó Cuinneagáin, and baton-charged the crowd. While they were thus engaged, a second Aiséirghe banner squad gathered outside the Metropole; 'Batons were again used freely, and a number of men were struck, whilst those not in the immediate vicinity booed lustily'.[63] Ninety minutes later, further 'wild scenes' ensued when an Aiséirghe member climbed the statue of Sir John Gray beside the Metropole and attempted to address crowds leaving the city centre cinemas. A third baton-charge was unleashed to prevent Aiséirghe demonstrators from mobbing guests entering and exiting the hotel, while the British Ambassador, Sir Gilbert Laithwaite, and the British Military Attaché in Dublin observed the mêlée from the balcony above.

Other than by its mere presence, the Royal Artillery Association had offered no such provocation to the people of Dublin as had the students of Trinity College in 1945. With the exception of the rioters themselves, few Irish citizens regarded the holding of a private function by a British ex-servicemen's organisation as an offensive act. Rather than being hailed as defenders of an outraged nation's honour, therefore, Aiséirghe demonstrators were treated as hooligans and firebrands. Two of them appeared in court. Liam Creagh, a newspaper-seller for the movement, was fined £2 for breaching the peace and using abusive and insulting language. The bench accepted the plea of Nora Brennan that she was not aware that the person she had struck on the back of the head was a police officer – 'I lashed out with my handbag and was not particular who I hit' – and dismissed the assault charges against her.

Aiséirghe's militant tactics in 1949, while undoubtedly successful in reminding the country of its continued existence, thus failed in their larger object. The haemorrhage of members proceeded unabated; the

62 *Irish Independent*, 11 November 1949.
63 *Belfast Telegraph*, 18 November 1949.

most talented officials had already left; finances remained in a critical state; and the party's policy seemed ever more ill-suited to Irish political realities. By now, Ó Cuinneagáin's actions appeared those of a man seeking to gain public attention by ever more desperate means. Such an impression undoubtedly contained an element of truth. To view the movement's drift towards direct action as nothing more than a cynical exercise in rabble-rousing, though, would be mistaken. In part, Aiséirghe's radicalism was the outward manifestation of an extremist mentality that had been growing more overt within party circles ever since the end of the Emergency. During the war years, Aiséirghe had been able to rely upon the existence of fascist regimes elsewhere in Europe to make part of its ideological case for it. With the worldwide defeat of fascism in 1945, however, the movement was compelled to state openly what had previously been implicitly understood. This sharper and more strident tone was evident in both in the party's rhetoric and in its associations with similar ultra-right bodies overseas.

The growth of intolerance

In the years following the Second World War, Aiséirghe's attacks upon those minority groups it held responsible for many of the country's social and economic problems became markedly more frequent, intense and bitter. It was, of course, to be expected that the quantity of anti-Semitic rhetoric emanating from the movement would have increased with the lifting of censorship at the close of the Emergency. Gearóid Ó Cuinneagáin, indeed, marked VE Day with a letter to three Dublin weeklies accusing them of 'discrimination against Aiséirghe' and expressing his suspicion that the press was boycotting his party because its success 'would endanger the Jewish-masonic clique'.[64] In reality, bearing in mind the part played by Aiséirghe in the Dublin disturbances that evening, the movement's invisibility within the mainstream press may have worked – not for the first time – to its advantage. Despite this, and despite the fact that two of the three journals of which Ó Cuinneagáin complained had been among the movement's staunchest supporters, Aiséirghe continued its campaign of anti-Jewish vilification. In what may have been the world's first instance of Holocaust denial to appear in print, the movement's film critic, Deasún Breathnach (who published under the pen-names of 'Rex Mac Gall' and 'Cú Scannán' ['Film Hound']) described in July

64 Ó Cuinneagáin to the editors of *An tIolar/The Standard*, the *Irish Catholic* and *Hibernia*, 7 May 1945, 11/2/1, GÓCP.

1945 the newsreel footage of the concentration camps at Belsen and Buchenwald as 'hate-mongering' fabrications.

> We're able to see through the lie: the corpses [in the newsreels] had been exhumed from the ground. Furthermore, I myself observed (from the Press Association!) that 4,700 people have died in Germany of typhus, and that of this number 1,500 were in Buchenwald. A couple of days afterward I was speaking with a German who said that the Germans place those suffering from typhus in typhus camps. Can it thus be seen that Belsen and Buchenwald were typhus camps? When people contract typhus they quickly become emaciated. It's easy to recognise typhus from this film.[65]

It must be acknowledged that such displays of bigotry did not place Aiséirghe far outside the Irish political mainstream. As noted in Chapter 6, the free circulation of information about the Nazi extermination programme in the immediate postwar years neither gave rise to increased popular sympathy for the Jews nor produced any visible diminution of the scale or intensity of Irish anti-Semitism. A revealing sidelight is provided in a letter by Joe Walshe, who had recently taken over as Irish ambassador to the Holy See, in October 1946, two weeks after the conclusion of the Nuremberg trials. Having had the opportunity to speak with many of the leaders of Ireland's male and female religious orders who were visiting Rome for the first time since the war, Walshe reported to the Department of External Affairs their 'unanimous' belief that 'something ought to be done to prevent the jews [*sic*] buying property and starting or acquiring businesses in Ireland. There was a general conviction that the jewish influence is in the last analysis anti-Christian and anti-national ... I could not but be struck by the fact that, in their view, our only serious problem was the Jewish infiltration'.[66] The prevalence of such views among 'men and women holding the highest positions in their respective orders' serves to indicate that anti-Jewish sentiment had lost little of its prewar appeal among leaders of Irish public opinion. As late as 1947, moreover, the American Legation was reporting to Washington the existence in Ireland of 'a feeling of sympathy with the German people rather than with the Allies which appears to be general'.[67] Aiséirghe's renewed emphasis upon such themes may have been based upon Ó Cuinneagáin's recognition of that fact.

65 *Aiséirghe*, July 1945. For Breathnach's obituary, see *Irish Times*, 5 October 2007.
66 Walshe to F. H. Boland, 17 October 1946, quoted in P. L. Wylie, *Ireland and the Cold War: Diplomacy and Recognition 1949–63* (Dublin: Irish Academic Press, 2006), p. 203.
67 Draft dispatch for State Department, n.d. [c. January 1947], Box 9, 'Ireland (Undated)' file, David Gray papers, Franklin D. Roosevelt Presidential Library, Hyde Park, New York.

A great deal of the party's journalistic energy after 1945 was devoted to re-fighting the war and defending Nazi Germany against its Anglo-American critics. Liam Ó hArgadáin complained bitterly of depictions of 'superior German officers being mocked and treated with scorn' in Movietone newsreels; Seosamh Mac Uidhir blasted Hugh Trevor-Roper's *The Last Days of Hitler* as 'hysterical vituperation' directed against Britain's latest 'victim'; and Micheál Ó Cinnéide equated 'pro-German' sentiment during the Emergency with Irish patriotism.[68] Additionally, articles expressing sympathy and support for ultra-right and extremist movements overseas became an increasingly prominent feature of the party paper – which was expanded to a broadsheet and incorporated the modernised spelling of its name, *Aiséirí* – in the late 1940s and early 1950s. The June 1950 issue, for example, carried a laudatory front-page feature devoted to the memory of Ferenc Szálasi, the genocidal head of the Arrow Cross, or Hungarian National Socialist movement, and puppet Prime Minister of Hungary during the last year of the Second World War.[69] Though the discovery of the Arrow Cross as an ideologically compatible movement came rather late to Aiséirghe, the parallels between the two were indeed significant. Szálasi, like Ó Cuinneagáin, regarded his own country as 'uniquely [qualified to] mediate between eastern and western civilizations. Along with the Germans and Japanese, [Hungarians] were destined to be one of the three "ruling peoples" of the world'.[70] The Arrow Cross's emphasis on Christian and Catholic social principles, anti-capitalism, organic nationalism and youth also dovetailed well with Aiséirghe ideas. Bizarrely characterising Szálasi as the 'Hungarian Prototype of Mac Piarais [Pádraig Pearse]', *Aiséirí* praised the Arrow Cross for its 'heroic' resistance, alongside its German allies, to the Soviet forces in the closing months of the Second World War. Depicting Szálasi, who was executed for crimes against humanity in 1946, as the victim of a Communist-inspired show trial, the *Aiséirí* author went on to describe him as a 'figure of nobility and integrity', possessed of 'high moral standards'.[71] The same issue included an article on German politics by Otto Strasser, one of Adolf Hitler's closest early collaborators who had fallen out with the *Führer* in 1930 but never found it necessary to modify his adhesion to the 'original' principles of National Socialism

---

68 *Aiséirghe*, December 1945; September 1950; September 1949.
69 So abject was Szálasi's devotion to the Nazi cause that in December 1944 he offered the throne of Hungary to Hermann Goering. N. M. Nagy-Talavera, *The Green Shirts and the Others: A History of Fascism in Hungary and Rumania* (Palo Alto, CA: Hoover Institution, 1970), p. 237.
70 M. Mann, *Fascists* (Cambridge: Cambridge University Press, 2004), p. 246.
71 *Aiséirí*, June 1951.

or his virulent anti-Semitism.

Aiséirí's own obsession with the Jewish menace had by this time become so ubiquitous and explicit as to arouse protest even from some of the movement's own adherents. A London-based supporter, protesting that 'the Jews have never done Ireland any harm', recalled the services of Robert Briscoe to the national cause during the War of Independence.[72] He was swiftly taken to task in print by Ristéard de Róiste [Richard Roche], an Ard-Chomhairle member and future deputy editor of the *Irish Independent*:

> With the Jew as a mere Jew 'Aiséirghe' has no quarrel. With the Jew as the agent of evil and pagan Naturalism 'Aiséirghe' is bound in duty to Irish Christian ideals to engage in righteous warfare.
>
> The Jews, having rejected the kingship of Jesus Christ … are therefor [*sic*] the principal agents of Naturalism in all its myriad shapes and forms, and *as such* they are the enemies of every Catholic and Christian Irishman.[73]

It was in keeping with such sentiments that, as an English newspaper reported in May 1949, Jews were declared ineligible to become Aiséirghe members.[74] In common with neo-fascist movements elsewhere in Europe, the party devoted much attention to the 'outing' of Jews in positions of power, especially within international organisations. The United Nations Organisation became a special preoccupation of Aiséirghe in the late 1940s, both for its 'artificial' internationalism and its role in creating a Jewish homeland in Palestine. The state of Israel, Seán Ó Riain argued in 1948, was an illegitimate entity: 'The Firbolgs, should their scattered descendants be brought together, would have a greater moral claim to the present ownership of Ireland than the Jews to Palestine'.[75] From this it was but a short step to asserting that the UN was itself a Jewish front organisation, a conclusion to which de Róiste duly proceeded in August 1950: 'To be blunt, U.N.O. is but the temporary World Government of the Jewish Communists or Zionists, whose plans for ultimate world domination draw nearer to realisation with every day that passes'.[76] It was no coincidence, he maintained, that the United Nations flag bore the 'Israeli colours of blue and white'.[77]

---

72 Letter by Liam Ó Maolalaidh, *ibid.*, September 1949.
73 R. de Róiste, 'This Anti-Semitism!', *ibid.*, October 1949. Emphasis in original.
74 *Sunday Empire News*, 29 May 1949.
75 S. Ó Riain, 'Much Promised Land', *Aiséirghe*, 13 March 1948. The Firbolgs [*fir bholg*], according to Irish mythology, were members of an aboriginal Irish tribe that was displaced by the invading Tuatha Dé Danann in the second millennium BC.
76 R. de Róiste, 'Holy Places–Unholy Plans', *ibid.*, August 1950.
77 H. Cotter & R. de Róiste, *World Government by 1955? Why Forrestal Threw Himself Out of the Window* (Framlingham, Suffolk: Nationalist Information Service, 1951), p. 67.

Aiséirghe's fervent racialism led it to take a series of equivocal and conflicting stances on some of the leading world issues of the day. The decolonisation of the British Empire, for example, raised the question of whether the party should support or co-operate with anti-colonial movements overseas. Since his Clann na Saoirse days, Ó Cuinneagáin had argued that Great Britain was itself the product of English imperialism, and sought to make common cause with Scottish and Welsh nationalist bodies. An organisation named Aontacht na gCeilteach ['Pan Celtic Union'], headed by his associate Éamonn Mac Murchadha, had been formed in November 1942. MI5 believed this to be an Aiséirghe front designed to act 'as a rallying point for Irish, Scottish, Welsh and Breton nationalists', a suspicion that, in light of the facts that its postal address was the same as that of Ailtirí na hAiséirghe and its meetings were held at the Red Bank restaurant, seems well-founded.[78] Ó Cuinneagáin advocated 'close liaison ... with the nationalists of Scotland and Wales ... and every encouragement offered them in their corresponding struggle'.[79] The movement maintained connections with Plaid Cymru, the mainstream Welsh nationalist party, and with the radical Scottish independence campaigner Wendy Wood (Gwendoline Cuthbert). On one occasion, Aiséirghe covered south Dublin city with posters bearing the Welsh-language slogan *Rhyddid i gCymru* ['Freedom for Wales'] and held a demonstration proclaiming their unity with the Welsh people 'in fighting for freedom from English domination'.[80]

It was to be expected, therefore, that Aiséirghe would adopt a broad anti-imperialist stance, and some influential officials did indeed do so. In January 1946, the movement sent telegrams to the head of the Egyptian Wafd, Nahas Pasha; the Indonesian independence movement; and the Iranian ambassador to Britain, expressing support for their efforts to remove 'alien forces' from their respective territories.[81] A speaker in 1946 – most probably the National Organiser, Éamonn Ó Ceallacháin

78 Aontacht na gCeilteach stated at its foundation that 'the present system is utterly repug-
    nant to the Celtic conception of life', and that it aimed at the creation of a new order
    based on the 'distinctive Celtic philosophy'. Mac Murchadha appears also to have been
    involved in an effort to revive Clann na Saoirse in February 1943; his publication, *A
    New Spirit*, was banned by censorship authorities because 'its supposed Irish nation-
    alist theme was actually a form of fascism'. *Irish Times*, 5 December 1942; unsigned
    minute, 30 November 1942, G2/X/1125, DDMA; 'Irish Affairs (The General Situation
    in Éire)', QRS/201, 1 March 1943, TNA DO 121/85; R. Cole, *Propaganda, Censorship and
    Irish Neutrality in the Second World War* (Edinburgh: Edinburgh University Press, 2006),
    p. 157.
79 'Anti-Partition Policy', 22 June 1949, 10/3/1, GÓCP.
80 *Y Ddraig Goch*, June 1954; *Empire News*, 14 March 1954.
81 *Irish Press*, 22 January 1946; *Irish Times*, 2 February 1946.

– pointed out that whereas India and Egypt were poised to regain their independence, 'the bulk of the Irish people reading of the fight for freedom in India, and sympathising with the oppressed, never realised that they themselves were in the same boat. It looks like we are now in the boat alone. Pity we did not form an anti-Imperialistic block with them. An extra pair of oars would get us to our destination much sooner'. Ó Cuinneagáin himself, three years later, was to call on the Irish government to work for 'the co-operation of all anti-British forces in the world (outside the Soviet sphere of influence)... so that anti-British imperialist activities may be co-ordinated to the greatest extent possible and maximum effort assured'.[82] In practice, however, consistent rhetorical sympathy for the plight of non-white peoples, far less active support, proved beyond Aiséirghe's capabilities. John C. (Seán) Tozer, later to become an ardent admirer of Iraq's Ba'ath ['Resurrection'] movement, set the tone when he lauded Daniel Malan, architect of the apartheid system in South Africa, in *Aiséirghe* for adopting 'a programme similar to that which Aiséirghe proposes for Ireland'.[83] A mock advertisement in a later issue, 'Island for Sale', was scarcely more diplomatic, declaring Ireland ideal for purchase by 'Indian Gackwars' and 'Jewish rack-renters', as well as 'English gentlemen'.[84]

The same inconsistency marked Aiséirghe's position on the Cold War. Its basic anti-Communist orientation, and its frequently reiterated insistence that Judaism and Marxism were two sides of the same coin, would seem to dictate a broadly pro-American and pro-Western policy, such as Clann na Poblachta had already embraced.[85] Even before the 'American Note' episode, however, a distinct strain of anti-Americanism could be directed in Aiséirghe's thought.[86] Certainly David Gray's lead-footed intervention on that occasion had temporarily coloured the Irish people's traditionally positive view of the United

---

82 'Anti-Partition Policy', 22 June 1949, 10/3/1, GÓCP.
83 *Aiséirghe*, April 1946. For Tozer's pro-Ba'ath sentiments, see his 'Progressive Developments in Iraq: A Personal View', *Irish and Arab News* 1:1 (Winter 1976). By 1976, Saddam Hussein had become de facto leader of Iraq. Amnesty International's first report on mass human rights abuses in that country appeared the previous year.
84 *Aiséirghe*, 7 November 1947. The reference was to a complaint by the Meath Fine Gael TD, Captain Giles, that 'Indian princes', 'Jews' and 'the English' were 'buying up the land of the country' and creating 'a gangster Ireland ... with nothing but deceit and fraud'. 108 *DP–Dáil*, cols 514–15 (15 October 1947).
85 For a useful discussion, see I. McCabe, *A Diplomatic History of Ireland, 1948–49: The Republic, the Commonwealth and NATO* (Dublin: Irish Academic Press, 1991), ch. 8.
86 In his 1942 Domhnach Phádraig address, Ó Cuinneagáin had alleged that Washington, DC was the fourth seat of Irish government, alongside Dublin, Belfast and London. This accusation was deleted from the published version by the censor. See 93/1/171, no. 158, Office of the Controller of Censorship files, NAI.

States, but any residual ill-feeling quickly dissipated.[87] Aiséirghe, on the other hand, continued to direct rhetorical broadsides against the specifically American component of 'Anglo-American pagan liberalism' long after the dispute, and even the Emergency itself, had come to an end. A speaker in July 1945, for example, promised that Aiséirghe would put an end not only to 'English imperialism' but 'American power' in God's good time.[88] In a similar vein, Peadar Ó Clamáin warned that Ireland must not allow the Anglo-Americans to use the 'Communist bogey' to push the country into support for a war between East and West in the interests of 'decadent capitalism'. Rather, the Irish people should resist hatred of ordinary Soviet citizens; 'In like manner we must assert our respect for the common people of both America and England and our desire to see them liberated from the Judaeo-Masonic bondage'.[89]

Extremist associations overseas

Paradoxically, Aiséirghe's anti-Americanism did not stand in the way of its cultivation of cordial relations with extremist bodies on the other side of the Atlantic. Perhaps the most exotic organisation with which the party was associated during these years was the Christian Nationalist Crusade (CNC), headed by the veteran US ultra-right agitator Gerald L. K. Smith. The most widely known American anti-Semite of his day and a figure whose prominence as a Red-baiter was second only to that of his fellow Wisconsinite, Senator Joseph McCarthy, Smith had enjoyed a chequered career in the 1930s as a leading lieutenant of the Louisiana governor Huey P. Long. After the latter's assassination in 1935 Smith went on to promote the career of Fr Charles Coughlin, whose racist and isolationist radio broadcasts reached a nationwide audience, before branching off to launch his own radical-right organisation, the 'Committee of One Million' – a body whose membership at its peak may in fact have justified its title. Two failed presidential campaigns, in 1944 and 1948, put an end to Smith's political ambitions; but through the CNC and its journals, *The Cross and the Flag* and *Attack*, he continued to attract a large following for his blend of Communist conspiracy theories, exposés of 'International Jewry' and white supremacist doctrines.[90]

87 This was partly a result of the widely-held view that the US government had been 'put up to it' by the British, and partly due to the replacement of Gray as Minister by the knowledgeable former OSS officer, George Garrett, in 1947.
88 M. Ó Murchadha to Ó Cuinneagáin, n.d. [c. 29 July 1945], 7/3/5, GÓCP.
89 *Aiséirghe*, 26 October 1947.
90 See G. Jeansonne, *Gerald L. K. Smith: Minister of Hate* (New Haven, CT: Yale University Press, 1988). The Darryl Zanuck film *Gentleman's Agreement* (1947), starring Gregory

Ailtirí na hAiséirghe came to Smith's attention after Ó Cuinneagáin wrote to request copies of a book by the CNC leader contending that Franklin D. Roosevelt's death had not been natural, and offering samples of his own literature in exchange.[91] After reviewing Ó Cuinneagáin's material, Smith asked him in April 1950 to act as Irish correspondent for the CNC's 'World Nationalist News Service', proposing payment in the form of supplies of free copy from the service's other bureaux. An agreement was reached on this basis, and within months a stream of Ó Cuinneagáin-composed items alleging the victimisation of a Dublin detective for investigating law-breaking by Jews; claiming that Clann na Poblachta was in receipt of 'Zionist cheques'; and describing Dublin as 'a place to provide suckers from whom Zionists can take and make money easily' had begun to appear in CNC publications.[92] *Aiséirí*, for its part, carried an equivalent number of articles provided or inspired by Smith and other leading members of the American extreme right.

By the autumn of 1950, co-operation with these organisations had become for Ó Cuinneagáin a profitable sideline. The October 1950 issue of *Aiséirí* carried a defamatory article, originally published in the *Chicago Tribune*, that accused three prominent Jewish Americans – Supreme Court justice Felix Frankfurter, former Treasury Secretary Henry Morgenthau, and senator for New York Herbert H. Lehman – as constituting the pro-Zionist 'secret government of the United States'. The article was both highly libellous and legally indefensible, and to avoid the threat of a court action the *Tribune*'s publisher, Colonel McCormick, was obliged to publish a full retraction and to undertake not to permit the libel to be repeated anywhere within the United States. Overseas journals like *Aiséirí*, however, were beyond the reach of the US civil courts. The same issue of *Aiséirí* in which this reprint appeared – and which, most unusually, sold out within three weeks of publication – carried what Ó Cuinneagáin described as a 'publicity blurb' in praise of Conde McGinley, a significant, albeit somewhat less prominent, American anti-Semite in the Smith mould, whose journal, *Common Sense*, sold 90,000 copies weekly.[93] The blurb

Peck, was intended in part to counter Smith's influence in the United States; it won three Academy Awards, including the Oscar for best picture, that year. Two lawsuits by the CNC leader against the film's makers and distributors were dismissed.

91 Ó Cuinneagáin to Christian Nationalist Crusade, 23 March 1950, 11/3/16, GÓCP.

92 Ó Cuinneagáin to Editor, World Nationalist News Service, 18 May 1950; 16 October 1950, *ibid.*

93 McGinley's publishing activities were bankrolled by an eccentric soap manufacturer, Benjamin Freedman, who after converting from Judaism to Catholicism declared himself an 'honorary Aryan' and spent the remainder of his life and much of his considerable fortune campaigning against the alleged machinations of his former co-religionists.

recommended readers to subscribe to *Common Sense* 'for straight talk on foreign policy', advice which can hardly have been addressed to *Aiséirí* subscribers in Ireland.[94] The strong likelihood, therefore, is that the reprint was carried at the behest of McGinley, who by having copies of *Aiséirí* containing the article sent directly from Ireland was able to put it in the hands of his subscribers without exposing himself personally to US libel law.

Detecting from the success of this experiment a promising commercial opportunity, Ó Cuinneagáin wrote to Gerald L. K. Smith in September offering him the same facility, including as an additional incentive 'a much larger boost to "Cross and Flag" [than that provided to McGinley]' at the post-paid rate of $50 in American currency per thousand copies.[95] The CNC leader responded enthusiastically to this suggestion, placing an initial order of 2,000 copies to be sent individually from Dublin to a select group of his US followers. To meet this request, Ó Cuinneagáin reprinted the *Tribune* article in its entirety a second time in the December 1950 issue and despatched the desired number of copies to the U.S., using a mailing list provided by Smith.

The arrangement with the CNC was advantageous personally to Ó Cuinneagáin – if not to regular readers of *Aiséirí* – providing him with a stream of dollar remittances at a time when US currency had immense scarcity value.[96] (At his request, part of his payment was taken in the form of anti-Semitic literature, including copies of Henry Ford's *The International Jew* which the CNC had recently reprinted in an abridged edition.) But alhough he may have benefited financially from the arrangement, Ó Cuinneagáin clearly regarded his association with Smith and the CNC as more than a purely commercial relationship. As a signed article in the August 1951 issue of *Aiséirí* showed, the *Ceannaire* viewed Smith as an ideological blood-brother in the global campaign against Jewish, Masonic and Communist influence. Hailing the CNC leader and his supporters as '[m]en and women who take risks and make big personal sacrifices in the fight for the triumph of Christian principles in public life', Ó Cuinneagáin went on to defend the CNC's white-supremacist doctrines against their Irish critics:

> If your sister were to marry a negro would you run out into the street and joyfully tell everybody? If only 10 out of 100 houses on your road were suddenly acquired and occupied by negro families wouldn't you

94 *Aiséirí*, October 1950. Ó Cuinneagáin did, however, circulate *Common Sense* among his own supporters. R. de Róiste to Ó Cuinneagáin, 1 September 1950, 7/10/8, GÓCP.
95 Ó Cuinneagáin to Smith, 22 September, 23 October, 31 October 1950, 11/3/15, *ibid*.
96 In a letter of May 1951, Ó Cuinneagáin assured Smith that he stood ready to reprint, 'on more or less similar terms', other articles the CNC leader might require. Ó Cuinneagáin to Smith, 17 May 1951, 11/3/14, *ibid*.

and almost all other whites there quickly seek residences in other localities? ... It is conceivable that in certain circumstances segregation could be a help to the negro in the States, not a hindrance. We can't judge accurately here in Ireland as that is one problem we have not on the plate before us awaiting solution.[97]

A still more unlikely association emerged between Aiséirghe and Sir Oswald Mosley's neo-fascist Union Movement in Britain. As noted earlier, scattered contacts had existed between Aiséirghe members and supporters and fascist leagues in Britain, notwithstanding the Hibernophobia customarily exhibited by the latter. After his release from internment during the Second World War, Mosley made a conscious bid for Irish support. It is possible that this tactic may have suggested itself to him by the need to ensure a warm welcome in the event that the attentions of the British security services should make a withdrawal to Ireland seem desirable – an eventuality that materialised in 1951, when Sir Oswald and his wife took up residence in Co. Galway. After its formation in 1948, the Union Movement declared itself in favour of the abolition of partition within the context of a far-right European federation, a stance that differed markedly from that advocated by the British Union of Fascists in the pre-war years.[98]

While there is no evidence suggesting that Ó Cuinneagáin and Mosley ever communicated directly with each other, Aiséirghe members, including the *Ceannaire* himself, took a keen interest in the Union Movement. Ó Cuinneagáin's attention had first been drawn to the Christian Nationalist Crusade by an Aiséirghe adherent of the British Union of Fascists, and other students of Mosleyism were to be found within the movement. Ristéard de Róiste, for example, wrote in July 1949 to the British extremist Arnold Leese, who, since the suppression of his prewar Imperial Fascist League, was engaged in the production of an extravagantly vile journal bearing the exotic title of *Gothic Ripples*.[99] Seemingly unaware of Leese's contempt for Mosley as a practitioner of what the former dismissed as 'kosher Fascism', de Róiste, after wishing the IFL leader 'Congratulations and more power to you!', explained that Ailtirí na hAiséirghe, an 'anti-Communist and therefore anti-Jewish' organisation, was 'more or less the Irish equivalent of Union Movement or [the Canadian fascist Adrien]

97 *Aiséirí*, August 1951.
98 See R. M. Douglas, 'The Swastika and the Shamrock: British Fascism and the Irish Question, 1918–1940', *Albion* 29:1 (Spring 1997): 71.
99 A regular feature of *Gothic Ripples* was its 'Nigger Notes' section. See R. Thurlow, *Fascism in Britain: From Oswald Mosley's Blackshirts to the National Front* (London: I. B. Tauris, 1998), p. 226.

Arcand's Unity Party'.[100] De Róiste went on to express his 'hope that the true Nationalist, Anti-Communist and Anti-Semitic movements and parties of all lands will get in touch with one another and contact each other much more than they do'.[101] Later the same year de Róiste submitted an article on Irish politics to the Union Movement's weekly newspaper, having first had it vetted by Ó Cuinneagáin, and requested from the secretary of the movement an autographed copy of Mosley's photograph.[102] Mosley's own articles were also reprinted in *Aiséirí*, which praised the fascist leader for his commitment to 'the cause of Irish independence'.[103]

In his quest for foreign neo-fascist and pro-Axis collaborators, the *Ceannaire* found himself casting his net increasingly widely. One of his more unusual initiatives was a bid to sign up the renegade Englishman Norman Baillie-Stewart as a contributor to *Aiséirí*. Popularly known to readers of the British tabloid press as 'the Officer in the Tower' and 'the first Lord Haw-Haw', Baillie-Stewart had been convicted in 1933 for selling military secrets to Germany. He was remanded in the Tower of London, the last man to be imprisoned there, and took up German citizenship upon his release in 1937. During the war he made propaganda broadcasts on behalf of the Nazis and was the first to earn the sobriquet of 'Lord Haw-Haw' for his exaggerated Oxonian accent, the title subsequently passing to his more celebrated counterpart William Joyce.[104] After a further term of imprisonment following the war, he emigrated to Ireland where he lived under the alias of 'James Scott'. In February 1950, Ó Cuinneagáin asked him to contribute articles to the party newspaper, presumably as an expert on Germany. Baillie-Stewart, however, declined. Expressing his private sympathy for Ailtirí na hAiséirghe, he pointed out that as a 'political refugee' who enjoyed 'the protection of no Government' he could not afford to jeopardise his status by becoming involved in Irish politics.[105]

100 Arcand was founder of the Nazi-inspired National Social Christian Party (renamed Unité Nationale after the Second World War); editor of its newspaper, *Le Fasciste Canadien*; and an admirer of Fr Denis Fahey, whose anti-Semitic works he translated into French. For particulars of his activites see S. Morisset, 'Adrien Arcand: sa vision, son modèle et la perception inspirée par son programme' (MA thesis, Université Laval, 1995); M. Robin, *Shades of Right: Nativist and Fascist Politics in Canada 1920–1940* (Toronto: University of Toronto Press, 1992); E. Delaney, 'Political Catholicism in Post-War Ireland: The Revd. Denis Fahey and *Maria Duce*, 1945–54', *Journal of Ecclesiastical History* 52:3 (July 2001): 496.
101 Richard F. Roche [de Róiste] to Leese, 6 July 1949, TNA KV 3/226.
102 De Róiste to Ó Cuinneagáin, 31 August 1949, 7/10/4, GÓCP; same to Alfred Flockhart, Union Movement, 16 January 1950, TNA KV 3/226.
103 *Aiséirghe*, 20 June 1948; January 1950.
104 Baillie-Stewart's self-serving and incredible account of his life is given in N. Baillie-Stewart, *The Officer in the Tower* (London: Leslie Frewin, 1967).
105 'James Scott' to Ó Cuinneagáin, 9 February 1950, 9/2/34, GÓCP.

The twilight years

Aiséirghe's rhetorical extremism led to a serious diplomatic incident between London and Dublin in the spring of 1950. Reacting to a controversial tour of North America by the Northern Ireland Prime Minister, Sir Basil Brooke, a banner headline in the April issue of *Aiséirí* offered a reward of £1,000 to any citizen of the United States or Canada for the capture of the Stormont leader. The accompanying article asserted that Brooke was 'wanted' for a number of offences including treason, war crimes and crimes against humanity.[106] Taking the threat seriously, Brian Maginnis, Northern Ireland Minister for Home Affairs, complained to his counterpart in London, James Chuter Ede, over what he described as 'a direct incentive to commit a most serious crime against the person of a Prime Minister of a Government of part of the United Kingdom'.[107] Maginnis went on to demand that the British government prevail upon its Irish counterpart either to suppress *Aiséirí* altogether or to prohibit the publication of such articles.

Opinion in Whitehall was divided as to the appropriate course of action. The Deputy Director of Public Prosecutions was asked on 6 April for a legal opinion, and advised that if a similar article were published in Britain advocating the abduction of a foreign political leader, he would initiate criminal proceedings provided that adequate evidence was available. The British Embassy in Dublin took a less serious view of the matter, informing the Commonwealth Relations Office that *Aiséirí* was 'the organ of a tiny fascist group ... published primarily for the personal profit of the editor' and not worth taking seriously. A Home Office official too considered that 'it might be wiser – and more dignified – to treat the article with the contempt it deserves', although he noted that a recent outbreak of IRA activity in Belfast made such a stance difficult to maintain.[108] Ministerial opinion held that a more robust response was called for, and the following week Patrick Gordon Walker, Secretary of State for Commonwealth Affairs, summoned the Irish ambassador to lodge an official protest on behalf of his government. Both the Ambassador, John Dulanty, and Freddie Boland at the Department of External Affairs worked assiduously to mollify their British counterparts, describing *Aiséirí* as unimportant and promising to have the Gardaí warn Ó Cuinneagáin as to his future conduct.[109]

---

106 *Aiséirí*, April 1950.
107 Maginnis to James Chuter Ede, 1 April 1950, TNA HO 45/25271/929144/2.
108 Minute by J. H. Walter, 6 April 1950, *ibid*.
109 B. Cockram, Commonwealth Relations Office, to A. W. Glanville, Home Office, 10 May 1950, *ibid*.

On this occasion the Irish diplomats were stating no more than the truth. Since the end of 1947, when the *Ceannaire* had stated that Aiséirghe's 'chief aim just now is the revival of the old fighting spirit and earnestness in the organisation' and announced that *'the time is here when we must try to reawaken national spirit more through action'*,[110] it had become apparent that conventional political campaigning was increasingly beyond Aiséirghe's means. At that time, financial exigencies had compelled the movement to lay off Gearóid Ó Broin, the National Organiser; Aindrias Ó Scolaidhe, the National Treasurer; and Éamonn Ó Ceallacháin, the last full-time worker at Harcourt Street with the exception of Ó Cuinneagáin himself. The *Ceannaire*, too, informed his subordinates in December 1947 that it would be 'utterly impossible' for him to continue to devote his full time to the movement, in view of the fact that the pay he received was not 'sufficient to provide me with a new pair of shoes each year'.[111] In the event, Ó Cuinneagáin was inhibited from carrying this intention into effect by the discovery that 'I would be unable to take such a step without letting the whole movement simply collapse'.[112]

Making a virtue out of necessity, Fionntán Mac Guill argued that with the exception of public meetings, Aiséirghe should devote its resources exclusively to the production of the party newspaper: 'Let us be patient; we can educate the people better with an attractive, bright, lively, outspoken paper than with anything else whatsoever. Those people who are embarrassed to be taken for "paper boys," you know what good they are'.[113] Even retrenchment on this scale, though, could not reverse the party's declining fortunes. Ó Cuinneagáin acknowledged in January 1949 that '[w]ithout the paper during the past year it is quite possible that Ailtirí na h-Aiséirghe would not exist to-day', but that nevertheless 'we must recommence practically from the beginning'.[114]

By the end of the 1940s, the Aiséirghe organisations in the country districts were largely being left to their own devices. Individual branches continued to pursue their customary activities, and from time to time new ones were formed – the Belfast branch, Cumann Wolfe Tone, was relaunched as late as August 1952.[115] As the 1949 convention was reminded, though, 'Often when a branch is formed,

110 'Annual Report to 30ú Meán Fomhair 1947 (Translation)', 2 December 1947, 5/5/4, GÓCP.
111 *Ibid.*
112 'Yearly Report up to 30st. [*sic*] Meán Fomhair, 1948', 23 January 1949, 5/6/3, *ibid.*
113 Mac Guill to Ó Cuinneagáin, 12 December 1947, 5/5/9, *ibid.*
114 'Yearly Report up to 30st. [*sic*] Meán Fomhair, 1948', 23 January 1949, 5/6/3, *ibid.*
115 *Irish News*, 4 August 1952.

and there is no organiser to help it, it soon goes under'.[116] Not only was there insufficient money for a paid staff, however, but for a headquarters either. In August 1949 Aiséirghe was compelled to relinquish the Harcourt Street premises.[117] Thereafter, Ard-Chomhairle meetings were convened at Ó Cuinneagáin's private residence in Blarney Park, Kimmage. This caused no great inconvenience. Only a single Ard-Chomhairle meeting was held in each of the years 1948 and 1949; the meeting scheduled for April 1950 was abandoned when the *Ceannaire* and Seán Ó hUrmoltaigh were the sole attendees (Dómhnall Ó Maolalaí arrived thirty minutes later).[118] A subsequent rule change provided that the Ard-Chomhairle would be quorate with just three members present. The infrequency of its meetings and the lack of business to transact rendered this modification unnecessary.

Aiséirghe's withdrawal from the political arena was signalled by Ó Cuinneagáin's demand at the end of 1949 that two of its councillors, Tomás Ó Muireagáin of Drogheda Corporation and Seán Ó Dubhghaill of New Ross Urban District Council, resign their seats on the grounds that they were no longer suitable persons to represent the party. Although neither man complied, the *Ceannaire* made clear that in future Aiséirghe would be 'in no hurry to nominate anyone, even if there is an excellent chance that he will be elected, unless we are certain that he will be a worthy Aiséirghe representative'.[119]

The falling-away of so many of his former collaborators compelled Ó Cuinneagáin to be considerably less fastidious than in the past. 'It was apparent', the *Ceannaire* waspishly remarked, 'that many old members, who had worked really hard for a long time, needed a rest, and indeed, it can be said they took it!'[120] Some of the new members, however, left much to be desired both in terms of efficiency and of the ascetic virtues for which the movement stood. A notable example was Liam Creagh, a drinking crony of Brendan Behan from the inner city of Dublin who first made his mark in Aiséirghe when he was arrested for his part in the Metropole riots of 1948. Creagh's readiness to undertake the less glamorous duties of a party member was equalled only by his proclivity for helping himself to whatever Aiséirghe funds came his way. The relationship between Creagh and Ó Cuinneagáin soon came to resemble a dysfunctional marriage, in which the former periodically drank the proceeds of the newspapers he sold while the latter bombarded him with furious letters threatening expulsion,

116 Minutes of seventh Comhdháil, 20 February 1949, 5/6/4, GÓCP.
117 'Tuarascbháil Bhliantúil go dtí 30ú Meán Fomhair, 1949', 8 December 1949, 5/7/2, *ibid.*
118 Ard-Chomhairle minutes, 6 March 1948; 18 December 1949; 30 April 1950, 5/123/1, *ibid.*
119 'Tuarascbháil Bhliantúil go dtí 30ú Meán Fomhair, 1949', 8 December 1949, 5/7/2, *ibid.*
120 'Yearly Report up to 30st. [sic] Meán Fomhair, 1948', 23 January 1949, 5/6/2, *ibid.*

legal action or both if full restitution was not made. But Creagh was above all loyal; disarmingly frank about his personal failings; and knew how to endear himself to the *Ceannaire* by his readiness to put himself outside the law on behalf of the movement. In an alcohol-fuelled excess of patriotic zeal in April 1953, for example, he hurled an ashtray wrapped inside a copy of *Aiséirí* through the plate-glass window of a Grafton Street shop containing a display of souvenirs of the coronation of Queen Elizabeth II, and then obligingly telephoned for the Gardaí to come and arrest him.[121] Such demonstrations of commitment covered a multitude of sins in Ó Cuinneagáin's eyes, and Creagh continued to serve the cause – with the exception of occasional interruptions caused by dipsomaniacal blackouts, arrests for assault and other unavoidable hiatuses – until his early death.

The retreat of Aiséirghe from the field of active campaigning left an opening on the extreme right of Irish politics that some new movement might have taken the opportunity to exploit. Fortunately, the potential candidates, the three most notable of whom were former Aiséirghe members, were both few and of exceedingly low calibre. Raymond Moulton Seán O'Brien, a wealthy landowner and one-time oil-company executive in New York, was the most exotic and least savoury of these would-be successors. Proclaiming himself a direct descendant of Brian Ború, the eleventh-century High King of Ireland, the English-born O'Brien had brought a claim before the Court of Privileges in London to have himself recognised as the true heir to the extinct Earldom of Thomond.[122] Although this petition was denied, there being no evidence of any kind to support it, he continued to style himself 'Prince of Thomond', in addition to a number of other equally fanciful titles.[123] While still resident in London he joined Aiséirghe in 1944, later taking up residence in Ireland with his wife, the 'Countess Gularis de Zante'. Appearing in public in a green Irish kilt and Highland jacket, he seemed to be nothing more than a well-to-do eccentric. O'Brien was, however, a compulsive child molester, most of whose time was spent in the parks, cinemas and buses of Dublin in search of children of both sexes upon whom to prey. He was

---

121 *Irish Times*, 17 April 1953.
122 *Ibid.*, 8 October 1936.
123 By 1951 O'Brien was describing himself as 'Colonel His Highness Réamonn Moulton Seaghan, The O'Brien, Prince of the Dalcassians of Thomond and Pogla, 14th Count of Thomond, 13th Baron Ibracken', and laying claim to medical and doctoral degrees, among other distinctions. A letter from the 'Dalcassian Legation', whose address was identical to O'Brien's Charlemont Street house in Dublin, to the London *Spectator* claimed that his sovereignty over the Principality was recognised by, *inter alios*, 'President [W. V. S.] Tubman of Liberia who holds our principal State Order of Chivalry'. *The Spectator*, 7 December 1951.

charged with the commission of indecent acts with three under-age girls in 1945; attempted carnal knowledge of a girl under the age of fifteen in 1946; indecent assault of a twelve-year-old girl in 1949; and assault and procurement of a ten-year-old boy for indecency a year later, although only one of these offences resulted in a conviction and custodial sentence.[124]

In September 1951 O'Brien announced the formation of the United Christian Nationalist Party. Although its founder hinted that he wished to see the re-establishment of the Irish monarchy with himself occupying the throne, the party's objectives were similar to those of Aiséirghe, with anti-Communism and anti-Semitism playing an especially prominent part in its ideology. It was also distinctly anti-feminist. Membership was to be restricted to males 'of Irish blood', although women could serve in an associate capacity. The UCNP issued a further call for recruits to a 5,000-strong paramilitary wing, the Black Legion, whose uniform was to consist of British Army attire dyed black.[125] Officers were to be between 35 and 45 years of age, a limitation that, if applied, would have excluded its commander-in-chief; ordinary recruits would be required 'to give a demonstration of their courage and determination if called upon after a period of training'.[126] According to G2, the party bore 'all the hall-marks of [an] orthodox Fascist movement'.[127] Its initial membership, however, did not exceed twenty-five, and 'although it printed and issued pamphlets and posters appealing for membership and financial aid, it never achieved anything except a certain amount of derision'. By 1953, following a leadership split, it was no longer in existence.[128]

Another ex-Aiséirghe activist with broader political ambitions was the former Ard Chomhairle member and Mosleyite enthusiast, Ristéard de Róiste. Unlike Ó Cuinneagáin, he had always seen Aiséirghe as the local manifestation of a transatlantic network of extreme-right and anti-Semitic organisations. That these groups should join together in a mutually reinforcing coalition in pursuit of their common goals seemed to him self-evident. To this end, de Róiste established contact with members of the British-based National Workers' Movement, a party founded in July 1948 as a successor to Arnold Leese's Imperial Fascist League. Its head, personally chosen by Leese, was Anthony F. X. Baron, an insurance clerk from Ipswich described by MI5 as 'a

124 *Irish Times*, 14 October 1945; 28 March 1946; 3 December 1949; 18 April 1950.
125 *The People*, 21 October 1951.
126 *Ibid.*, 14 October 1951.
127 Dan Bryan to Seán Nunan, Department of External Affairs, 19 December 1951, P 168/5, Department of External Affairs files, NAI.
128 Unsigned G2 memorandum for MI5 (G2/C.550), 17 January 1953, TNA KV 3/226.

strict Roman Catholic' who had been 'led to his present Nazi stance by way of his hatred of Communism and Soviet Russia'.[129] Baron was assisted by another Englishman, an ex-member of Mosley's Union Movement named Hilary James Coughtrie Cotter who had been a student at Trinity College, Dublin and lived at Glenageary on the south side of the city. By 1951 Baron and Cotter had established a Nationalist Information Bureau, run out of the former's residence in Framlingham, Suffolk, to provide a steady supply of neo-Nazi literature to the European extreme right. As part of this effort, Cotter and de Róiste collaborated on a book that sought to expose the Cold War as a sham fight orchestrated by Jews manipulatng both the capitalist and Communist blocs for the purpose of bringing the world under a single dictatorial government. Quoting *Mein Kampf* on the importance of racial purity, the two authors laid particular stress upon the danger of attempts to break down race prejudice, especially in the United States of America. These they saw as part of an effort to create 'a weakened, degenerate mulatto world over which it will be easy for the Jews to establish their dictatorship'.[130] The *Protocols of the Elders of Zion*, they maintained, were an authentic 'blue-print for Jewish world conquest'. Their book concluded with the rallying-cry: 'NATIONALISTS OF ALL LANDS UNITE: YOU HAVE NOTHING TO LOSE BUT YOUR JEWS'.[131]

Cotter's and de Róiste's manifesto exemplified the fascist internationalism for which they appealed. Adrien Arcand provided a foreword to the book, which was printed by the former Catholic Confederation of Occupational Guilds leader W. J. Brennan-Whitmore. After its appearance, the Nationalist Information Bureau took an even larger step toward co-ordinating the activities of the global ultra-right. At a meeting of its principal activists in the German town of Oldenburg in October 1952 it was agreed to organise a conference of extremist movements under the guise of a 'World Congress of Ex-Soldiers' in Dublin for the following January. Responsibility for making the local arrangements was entrusted to the Director of Political Education and Culture of Raymond O'Brien's United Christian Nationalist Party, a Dublin taxi-driver named James (Sonny) Murphy who had recently enlisted in the

---

129 Baron had spent part of the war years in Northern Ireland working in a psychiatric hospital as a member of the Royal Army Medical Corps. He was found unsuitable for training as a mental nursing orderly because of his commanding offier's fears that he might himself be mentally unbalanced. 'B.1.C. Report on Fascist Activities for Inclusion in Home Office Monthly Bulletin', July 1948, TNA KV 3/52; 'Fascist Activities May–June 1948', 2 July 1948, TNA KV 3/51.

130 Cotter & de Róiste, *World Government by 1955?*, p. 48.

131 *Ibid.*, pp. 66, 70. Emphasis in original.

Royal Air Force.[132] This proved to be an infelicitous choice. Considered 'slightly unbalanced' by G2, Murphy succeeded in attracting the attention of the international press to the proposed event,[133] which was abandoned after the manager of the Bray, Co. Wicklow hotel in which it was due to take place, exasperated by endless media inquiries from London, cancelled the Nationalist Information Bureau's reservation.[134] By then de Róiste had already taken fright and severed his connections with the organisation. Alarmed by the appearance of an item in the newspaper of Baron's German collaborator, Wolfgang R. Sarg, claiming that the ex-Aiséirghe man had undertaken to produce articles for the German neo-Nazi press, de Róiste disavowed all connection with such politics as inconsistent with 'my Irish Catholic ideals' and publicly announced in March 1952 that he was 'no longer associated with Mr. Baron, who had no authority to pledge my name in any cause whatsoever'.[135] With the exception of a later flirtation with Sinn Féin, de Róiste took no further part in active politics.

The third competing body was launched in the winter of 1950 by Seán Brady [Seán Ó Brádaigh], another former Aiséirghe member who worked as an advertising agency clerk. Named Aontas Náisiúnta ['National Union'], this organisation was, according to Risteárd de Róiste, 'more fascist than Aiséirghe' in ideology.[136] Its members, most of whom had previously been connected with Maria Duce, signified their allegiance by wearing green shirts and were responsible for a cyclostyled periodical named *Saoirse* ['Freedom'], the principal aim of which was to demonstrate the Jewish antecedents of Communism.[137] Neither the movement nor its journal achieved any significance, and both quickly disappeared from view.

In however tenuous a form, then, Aiséirghe continued to enjoy an effective monopoly position on the extreme right of Irish politics. Indeed, throughout the 1950s and 1960s, the movement experienced a new lease of life as a publishing enterprise. Sales of *Aiséirí* remained surprisingly robust, especially in view of the somewhat stale quality of the product. Ó Cuinneagáin's need to provide for his growing family inspired him to launch the first Irish-language women's magazine,

132 Unsigned G2 'Memorandum on Proposed World Congress of Ex-Soldiers in Dublin', 26 January 1953, P 168/5, Department of External Affairs files, NAI.
133 See, e.g., *Newsweek*, 2 February 1953.
134 G2 to MI5, 28 January 1953, TNA KV 3/226.
135 Letter by de Róiste, 28 March 1952, 7/10/8, GÓCP.
136 R. de Róiste, author interview, 25 June 1999.
137 A. Costigan, Department of Justice, 'Saoirse – Anti-Jewish Periodical', 8 November 1950; Garda Síochána memorandum for the Secretary, Department of Justice, 3 November 1950, JUS 8/984, NAI.

Deirdre, in 1954. Though this provided him with a modest income, it sharply reduced the time available for political journalism. *Aiséirí* suffered as a result, consisting mainly of caustic commentaries by Ó Cuinneagáin on the numerous deficiencies he perceived in Irish life. The campaigns pursued in the newspaper – against what the *Ceannaire* characterised as the Irish government's 'compulsory English' policy, the hypocrisy and corruption of party politics, the corrosive effects of foreign cultural influences – became repetitive to the point of tedium. So too did Ó Cuinneagáin's insistence that the nostrums advanced by Aiséirghe in the early 1940s remained the only means of national salvation, years or even decades after they were first elaborated.

This is not to suggest, though, that *Aiséirí* was fixated upon the past. Ó Cuinneagáin's fascination with the technological possibilities of modernity remained unabated throughout his life, and he was quick to point out how these could be applied to the task of Irish economic and cultural renewal. Some of the positions taken by the paper could cause surprise, notably its support for the ideal of European federation and of Ireland's membership of the European Economic Community. If Ó Cuinneagáin was unable to adapt his fundamental *weltanschauung* to the course of world events, his unshakeable conviction that the social order he advocated must come sooner or later lent even his many jeremiads an underlying if often perverse element of optimism. He welcomed, for example, the upsurge of national consciousness on both sides of the Border that accompanied the outbreak of violence in Northern Ireland, even as he deplored the leaving to a paramilitary organisation of a task that he considered properly fell to the Irish government.

Ó Cuinneagáin's interest in and willingness to encourage youth, especially in the form of column-inches offered to aspirant journalists whose opinions did not always mirror his own, helped to maintain his paper beyond its expected lifespan. By the mid-1970s, though, the costs of publishing *Aiséirí*, even as a quarterly, were becoming insupportable. Only a single issue appeared in 1975, after which the journal was discontinued altogether.[138] Little or no trace remained by then of the movement it had once represented. Some Aiséirghe adherents, like Gearóid Ó Broin and Ó Cuinneagáin's own brother Seosamh, had found an outlet for their political energies in the republican movement.[139] Others abandoned politics altogether, turning their

138 Ó Cuinneagáin to the Secretary, Harvard College Library Serials Record Division, 21 January 1977, 12/3/6, GÓCP.
139 Some authorities have claimed that Seán South, an IRA member and head of the Limerick branch of Maria Duce who died in a clash with the RUC during the so-called

attentions to various language revival organisations. A considerable number made their peace with an imperfect Ireland, building professional careers and viewing their involvement with Aiséirghe as an embarrassing episode of which they preferred not to be reminded. A few defiantly insisted to the end of their lives that, regardless of its failure to achieve its objectives, Aiséirghe's diagnosis of the nation's ills and its prescription for their cure remained correct.[140]

Even in the closing years of his own life, Ó Cuinneagáin never lost faith in either the relevance or the inevitability of Aiséirghe's programme. Responding to an enquiry from a researcher in 1978, he pointed out that the movement had never formally disbanded and that it 'could spring to life again!'.[141] Shortly before his death in 1990, he startled Risteárd Ó Glaisne by saying, 'You think we're all washed up. We're not. You wait and see – our day is coming.'[142]

'Border Campaign' of 1956, was an Aiséirghe member. Though his biographer, Mainchín Seoighe, notes that South was strongly influenced by Aiséirghe publications, there is no evidence in the Ó Cuinneagáin papers to suggest that he was ever connected with the movement. It is extremely unlikely that the *Ceannaire* would have failed to publicise South's membership had the case been otherwise. See M. Seoighe, *Maraíodh Seán Sabhat Aréir* (Dublin: Sairséal & Dill, 1964), p. 44.

140 Caoimhín de Eiteagáin points to materialism, corruption and greed in modern Ireland as examples of why he continues not to 'believe in democracy'. He does not deny that Aiséirghe was hostile to Jews, but maintains that it was anti-Semitic 'with good reason'. C. de Eiteagáin, author interview, 27 July 1999.

141 Ó Cuinneagáin to Gerry Moore, Jordanstown Polytechnic (now University of Ulster at Jordanstown), 25 September 1978, 12/2/1, GÓCP. He added that *Aiséirí* too 'could re-appear if printing costs become tolerable'.

142 Risteárd Ó Glaisne, author interview, 2 August 2003.

Conclusion

Though continuing to the end of his life to profess his 'great regard' for Benito Mussolini,[1] Gearóid Ó Cuinneagáin was sincere in disavowing any intention blindly to follow where the *Duce* or any other Continental European totalitarian dictator had led. If Aiséirghe was not an imitative Irish version of the Italian or German fascist movements, however, neither was it *sui generis*: a response to purely internal concerns with little relevance to events beyond the island of Ireland. On the contrary, Aiséirghe was a local manifestation of a broader political movement whose dynamics are as yet poorly understood: a variety of fascism whose energy and appeal derived not from its response to a perceived threat of social dissolution from the Marxist left, but rather to the stresses experienced by relatively *homogeneous* societies, especially those engaged with or emerging from colonial encounters, while confronting the twin challenges of a modernisation crisis and the necessity of national self-definition.

An example of the seductiveness of such a programme in what might be thought an even unlikelier milieu than mid-twentieth-century Ireland can be found in the early political development of the future Canadian Prime Minister, Pierre Elliott Trudeau. The Québec into which Trudeau was born in 1919 had many similarities to Ireland of the same era – an intensely Catholic society with a legacy of British imperial domination, a strong national consciousness, and a perception that its embattled language and culture were in danger of being snuffed out by the powerful Anglophone and liberal influences that surrounded it. Canada's participation in the Second World War was far from popular in Québec, which retained memories of a 'conscription crisis' in 1917 rivalling in scale and bitterness the one that occurred in Ireland the following year.[2] It was in the course of

---

1 Radio interview of Ó Cuinneagáin by Proinsias Mac Aonghusa, Raidió Teilifís Éireann, 11 August 1981 (transcript by Fionán Ó Cuinneagáin).
2 K. See, *First World Nationalisms: Class and Ethnic Politics in Northern Ireland and Quebec* (Chicago, IL: University of Chicago Press, 1986), p. 87.

a renewed protest by French-Canadians against the reimposition of conscription in 1942 that Trudeau, as a student activist, made his first intervention in politics, describing the Ottawa government's decision to bring Canada into the war on the side of Great Britain as 'imbecilic, when it wasn't disgusting', and condemning the 'dishonest aliens' [*métèques*] who had made 'suckers' of their naive French-Canadian hosts.[3] In the same year he was to express his admiration for the leader of the Rexist movement in Belgium, Léon Degrelle, who 'fire[s] me up with enthusiasm. Degrelle ... is a young man who must be imitated ... idealistic, Catholic, cultural, mystical'. Strongly influenced by the anti-democratic and anti-Semitic writings of Charles Maurras, Trudeau hailed the advent of Pétain's 'National Revolution' and shared the disdain of both for 'the ineptitude of democracy ... [since] the very idea of organization excludes that of equality'. Drawing upon these inspirations, Trudeau drafted with two contemporaries a scheme for a similar 'National Revolution' for Québec. 'We believe', he wrote, 'that the state cannot pursue effectively the common good of the nation unless it answers to a single leader ... We must remember that authority comes from above, not from below: we condemn parliamentary democracy and liberalism.'[4] The revolutionary manifesto thus called for a 'Sovereign French Canadian State' whose guiding principles were to be 'Catholic', 'authoritarian' and 'corporatist'.[5]

Like Gearóid Ó Cuinneagáin, who never travelled beyond his country's borders, Pierre Trudeau formed his early political views in a highly parochial environment; few of them were to survive after he began legal studies in the United States at the age of twenty-five. But while it may seem tempting to regard the rise of 'spiritually synthesised fascism' as the political expression of dogmatic Christianity's inability generally – or that of Catholicism specifically – to reconcile itself to the advent of twentieth-century secular modernity, a sort of political arrested development, the complexities of its historical development in Ireland as elsewhere defy such a reductive interpretation. To be sure, explanations like these were once popular among socialist and Marxist commentators, who coined the expression 'clerico-Fascism' to describe the supposed unholy alliance of the 'black' and 'brown' internationals against their common enemies, democratic and working-class movements. The tendency of this school to select as its examples regimes like those of Franco and Salazar, which were demonstrably not

3 M. & M. Nemni, *Young Trudeau: Son of Québec, Father of Canada, 1919–1944*, vol. 1 (Toronto: McClelland & Stewart, 2006), pp. 122, 267.

4 *Ibid.*, p. 122.

5 *Ibid.*, pp. 222, 225–6.

fascist; its inability to identify any frankly fascist movement in which 'clerics' took the leading role;[6] and the general hostility of the Vatican throughout the period to the involvement of ministers of religion in political parties of whatever stripe, led to the virtual abandonment of 'clerico-Fascism' as a category of analysis by the end of the 1950s, although attempts have periodically been made to revive it in a much-diluted form in such polemical works as John Cornwell's *Hitler's Pope*. An even more compelling counter-argument, however, is the fact that perhaps the closest overseas analogue to Ailtirí na hAiséirghe is to be found not anywhere in the Christian world, but in Egypt during the last years of British administration.

The parallels between Aiséirghe and the Young Egypt [*Misr al-Fatah*] movement of the 1930s and 1940s are striking, and fascinating.[7] Founded in October 1933 as an organisation of nationalist students – among whom Ahmed Hussain, born a year after Gearóid Ó Cuinneagáin, quickly emerged as the leading figure – Young Egypt drew up a thirty-eight-point programme that sought the cultural renewal of Egyptian society, a corporatist economic modernisation programme, the purging of all British influences, a boycott of Jews, the cultiva-tion of a 'martial spirit' among youth, and the international promo-tion of Islam under an Egyptian-dominated Arab federation. In the movement's journal, activists assailed the British for 'dividing' the nation through the introduction of an alien party-political system, and called for the exclusive use of the Arabic language in all public and private business. Though Hussain, like Ó Cuinneagáin, saw the totali-tarian systems of Hitler and Mussolini as imperfect models – 'They believe primarily in material force. We believe primarily in spiritual force, in faith in God and in religion' – Young Egypt openly admired the achievements of European fascism and sought to replicate them at home.[8] Nazi Germany and Fascist Italy, Hussain declared after visiting both countries in 1938, were 'the two democratic states in Europe,

---

6 The most frequently-cited counter-example – the Tiso regime in Slovakia – is a special case, in light of the fact that, as a German puppet, the fate of the country it professed to govern was determined in Berlin rather than Bratislava. In any event, Tiso's admin-istration 'remained a Catholic right authoritarian system with a limited semipluralism, though under one-party government'. As Stanley Payne has noted, 'Hitler found it more satisfactory to deal with conservative right-wing authoritarians as satellites, for they were more compliant and less challenging'. S. G. Payne, *Fascism: Comparison and Definition* (Madison, WI: University of Wisconsin Press, 1980), p. 136.

7 I am grateful to Dr Elizabeth Bishop of the American University in Cairo for drawing the example of Young Egypt to my attention.

8 Quoted in J. P. Jankowski, *Egypt's Young Rebels: 'Young Egypt', 1933–1952* (Stanford, CA: Hoover Institution Press, 1975), p. 59. See also S. Shamir, 'The Influence of German National-Socialism on Radical Movements in Egypt', *Jahrbuch des Instituts für Deutsche Geschichte* (1975), suppl. 1: 200–9.

the other states being capitalist-parliamentary organizations'; their social programmes represented a practical demonstration of ideals they shared with Islam.[9] His lieutenant Fathi Radwan concurred: 'If it is dictatorship which can fill youth with power, fill the nation with the military spirit, and fill the people with electricity, vigour and dynamism, then we will be dictators to the bone'.[10] As with Christianity in Aiséirghe's case, Young Egypt saw the enshrinement of Islam as a modern, relevant ideology as the key to social justice at home and political influence abroad. The movement accordingly framed the Muslim faith, as James Jankowski notes, 'as a twentieth-century belief system through emphasis on its secular efficiency in comparison to contemporary schools of thought'.[11]

There was one other respect in which Young Egypt's history closely matched that of Aiséirghe. Although it was always more influential than its numbers suggested and drew thousands to its meetings before the Second World War, it made little headway in electoral politics. Its membership base was weak – at its prewar peak, Young Egypt may actually have had a smaller paid-up membership than Aiséirghe, in a country whose population was eight times as large – and, once the war began, it found itself operating in an even more forbidding legal climate than its Irish counterpart. A combination of martial law, rigorous censorship and selective internment had already sapped Young Egypt's vitality before its leading members were arrested in May 1941 on suspicion of planning a pro-Axis insurrection. Although the party's vice-president evaded the round-up and eventually found his way to Berlin, where he was killed by an Allied bomb in the spring of 1945, little remained of its organisation, and still less of its foundational ideology, by the time the British authorities brought internment to an end in 1944. At that point, of the twenty members of Young Egypt's Administrative Council, only four had been represented on that body in 1939. Most of the party's original programme was jettisoned shortly afterwards, a shift symbolised by its adoption of a new name. As the 'Socialist Party of Egypt', Hussain's movement advocated a pro-Soviet stance in foreign policy, an orientation that sat uneasily with its ambivalence toward Marxism-Leninism and its views on such questions as state-sponsored atheism. By the early 1950s, it had come to be perceived largely as a front for the banned Moslem Brotherhood, with the architect of modern Salafism, Sayyid Qutb, contributing frequently to the party newspaper. The Free Officers' *coup* of 1952,

9 Jankowski, *Egypt's Young Rebels*, p. 60.
10 *Ibid.*, p. 62.
11 *Ibid.*, p. 73.

quickly followed by the suppression of all political organisations, would ultimately relieve Young Egypt of the problem of attempting to resolve its many contradictions.

That the embrace of a similar programme need not constitute a recipe for political marginality, however, was demonstrated by another and considerably more successful group with strong ideological parallels to Aiséirghe, Plinío Salgado's *Ação Integralista Brasiliera* (AIB). Launched in 1932, the Integralist movement ranged itself in opposition to both the liberal-democratic system inaugurated in Brazil by the Constitution of 1891 and the personalist regime set in place by Getúlio Vargas after the 1930 Revolution. Its founder, Salgado, was a considerably more cosmopolitan and intellectual figure than Ó Cuinneagáin. Strongly influenced by artistic and literary modernism and in his own right a novelist of no mean ability, he had travelled to Europe, seen Mussolini's Italy at first hand, and was well acquainted with the theoretical works of Marinetti, Gentile and Prezzolini, among others.[12] The Italian influence on the movement Salgado led was obvious, manifested in such familiar symbols as the straight-arm salute, a uniform shirt (green in colour), and a marching song set to the tune of the Mussolinian anthem *Giovinezza*. Like its European counterparts, the AIB was an 'anti-party party', participating reluctantly in the political system only for the purpose of destroying it. But in contrast to Italian fascism, and to a still greater degree National Socialism – which Salgado criticised severely for its racial prejudice – Integralism was explicitly religious in its ideological approach. Salgado himself, a repentant ex-atheist, believed as firmly as Ó Cuinneagáin that the Almighty was guiding his footsteps. The first line of his 'October Manifesto', a statement of principles calling for the creation of a totalitarian, Christian, nationalist and corporatist state as the only means of overcoming Brazil's regional and racial differences as well as the menace of Communism, declared unambiguously: 'God directs the destinies of peoples'.[13] Integralism thus stood for a 'spiritual revolution' to be accomplished by a small, dedicated cadre of AIB 'apostles' whose function, as Ricardo Benzaquen de Araujo observes, was to act as 'veritable mediators between the spirit and the world'.[14] Accepting the AIB's nomination as its presiden-

---

12 E. R. Broxson, 'Plinío Salgado and Brazilian Integralism, 1932–1938', PhD diss., Catholic University of America, 1972.

13 *Ibid.*, p. 65. For a discussion of the AIB's fascist lineage, see H. Trinidade, 'Fascism and Authoritiarianism in Brazil under Vargas (1930–1945)', in S. U. Larsen, ed., *Fascism Outside Europe: The European Impulse Against Domestic Conditions in the Diffusion of Global Fascism* (Boulder, CO: Social Science Monographs, 2001).

14 R. Benzaquen de Araujo, 'As Classificações de Plínio: Uma Análise do Pensamento de Plínio Salgado entre 1932 e 1938', *Revista de Cieñcia Política* 21:3 (January 1978): 172.

tial candidate in June 1937, Salgado proclaimed his conviction that 'the Integral State, essentially, is for me the State that comes from Christ, is inspired by Christ, acts for Christ and moves toward Christ'.[15]

Within a very few years of its foundation, Integralism had emerged as a major political force. While its claim in 1935 to have enrolled 400,000 members nationwide may be exaggerated, a figure comfortably in the six-figure range is by no means improbable. An important part of the explanation for its success, in contrast to that of Aiséirghe, is to be found in the attitude taken by the Brazilian Catholic Church. Deeply alarmed by the threat of proletarian revolution and 'lacking a widespread following within its own, elitist-oriented associations', the Church in Brazil 'tacitly relied on the Integralist organizational grid and mass membership to disseminate Catholic political messages'.[16] While refusing to endorse the AIB and insisting that the Church stood 'outside and above' the political realm, prominent Catholic clergymen took highly visible positions in Integralist affairs. Fr Hélder Câmara, for example, a diocesan priest, served as Salgado's personal secretary and eventually rose to become the AIB's Secretary-General, in defiance of the wishes of the Cardinal-Archbishop of Rio, Sebastião Leme. Though some members of the episcopacy like Dom Gastão Liberal Pinto of São Carlos pointed to the dangers of too close an association with totalitarianism, warning his brother bishops that 'Integralism puts its doctrines forward as the only salvation of society…[i]t advocates its own methods before those preached by the Popes', his words of caution fell on deaf ears.[17] Some 20% of the Brazilian archbishops and bishops at one time or another publicly indicated their approval of Integralism and, as Margaret Williams points out, so long as it appeared that the AIB might achieve political power 'the Church continued to treat the movement with benevolence'.[18]

Had the 1938 presidential election gone ahead, it is certain that the AIB would have become a major player in the Brazilian political scene. President Vargas, however, was determined that it should not. In the autumn of 1937, street clashes between the AIB militia and the Brazilian Communist Party gave him a pretext for declaring a personal dictatorship on the Portuguese model, to which, like Salazar, he attached the name of the *Estado Novo*. Salgado unwisely opted to take no action,

---

15 Broxson, 'Plinío Salgado and Brazilian Integralism', p. 242.

16 S. M. Deutsch, *Las Derechas: The Extreme Right in Argentina, Brazil, and Chile, 1890–1939* (Palo Alto, CA: Stanford University Press, 1999), p. 295; M. T. Williams, 'Integralism and the Brazilian Catholic Church', *Hispanic American Historical Review* 54:3 (August 1974): 435.

17 Williams, 'Integralism and the Brazilian Catholic Church', 448.

18 *Ibid.*, 450.

accepting at face value the President's mendacious assurances that 'Integralismo would form the base of the new regime' and believing that this 'revolution from above' would serve his purposes by putting paid to the last vestiges of the democratic system.[19] Vargas repaid the Integralist leader's forbearance by promptly outlawing all political parties and, after a belated and futile attempt by the AIB to orchestrate a counter-*coup*, arresting and exiling Salgado to Portugal shortly before the outbreak of the Second World War.

Whether Aiséirghe's fortunes would follow those of Young Egypt or of the AIB in its heyday – or somewhere in between, like some of the other fascist and fascistoid movements of the period with which suggestive affinities can also be discerned[20] – was never, of course, wholly in the party's own power to determine. As in the case of Bolesław Piasecki's *Ruch Narodowo-Radykalny* [Radical National Movement[in Poland, the unwillingness of the Catholic Church to accord it even a benevolent neutrality was a major constraint on its potential for growth, as was the steadiness and resolve of those who directed the affairs of the Irish democratic state. This is not to say, however, that there was no place for Aiséirghe at the political table, or that, had it been more astutely directed, the movement's history and that of the country might not have taken a different course.

Any assessment of the reasons for Aiséirghe's ultimate failure must start with its leader. Gearóid Ó Cuinneagáin was at once the party's greatest strength and gravest liability. Without him, it is unlikely that it would have persisted at all; with him at its head, its potential was constantly held in check by his personal shortcomings. With the passage of time, moreover, those deficiencies became increasingly obvious and damaging. The *Ceannaire*'s inability to delegate authority even in comparatively trivial matters, his preference for ideological purity over pragmatism, his tendency to regard counsel as falling in the same general category as dissent, and his intellectual inflexibility would have been serious handicaps even to a movement less beholden to the leadership principle than Ailtirí na hAiséirghe. The fact that there was no counterweight to his influence within the party he led, however, exponentially magnified his errors. In 1944 this reality was apparent to well-disposed outsiders like Ernest Blythe; by the end of 1945 it had been grasped by a large proportion of the membership. The

19 Deutsch, *Las Derechas*, p. 304.
20 Among these are the early Rexist movement in Belgium, João de Castro Osório's Nacionalismo Lusitano party in Portugal, and what some commentators have described as the *fascismo frailuno* ('friar fascism') wing of the *Falange Española Tradicionalista* in Spain. Additional study of the 'spiritually synthesised' components of all three movements is, however, necessary.

only person who remained oblivious to it was Ó Cuinneagáin himself: but his was the only opinion that counted.

Individual personalities alone – however dominant they may be – rarely account, though, for the destinies of political movements. It is no less clear that Aiséirghe suffered from serious structural failings. Ironically for a party that never ceased to condemn the 'civil service mentality' as one of the leading causes of Ireland's national underperformance, Aiséirghe experienced most of the constraints of bureaucratic procedure while failing to reap any of the corresponding benefits. Its unworkable financial apparatus led branches, with some justification, to regard Harcourt Street as a parasite draining their own resources while offering little in return. The only way in which local organisations could stay afloat was to starve the national headquarters of both funds and information, to such a degree that after three years in existence the Ard-Chomhairle was unable even to say how many branches the party had. The excessive centralisation of the movement not only stifled initiative at the lower levels but, as the Cork officials perceptively noted in September 1945, laid so heavy a burden on 'a full-time staff in Áth Cliath [Dublin] harassed by overwork' as in itself to constitute 'at least a contributory factor to disunity'.[21]

Lastly, Aiséirghe's inability to build alliances with powerful institutions – including but by no means limited to the Catholic and other Christian denominations, whose interests it purported to serve – deprived it of critical sources of assistance in its early years, and almost certainly foreclosed the possibility of its making a nationwide political breakthrough. This was in large measure an outcome of the party's own choosing. Rather than cultivate support from those quarters where it might have been obtained, from its earliest days as a branch of Conradh na Gaeilge it gloried in its prickly independence, systematically alienating even those who desired to assist it the better to assert its anti-establishment credentials. The price it paid was a heavy one, whether measured in financial terms or in its ability to disseminate its message.

The irony was that notwithstanding this hyper-isolationist stance, Aiséirghe did not in the end succeed in persuading the Irish people that it stood for something dramatically new in political life. An important part of the reason is that, contrary to its grandiose party slogan, its deeds did not in fact match its words. The peculiar course of Irish history, by the time Aiséirghe appeared on the scene, had produced a citizenry and a governing class each of which was exquisitely attuned to the essential differences between constitutional methods

---

21 'Ráiteas Ó Cumann Corcaighe d'Aiséirghe', September 1945, 7/2/8, GÓCP.

and physical force as alternative routes to power. Nearly all successful fascist movements have been able to blur that distinction, outflanking the liberal-democratic state by oscillating between political mobilisation and paramilitary violence as circumstances require. Without being able to call upon the services of the *fasci di combattimento* in Italy or the SA in Germany, it is profoundly unlikely that either Benito Mussolini or Adolf Hitler would ever have gained control over their respective countries. Aiséirghe, however, was confronting a political establishment the great majority of whose members, on both sides of the Dáil chamber, possessed postgraduate-level qualifications in both the physical-force and constitutional traditions, and understood far better than Gearóid Ó Cuinneagáin the potentialities and limitations of each. Such people were not easily impressed, or intimidated, by alarmist rhetoric alone. They quickly perceived that for all its invocations of martyrdom and blood sacrifice, Aiséirghe was not prepared to step far outside the bounds of legality. It hardly helped in this context that the movement was launched at a moment when the repressive powers of the state were stronger than they had been at any time since the Civil War.

The Ó Cuinneagáin formula for political success, therefore, could only carry Aiséirghe so far. At some point, if the movement was to make the breakthrough it required, it needed to accommodate itself to the realities of Irish political life – something that, as Tomás Ó Dochartaigh and the Cork County organisation realised in 1945, could only be accomplished under another leader. A fascinating question is what might have then transpired had such an alternative been available.

The strong likelihood is that Aiséirghe would have found itself compelled, as were most of its postwar European counterparts, to move away from out-and-out fascism in the direction of the 'radical right'. Many cherished policies would have had to be jettisoned in the process, something that would no doubt have produced protests and defections in its own right. But there is no reason to believe that a significant number of Irishmen and women would not have been attracted by such a movement. The fact that so many were prepared to back Aiséirghe even in its most unreconstructed form in the 1945 local government elections is sufficient evidence of that. It may well be that Aiséirghe's true 'twentieth century destiny', had it continued under alternative leadership, was to become an Irish equivalent of the French *Front National*, the German *Republikaner* or the Italian *Alleanza Nazionale*, rather than a Hibernian version of Hitlerism. Certainly today, in an Ireland whose foreign-born population has risen almost overnight to more than 10% of the total, it would be a reckless prognosticator who would maintain that no such party could yet emerge.[22] Gearóid Ó Cuinneagáin's most lasting and significant – if distinctly paradoxical – contribution to his country's political history, therefore, may have been, by his own unbending extremism, to help postpone the hour at which a serious Irish manifestation of far-right populist politics could be expected to materialise.

---

22 For an examination of the potential of radical-right populist politics in Ireland, see M. O'Connell, *Right-Wing Ireland? The Rise of Populism in Ireland and Europe* (Dublin: Liffey Press, 2003).

Select bibliography

Archival and unpublished sources

Cork Archive Institute
Liam de Róiste diaries.

Department of Defence Military Archive, Cathal Brugha Barracks, Rathmines.
G2 (Irish Military Intelligence) files.
Gearóid Ó Cuinneagáin papers.

Franklin D. Roosevelt Presidential Library, Hyde Park, New York.
David Gray papers.

National Archives, College Park, Maryland.
Department of State records.
Office of Strategic Services records.

National Archives of Ireland, Dublin.
Department of External Affairs records.
Department of Justice records.
Department of the Taoiseach records.

National Library of Ireland.
W. J. Brennan-Whitmore papers.
Liam D. Walsh papers.

Private collections
Seán Ó hUrmoltaigh papers (in the possession of Hugo Hamilton, Dún Laoghaire).

The National Archive, Kew (formerly Public Record Office)
Auswärtiges Amt [German Foreign Ministry] records.
Cabinet Office records.
Dominions Office records.
Foreign Office records.
MI5 records.

University College, Dublin.
Frank Aiken papers.

Ernest Blythe papers.
Dan Bryan papers.
Patrick Moylett papers.
Richard Mulcahy papers.

Printed primary sources

Ailtirí na hAiséirghe. *Aiséirghe Says … The New Order in the New Ireland.* Dublin: Ailtirí na hAiséirghe, 1943.
——. *For National Government and Action.* Dublin: Ailtirí na hAiséirghe, n.d. [c. 1943].
——. *Le Linn an Choghaidh Mhóir.* Dublin: Ailtirí na hAiséirghe, n.d. [c. 1943].
——. *Whither Ireland's Students??!!??* Dublin: Cumann Aiséirghe na Mac Léighinn, n.d. [c. 1943].
——. *Aiséirghe For the Worker.* Dublin: Ailtirí na hAiséirghe, 1946.
——. *Partition: A Positive Policy.* Dublin: Ailtirí na hAiséirghe, 1946.
'Anelius, Josephus' [Joseph Hanly]. *National Action: A Plan for the National Recovery of Ireland.* Dublin: Gaelic Athletic Association, 1942.
Breathnach, R. *An Dá Shruth – The Two Currents.* Cork: Glún na h-Aiséirghe, 1943.
Brennan-Whitmore, W. J. *With the Irish in Frongoch.* Dublin: Talbot, 1917.
——. *Dublin Burning.* Dublin: Gill & Macmillan, 1996.
Brown, S. J. *Poison and Balm.* Dublin: Browne & Nolan, 1938.
Cahill, E. J. *The Framework of a Christian State: An Introduction to Social Science.* Dublin: M. H. Gill, 1932.
Cockerill, G. K. *What Fools We Were.* London: Hutchinson, 1944.
Cotter, H. & de Róiste, R. *World Government by 1955? Why Forrestal Threw Himself Out of the Window.* Framlingham, Suffolk: Nationalist Information Service, 1951.
Coyle, E. *Freemasonry in Ireland.* Dublin: S. O'Doherty, 1932.
Craobh na hAiséirghe. *Aiséirghe 1942.* Dublin: Craobh na hAiséirghe, n.d. [1942].
Dáil Éireann. *Díospóireachtaí Páirliminte: Tuairisc Oifigiúil.* Dublin: Oifig an tSoláthair, 1919–.
De Blacam, A. *Gentle Ireland: An Account of a Christian Culture in History and Modern Life.* Milwaukee, WI: Bruce, 1935.
Department of Foreign Affairs. *Documents on Irish Foreign Policy,* vol. V: *1937–1938.* Dublin: Royal Irish Academy, 2006.
Donovan, T. M. *Revolution: Christian or Communist?* n.d. [c. 1937].
Fahey, D. *The Kingship of Christ and Organized Naturalism.* Cork: Forum, 1943.
Hanly, J. *The National Ideal: A Practical Exposition of True Nationality Appertaining to Ireland.* Dublin: Dollard, 1931.
Hogan, J. *Could Ireland Become Communist? The Facts of the Case.* Dublin: Cahill, n.d. [1935].
——. *Modern Democracy.* Cork: Cork University Press, 1938.

Imperial Fascist League. *Race and Politics: A Counter-Blast to the Masonic Teaching of Universal Brotherhood.* London: Imperial Fascist League, n.d. [c. 1934]

Murphy, J. V. *Adolf Hitler: The Drama of His Career.* London: Chapman & Hall, 1934.

Ní Dhubhshláine, M. *A Chailíní, Éistigidh! nó, For Girls Only.* Dublin: Craobh na hAiséirghe, 1942.

Ní Sheaghdha, R. *Jeanne d'Arc (Eisiompláir Tír-Ghrádha).* Dublin: Craobh na hAiséirghe, 1942.

Ó Cuinneagáin, G. *Ireland's Twentieth Century Destiny.* Dublin: Ailtirí na hAiséirghe, n.d. [1942].

O'Donnell, P. *There Will Be Another Day.* Dublin: Dolmen Press, 1963.

Ó Drisceóil, P. *Youth Marches Chun Buaidhe.* Dublin: Glún na Buaidhe, n.d. [1943].

Ó Fiannghúsa, P. & Ó Ceallaigh, S. G. *Aiséirghe 1842, nó Young Ireland Spoke Out.* Dublin: Craobh na hAiséirghe, 1942.

Ó Gráda, M. & Ó Ceallaigh, S. G. *Náire Náisiúnta, nó Seán Treacy's Shame.* Dublin: Craobh na hAiséirghe, 1942.

O'Higgins, B. *My Songs and Myself* (Wolfe Tone Annual). Dublin: The author, 1949.

Ó Laoghaire, L. *Invitation to the Film.* Tralee: The Kerryman, 1945.

Pearse, P. H. *The Murder Machine and Other Essays.* Cork: Mercier, 1986.

Seanad Éireann. *Díospóireachtaí Páirliminte: Tuairisc Oifigiúil.* Dublin: Oifig an tSoláthair, 1922–.

Stuart, F. *Things to Live For: Notes for an Autobiography.* London: Jonathan Cape, 1934.

——. *Pigeon Ireland.* New York: Macmillan, 1932.

Walsh, J. J. *Recollections of a Rebel.* Tralee: The Kerryman, 1944.

Books

Akenson, D. H. *A Mirror to Kathleen's Face: Education in Independent Ireland 1922–1960.* Montreal: McGill-Queen's University Press, 1975.

Allen, K. *Fianna Fáil and Irish Labour: 1926 to the Present.* London: Pluto Press, 1997.

Ambrose, J. *Dan Breen and the IRA.* Cork: Mercier, 2006.

Andrews, C. S. *Autobiography,* vol. I, *Dublin Made Me;* vol. II, *Man of No Property.* Dublin: Mercier, 1979, 1982.

Arnold, B. *Haughey: His Life and Unlucky Deeds.* London: HarperCollins, 1993.

Athans, M. C. *The Coughlin–Fahey Connection: Father Charles E. Coughlin, Father Denis Fahey, C.S.Sp., and Religious Anti-Semitism in the United States, 1938–1954.* New York: Peter Lang, 1991.

Baillie-Stewart, N. *The Officer in the Tower.* London: Leslie Frewin, 1967.

Bartlett, T. & Jeffery, K., eds. *A Military History of Ireland.* Cambridge: Cambridge University Press, 1996.

Barton, B. *The Blitz: Belfast in the War Years*. Belfast: Blackstaff, 1989.

Body, R. *England for the English*. London: New European Publications, 2001.

Bowman, J. *De Valera and the Ulster Question 1917–1973*. Oxford: Clarendon Press, 1982.

Boyce, D. G. *Nationalism in Ireland*, 3rd edn. London: Routledge, 1995.

Bronner, S. E. *A Rumor About the Jews: Antisemitism, Conspiracy, and the Protocols of Zion*. Oxford: Oxford University Press, 2000.

Brown, S. J. & Miller, D. W., eds. *Piety and Power in Ireland 1760–1960: Essays in Honour of Emmet Larkin*. South Bend, IN: University of Notre Dame Press, 2000.

Brown, T. *Ireland: A Social and Cultural History, 1922 to the Present*. Ithaca, NY: Cornell University Press, 1985.

Browne, N. *Against the Tide*. Dublin: Gill & Macmillan, 1986.

Burleigh, M. *Earthly Powers: The Clash of Religion and Politics in Europe from the French Revolution to the Great War*. New York: HarperCollins, 2005.

Campbell, C. *Emergency Law in Ireland, 1918–1925*. Oxford: Clarendon Press, 1994.

Chubb, B. *The Government and Politics of Ireland*, 2nd edn. Palo Alto, CA: Stanford University Press, 1982.

Cole, R. *Propaganda, Censorship and Irish Neutrality in the Second World War*. Edinburgh: Edinburgh University Press, 2006.

Conquest, R. *The Dragons of Expectation: Reality and Delusion in the Course of History*. New York: Norton, 2005.

Coogan, J. W. *The End of Neutrality: The United States, Britain, and Maritime Rights, 1899–1915*. Ithaca, NY: Cornell University Press, 1981.

Coogan, T. P. *Ireland in the Twentieth Century*. London: Hutchinson, 2003.

Cooney, J. *John Charles McQuaid: Ruler of Catholic Ireland*. Dublin: O'Brien Press, 1999.

Corkery, D. *The Hidden Ireland: A Study of Gaelic Munster in the Eighteenth Century*. Dublin: M. H. Gill, 1925.

Cornwell, P. *Only By Failure: The Many Faces of the Impossible Life of Terence Gray*. Cambridge: Salt, 2004.

Costello, F. J. *The Irish Revolution and Its Aftermath 1916–1923: Years of Revolt*. Dublin: Irish Academic Press, 2003.

Couturié, S. *No Tears in Ireland: A Memoir*. New York: Free Press, 2001.

Cronin, M. *The Blueshirts and Irish Politics*. Dublin: Four Courts Press, 1997.

Crowley, T. *Wars of Words: The Politics of Language in Ireland 1537–2004*. Oxford: Oxford University Press, 2005.

Cullingford, E. *Yeats, Ireland and Fascism*. New York: New York University Press, 1981.

Daly, M. E. *Industrial Development and Irish National Identity, 1922–1939*. Syracuse, NY: Syracuse University Press, 1992.

DeJong, L. *The German Fifth Column in the Second World War*. Chicago, IL: University of Chicago Press, 1956.

Deutsch, S. M. *Las Derechas: The Extreme Right in Argentina, Brazil, and Chile, 1890–1939*. Palo Alto, CA: Stanford University Press, 1999.

Diner, H. R. *Erin's Daughters in America: Irish Immigrant Women in the Nineteenth Century*. Baltimore, MD: Johns Hopkins University Press, 1983.

Duggan, J. P. *A History of the Irish Army*. Dublin: Gill & Macmillan, 1989.

———. *Neutral Ireland and the Third Reich*. Dublin: Gill & Macmillan, 1989.

———. *Herr Hempel at the German Legation in Dublin, 1937–1945*. Dublin: Irish Academic Press, 2003.

Dunphy, R. *The Making of Fianna Fáil Power in Ireland 1923–1948*. Oxford: Clarendon Press, 1995.

Durham, M. *Women and Fascism*. New York: Routledge, 1998.

Dwyer, T. Ryle. *Irish Neutrality and the U.S.A. 1939–47*. Dublin: Gill & Macmillan, 1977.

———. *Strained Relations: Ireland at Peace and the U.S.A. at War 1941–45*. Dublin: Gill & Macmillan, 1988.

Eatwell, R. *Fascism: A History*. London: Chatto & Windus, 1995.

Elborn, G. *Francis Stuart: A Life*. Dublin: Raven Arts Press, 1990.

English, R. *Radicals and the Republic: Socialist Republicanism in the Irish Free State, 1925–1937*. Oxford: Clarendon Press, 1994.

———. *Armed Struggle: The History of the IRA*. New York: Oxford University Press, 2003.

———. *Irish Freedom: The History of Nationalism in Ireland*. London: Macmillan, 2006.

Evans, R. *The Coming of the Third Reich*. London: Allen Lane, 2003.

Falasca-Zamponi, S. *Fascist Spectacle: The Aesthetics of Power in Mussolini's Italy*. Berkeley, CA: University of California Press, 2000.

Fallon, B. *An Age of Innocence: Irish Culture 1930–1960*. Dublin: Gill & Macmillan, 1998.

Fanning, B. *Racism and Social Change in the Republic of Ireland*. Manchester: Manchester University Press, 2002.

Farrell, B., ed. *The Creation of the Dáil*. Dublin: Blackwater, 1994.

Farry, M. *The Aftermath of Revolution: Sligo 1921–23*. Dublin: University College Dublin Press, 2000.

Ferriter, D. *The Transformation of Ireland 1900–2000*. London: Profile, 2004.

———. *Judging Dev: A Reassessment of the Life and Legacy of Éamon de Valera*. Dublin: Royal Irish Academy, 2007.

Fischer, J. *Das Deutschlandbild der Iren 1890–1939: Geschichte, Form, Funktion*. Heidelberg: Universitätsverlag C. Winter, 2000.

Fisk, R. *In Time of War: Ireland, Ulster and the Price of Neutrality 1939–1945*. London: André Deutsch, 1983.

Fitzpatrick, D. *The Two Irelands 1912–1939*. Oxford: Oxford University Press, 1998.

Freyer, G. *W. B. Yeats and the Anti-Democratic Tradition*. Dublin: Gill & Macmillan, 1981.

Gallagher, M. *Political Parties in the Republic of Ireland*. Dublin: Gill & Macmillan, 1985.

Garvin, T. *1922: The Birth of Irish Democracy*. Dublin: Gill & Macmillan, 1996.

———. *The Evolution of Irish Nationalist Politics*. Dublin: Gill & Macmillan, 2005.

Gentile, E. *Il culto del littorio: la sacralizzazione della politica nell'Italia fascista.* Bari: Laterza, 1993.

Girvin, B. *From Union to Union: Nationalism, Democracy and Religion in Ireland – Act of Union to EU.* Dublin: Gill & Macmillan, 2002.

——. *The Emergency: Neutral Ireland, 1939–45.* London: Macmillan, 2006.

Gmelch, S., ed. *Irish Life.* Dublin: O'Brien, 1979.

Goldring, M. *Tu ne voteras point: l'exclusion du suffrage universel dans l'Irlande du XIXe siècle.* Biarritz: Atlantica, 2005.

Gottlieb, J. V. *Feminine Fascism: Women in Britain's Fascist Movement, 1923–1945.* New York: I. B. Tauris, 2000.

Gray, T. *The Lost Years: The Emergency in Ireland 1939–45.* London: Little, Brown, 1997.

Greacen, L. *Chink: A Biography.* London: Macmillan, 1989.

Griffin, R. *The Nature of Fascism.* London: Routledge, 1993.

——. ed. *Fascism.* Oxford: Oxford University Press, 1995.

——. *International Fascism: Theories, Causes and the New Consensus.* London: Arnold, 1998.

Grob-Fitzgibbon, B. *The Irish Experience During the Second World War: An Oral History.* Dublin: Irish Academic Press, 2004.

Hamilton, H. *The Speckled People.* London: Fourth Estate, 2003.

——. *The Sailor in the Wardrobe.* London: Fourth Estate, 2006.

Hanley, B. *The IRA, 1926–1936.* Dublin: Four Courts Press, 2002.

Henderson, N. *Water Under the Bridges.* London: Hodder & Stoughton, 1945.

Hill, J. R., ed. *A New History of Ireland*, vol. VII: *Ireland, 1921–84.* Oxford: Oxford University Press, 2003.

Hobsbawm, E. J. *Nations and Nationalism Since 1780: Programme, Myth, Reality*, 2nd edn. Cambridge: Cambridge University Press, 1992.

Holfter, G., ed. *German-Speaking Exiles in Ireland 1933–1945.* Amsterdam: Rodopi, 2006.

Hull, M. M. *Irish Secrets: German Espionage in Wartime Ireland 1939–1945.* Dublin: Irish Academic Press, 2003.

Inglis, T. *Moral Monopoly: The Rise and Fall of the Catholic Church in Modern Ireland*, 2nd edn. Dublin: University College Dublin Press, 1998.

Ioanid, R. *The Sword of the Archangel: Fascist Ideology in Rumania.* Boulder, CO: East European Monographs, 1990.

Jankowski, J. P. *Egypt's Young Rebels: 'Young Egypt', 1933–1952.* Stanford, CA: Hoover Institution Press, 1975.

Jeansonne, G. *Gerald L.K. Smith: Minister of Hate.* New Haven, CT: Yale University Press, 1988.

Jeffery, K. *Ireland and the Great War.* Cambridge: Cambridge University Press, 2000.

Keane, E. *An Irish Statesman and Revolutionary: The Nationalist and Internationalist Politics of Seán MacBride.* London: I. B. Tauris, 2006.

Kee, R. *In Time of War? Éire, Ulster and the Price of Neutrality 1939–1945.* London: André Deutsch, 1983.

Kennedy, L. *Colonialism, Religion and Nationalism in Ireland.* Belfast: Institute of Irish Studies, 1996.

Kenny, M. *Goodbye to Catholic Ireland*. London: Sinclair-Stevenson, 1997.

Keogh, D. *The Vatican, the Bishops and Irish Politics 1919–1939*. Cambridge: Cambridge University Press, 1986.

——. *Ireland and Europe 1919–1948*. Dublin: Gill & Macmillan, 1988.

——. *Twentieth Century Ireland: Nation and State*. Dublin: Gill & Macmillan, 1994.

——. *Ireland and the Vatican: The Politics and Diplomacy of Church–State Relations, 1922–1960*. Cork: Cork University Press, 1995.

——. *Jews in Twentieth-Century Ireland: Refugees, Anti-Semitism and the Holocaust*. Cork: Cork University Press, 1998.

—— & O'Driscoll, M., eds. *Ireland in World War Two: Diplomacy and Survival*. Cork: Mercier, 2004.

—— & McCarthy, A. *Limerick Boycott 1904: Anti-Semitism in Ireland*. Cork: Mercier, 2005.

Keogh, N. *Con Cremin: Ireland's Wartime Diplomat*. Cork: Mercier, 2006.

Kershaw, I. *The 'Hitler Myth': Image and Reality in the Third Reich*. Oxford: Oxford University Press, 1987.

Kissane, B. *Explaining Irish Democracy*. Dublin: University College Dublin Press, 2002.

Klemperer, V. *LTI–Lingua Tertii Imperii: The Language of the Third Reich*, trans. M. Brady. London: Continuum, 2000.

Laffan, M. *The Resurrection of Ireland: The Sinn Féin Party, 1916–1923*. Cambridge: Cambridge University Press, 1999.

Larsen, S. U., ed. *Fascism Outside Europe: The European Impulse Against Domestic Conditions in the Diffusion of Global Fascism*. Boulder, CO: Social Science Monographs, 2001.

Ledeen, M. A. *Universal Fascism: The Theory and Practice of the Fascist International, 1928–1936*. New York: Howard Fertig, 1972.

Lee, J. J. *Ireland 1912–1985: Politics and Society*. Cambridge: Cambridge University Press, 1989.

Legg, M.- L. *Newspapers and Nationalism: The Irish Provincial Press 1850–1892*. Dublin: Four Courts Press, 1999.

Levitas, B. *The Theatre of Nation: Irish Drama and Cultural Nationalism 1890–1916*. Oxford: Clarendon Press, 2002.

Linklater, A. *An Unhusbanded Life: Charlotte Despard: Suffragette, Socialist, and Sinn Féiner*. London: Hutchinson, 1980.

Linz, J. J. *Totalitarian and Authoritarian Regimes*. Boulder, CO: Lynne Rienner, 2000.

Lipstadt, D. *Denying the Holocaust: The Growing Assault on Truth and Memory*. New York: Free Press, 1993.

Mac an Bheatha, P. *Téid Focal le Gaoith*. Dublin: Foilseacháin Náisiúnta, 1967.

——. *Téann Buille le Cnámh*. Dublin: Foilseacháin Náisiúnta, 1983.

Mac Aonghusa, P. *Ar Son na Gaeilge: Conradh na Gaeilge, 1893–1993*. Dublin: Conradh na Gaeilge, 1993.

McCabe, I. *A Diplomatic History of Ireland, 1948–49: The Republic, the Commonwealth and NATO*. Dublin: Irish Academic Press, 1991.

McCann, D. *Step Together! The Story of Ireland's Emergency Army as told by its Veterans*. Dublin: Irish Academic Press, 1999.

McCartney, D. *Democracy and its Nineteenth Century Irish Critics*. Dublin: National University of Ireland, 1979.

Mac Con Iomaire, L. *Breandán Ó hEithir: Iomramh Aonair*. Indreabhán, Co. Galway: Cló Iar-Chonnachta, 2000.

McCullagh, D. *A Makeshift Majority: The First Inter-Party Government, 1948–51*. Dublin: Institute of Public Administration, 1998.

McDowell, R. B. & Webb, D. A. *Trinity College Dublin 1592–1952: An Academic History*. Cambridge: Cambridge University Press, 1982.

McGarry, F. *Irish Politics and the Spanish Civil War*. Cork: Cork University Press, 1999.

——, ed. *Republicanism in Modern Ireland*. Dublin: University College Dublin Press, 2003.

——. *Eoin O'Duffy: A Self-Made Hero*. Oxford: Oxford University Press, 2005.

McMahon, D. *Republicans and Imperialists: Anglo-Irish Relations in the 1930s*. New Haven, CT: Yale University Press, 1984.

Mann, M. *Fascists*. Cambridge: Cambridge University Press, 2004.

Manning, M. A. *James Dillon: A Biography*. Dublin: Wolfhound, 1999.

——. *The Blueshirts*, 3rd edn. Dublin: Gill & Macmillan, 2006.

Mathews, P. J. *Revival: The Abbey Theatre, Sinn Féin, the Gaelic League and the Co-Operative Movement*. Cork: Cork University Press, 2003.

Maume, P. *The Long Gestation: Irish Nationalist Life 1891–1918*. New York: St Martin's Press, 1999.

Maye, B. *Fine Gael 1923–1987: A General History with Biographical Sketches of Leading Members*. Dublin: Blackwater, 1993.

Milotte, M. *Communism in Modern Ireland: The Pursuit of the Workers' Republic Since 1916*. Dublin: Gill & Macmillan, 1984.

Molohan, C. *Germany and Ireland 1945–1955: Two Nations' Friendship*. Dublin: Irish Academic Press, 1999.

Mulholland, M. *The Politics and Relationships of Kathleen Lynn*. Dublin: Woodfield Press, 2002.

Mullins, G. *Dublin Nazi No. 1: The Life of Adolf Mahr*. Dublin: Liberties Press, 2007.

Murray, P. *Oracles of God: The Roman Catholic Church and Irish Politics, 1922–37*. Dublin: University College Dublin Press, 2000.

Nagy-Talavera, N. M. *The Green Shirts and the Others: A History of Fascism in Hungary and Rumania*. Palo Alto, CA: Hoover Institution, 1970.

Nemni, M. & M. *Young Trudeau: Son of Québec, Father of Canada, 1919–1944*. Toronto: McClelland & Stewart, 2006.

Nolan, J. A. *Ourselves Alone: Women's Emigration from Ireland, 1885–1920*. Lexington, KY: University Press of Kentucky, 1989.

Novick, B. *Conceiving Revolution: Irish Nationalist Propaganda During the First World War*. Dublin: Four Courts Press, 2001.

O'Brien, H. *The Real Ireland: The Evolution of Ireland in Documentary Film*. Manchester: Manchester University Press, 2004.

O'Brien, M. *De Valera, Fianna Fáil and the Irish Press*. Dublin: Irish Academic Press, 2001.

Ó Conaire, B. *Myles na Gaeilge: Lámhleabhar ar Shaothar Gaeilge Bhrian Ó Nualláin*. Dublin: An Clóchomhar, 1986.

O'Connell, M. *Right-Wing Ireland? The Rise of Populism in Ireland and Europe*. Dublin: Liffey Press, 2003.

O'Connor, E. *A Labour History of Waterford*. Waterford: Waterford Trades Council, 1989.

——. *Reds and the Green: Ireland, Russia and the Communist Internationals 1919–43*. Dublin: University College Dublin Press, 2004.

Ó Corráin, D., ed. *James Hogan: Revolutionary, Historian and Political Scientist*. Dublin: Four Courts Press, 2001.

O'Donoghue, D. *Hitler's Irish Voices: The Story of German Radio's Wartime Irish Service*. Belfast: Beyond the Pale Publications, 1998.

Ó Drisceoil, D. *Censorship in Ireland 1939–1945: Neutrality, Politics and Society*. Cork: Cork University Press, 1996.

——. *Peadar O'Donnell*. Cork: Cork University Press, 2001.

Ó Duibhginn, S. *Ag Scaoileadh Sceoil*. Dublin: An Clóchomhar, 1962.

Ó Glaisne, R. *Gaeilge i gColáiste na Tríonóide 1892–1992*. Dublin: Preas Choláiste na Tríonóide, 1992.

——. *Denis Ireland*. Dublin: Coiscéim, 2000.

Ó Gráda, C. *Jewish Ireland in the Age of Joyce: A Socioeconomic History*. Princeton, NJ: Princeton University Press, 2006.

O'Halpin, E. *Defending Ireland: The Irish State and Its Enemies Since 1922*. Oxford: Oxford University Press, 1999.

O'Leary, D. *Vocationalism and Social Catholicism in Twentieth-Century Ireland: The Search for a Christian Social Order*. Dublin: Irish Academic Press, 2000.

O'Leary, P. *Gaelic Prose in the Irish Free State 1922–1939*. University Park, PA: Pennsylvania State University Press, 2004.

Ó Longaigh, S. *Emergency Law in Independent Ireland 1922–1948*. Dublin: Four Courts Press, 2006.

Ó Murchadha, D. *Liam de Róiste*. Dublin: An Clóchomhar, 1976.

Orwell, G. *Homage to Catalonia*. Harmondsworth, Middlesex: Penguin, 1989.

Ó hUid, T. *Faoi Ghlas*. Dublin: Foilseacháin Náisiúnta, 1985.

Palmer, S. H. *Police and Protest in England and Ireland 1750–1850*. Cambridge: Cambridge University Press, 1988.

Passmore, K., ed. *Women, Gender and Fascism in Europe, 1919–45*. Manchester: Manchester University Press, 2003.

Patterson, H. *Ireland Since 1939*. Oxford: Oxford University Press, 2002.

Paxton, R. O. *The Anatomy of Fascism*. New York: Knopf, 2004.

Payne, S. G. *Fascism: Comparison and Definition*. Madison, WI: University of Wisconsin Press, 1980.

——. *Franco and Hitler: Spain, Germany, and World War II*. New Haven, CT: Yale University Press, 2008.

Pinto, A. Costa. *Salazar's Dictatorship and European Fascism: Problems of Interpretation*. Boulder, CO: Social Science Monographs, 1995.

——. *The Blue Shirts: Portuguese Fascists and the New State*. Boulder, CO: Social Science Monographs, 2000.

Prager, J. *Building Democracy in Ireland: Political Order and Cultural Integration in a Newly Independent Nation*. Cambridge: Cambridge University Press, 1986.

Puirséil, N. *The Irish Labour Party 1922–73*. Dublin: University College Dublin Press, 2007.

Rafter, K. *The Clann: The Story of Clann na Poblachta*. Cork: Mercier, 1996.

Regan, J. M. *The Irish Counter-Revolution: Treatyite Politics and Settlement in Independent Ireland, 1921–1936*. Dublin: Gill & Macmillan, 1999.

Robin, M. *Shades of Right: Nativist and Fascist Politics in Canada, 1920–1940*. Toronto: University of Toronto Press, 1992.

Roth, A. *Mr Bewley in Berlin: Aspects of the Career of an Irish Diplomat, 1933–1939*. Dublin: Four Courts Press, 2000.

Rubinstein, W. D. *A History of the Jews in the English-Speaking World: Great Britain*. Basingstoke: Macmillan, 1996.

Samuel, R. *The Lost World of British Communism*. London: Verso, 2006.

Schmitt, D. E. *The Irony of Irish Democracy: The Impact of Political Culture on Administration and Democratic Political Development in Ireland*. Lexington, MA: Lexington Books, 1973.

See, K. *First World Nationalisms: Class and Ethnic Politics in Northern Ireland and Quebec*. Chicago, IL: University of Chicago Press, 1986.

Seoighe, M. *Maraíodh Seán Sabhat Aréir*. Dublin: Sáirséal & Dill, 1964.

Shermer, M. & Grobman, A. *Denying History: Who Says the Holocaust Never Happened and Why Do They Say It?* Berkeley, CA: University of California Press, 2000.

Simpson, A. W. B. *In the Highest Degree Odious: Detention Without Trial in Wartime Britain*. Oxford: Clarendon Press, 1992.

Sørensen, G. & Mallett, R., eds. *International Fascism 1919–45*. London: Frank Cass, 2002.

Sperber, J. *The European Revolutions, 1848–1851*. Cambridge: Cambridge University Press, 1984.

Stern, F. *The Politics of Cultural Despair: A Study in the Rise of the Germanic Ideology*. Berkeley, CA: University of California Press, 1961.

Stillman, B. *A Short History of the Jews in Ireland*. Dublin: The author, 1945.

Stradling, R. A. *The Irish and the Spanish Civil War 1936–1939: Crusades in Conflict*. Manchester: Manchester University Press, 1999.

Strobl, G. *The Germanic Isle: Nazi Perceptions of Britain*. Cambridge: Cambridge University Press, 2000.

Sturm, H. *Hakenkreuz und Kleeblatt: Irland, das Allierten und das 'Dritte Reich', 1933–1945*. Frankfurt am Main: Peter Lang, 1984.

Tanner, M. *Ireland's Holy Wars: The Struggle for a Nation's Soul, 1500–2000*. New Haven, CT: Yale University Press, 2001.

Tauber, K. P. *Beyond Eagle and Swastika: German Nationalism Since 1945* (2 vols). Middletown, CT: Wesleyan University Press, 1967.

Thomas, H. *The Spanish Civil War*. Harmondsworth, Middlesex: Penguin, 1979.

Thurlow, R. *Fascism in Britain: From Oswald Mosley's Blackshirts to the National Front*. London: I. B. Tauris, 1998.

Valiulis, M. G. *Almost a Rebellion: The Irish Army Mutiny of 1924*. Cork: Tower, 1985.

——. *Portrait of a Revolutionary: General Richard Mulcahy and the Founding of the Irish Free State*. Dublin: Irish Academic Press, 1992.

Wasserstein, B. *Britain and the Jews of Europe 1939–1945*. Oxford: Oxford University Press, 1988.

Wills, C. *That Neutral Island: A Cultural History of Ireland During the Second World War*. London: Faber & Faber, 2007.

Wohl, R. *The Generation of 1914*. Cambridge, MA: Harvard University Press, 1979.

Wood, I. S. *Ireland During the Second World War*. London: Caxton, 2002.

Wylie, P. L. *Ireland and the Cold War: Diplomacy and Recognition 1949–63*. Dublin: Irish Academic Press, 2006.

Articles

Armon, T. 'Fra tradizione e rinnovamento. Su alculi aspetti dell'antisemitismo della Guardia di ferro', *Storia contemporanea* 11:1 (January 1980): 5–23.

Benzaquen de Araujo, R. 'As Classificações de Plínio: Uma Análise do Pensamento de Plínio Salgado entre 1932 e 1938', *Revista de Ciêcia Política* 21:3 (January 1978): 161–79.

Clear, C. '"Too Fond of Going": Female Emigration and Change for Women in Ireland, 1946–1961'. In D. Keogh, F. O'Shea & C. Quinlan, eds, *The Lost Decade: Ireland in the 1950s* (Dublin: Mercier, 2004): 135–46.

Cole, R. '"Good Relations": Irish Neutrality and the Propaganda of John Betjeman, 1941–43', *Éire-Ireland* 30:4 (Winter 1996): 33–46.

Colignon, A. 'Les droites radicales en Roumanie: 1918–1941', *Transitions* 34:1 (1993): 145–71.

Crawford, E. M. 'Food and Famine'. In C. Póirtéir, ed., *The Great Irish Famine* (Dublin: Mercier, 1995): 60–73.

Cronin, M. '"Putting New Wine Into Old Bottles": The Irish Right and the Embrace of European Social Thinking in the Early 1930s', *European History Quarterly* 27:1 (1997): 93–125.

Cullen, S. M. 'Leaders and Martyrs: Codreanu, Mosley and José Antonio', *History* 71:233 (October 1986): 408–30.

Curtis, L. P. Jr. 'Moral and Physical Force: The Language of Violence in Irish Nationalism', *Journal of British Studies* 27:2 (April 1988): 150–89.

Delacor, R. M. 'From Potential Friends to Potential Enemies: The Internment of "Hostile Foreigners" in France at the Beginning of the Second World War', *Journal of Contemporary History* 35:3 (July 2000): 361–8.

Delaney, E. 'Political Catholicism in Post-War Ireland: The Revd. Denis Fahey and *Maria Duce*, 1945–54', *Journal of Ecclesiastical History* 52:3 (July 2001): 487–511.

Douglas, R. M. 'The Swastika and the Shamrock: British Fascism and the Irish Question, 1918–1940', *Albion* 29:1 (Spring 1997): 57–75.

——. 'The Pro-Axis Underground in Ireland, 1939–42', *Historical Journal* 49:4 (December 2006): 1155–83.

Eatwell, R. 'On Defining the Fascist Minimum: The Centrality of Ideology', *Journal of Political Ideologies* 1:3 (October 1996): 303–19.

Farrell, B. 'The First Dáil and After'. In B. Farrell, ed., *The Irish Parliamentary Tradition*. Dublin: Gill & Macmillan, 1973: 208–20.

Fitzpatrick, D. 'A Share of the Honeycomb: Education, Emigration and Irish-women', *Continuity and Change* 1:2 (1986): 217–34.

Gageby, D. 'The Media, 1945–70'. In J. J. Lee, ed., *Ireland, 1945–70*. Dublin: Gill & Macmillan, 1979: 124–35.

Garvin, T. 'The Rising and Irish Democracy'. In M. Ní Dhonnchadha & T. Dorgan, eds, *Revising the Rising*. Derry: Field Day, 1991: 21–8.

——. 'Unenthusiastic Democrats: The Emergence of Irish Democracy'. In R. J. Hill & M. Marsh, eds, *Modern Irish Democracy: Essays in Honour of Basil Chubb*. Dublin: Irish Academic Press, 1993: 9–23.

Gentile, E. 'The Sacralisation of Politics: Definitions, Interpretations and Reflections on the Question of Secular Religion and Totalitarianism', *Totalitarian Movements and Popular Religions* 1:1 (Summer 2000): 18–55.

——. 'Fascism, Totalitarianism and Political Religion: Definitions and Critical Reflections on Criticism of an Interpretation', *Totalitarian Movements and Political Religions* 5:3 (Winter 2004): 326–75.

Gibbons, L. 'Labour and Local History: The Case of Jim Gralton, 1886–1945'. In *Transformations in Irish Culture*. South Bend, IN: University of Notre Dame Press, 1996: 95–106.

Grynberg, A. '1939–40: l'internement en temps de guerre: les politiques de France et de la Grande Bretagne', *XXe Siècle* 54 (April–June 1997): 24–33.

Jennings, E. 'Reinventing Jeanne: The Iconology of Joan of Arc in Vichy Schoolbooks, 1940–44', *Journal of Contemporary History* 29:4 (October 1994): 711–34.

Keogh, D. 'De Valera, the Catholic Church, and the "Red Scare," 1931–1932'. In J. P. O'Connell & J. A. Murphy, eds, *De Valera and His Times*. Cork: Cork University Press, 1983: 134–59.

Lee, J. J. 'Aspects of Corporatist Thought in Ireland: The Commission on Vocational Organisation 1939–43'. In A. Cosgrove & D. McCartney, eds, *Studies in Irish History, Presented to R. Dudley Edwards*. Dublin: University College Dublin Press, 1979: 324–46.

Linz, J. J. 'Some Notes Toward a Comparative Study of Fascism in Sociological Historical Perspective'. In W. Laqueur, ed., *Fascism: A Reader's Guide*. Harmondsworth, Middlesex: Penguin, 1982: 13–78.

Loughlin, J. M. 'Northern Ireland and British Fascism in the Inter-War Years', *Irish Historical Studies* 29:116 (November 1995): 537–52.

McKee, E. 'Church–State Relations and the Development of Irish Health Policy: The Mother and Child Scheme, 1944–53', *Irish Historical Studies* 25:98 (November 1986): 159–94.

McLoughlin, B. 'Die Irischen Blauhemden: Faschisten oder Radikale Konservative?' *Zeitgeschichte* 8:5 (1981): 169–91.

Mac Póilin, A. 'Irish in Belfast, 1892–1960: From the Gaelic League to Cumann Chluain Árd'. In F. de Brún, ed., *Belfast and the Irish Language*. Dublin: Four Courts Press, 2006: 114–35.

Mair, P. 'The Break-up of the United Kingdom: The Irish Experience of Regime Change, 1918–1949', *Journal of Commonwealth and Comparative Politics* 16:3 (November 1978): 288–302.

——. 'De Valera and Democracy'. In T. Garvin, M. Manning & R. Sinnott, eds, *Dissecting Irish Politics: Essays in Honour of Brian Farrell*. Dublin: University College Dublin Press, 2004: 31–47.

Meenan, J. F. 'The Irish Economy during the War'. In K. B. Nowlan & T. D. Williams, *Ireland in the War Years and After 1939–51*. Dublin: Gill & Macmillan, 1969: 28–38.

Moore, G. 'Socio-Economic Aspects of Anti-Semitism in Ireland, 1880–1905', *Economic and Social Review* 12:3 (April 1981): 187–201.

Murphy, J. A. 'The Irish Party System, 1938–51'. In K. B. Nowlan & T. Desmond Williams, eds, *Ireland in the War Years and After, 1939–51*. Dublin: Gill & Macmillan, 1969: 147–66.

Newsinger, J. 'Blackshirts, Blueshirts, and the Spanish Civil War', *Historical Journal* 44:3 (September 2001): 825–44.

O'Brien, C. C. 'The Roots of My Preoccupations', *Atlantic Monthly* 274:1 (July 1994): 73–81.

O'Callaghan, M. 'Language, Nationality and Cultural Identity in the Irish Free State, 1922–7', *Irish Historical Studies* 24:94 (November 1984): 226–45.

Ó Drisceoil, D. '"Jews and Other Undesirables": Anti-Semitism in Neutral Ireland During the Second World War'. In E. Crowley & J. Mac Laughlin, eds, *Under the Belly of the Tiger: Class, Race, Identity and Culture in the Global Ireland*. Dublin: Irish Reporter, 1997: 71–8.

—— '."Whose Emergency Is It?" Wartime Politics and the Irish Working Class, 1939–45'. In F. Lane & D. Ó Drisceoil, *Politics and the Irish Working Class, 1830–1945*. Basingstoke, Hampshire: Palgrave Macmillan, 2005: 262–80.

O'Halpin, E. 'Army, Politics and Society in Independent Ireland 1923–1945'. In T. G. Fraser & K. Jeffrey, eds, *Men, Women and War: Papers Read Before the XXth Irish Conference of Historians, Held at Magee College, University of Ulster, 6–8 June 1991*. Dublin: Lilliput Press, 1993: 158–74.

——. 'Irish Neutrality in the Second World War'. In N. Wyllie, ed., *European Neutrals and Non Belligerents During the Second World War*. Cambridge: Cambridge University Press, 2002: 283–303.

——. 'British Intelligence, the Republican Movement and the IRA's German Links, 1939–45'. In F. McGarry, ed., *Republicanism in Modern Ireland*. Dublin: University College Dublin Press, 2005: 108–31.

Oltra, B. & de Miguel, A. 'Bonapartismo y catolicismo: Una hipótesis sobre los orígenes ideológicos del franquismo'. In B. Oltra, ed., *Papers: Revista de sociología: El regimen franquista*. Barcelona: Peninsula, 1978: 53–102.

Paxton, R. G. 'The Five Stages of Fascism', *Journal of Modern History* 70:1 (March 1998): 1–23.

Pocock, J. G. A. 'The Union in British History', *Transactions of the Royal Historical Society* 10 (6th ser.) (Cambridge: Cambridge University Press, 2000): 181–96.

Ryan, L. 'Leaving Home: Irish Press Debates on Female Unemployment, Domesticity and Emigration to Britain in the 1930s', *Women's History Review* 12:3 (2003): 387–406.

Savage, R. B. 'The Church in Dublin, 1940–1965: A Study of Most Reverend John Charles McQuaid, D.D'., *Studies* 54:216 (Winter 1965): 297–338.

Shamir, S. 'The Influence of German National-Socialism on Radical Movements in Egypt', *Jahrbuch des Instituts für Deutsche Geschichte* (1975) (Supplement 1): 200–9.

Shander, J. 'The Testimony of Images; The Allied Liberation of Nazi Concentration Camps in American Newsreels'. In R. M. Shapiro, ed., *Why Didn't the Press Shout? American and International Journalism During the Holocaust.* Jersey City, NJ: Yeshiva University Press, 2003: 109–25.

Shapiro, P. A. 'Faith, Murder, Resurrection: The Iron Guard and the Romanian Orthodox Church'. In K. P. Spicer, ed., *Antisemitism, Christian Ambivalence, and the Holocaust.* Bloomington, IN: Indiana University Press, 2007: 136–72.

Swift, J. 'Report of Commission on Vocational Organisation (and its Times, 1930–40s)', *Saothar* 1:1 (May 1975): 54–63.

Sznajder, M. 'A Case of Non-European Fascism: Chilean National Socialism in the 1930s', *Journal of Contemporary History* 28:2 (April 1993): 269–96.

Tozer, J. C. 'Progressive Developments in Iraq: A Personal View', *Irish and Arab News* 1:1 (Winter 1976).

Travers, P. '"There Was Nothing For Me There": Irish Female Emigration, 1922–71'. In P. O'Sullivan, ed., *The Irish World Wide: History, Heritage, Identity*, vol. 4: *Irish Women and Irish Migration.* London: Leicester University Press, 1995: 146–67.

Varley, T. & Curtin, C. 'Defending Rural Interests Against Nationalists in 20th-Century Ireland: A Tale of Three Movements'. In J. Davis, ed., *Rural Change in Ireland.* Belfast: Institute of Irish Studies, 1999: 58–83.

Williams, M. T. 'Integralism and the Brazilian Catholic Church', *Hispanic American Historical Review* 54:3 (August 1974): 431–52.

Wills, C. 'Women Writers and the Death of Rural Ireland: Realism and Nostalgia in the 1940s', *Éire-Ireland* 41:1 (Spring 2006): 192–212.

Zink, A. 'Ireland: Democratic Stability Without Compromise'. In D. Berg-Schlosser & J. Mitchell, eds, *Conditions of Democracy in Europe, 1919–39: Systematic Case Studies.* Basingstoke, Hampshire: Macmillan, 2000: 263–93.

Dissertations

Audrain, X. 'Les milieux fascisants en Irlande du Sud durant la seconde guerre mondiale'. MA, Université Pierre Mendès-France, Grenoble II, 1999.

Broxson, E. R. 'Plínio Salgado and Brazilian Integralism, 1932–1938'. PhD, Catholic University of America, 1972.

Cotter, C. M. 'Anti-Semitism and Irish Political Culture, 1932–1945'. MPhil, University College, Cork, 1996.

Crain, T. J. 'The Triumph of Intolerance: Fr. John Creagh and the Limerick Pogrom of 1904'. PhD, Arizona State University, 1998.

Heyck, H. 'The Reich Labour Service in Peace and War: A Survey of the *Reichsarbeitsdienst* and its Predecessors 1920–1945'. MA, Carleton University, Ottawa, 1997.

Hurlburt, S. 'Enemy Within Our Gates: The National Press and the Fifth Column Scare in Britain, April–June 1940', BA, Colgate University, 2001.

Kunicki, M. S. 'The Polish Crusader: The Life and Politics of Bolesław Piasecki, 1915–1979'. PhD, Stanford University, 2004.

Moore, G. 'Anti-Semitism in Ireland'. PhD, Ulster Polytechnic, Jordanstown, 1984.

Morisset, S. 'Adrien Arcand: sa vision, son modèle et la perception inspirée par son programme'. MA, Université Laval, 1995.

O'Duffy, B. 'Violent Politics: A Theoretical and Empirical Analysis of Two Centuries of Political Violence in Ireland'. PhD, University of London, 1996.

O'Malley, P. F. 'The Origins of Irish Neutrality in World War II, 1932–1938'. PhD, Boston College, 1980.

White, M. 'The Greenshirts: Fascism in the Irish Free State, 1935–45'. PhD, University of London, 2004.

Periodicals

Aicéin
Aiséirighe [Córas na Poblachta]
Aiséirghe/Aiséirí
An Aimsir Cheilteach
An Claidheamh Soluis
An t-Éireannach
An Glór
An tIolar/The Standard
An Síol
An t-Ultach
Aontas Gaedheal Weekly Post
Belfast Telegraph
Blueshirt
Catholic Bulletin
Catholic Herald
Catholic Mind
Clonmel Nationalist
Church of Ireland Gazette
Club News
Comhar
Cork Examiner
Deirdre
Drogheda Argus
Drogheda Independent
Dublin Evening Mail
Dundalk Examiner
Dungarvan Observer
Empire News
Fiat
Holiday
Indiú
Irish and Arab News
Irish Catholic
Irish Christian Front
Irish Ecclesiastical Record
Irish Examiner
Irish Freedom
Irish Independent
Irish News

Irish People
Irish Press
Irish Rosary
Irish Times
Irish Workers' Voice
Irish Workers' Weekly
Kerryman
Kilkenny People
Labour News
The Leader
Manchester Guardian
Meath Chronicle
Midland Tribune
Munster Express
Munster News
Nationalist and Leinster Times
New Statesman and Nation
Newsweek
New York Herald Tribune
Penapa
Plain English
Sunday Empire News
The Bell
The Cross and the Flag
The Fascist
The Hidden Hand
The Tablet
The Times
Tipperary Star
Torch
Union
Völkischer Beobachter
Waterford Evening News
Waterford News
Waterford Standard
Wolfe Tone Weekly
Y Ddraig Goch
Youghal Tribune

Index

Abwehr 66, 67, 79, 223
Ação Integralista Brasiliera 291–3
Action 53
Aicéin 80, 82–3
Aiken, Frank 175, 199, 252
Aiséirghe (newspaper) 195, 199, 244, 261, 263, 269, 272, 274–5, 277, 278–9, 281, 284–5
Aisling 226
Alleanza Nazionale 295
'American Note' 200–1, 208–9, 210, 218, 234, 272
Andrews, C. S. ('Todd') 17, 19, 52, 167
Andrews, Joseph 79
An tÉireannach 61, 167
An Fánaí 71
An tIolar 33–4, 49, 50, 150, 151, 180
An Sgian 181–2
Anti-British Propaganda Committee 166
Anti-Jewish Information Bureau 211
Anti-Partition League 255
anti-semitism 19, 31–2, 34–40, 48, 51, 52, 58, 65, 71, 79, 81, 83, 126–35, 173, 187, 188, 193, 195, 203, 211–12, 221, 267–8, 270, 272–7 *passim*, 282–4, 288, 289
Aontacht na gCeilteach 271
Aontas Gaedheal 38
Aontas Náisiúnta 284
Arcand, Adrien 277, 283
Archer, Norman 214

Army Comrades' Association *see* Blueshirts
'Army Mutiny' 16
Arrow Cross 269
Ashe, Nora 154
Ashe, Thomas 35, 154
Attack 273

Ba'ath movement 272
Baillie-Stewart, Norman 277
Balfour, Arthur J. 217
Bandon Town Council 228
Baron, Anthony F. X. 282–4
Beaumont, Seán 61
Becker, Heinrich 71
Behan, Brendan 280
Belsen 220, 221, 268
Belton, Patrick 32, 57
Betjeman, John 55, 172
'Black Legion' 282
Blueshirts 1, 9–10, 12, 18, 19, 20, 21, 23, 24, 26, 36, 41, 65, 68, 135, 162, 169, 171, 172, 174
Blythe, Ernest 51, 98, 152, 154, 156, 165, 191–2, 203–4, 208, 210, 234, 237, 293
Boland, Frederick H. ('Freddie') 53–4, 265, 278
Bourke, Dan 55–6
Boyle, Det.-Garda Thomas 154
Brady, Seán 284
Brasillach, Robert 92
Bray Tribune 52
Breathnach, Deasún 138, 231, 267–8

Breathnach, Liam *see* Walsh, Willie
Breathnach, Riobárd 82, 122–3, 126,
    130, 195, 198, 206–7, 209, 233,
    240, 245, 248
Breathnach, Seán 227
Breen, Dan 205, 206, 223, 234, 244
Brennan, Dermot 79, 191
Brennan, Dr Joseph P. 253
Brennan, Nora 266
Brennan-Whitmore, William James
    65–6, 283
Brewster, Mairéad 164
Brioscú, Aodhagán 75
Briscoe, Robert 37, 135, 270
British Union of Fascists 53, 229, 276
Brooke, Sir Basil 227, 278
Brown, Fr. Stephen J. 50
Browne, Bishop Michael 52
Browne, Noël 125, 253, 256
Bruce, Col. David 217
Bryan, Col. Dan 69, 70, 129, 152, 154,
    218
Buchenwald 221, 268

Cadell, Maurice 155
Cahill, Fr. Edward J. 37, 127
Cahill, Kevin 223
Camâra, Fr. Hélder 292
Cameron, Elizabeth (Bowen) 44, 222
Carey, Fr. Alexander P. 39, 79
Carr, Frederick 187–8, 190–1
Catholic Bulletin 49
Catholic Church 23–4, 31–2, 49, 111,
    123–6, 139–40, 288–9, 292, 293
Catholic Herald 264
Catholic Mind 22, 49
Catholic Union 193
Celtic Confederation of
    Occupational Guilds 66, 191,
    283
Celtic (Belfast) F. C. 53
Censorship 44, 130, 152, 175, 182,
    195–6, 198–9, 202, 219, 227
Chamberlain, Houston Stewart 127
Chicago Tribune 274, 275
Childers, Erskine 216–17

Christian Nationalist Crusade 273–6
Churchill, Winston S. 222, 247
Church of Ireland Gazette 49
Civil Authorities (Special Powers)
    Act 15
Clann na Poblachta 80, 252–7, 264,
    272, 274
Clann na Saoirse 66–7, 70, 271
Clann na Talmhan 129, 134, 148, 172,
    194, 205, 255, 256
Clarke, Kathleen 254
Clarke, Chief Supt. T. 27, 28
Cleeve, Brian 163
Cobh Urban District Council 227,
    230
Codreanu, Corneliu Z. 141
Colahan, Bishop Daniel 49, 50
Collier, Bishop Matthew 25
Collins, Michael 6, 7, 35
Comhar 150, 151
Comhdháil Laochra Poblacht na
    hÉireann 245
Comhdháil Náisiúnta na Gaeilge 196
Committee of One Million 273
Common Sense 274–5
Communist Party of Great Britain
    22
Communist Party of Ireland 29, 39,
    92, 135, 178
Condon, Timothy 227
Connolly, James 80, 170
Conradh na Gaeilge 69, 72–4, 82–5,
    86, 167, 172, 182, 294
Conway, Cardinal William 60
Cooney, Patrick 220
Córas Gaedhealach 39, 79
Córas na Poblachta 78–81, 138, 152,
    153, 167, 171–2, 187, 188, 191,
    192, 204, 223, 253
Corcoran, Thomas *see* Ó Corcráin,
    Tomás
Corish, Brendan 252
Cork Corporation 227, 230
Cork Examiner 195, 221
Cork Socialist Party 178
Cosgrave, William T. 7, 8, 9, 10

Costello, John A. 261–2
Cotter, Hilary J. C. 283
Coughlin, Fr Charles 273
Couturié, Sylvia 56
Craobh na hAiséirghe 69, 70–8,
    80–91, 110, 118, 150, 166, 167,
    174, 175, 179, 231
Craig, William *see* Creagh, Liam
Creagh, Liam 266, 280–1
Cremin, Cornelius (Con) 221
Cromwell, Oliver 150
Cronin, Edmund ('Ned') 19
Cullen, Archbishop Matthew 24
Cumann Cultúrdha na hAiséirghe
    179, 180
Cumann Díth-Shnadhmtha 61–2
Cumman na nGaedheal 6–10, 16, 17,
    18–19, 23, 30, 37, 101, 102, 157
Cumann na gCailíní 164, 242–3
Cumann Náisiúnta *see* Irish Friends
    of Germany
Cunningham, Bernadette 171
Cunningham, Gerald *see* Ó
    Cuinneagáin, Gearóid
Cunningham, Joseph *see* Ó
    Cuinneagáin, Seosamh
'Cú Scannán' *see* Breathnach,
    Deasún
Cuthbert, Gwendoline *see* Wood,
    Wendy

Dáil Éireann 5–6, 8, 11, 50, 157, 179,
    181, 183, 187, 193, 195, 230,
    255, 262, 295
Davern, Owen 250
Davis, Thomas 126
De Blacam, Aodh ('Roddy the
    Rover') 22, 63, 253
De Eiteagáin, Caoimhín 159, 170,
    175, 233, 257
Defence Conference 44
Defence of the Realm Act 14–15
De Gobineau, Joseph 127
Degrelle, Leon 51, 288
Deighan, Joseph *see* Ó Duibhginn,
    Seosamh

Deirdre 285
De Leigh, Seosamh 256
De Man, Henri 92
De Róiste, Éamonn 227
De Róiste, Liam 31, 56–8, 182, 189,
    222
De Róiste, Risteárd 160, 270, 276–7,
    282–4
Despard, Charlotte 23, 26
De Stocdáil, Tomás *see* Stockdale,
    Thomas
Deutscher Fichte-Bund 127
De Valera, Éamon 7, 8, 37–8, 44, 46,
    54, 64, 70–1, 78, 87, 172, 174,
    185, 200–1, 203, 211–12, 216,
    217, 218, 221, 232, 247, 252
Devane, Fr. R. S. 50
Dignan, Bishop John 36
Dillon, James 47, 174, 222, 261
Diskin, Maureen 48
Disraeli, Benjamin 13
Dobbyn, Séamus 79
Dollfuss, Engelbert 33
Donnellan, Michael 129
Donnelly, Simon 78, 172
Donohoe, Archdeacon P. 24
Donovan, T. M. 30
Doriot, Jacques 51, 92
Douglas, George 53
Dowling, Seán 172
Doyle, Seán 227
Drogheda Corporation 160, 227, 230,
    280
Drogheda Independent 164, 228
Duane, Dr T. J. 252
Dublin Corporation 169, 212, 235
Dublin Evening Mail 181
Dublin Jewish Youth Monthly 197
Duff, Frank 31
Duffy, George Gavan 36
Dulanty, John 278

Eager, Reginald 68, 69, 79
Easter Rising 6, 15
Economic War 9, 22
Ede, James Chuter 264, 278

Egypt 272, 289–91
Eliade, Mircea 141
Emergency Powers Acts 65, 185
Esmonde, Sir Osmond 50
Etchingham *see* de Eiteagáin,
    Caoimhín
European Economic Community 285

Fahey, Fr Denis 37, 125, 127, 130
Fallon, Brian 44
Farrell, Stephen J. 226–7
Fascism 98, 134, 135–42, 152, 168,
    172–3, 175, 182, 184, 211, 224,
    267, 269, 282, 284, 287
Fennessy, Patrick *see* Ó Fiannghusa,
    Pádraig
Fianna Éireann 257
Fianna Fáil 8–10, 17, 30, 37, 39, 78,
    101, 104, 134, 135, 136, 147, 155,
    157, 171, 174, 175, 185, 191, 194,
    199, 201, 205, 207, 208, 223, 230,
    232, 247, 252, 256, 262
Financial Freedom Federation 39
Fine Gael 10, 41, 44, 47, 50, 54, 129,
    134, 135, 147, 172, 174, 175, 192,
    194, 197, 207, 256, 262
Fitzgerald, Lord Edward 126
Fitzgibbon, P. J. 228
Flanagan, Oliver J. 36, 135, 192–3,
    195–7, 234
Ford, Henry 276
Franco, Francisco 32–3, 139, 244, 288
Frankfurter, Felix 274
Freemasonry 78, 105, 129, 130, 131,
    150, 188, 203, 211, 226, 267–8,
    273, 276
Front National 295

G2 (Irish military intelligence) 69, 71,
    129, 152, 153, 166–7, 168, 171,
    174, 192, 218, 282, 284
Gaelic Athletic Association 148
Gaelic League *see* Conradh na
    Gaeilge
Gaffney, Gertrude 51
Gallacher, Willie 30

Garda Síochána 7, 9, 25, 26–8, 30, 79,
    154, 177–8, 214–15, 259, 262,
    266, 278, 281
Gasraí na hAiséirghe *see* Óige na
    hAiséirghe
Geary, Frank 32
Gentile, Giovanni 123, 291
Giles, Capt. Patrick 36
Glanbhille, Seán 240
Glennon, Patrick 25, 28
Glún na Buaidhe 90, 172, 181
Goebbels, Joseph 53
Goering, Hermann 223
Goertz, Hermann 223
Gogán, Liam 51, 223
Gogarty Jr., Francis *see* Mac
    Fógataigh, Prionnsias
Gogarty, Oliver St John 36
Goldberg, Gerald 135
Gorey, Denis 36
Gothic Ripples 276
Gough Monument 213
Gralton, James 23
Grant, Madison 127
Gray, David 55, 78, 154, 200–1, 209,
    216, 217–18, 272
Gray, Terence 154
Green Cross Fund 168
Green Front 191
Griffin, George 79
Griffith, Arthur 6, 7, 18, 35
Günther, Hans F. K. 127

Hanly, Joseph 20, 148–9
Hannington, Walter ('Wal') 23
Hargadon, William *see* Ó hArgadáin,
    Liam
Harte, Patrick 78
Hartnett, Noel 253
Haughey, Charles J. 213–14
Hayes, Fr. John M. 50, 124
Healy, T. M. 35
Held, Stephen Carroll 67
Hempel, Eduard 38, 152
Henchy, Séamus *see* Ó hInnse,
    Séamus

Hendrick, Seán *see* Ó hÉanraic, Seán
Himmler, Heinrich 223
Hiroshima 223
Hitler, Adolf 24, 48, 51, 56, 57, 83, 92, 93, 96, 129, 137, 138, 216, 223, 236, 244, 269, 289, 295
Hobson, Bulmer 39
Hogan, James 21, 29, 135
Holocaust 48, 220–1, 267–8
Home Rule 13
Hore-Belisha, Leslie 79
Hull, Cordell 55
Humbert, Jean Joseph 59
Hussain, Ahmed 289–90
Hyde, Douglas 72

Imperial Fascist League 211, 276, 282
India 272
Indonesia 271
Iran 271
Iraq 272
Ireland Bill 261–2, 264
Ireland, Denis 76, 150
Irish Brigade 32
Irish Catholic 49, 150
Irish Christian Front 32, 38, 57, 193
Irish Civil War 6, 11, 15, 16, 18, 149, 185
Irish Friends of Germany 66–70, 79, 80, 152, 168, 192, 253
Irish Friends of the Soviet Union 23
Irish Hospitals' Trust 128
Irish Independent 24, 32, 51, 52, 270
Irish National Volunteers 14
Irish People 223
Irish Press 22, 29, 49, 51, 61, 221
Irish Republican Army 10, 19, 22, 23, 59, 67, 73, 78, 79, 80, 81, 84, 110, 165, 166, 167–8, 170, 171–2, 174, 209, 210, 234, 252, 257, 262, 263, 278
Irish Republican Brotherhood 59, 72, 73
'Irish Republican Radio' 168
Irish Social Credit Party 39–40
Irish Times 24, 108, 151, 215, 221, 223

Irish Unemployed Workers' Movement 23
Irish Unity Association 25
Irish Workers' Voice 26
'Iron Guard' *see* Legion of the Archangel Michael
Israel 113, 270

Jammet's restaurant 215
Japan 94, 107, 223
Jeunesses patriotes 38
Joyce, William 277

Kelleher, Derry 178
Kelleher, Monsignor John 193
Kelly, James *see* Ó Ceallaigh, Séamus
Kelly, Michael 253
Kelly, Michael O'Brien 228
Kennedy, Hugh 18
Kent, William 50
Kerryman 51
Kildare County Council 227
Kostal, D. K. 54

Labour Party 8, 44, 134, 135, 148, 151, 172–4, 175, 178, 191, 194, 207, 252, 255
Labour Youth 174
Laithwaite, Sir Gilbert 266
Land War 20
Larkin, James Jr. 25
League of Christian Social Justice 31
League for Social Justice 39
Leese, Arnold S. 211–12, 276, 282
Legion of the Archangel Michael 141
Legion of Mary 31
Lehane, Con 80, 253
Lehman, Herbert H. 274
Lemass, Seán 7, 19, 196, 197, 198, 252
Leme, Cardinal Sebastião 292
Lenihan, Patrick 60
'Limerick Pogrom' 34
Linfield (Belfast) FC 53
Local Defence Force 231
Long, Huey P. 273
Louth County Council 225, 227

Lynn, Kathleen 80

Mac an Bhaird, Seán 257
Mac an Bheatha, Prionsias 71, 72, 77, 83, 84, 86, 87, 90
MacBride, Maud Gonne 39
MacBride, Seán 252–6
McCabe, Alec 32, 79
Mac Cártaigh, Caoimhín *see* McCarthy, Kevin
McCartan, Dr Patrick 253
McCarthy, Joseph 273
McCarthy, Kevin 227, 230, 248–9
McCaughey, Seán 252
McCorley, Roger 78, 172
McCormack, Patrick 29
McCormick, Col. Robert 274
Mac Eoin, Seán 262
Mac Fógartaigh, Prionnsias 189
'Mac Gall, Rex' *see* Breathnach, Deasún
Mac Gearailt, Muiris 170, 239
McGilligan, Patrick 7
McGinley, Conde 274–5
Mac Giobúin, Pádraig *see* Fitzgibbon, P. J.
McGrath, Patrick 78
Mac Guill, Fionntán M. 244, 251, 279
McHugh, Roger 78, 168
Mac Maghnúsa, Piaras 240
Mac Maghnusa, Risteárd 111
Mac Murchadha, Éamonn 271
MacNeill, Eoin 72
McQuaid, Archbishop John Charles 125, 128, 223
McQuillan, Jack 253
Macra na Feirme 124
Mac Réamoinn, Daithí *see* Redmond, David
McRory, Cardinal Joseph 24, 55
Mac Siacuis, Risteárd 240
MacSwiney, Terence 195, 210
Mac Uidhir, Seosamh 269
McVeigh, Francis *see* Mac an Bheatha, Prionsias
Maffey, Sir John 200, 216, 220

Mageean, Tom 53
Maginnis, Brian 278
Malan, Daniel 272
Maria Duce 125, 284
Marinetti, Filippo Tommaso 291
Maritain, Jacques 122
Marsh, Arnold 173
Matthew, Fr Theobald 210
Maurras, Charles 288
Maxwell, Sir John 15
Mehigan, Cornelius 227
Mein Kampf 283
MI5 (British security service) 72, 154, 172, 174, 179, 181, 191, 264, 271, 282
Midland Tribune 151
Misr Al-Fatah see Young Egypt
Mitchel, John 126
Moloney, Helena 80
Monetary Reform Party 192
Moran, David Patrick 35
Moreno, Gabriel Garcia 140
Morgan, Thomas 227, 280
Morgenthau, Henry 274
Moslem Brotherhood 290
Mosley, Sir Oswald 276–7
Mounier, Emmanuel 122
Moylett, John 79
Moylett, Patrick 79
Muintir na Tíre 50, 197
Mulcahy, Richard 54
Mulhern, Bishop Edward 31
Murphy, James ('Sonny') 283–4
Murphy, James Vincent 51
Murray, Fr. Laurence 61
Murray, Thomas *see* Ó Muireadh-aigh, Tomás
Mussolini, Benito 24, 33, 34, 48, 50, 62, 92, 96, 137, 138, 140, 170, 182, 216, 223, 287, 289, 295

Nahas Pasha, Mustafa 271
National Action Party 149
National Agricultural and Industrial Development Association 128
National Association of Old IRA 78

National Centre Party 50
National Corporate Party 20
National Workers' Movement 282
Nationalist Information Bureau
    283–4
Nazism 48–50, 51–2, 63, 66, 71, 79,
    93, 114, 134, 138, 141, 152, 184,
    217, 221, 269
New Ross Urban District Council
    227, 280
Ní Chochláin, Nóra *see* Uí
    Mhaolalaí, Nóra
Ní Chochláin, Síle *see* Uí
    Chuinneagáin, Síle
Ní Dhubhshláine, Máire 116, 118–19,
    120
Ní Mhurchadha, Moinice 118–19
Nic Giuolla Choilín, Barbara 239
Nic Réamoinn, Denise 118, 242–3,
    257
Northern Ireland 44, 54, 67, 106–10,
    112, 118, 164, 189–90, 208, 227,
    230, 234, 259–65, 285

Ó hÁinle, Daithí P. 103
Ó hAodha, Gearóid 240
Ó hArgadáin, Liam 243–4, 255, 256,
    257, 269
Ó Baoghill, Seán 151
Ó Beinéid, Tomás 257, 259
O'Brádaigh, Seán *see* Brady, Seán
O'Brien, Gerry *see* Ó Broin, Gearóid
O'Brien, J. E. 28
O'Brien, Nora Connolly 80
O'Brien, Raymond Seán Moulton
    155, 281–2, 283
Ó Broin, Gearóid 131, 168, 177, 213,
    235, 256, 259, 279, 285
O'Byrne, J. J. 223
Ó Carra, Feardorcha *see* Carr,
    Frederick
Ó Casáide, Pádraig 86–7
Ó Ceallacháin, Éamonn 251, 271, 279
Ó Ceallaigh, Micheál Brianach *see*
    Kelly, Michael O'Brien
Ó Ceallaigh, Peadar 90

Ó Ceallaigh, Séamus G. 82, 100, 166
Ó Ceallaigh, Seosamh 174, 202, 251,
    255
Ó Cearnaigh, Stiofán 75
Ó Cinnéide, Micheál 269
Ó Clamháin, Peadar 273
Ó Coigligh, Caoimhín 160
Ó Coigligh, Eoin 177, 187, 202, 216,
    225, 227, 230–1, 240
Ó Coigligh, Séamus 244
Ó Coigligh, Seosamh 204, 206–7,
    209, 238, 239, 240, 245, 248
Ó Condúin, Tadhg *see* Condon,
    Timothy
Ó Conluain, Prionsias 75, 89
O'Connell, Daniel 13
O'Connor, James 172
O'Connor, Maurice 68–70, 71, 79, 80,
    192, 223
Ó Cuinneagáin, Gearóid
    anti-semitism 126, 130–5, 195, 274
    arrest in Belfast 189–90
    birth and background 60–1
    breach with Conradh na Gaeilge
        82–5
    directs Clann na Saoirse 66–7
    Dáil candidacies 187–91, 202–4
    Domhnach Phádraig address
        85–6, 87, 92, 95–6, 97, 100, 181
    early political activity 61–2
    electoral strategy 181, 185–92,
        201–4, 224–9, 256
    'exemplary Christian state' 94–7,
        123–6, 140–1
    formation of Ailtirí na hAiséirghe
        85–91
    feud with Aiséirghe dissidents
        207–11, 231–51
    heads Craobh na hAiséirghe 70–8
    involvement with Córas na
        Poblachta 80–3, 171–2
    Irish language policy 110–13
    participation in Irish Friends of
        Germany 68–70
    Partition policy 106–10, 259–65
    personality 77, 88–9, 152–3

racism 274–6
subversive activities 165–9
suggests alliance with fascist Italy
   34, 62, 64
totalitarian ideology 63–5, 100,
   151
views on women 113, 114–21, 162,
   164
Ó Cuinneagáin, Seosamh 162, 285
Ó Dabharáin, Eoghan *see* Davern,
   Owen
Ó Dálaigh, Cearbhall 51
Ó Dochartaigh, Tomás 111, 117, 130,
   155, 173, 176, 177, 187, 193,
   202, 204–6, 208, 226, 231, 233,
   234–41, 243, 244, 245, 248, 251,
   295
O'Donnell, Frank Hugh 35
O'Donnell, Peadar 23, 30
O'Donovan, James 79
Ó Droighneáin, Oisín 202, 204
Ó Dubhghaill, Seán 227, 280
Ó Dubhghaill, Seán S. 187, 202, 227,
   230, 248
Ó Dubhghaill, Tomás 168
O'Duffy, Eoin 1, 9, 16, 18, 20, 33, 75,
   135, 139, 162, 170
Ó Duibhginn, Seosamh 85, 168
Ó hÉanraic, Seán 131
Ó hÉigeartaigh, Seán 71, 150, 151
Ó hEithir, Breandán 163
Ó Fearghail, Micheál 78
Ó Fearghail, Stiofáin *see* Farrell,
   Stephen J.
Office of Strategic Services 154,
   217–18
Ó Fiannghusa, Pádraig 82, 98, 106,
   130–1
Ó Glaisne, Risteárd 109, 286
O'Gowan, Eric Dorman 262–4
Ó Gríobhtha na Coille, Pádraig 250
O'Growney, Eugene 72
O'Hegarty, P. S. 217
O'Higgins, Kevin 16
Óige na hAiséirghe 164, 179
Ó hInnse, Séamus 75

Oireachtas 185, 199
O'Kelly, John Joseph (J. J.) 154
O'Kelly, Seán T. 247
O'Leary, Fr. Patrick 22, 63
Ó Liatháin, Annraoi 75, 88–9
Ó Laoghaire, Liam 75, 254
Ó Maolalaí, Dómhnall 127, 135, 158,
   159, 160, 188, 255, 256, 280
Ó Maothagáin, Conchúbhar *see*
   Mehigan, Cornelius
O'Moore, Fergus *see* Ó Mordha,
   Feargus
Ó Mordha, Feargus 198
Ó Muireadhaigh, Tomás 249
Ó Muireagáin, Tomás *see* Morgan,
   Thomas
O'Mullane, Michael 78
Ó Murchadha, Micheál 250
Ó Murchadha, Risteárd 240
Ó Murchadha, Tomás (Óg) 170, 181,
   234, 237, 239–40, 242
O'Neill, Hugh 39, 79, 80
O'Nolan, Brian ('Myles na
   gCopaleen') 151, 181
Ó Nualláin, Ciarán 75, 84, 89, 151
O'Rahilly, Alfred 31
O'Reilly, Dónal 23
O'Reilly, Frank 31
Ó Riain, Aindrias 225
Ó Riain, Éamonn 226
Ó Riain, L. J. 38
Ó Riain, Seán 270
Ó Rinn, Liam 49
Orwell, George 31
Ó Sandair, Cathal 75
Ó Scolaidhe, Aindrias 138, 156, 158,
   160, 171, 176, 202, 250, 256, 258,
   279
Ó Seachnasaigh, Ciarán 71, 72, 76
O'Sheehan, Jack 128
O'Shiel, Kevin 18
Ó Sleibhín, Tomás 177
O'Sullivan, J. M. 22
O'Sullivan, P. S. 223
Ó Tuama, Seán 84, 167
Ó hUid, Tarlach 168

Ó hUiginn, Pádraig 75, 87, 89
Ó hUrmoltaigh, Seán Gearóid 96, 130–4, 236–9, 243, 245, 256, 257, 280
Our Country 254

Pan Celtic Union *see* Aontacht na gCeilteach
Parnell, Charles Stewart 126
Parti populaire français 51
Pearse, Pádraig 73, 87, 126, 170, 210, 269
People's National Party 40, 79
Perón, Juan 138
Pétain, Philippe 139, 148, 288
Petersen, Carl Heinz 79
Piasecki, Bolesław 293
Pinto, Gastão Liberal 292
Pius XI, Pope 49, 105
Plaid Cymru 271
'Plan Kathleen' 67
Pobedonostsev, Konstantin 34
Prezzolini, Giuseppe 291
Pro-Axis sentiment 46–58, 65–70, 71, 78–82, 107, 138, 153, 215–17, 222–3, 268–9
Protestantism 109–10
Public Safety Acts 15

Quigley, Joseph *see* Ó Coigligh, Seosamh
Quigley, Owen *see* Ó Coigligh, Eoin
Quisling, Vidkun 92
Qutb, Sayyid 290

Radwan, Fathi 290
Raidió Éireann 76, 194
Red Bank restaurant 66, 166, 271
Redmond, David 257
Republican Congress 61
Republikaner 295
Restoration of Order in Ireland Act 15
Revolutionary Workers' Groups 26
Rexist movement 38, 51, 288
Riefenstahl, Leni 75

Roberts, Henry Nevile 39
Roche, Richard *see* de Róiste, Risteárd
Roche, Éamonn *see* de Róiste, Éamonn
Rommel, Erwin 222
Roosevelt, Eleanor 200
Roosevelt, Franklin D. 64, 96, 217, 274
'Rosary Riots' 25–9
Rosenberg, Alfred 51
Royal Artillery Association 266
Royal Ulster Constabulary 118, 189, 190, 259
Ruch Narodowo-Radykalny 293
Ryan, Harry 173

St Patrick's Anti-Communist League 25, 28, 38
Salazar, António de Oliveira 33–4, 138, 139, 148, 198, 288
Salgado, Plínio 291–3
Saoirse 284
Saoirse Gaedheal 79
Saor Éire 23, 61, 167
Sarg, Wolfgang R. 284
Save the German Children Society 223
Seanad Éireann 169, 262
Sheehy Skeffington, Hanna 28–9
Sheehy Skeffington, Owen 173
Sinn Féin 1, 8, 10, 73, 86, 170, 174, 182, 185, 186, 189, 207, 209, 229, 254–5, 284
Smiddy, Patrick 38
Smith, Gerald L. K. 273–5
Socialist Party of Egypt *see* Young Egypt
Solove'ev, Vladimir 122
Southern Star 196–7
Spanish Civil War 31
Special Infantry Corps 15
Stakelum, John P. ('Jack') 205, 206, 244
Stalin, Josef Vissarionovich 93, 96, 223, 236

Stockdale, Thomas 227, 231, 250
Strasser, Gregor 236
Strasser, Otto 269
Stuart, Francis 21, 188
Sunday Empire News 264
Sunday Independent 217
Synge, John Millington 18
Szálasi, Ferenc 269

The Cross and the Flag 273, 275
The Fascist 211
The Leader 152, 162, 165, 191, 203, 204, 220, 224, 235, 250
The Nation 85
The Standard see *An tIolar*
The Times 1, 264
Thurles Urban District Council 227
Tierney, Michael 135
Tipperary Star 195
Tone, Theobald Wolfe 58
Torch 173
Tozer, John Carson 272
Treacy, Seán 179, 250
Trevor-Roper, Hugh 269
Trinity College, Dublin 70, 75, 79, 110, 179, 213–14, 216, 283
Trudeau, Pierre Elliott 287–8
Tunisian Victory 222

Ui Chuinneagáin, Síle 213, 235
Uí Nuanáin, Máire 226
Ulster Union Club 76, 150–1
Ulster Volunteer Force 14
Union Movement 276–7, 283
Union of Soviet Socialist Republics 47, 57, 93, 273, 283
United Christian Nationalist Party 282, 283

United Nations 270
United States of America 47, 59, 64
Unité Nationale 277
University College, Cork 29, 75, 122, 135
University College, Dublin 75, 78, 214
University College, Galway 216

Vargas, Getúlio 291–3
V-E Day riots 213–17, 222
Versailles, Treaty of 93–4
Vichy France 11, 56

Wafdist movement 271
Walker, Patrick Gordon 278
Walsh, James Joseph (J. J.) 18, 83, 87, 153–4, 171
Walsh, Willie 174, 202–3
Walshe, Joseph ('Joe') 50, 55, 216, 218, 268
War of Independence, Irish 6, 15, 189, 212
War News 168
Weenick, I.R.A. 54
Wilson, Woodrow 42
Wolfe Tone Weekly 34, 167
Wood, Terence see Ó hUid, Tarlach
Wood, Wendy 271
'World Congress of Ex-Soldiers' 283–4
World Nationalist News Service 274

Yorkshire Post 55
Young Egypt 289–91, 293
Young Ireland 85
Young Ireland Association 81, 152, 166, 191